Stirrings in the Jug

Stirrings in the Jug

Black Politics in the Post-Segregation Era

Adolph Reed Jr.

Foreword by Julian Bond

University of Minnesota Press

Minneapolis • London

Published by the University of Minnesota Press
111 Third Avenue South, Suite 290
Minneapolis, MN 55401-2520
http://www.upress.umn.edu

Library of Congress Cataloging-in-Publication Data

Reed, Adolph L., 1947–
    Stirrings in the jug : Black politics in the post-segregation era /
    Adolph Reed, Jr. ; foreword by Julian Bond.
        p.   cm.
    Includes index.
    ISBN 0-8166-2680-4 (hc.). — ISBN 0-8166-2681-2 (pbk.)
    1. Afro-Americans — Politics and government — 20th century.   2. Afro-
Americans — Social conditions — 1964–1975.   3. Afro-Americans — Social
conditions — 1975–   I. Title.
E185.615.R39   1999
324'.089'96073—dc21   99-27301

To Alex W. Willingham and Arthur V. "Val" Hawley—
friends, comrades, brothers, compass, and long marchers,
through all the twists and turns of all these years

Contents

Foreword

Julian Bond

In the early years of the twentieth century, two strong voices offered black Americans general and markedly different visions of how they might make a home for themselves in America. One voice came from the South: Booker T. Washington, the founder of the Tuskegee Institute and the greatest proponent of self-help. Black Americans — black southerners in particular — should forgo seeking political and social equality, Washington argued. Political strength and social respect would follow naturally when blacks had proven themselves in agriculture, in the professions, and as tradesmen. The other voice, W. E. B. Du Bois, argued that it was impossible to obtain economic sufficiency without political rights. Without access to the ballot and the ability to influence public policy, black Americans could not possibly hope to win equal protection from the state, equal spending for their schools, or equal rights before the law. Conventional wisdom has it that Du Bois won that argument; the truth is that both his and Washington's visions have competed for primacy until today.

Now Adolph Reed revisits these arguments, adds nuance to them, and reminds us of their current application. Reed focuses on the modern era from the demise of legal segregation through the mid-1990s. He uses specific cases to draw a general outline of the ongoing debates as they are expressed, from Montgomery's bus boycott in 1955–56 through the elimination of state-sanctioned segregation in 1964 and 1965 through the black power movement of the late 1960s and early 1970s to the Jesse Jackson campaigns of 1984 and 1988.

Reed's arguments hold special meaning for us now. In less than a quarter of a century, by 2010, America will be an older and more varied nation, less white, less female, and less northern. We will not look like Du Bois's and Washington's America, nor will we be the America of today. The population of minorities will grow rapidly. Ratios of sex and age will undergo rapid shifts. This new America's racial views, attitudes, and actions will grow from the American past, both recent and distant.

In 1954 the U.S. Supreme Court's *Brown v. Board of Education* decision ruled school segregation illegal. The decision prompted an army of nonviolent protesters to challenge segregation's morality as well. The southern movement battled segregation on buses, at lunch counters, and then at ballot boxes. It won these battles through a combination of legal action in courts and the Congress and extralegal tactics in the streets. What had begun as a movement for elemental civil rights became a movement for political and economic power, and black men and women won office and wielded power in numbers only dreamed of before.

Reed writes that the southern movement's demand for integration was superfluous outside the South; he argues that "the gains of the 1960s" have yet to be realized, since the removal of segregation and state-sponsored oppression, though undoubtedly a benefit, merely revealed the oppressive nature of racism on the national scene and the successes of midcentury capitalism in reordering social control. Reed's focus is on the post-segregation era, that period in American life from Martin Luther King Jr.'s elevation as the premier figure in the freedom movement to today, from the time when an American majority seemed single-mindedly in pursuit of racial integration to the post-Reaganite present.

In popular memory, the southern Freedom movement was a second Reconstruction whose ripples were felt far beyond the southern states and whose victories benefited more than blacks. Like the first Reconstruction, almost a hundred years earlier, it focused on making civil rights protections of America's half-citizens more secure. Like the first, it saw gains for blacks extended to civil rights protections for others—women, the elderly, and the handicapped. Like the first, it gave new life to other movements of disadvantaged Americans, and like the first, it ended when the national purpose wavered and reaction swept the land.

Before the second Reconstruction ended, it was our modern democracy's finest hour. A voteless people voted with their bodies and their feet and showed the way for other social protest. The antiwar movement drew its earliest soldiers from the southern freedom army; the reborn movement for women's rights took many of its cues and much of its momentum from the southern movement for civil rights. Three great impediments to democracy's success—gender and race discrimination and abusive power—were all weakened by the movement's drive, and we are all better for it today.

There were lives lost along the way, but civil rights laws were passed; by 1965 Jim Crow was legally dead. The early 1960s civil rights movement—interracial and nonviolent—gave way to black power and urban riots. Appeals to justice gave way to nonnegotiable demands. The farther north it was demanded, the less desirable racial integration became. The bigots of Birmingham, Alabama, transferred to Boston, Massachusetts, became unmeltable ethnics, and violent defense of white skin privilege in the South became community preservation in the North.

But black women and men did begin to win public office. As they did so, they became the old movement's new standard-bearers, upsetting entrenched and powerful interests. In 1964, only about 300 blacks held elective office. By 1970, 1,469 blacks had been elected nationally, and by 1989, 7,226 blacks held office throughout the United States.

At the same time that a new stratum of leadership arose in black America, conditions for most blacks in the post-segregation era remained the same. By the mid-1980s the number of black mayors, legislators, and members of Congress was reaching record heights. The 1990 census reported that the number of people living in poverty had increased over the previous four years by more than nine million, the biggest increase since these statistics were first reported. For those Americans whose skins were black or brown, the rate of poverty went up, median family income went down, children who were poor got poorer, and the gap between rich and poor grew wider. At the end of the 1960s, three-fourths of all black men were working; by the end of the 1980s, only 57 percent had a job.

By the middle 1970s, the growing number of blacks and women and other minorities pushing for entry into power in the academy, the media, business, government, and other traditionally white male institutions fed a backlash in the discourse about race. Opinion leaders — in government and private life — began to redefine and reformulate the terms of the discussion, returning to a pre–Montgomery bus boycott analysis. Black behavior came to be identified as the reason blacks and whites lived in separate worlds. Racism retreated, and pathology advanced. The color-blind society that was the 1960s ideal became today's imagined reality. The failure of the lesser breeds to share society's fruits became their fault alone. Pressure for additional civil rights laws became special pleading. America's most privileged population, white men, suddenly became a victim class. Aggressive blacks and pushy women were responsible for America's decline. Reed has written about a "nonsensical tautology — these people are poor because they are pathological, they are pathological because they are poor."

A second front against racial and economic justice was opened in the late 1970s and has gained strength and power ever since. Led by scholars and academicians, funded by corporate America, this movement of neoconservatives has aimed its efforts at removing government regulation from every aspect of our lives, and they found a handy, hated target in civil rights. Central to their argument was the failure of politics to gain advances for blacks. More important, Reed writes, these forces found unsuspected allies in the new black elites, who, no more wanting to jeopardize their status than did elites of the past, accepted establishment initiatives without criticism if they contained affirmative action components. Elsewhere in this volume Reed details specific instances of this cooperation and co-optation. Anyone interested in the future of American cities should read this book.

But Reed's vision of politics is larger than elites and elections and larger than the limits frequently imposed on routine political activity when the actors are black. Limits imposed on discussions of solutions are equally abhorrent. Reed reserves a special place in his private hell for those who question "the legitimacy of black Americans' demands on the state" or who promote "social policy on the cheap."

He skewers the "self-help" models for avoiding responsibility for public policy failures and "underclass" depictions of black communities as shrugging off public responsibility. Poverty, he rightly notes, stems from the economic system in which we all strive, from racial discrimination, not from characteristics — drug abuse, teenage childbearing — that hardly distinguish the urban poor from their fellow citizens. These descriptions, of course, are designed to do exactly that: to make the poor a separate and feared "Other" whose problems are beyond the reach of organized politics and thus can be solved only by the victims themselves.

Adolph Reed occupies an important place in discussions of our modern American dilemma. His pen is pointed and often draws blood. His critiques of the failures of blacks, leftists, and liberals to develop effective oppositional politics probably will and certainly should wound many. This book is an invaluable contribution to ancient debates. It should be the beginning of fresh action to set our politics again on the road toward solving our problems rather than blaming victims.

Acknowledgments

Any book is the product of multiple influences. That is especially true of this one, which records a project both of lengthy duration and enacted in many venues within several, quite disparate domains. Therefore, any attempt to recall, much less acknowledge, even all the individuals who have had substantial influence on what is now this book would be hopelessly incomplete, a self-defeating pretense. I shall use this conventional space instead to express my gratitude to a smaller universe of those who have contributed most immediately and concretely to bringing this project to fruition in this form and as it is: Janaki Bakhle, Lisa Freeman, and Carrie Mullen, my editors at the University of Minnesota Press. I cannot adequately express how much I have appreciated their informed enthusiasm, encouragement, gentle and sometimes strikingly creative prodding (extending to the gambit of enlisting one of my friends to open a second flank), sympathetic understanding, and especially their patience. I am fortunate to be the beneficiary of their talents and, I hope, their friendship.

1. The Jug and Its Content
A Perspective on Black American Political Development

This book represents nearly two decades of effort to make sense of black American politics in the aftermath of the civil rights and black power movements. The essays collected here are united by a concern to characterize the fundamental shift in black politics that has occurred as a direct outcome of the successes of the civil rights movement and to assess the significance of that shift for those who would pursue egalitarian interests. As Professor Willie Legette has recently remarked, the only thing that has not changed about black politics since 1965 is how we think about it. This book attempts to take up the challenge implied in that observation.

In fact, the general concern from which the book originates is older still. I went to graduate school in the early 1970s, after several years working as a political organizer, partly because of a perception that movement politics had lost momentum. There were already significant institutional signs that a more radical politics of popular mobilization was on the decline. Largely at the behest of private foundation and government funding sources, programs and agencies that had previously supported what is now called social movement organizing were reorienting to "economic development" and technocratic models of service provision. It was also possible to see a new, mainstream black political establishment — what Martin Kilson would describe as the "new black political class"[1] — emerging from and merging into the old one. Activists were gradually being absorbed into a developing apparatus of race relations management, as either public officials or quasi-public functionaries (for example, in Model Cities or Office of Economic Opportunity programs). At the same time, the contentious edges of activist politics were being beveled away by the processes whose benign dimension Rufus Browning, Dale Marshall, and David Tabb later characterized as political incorporation.[2] What remained of black radicalism turned increasingly toward an ideological formalism — either cultural nationalist, pan-Africanist, or Marxist-Leninist/anti-imperialist — that seemed less and less adequate either for critically interpreting the dynamics forming and gathering steam in black politics or for reen-

1

ergizing radical alternatives. Left or oppositional forces were losing ground and seemed to be blocked from generating effective responses to the changing context and our deteriorating position in it.

In that environment I decided to repair to the university for reflection and study, to prepare in concert with like-minded others to meet the new situation, which increasingly exposed the limitations of the presumptions and strategies that had undergirded our political practice. The questions that I took with me, all driven by the objective of rejuvenating a popularly based left activism, are those that ultimately frame this book: What are the forces—both internal and external—most significant in shaping black American political life? How should we account for the decline of left-critical tendencies in black politics, for their failure even to secure institutional niches? To what extent have the interpretations and strategies associated with those tendencies contributed to their failure? How should an autonomous left critique interpret and respond to the dynamics actually operating in mundane black politics—for example, to the rise of black officialdom and the collapse of the "nationalist"/"integrationist" dichotomy that had been the conceptual foundation of black power radicalism's analysis and judgment inside Afro-American political activity?

Although I disliked the city practically from my arrival, I was nonetheless fortunate to spend the greater part of the 1970s in Atlanta. The graduate political science program at Atlanta University (now Clark-Atlanta University) uniquely encouraged the study of politics from left-critical perspectives. The faculty themselves were in various ways concerned with, or at least open to, approaches to scholarly activity that emanated from the imperatives of black radicalism. And for several years each incoming class contained at least one or two students who had come to graduate school directly from the front lines of movement activism. (The enrollment of a Marxist theory seminar, for instance, was virtually isomorphic with the leadership of the Atlanta chapter of the African Liberation Support Committee.) The program to that extent facilitated development of a radical discursive community that was anchored conceptually in the discipline yet provided some autonomy from the often suffocating conventions of the triumphalist behavioralism dominant at that time in American political science.

Because my years there happened to coincide with the rise and consolidation of black governance, Atlanta also turned out to be a natural laboratory in which I could observe the larger transition in black politics. I arrived in the city on the eve of Andrew Young's initial election to Congress, as the first black person sent from the Deep South in this century, and a year before Maynard Jackson's election as the city's first black mayor, also a first for a large southern municipality.

These two electoral victories affirmed and enhanced Atlanta's reputation for racial progressivism, at least by regional standards. As Floyd Hunter had already documented in the 1950s, however, this reputation was built on a regime of biracial "cooperation" among elites that presumed blacks' subsidiary role as cue-takers; black elites' participation was both largely unofficial and predicated upon acceptance of whites' absolute prerogative for defining policy imperatives. Cooperation meant negotiation of the terms of black acquiescence to policy agendas that unfailingly reproduced, and as likely as not intensified, a pattern of racial inequality.[3]

The rise of black public officialdom in Atlanta, therefore, presented an unusually clear opportunity to observe the entailments of the post-segregation era's regime of race relations management as it evolved and congealed institutionally. The perspective that proximity to Atlanta's transition allowed was particularly distinct in two ways. First, the transition occurred relatively early; by 1974 blacks controlled the executive and legislative branches of municipal government and the housing authority and held elective and administrative leadership positions on the board of education. Second, the intermediate institutions in black politics were already fully integrated into the semiformalized regime of "cooperative" racial subordination. This was true not only of the local chapters of the Southern Christian Leadership Conference (SCLC), Urban League, and National Association for the Advancement of Colored People (NAACP) but also of antipoverty agencies such as Economic Opportunity Atlanta and the Model Cities program. Those agencies also, along with the clubhouse-style, elite-led political organizations, became conduits for linking even ostensibly independent, "grassroots" groups — such as neighborhood, tenant, welfare rights, and other protest-advocacy organizations — into the regime. Ideological and programmatic incorporation proceeded most subtly through superficially apolitical, even democratizing, features of governmental structure as well as through the more conspicuous expressions of racial transition in officeholding. The new strong-mayor/council municipal charter that came into effect with Mayor Jackson's accession to office institutionalized this integration.

The Model Cities program became, virtually intact, the newly created Department of Community and Human Development (DCHD), which in turn operated partly as a vehicle for channeling resources to neighborhood-based or otherwise "grassroots" organizations. Access to those resources conferred legitimacy on the recipient organizations, both by officially validating their claims to representativeness and by providing them with the material and ideological bases for securing palpable constituencies for their efforts. This dynamic was reinforced when DCHD took over adminstration of the city's Community Development Block Grant program.

Similarly, the new charter established a mandate for citizen participation, which was implemented through the creation of a citywide network of neighborhood planning units (NPUs) that incorporated community groups into the process of constructing the city's annual Comprehensive Development Plan. The municipal Planning Bureau, in the newly created Department of Budget and Planning, set up a Division of Neighborhood Planning to formalize the NPUs' connection to the planning process. Especially because planning and municipal budget preparation were linked, the effect was to plug designated community groups directly into the public distributive apparatus. What appeared to be a move to decentralization, though, was more the opposite. The Planning Bureau, which set the overarching frame for the planning process and its large-scale objectives, reflected the hegemonic priorities of the dominant local pro-growth coalition centered in the Metropolitan Atlanta Chamber of Commerce and its downtown counterpart, Central Atlanta Progress (CAP). The NPU system rooted those priorities at the grass roots by cementing to them the loyalties of neighborhood or community groups. Articulation of posttransition "community" concerns and agendas came, ever more automatically and uncontroversially, to be shaped within the framework of a pragmatic politics whose common sense was defined by the large interests that had always governed the city.[4]

By the mid-1970s, therefore, the contours of what would be the new regime of race relations management in American politics were already clearly delineated in Atlanta. The imagery of populist, participatory action that had grounded black radical discourse lost its critical power in a context in which popular participation collapsed into ratification of elite-driven agendas. Ideologically, the new black political elite held a monopoly on the authenticating symbols of grassroots racial community from which radicalism had drawn the affective force that supported adversarial political mobilization. The driving rhetoric of the political transition presumed a model of descriptive representation[5] that treated shared racial status unproblematically as a vehicle for expressing authentic group interests. Because officials' actions were authenticated by their race, the insurgent language of transition facilitated tendencies among the emergent elite to define the substance of legitimate black interests tautologically, as whatever official black representatives said or did. Materially, the new black political class's capacity for delivering concrete benefits to individuals and ostensibly grassroots organizations made that tautological assertion a political reality. Politics is processual, and access to resources shapes and defines constituencies, which then become significant nodes in the matrix of community political life. A neighborhood group that becomes embedded in the public funding stream — say, through administering a housing rehabilitation program or summer youth employment program—solidifies a political base of actual and aspiring employees and beneficiaries; this base strengthens the group in relation to other voices that might endeavor to speak in the name of the neighborhood. Such groups are naturally inclined to accept the larger political and policy framework on which their access to resources is predicated. To that extent, the source of their legitimacy as representatives of neighborhood or community interests simultaneously biases them toward accommodation to the governing elite's agendas.

The new black elite's political capacity, however, presumed acceptance of overarching programmatic frameworks and priorities for governance and administration—a larger system of political rationality—defined by the pro-growth, pro-business interests that reproduce entrenched patterns of racialized inequality. These commitments constrain elite responsiveness to "grassroots" concerns and initiatives, typically by inducing elites to convert those concerns into forms that fit them into—or at least pose no threat to—the imperatives of those larger pro-business, pro-growth priorities. Grassroots groups, therefore, are also constrained to accommodate those priorities as a condition for maintaining access to the resources that legitimize them and buttress their support even among their own publics and constituents.

In Atlanta this contradiction appeared most strikingly in Mayor Jackson's success in preempting popular black support for a 1977 strike by municipal sanitation workers, nearly all of whom were black and who were easily the lowest-paid workers on the city government's payroll. Jackson short-circuited the union's attempt to build community support for the strike by portraying it as a racial attack by the white-led American Federation of State, County, and Municipal Employees on his black-led administration.

The 1977 strike triply illustrates the character of the post-segregation racial transition. First, it attests to the extent of the new political class's ideological victory within black politics. Jackson's hegemonic control of the idea of black interest enabled him to subvert and co-opt the moral force of racial populism even in opposition to a militant insurgency by one of the most vulnerable, conspicuously "grassroots" elements of the black population: public sector workers employed to do unappealing work for poverty-level wages. Second, the 1977 strike exemplifies the contradictory pattern of allegiance on which the new black power rests. The mayor had been dissuaded by the white business elite from seeking to replace Andrew Young in Congress, largely on the argument that Jackson would be better able than the white City Council president, Wyche Fowler (who would have succeeded him in the mayoralty), to "handle" the municipal unions. Jackson received enthusiastic support from the Chamber of Commerce, CAP, and their ideological organ, the *Atlanta Constitution,* for his reelection after the strike. Finally, the incident suggests how dramatically the new regime had altered the foundation of black politics in a very little while. As vice mayor under the old city charter, Jackson had flamboyantly walked out of City Hall in 1970 to join protesting sanitation workers on their picket line.[6] And it was, after all, the justice of this consitutency's cause that had been memorialized in the 1968 Memphis campaign that brought Martin Luther King Jr. to the site of his assassination.

Attempting to enact a left practice within black politics in Atlanta, as in the other cities that experienced racial transition in local governance during those years, exposed the limitations of the pro forma styles of political radicalism that had grown out of black power ideology. The global, axiomatic narratives of pan-Africanism (eight points), cultural nationalism (Seven Principles), and the potted Marxism-Leninism (mechanistic laws of "scientific" socialism) that collectively defined the discursive arena of black radicalism offered neither conceptual space nor analytical tools that could be brought to bear to make sense of the dynamics shaping the new black politics.[7] Those narratives, and the common mind-set in which they were embedded, in several related ways hindered confrontation of the emerging political realities.

Their abstractness posited interpretive categories too remote from the concrete, often prosaic milieus within which the relations and patterns of behavior constituting the new regime took shape. As languages of political criticism and legitimation, those narratives pivoted on normative criteria — contribution to the liberation of Africa and peoples of African descent elsewhere, propagation of an authentically black value system, or consonance with global laws of socialist revolution — that were so distant from mundane political life that they could not provide clear bases for apprehending the significance of the everyday micropolitical processes around which the new black political order congealed. Much less could they guide an evaluation of those processes or the project of locating them substantively either in a coherent approach to oppositional practice or even in more elaborately theoretical arguments regarding strategic action.

Each of those narratives of radicalism rested on fundamentally idealist intellectual commitments that supported summary rejection of the actually existing forms of black political action in favor of preferred alternatives in a millennial future. In relation to those ideal alternatives, mundane politics seemed both picayune and inauthentic. This idealist orientation was also linked to apocalyptic notions of political change that only reinforced a dismissive attitude toward the routine politics of the day. For each tendency, the goal of political action was the establishment of an ideal order unconnected to the existing world. They differed significantly regarding the nature of that new order and the features defining it, and they clustered around quite different, often incompatible views of the constituencies central to the ideal order and of the alliances deemed necessary to bring it into existence. Nevertheless, the tendencies shared a presumption that the route to the millennial order, however defined, required an absolute rupture from the institutions and practices of politics in the present. For each, the substance of political theorizing was a hermetic exercise in sketching a utopian alternative to current social relations, a world from which tension and contradiction—and thus, in effect, politics and history—had been eliminated. For each, progress toward the goal came through proselytizing for its alternative utopia and the ontological shifts required to enact it. Therefore, debate within and between the tendencies, when not simply competing assertions of faith, centered much more on the abstract logical standard of the arguments' internal consistency than on their apparent fit with the facts of an external, lived world or verifiably demonstrable capacities for intervening in it. All relied in practice on exhorting prospective adherents to devalue conventional—one might say this-worldly—forms of political participation linked to government institutions and public policy as inadequate for pursuit of the millennial goals. Instead, each of the radical tendencies encouraged, as an expression of theoretical sophistication and rectitude, a cavalier attitude toward the new, systemically incorporated black politics.

This approach to radicalism could not provide criteria for systematically assessing the performance and programs of the new political elite; nor could it propose institutional alternatives that were credible in the context of the time. It was too abstract and theoretically hermetic either to anchor discussion of middle-range questions concerning the possibilities and limits of the new black governance or even to guide a more general reflection on normative issues that—by articulating positive models and enabling conditions of just, egalitarian, and democratic institutions—could generate a basis for challenging the increasingly tight circumscription of black political aspiration by officials' routine practices.[8] This radicalism, in any of its utopian or ontological varieties, could neither extrapolate from current institutional arrangements to propose more desirable approaches to housing, development, or education policy, for example, nor comment effectively on such matters as the proper role of political institutions in shaping social life or the relations that should pertain between the state and the citizenry.

These limitations were strikingly exposed in Atlanta during the missing and murdered children episode at the beginning of the 1980s. Activists responded to low-income public housing residents' complaints of insufficient police protection by attempting to organize vigilante "bat patrols" in the housing projects rather than by mobilizing to demand improvements in the delivery of police services from the black-led municipal government. The vigilante option was appealing because it was consistent with the inclination simply to dismiss the exercise of political authority as at best a diversion and an inauthentic arena for transformative black politics. Yet taking that option sacrificed an opportunity to provoke public discussion of the black administration's obligations to its constituents and, perhaps, to dramatize the contradictions of political incorporation. Ironically, bat patrol vigilantism also appealed to a self-help, communitarian strain that was carried forward from black power ideology; this was in effect the alternative to a politics for the here-and-now, and its intrinsically conservative character would become clearer over the succeeding decade.[9]

Beneath its exhortations to epic political change and its embrace of apocalyptic rhetoric, this radicalism remained powered by the protest reflex that had been the default position in black politics during the direct action phases, at least, of the struggle against Jim Crow. As an oppositional style, therefore, post–black power radicalism was reactivist rather than strategic. Notwithstanding a penchant for references to protracted struggle, it could not generate a practice or critique directed toward cultivating and solidifying bases among specific populations within the really existing black politics and expanding them over time. (This disjunction of behavior and pronouncement suggests that the language of protracted struggle — most common among those who identified themselves as Marxists or scientific socialists — was pro forma and affective, an incantation affirming symbolic ties to Maoist or Third Worldist notions of revolution; to that extent, it reflected the concern to blend Marxism and nationalism by establishing a non-European, nonwhite revolutionary canon.)

Moreover, the combination of a trivializing attitude toward the operations of extant political institutions and the remoteness of the millennial goals removed restraints on opportunistic alliances with mainstream politicians. Not taking the new black official politics seriously enabled radicals to judge officials on criteria extrinsic to their policy priorities and routine political behavior. This underwrote a simplistic standard according to which supporting or making gestures toward radicals and their immediate, nonthreatening initiatives (for example, adopting an honorific street name or issuing a proclamation to acknowledge African Liberation Day, or appointing an activist to a commission or a job) qualified an official or aspirant as progressive or racially authentic. This was an unacknowledged concession to the ascendancy of the new political elite, of course; it amounted to a de facto agreement not to challenge the latter's hegemony in exchange for occasional symbolic nods of recognition in a perverse pageantry of legitimation through dependence. This orientation both reflected and reinforced radicalism's increasing marginalization in black politics.

The project that informs this volume grows from the environment I have just described. The three essays in Part I — chapters 2, 3, and 4 — build on one another both chronologically and theoretically; they chart a continuing effort to characterize the evolving political shift by examining its general features and the salient forces driving it. Each seeks to provide an account from within the new regime's sources and foundations. Their undergirding premise is that the post-segregation regime emerged no less from autonomous dynamics — both ideological and institutional — *within* black politics than from external pressures. The first, "The 'Black Revolution' and the Reconstitution of Domination," was written in the late 1970s, as the post-segregation regime was consolidating, and was revised (though not fundamentally) as the Reagan administration was moving toward its second term in the early 1980s. It focuses principally on reconstructing the ideological and programmatic trajectory of civil rights and black power activism to locate tendencies within them that were open to articulation in the direction of what became the new black politics. Chapter 3, "The Black Urban Regime," lays out an account of the conditions — demographic, economic, political, and ideological — that enabled the rise of black urban governance in the 1970s and 1980s and the emergence of that governance from the movement politics of the black power era. This chapter also analyzes the structural forces, programmatic and ideological commitments, and patterns of alliance and cleavage that have shaped the character of black governance and assesses its potential and actual significance for democratic interests. Chapter 4, "Sources of Demobilization in the New Black Political Regime," builds on the earlier critiques to provide an overall assessment of the state of black American politics in the mid-1990s. It examines pivotal features of the contemporary institutional and ideological situation that exert demobilizing pressures on black political activity, thus undercutting its capacity to respond to the major challenges posed by corporate reorganization of American life, and suggests alternative possibilities for refocusing a black politics in pursuit of egalitarian interests.

The three chapters of Part II are case studies of different facets of the new black politics as it has been institutionalized. Chapter 5, "A Critique of Neoprogressivism in Theorizing about Local Development Policy," focuses on Mayor Maynard Jackson's role in an Atlanta airport construction controversy to examine how black officials define black political interests to fit within the objectives of the pro-growth, corporate forces that set the larger agendas in their governing coalitions. Chapter 6, "The 'Underclass' as Myth and Symbol," is a critique of the sources, premises, content, and political consequences of a key ideological legitimation of the new American racial politics in general and black political discourse in particular. Chapter 7, "The Allure of Malcolm X and the Changing Character of Black Politics," explores specific features and consequences of the decline of radicalism in black politics through consideration of the proliferation of Malcolm X iconology during the early 1990s. Each of these essays recapitulates in concrete contexts the theoretical arguments laid out in Part I, thereby further grounding and refining them; at least, that is what I hope readers will find.

I have resisted the urge to revise the essays. I have only corrected typos, edited notes and style for consistency throughout the volume, and here and there clarified an awkward or dissonant construction, while trying not to alter original meanings. The temptation to do more was particularly great with respect to chapter 2, which is the oldest and represents an initial attempt to apprehend, describe, and characterize the political dynamics then shaping themselves. The essay's basic critique and argumentative thrust persist and are elaborated and refined through the entire book; indeed, I confess to being reassured at how well its central formulations and arguments have held up over time. However, as an early effort to catch up with and characterize emergent, at the time apparently quite open-ended, and rapidly evolving historical patterns, it is necessarily at least incomplete and vulnerable to conceptual awkwardness. The challenge of capturing such an unsettled and novel political moment from within was all the greater because virtually no directly satisfactory theoretical or discursive road map was available to guide the undertaking. In that regard, the essay is as much the beginning of an argument about how to think theoretically about contemporary black American politics as it is an interpretation of specific elements and tendencies in specific historical conditions. Therefore, presenting the early argument in its original form can be useful as a sort of case study in the development of a critique.

This is a historicist, rather than an autobiographical, point. The main conceptual difficulties that bedeviled the early articulation of my critique of the reorganization of black politics derived partly from its own foundation in the discourse of post–black power radicalism. To that extent, taking note of this essay's occasionally naive or insufficiently nuanced constructions and struggles to negotiate what turned out to be intellectual culs-de-sac exposes, in a very concrete way, the practical and interpretive limitations of that discourse and of the political sensibility that undergirds it. Especially because that discourse and sensibility continue to shape the language of insurgency in black politics, the essay may be informative as such an object of excavation, as well as through its intentional accomplishments.

From this archaeological perspective, two issues concerning chapter 2 in particular warrant review. The first is a tendency toward overstatement of the limits of the reforms associated with the prior period of civil rights activism. Post–black power radicalism shared this disposition with other strands of the broader discourse of left or oppositional politics that originated in the 1960s. Rhetorically, it was an imprecise reaction against an orthodox narrative that treated those reforms as tantamount to exhaustive fulfillment of the ideal of social justice. Frustration with the liberal establishmentarian view that celebrated the "gains of the 1960s" as a final victory gave rise to an analytical impatience because that view threatened to allow criticism and struggle to dissolve prematurely into a self-satisfied quiescence. This frustration overlapped the ideological dismissiveness toward institutional politics that I have already discussed in relation to black radicalism and that was also common more widely within the discursive streams flowing from the generic (that is, with reference to both black and white movement nodes) New Left.

In the initial formulations, the tendency to diminish the significance of institutional reforms coincided with an incipient but active critique of the welfare state's demobilizing role as an instrument for administering and displacing the class and racial contradictions of American capitalism. Frances Fox Piven's and Richard A. Cloward's account of the system-maintaining functions of public assistance was the most prominent exposition of this theoretical development.[10] Their discussion of the embeddedness of black power politics in the programmatic apparatus of the Great Society and the dynamics of racial transition in urban political systems amplified and deepened Robert L. Allen's earlier critical examination of black power's practical convergence with corporate and other elite political agendas.[11] The focus on establishing the conservative functions of the institutional accommodations to activism reinforced the tendency to minimize the "gains of the 1960s." By the end of the 1970s a coherent, textured left critique of the liberal American welfare state had begun taking shape — ironically, just as Reaganism trumped it from the right.[12]

Although "The 'Black Revolution'" (chapter 2) also tends to overstate the limits of the democratizing effects of the reforms of the 1960s,[13] I do not believe that it does so to the detriment of its larger critique. That critique does not necessarily depend on a claim that the beneficial outcomes of political incorporation were absolutely class-skewed. I draw attention to this issue principally to situate the essay within its own historical context and to indicate an aspect that I would now formulate differently. Still, the tendency to diminish the importance of earlier, partial victories stands out as an issue in the first place because of its problematic legacy in the present.

As a trope of urgency, the formulation minimizing those victories has become an unfortunate bequest to attempts to craft radical critique in the black political discourse of the 1990s, in the same way as have certain of Malcolm X's pithy utterances (see chapter 7). Originally, the minimizing of victories was enmeshed in the activist political culture that had won those victories and was therefore likely to be, as it is in chapter 2 here, a rhetorical device of strategic arguments for extending the content and scope of institutional reform—in some cases demanding radical transformation, in some cases only demanding more. Its more recent incarnation, however, comes in a context in which left activism with any popular momentum is not part of the lived memory or experience of those younger than middle-aged and in which triumphant Reaganism has besmirched the very idea that public institutions can be efficacious in the pursuit of egalitarian ends.

In this context, the trope, while still no doubt expressing frustration, no longer typically suggests urgent demands for public action or critical analysis aimed at expanding the scope and functions of public institutions. Instead, it is more likely to be harnessed to appeals to "self-help," the fundamentally conservative—and futile—politics of resignation that acquiesces in the Reaganite view of the world. In fact, the borrowed trope, by virtue of its vestigial association with militant activism, serves to mask this stance's conservative foundation. Resuscitation of post–black power radicalism's dismissive posture toward institutional politics operates to similar effect. Rhetorical evocation of that posture both replaces strategically oriented analyses of questions bearing on governance and the role of public institutions and also endows self-help antistatism with a rhetorical militance and represents it as an expression of racial authenticity.

The status of the idea of authenticity in black political argument is the second problematic issue that I wish to raise regarding "The 'Black Revolution,'" partly by correcting an always-unsatisfying interpretive tension in the essay. As formulated there, my critique, on the one hand, rejected claims to racial or cultural authenticity as the basis for black political legitimation on the grounds that such claims are ahistorical, rest on a folkish or otherwise organicist mythology, and deny the realities of interest differentiation among black Americans. On the other hand, I proposed an account of black popular culture's embeddedness in the ideological and marketing matrices of mass culture that unnecessarily juxtaposes a notion of an "authentic Afro-American particularity" to an "artificial particularity."

This juxtaposition is a spur of an argument that stresses mass capitalism's homogenizing and integrative capacities as a social system. That argument is propelled partly by an interpretation of the trajectory of Afro-American cultural and ideological integration as a strand in a process of social reorganization driven by the institutional logic of a corporate industrial culture, a process that also included the "Americanization" of eastern and southern European immigrants during the late nineteenth and early twentieth centuries. This interpretation represents the process of homogenization as consisting of the reformulation of relatively autonomous ethnic particularities in ways that displace the "[distinctive] institutional forms that were the source of group consciousness" in favor of the imperatives of mass capitalism; the upshot of this process has been replacement of "traditional ethnic ways of life" by the standardized fare of mass culture, packaged within "residues of the lost cultures — empty mannerisms and ambivalent ethnic identities."

This perspective leads to the following formulation: "Although authentic Afro-American particularity had been undermined by the standardizing imperatives of mass capitalism, the black nationalist reaction paved the way for the constitution of an artificial particularity." The latter I characterize as the product of loading mass cultural content and meanings into the residual trappings of earlier, more autonomous forms of black Americans' cultural expression. Grounding the distinction between authentic and artificial particularities was always a problem; I did not want to posit an essentializing notion of group authenticity, a less forthright version of the nationalists' presumptions of a definitive, racially pure culture. Rather, I saw the distinction as indicating the extent to which the normative substance of ostensible cultural particularity is reproduced within or outside of the logic of capitalist mass culture. My effort to clarify this distinction relied crucially on Jürgen Habermas's notion of "living" versus "objectivistically prepared and strategically employed" cultural traditions.[14]

I now believe that that distinction cannot be sustained; it does not comport with the actual practice of culture. The distinction, like the larger narrative of the incorporation of autonomous cultures in which it is embedded, is faulty in two related respects: First, though it does not necessarily assert a halcyon past, it too nearly approximates a nostalgic narrative of decline from a prelapsarian condition of autonomously self-reproducing groups. Second, in presuming the existence of such groups, the juxtaposition of authentic and artificial particularities also has resonances of a suspect distinction between "traditional" and "modern" cultures. Habermas's formulation certainly rests on this distinction, as it construes "living" cultural traditions as most fundamentally those that "take shape in an unplanned, nature-like manner." Habermas may hedge this view by representing the "nature-like" state of his living cultures as mere appearance. Nevertheless, the construction at least implicitly treats the "living" cultural traditions or traditional ways of life as if they were organic, bounded entities, pristine with respect to — or at least clearly distinguishable from — surrounding structures of social relations or formal institutions. To that extent, this conception of cultural traditions reifies and dehistoricizes them.

As much recent scholarship has shown,[15] characterizing supposedly traditional cultures as autonomous entities is simplistic and inaccurate; despite superficial appearances that may suggest otherwise, those cultures are neither isolated nor insulated from the rationalizing imperatives of the capitalist market and state systems. Appearances to the contrary, moreover, rest on presumptions that derive from, and in their commonsensical quality thereby attest to, the persisting ideological power of the nature/culture dichotomy and of its master trope, the imagery of the state of nature. From this perspective the distinction of "nature-like" traditional cultures and strategic modern ones evokes conventional Victorian narratives contrasting primitive simplicity and civilized complexity.[16]

Victorian social science is also the ultimate source of this mind-set's academic frame of reference and heuristic: the sociocultural evolutionism of the "comparative method" in anthropology — which expressly assumed that extant small-scale societies were transparent representations of earlier stages through which contemporaneous "civilized" societies had already passed and that such small-scale societies were outside of and untainted by the institutions and dynamics simultaneously shaping the world around them.[17] As such, this way of thinking about cultures emerged from an ideological environment shaped by the racialized imperialism ascendant in that era. Not surprisingly, therefore, the current distinction between traditional and modern cultures has a more proximate theoretical foundation in a social scientific artifact of another moment of imperialist enthusiasm — the "modernization" theory that emerged in American political science after World War II.[18]

In advancing the claim regarding the distinction between authentic and artificial particularities I consciously intended to avoid such normatively laden constructions as "traditional" versus "modern" cultures. Habermas's formulation seemed to provide a way of rendering the former distinction without the normative baggage of the latter. In the intervening years I have come to the view that though Habermas's formulation may avoid pejorative evaluation of "traditional" cultures, it nonetheless, like my "authentic" versus "artificial" dichotomy, tacitly reproduces the fundamental mischaracterization of supposedly autonomous or pristine cultural forms.[19] Both his characterization and mine, moreover, at least implicitly warrant a predisposition to distrust the "objectivistically prepared and strategically employed" forms, and that predisposition is a species of the same conceptual genus as the orientation underlying the romantic, nostalgic, and millennarian standards of political legitimacy that I criticize consistently otherwise in chapter 2 and throughout this book.

Rejecting the distinction between authentic and artificial particularities does not alter the encompassing argument that contemporary black American popular culture is structured by the imperatives of corporate mass culture and marketed as folkish authenticity. If anything, jettisoning the idea of authentic particularity strengthens that argument because doing so underscores the foundation of all culture within dynamic social structures. All "unquestionable" traditions are invented and reinvented pragmatically and are shaped through contestation. There is no primordial, nature-like community that exists unproblematically apart from the warp and woof of dynamic social relations within concrete, lived history. And there are no eddies of timeless tradition unaffected by surrounding state and market systems. No cultural traditions, therefore, are "authentic" even in the restricted sense in which I have used the term.

Clarifying this issue also throws into bolder relief the conceptual inadequacy of the presumption that there are, or can be, authentic or automatically discernible community interests and that, therefore, political legitimacy rests on appeal to such interests. This presumption is most immediately a conceptual legacy of black power radicalism that continues to constrain and distort black political critique. Not only does it proceed from an impossibly idealist and essentializing notion of the black American population, but it, along with the approach to political critique and action that ensues from it, is now the greatest single intellectual impediment to construction of a left-egalitarian black politics.

If culture does not exist independently of concrete social relations — including hierarchy and ideology — and is a contested domain, then attempts to determine which voices or programs represent the group's *genuine* interests are pointless. Unraveling all the partial, hortatory, and ideological constructions of the group's nature and interests, like peeling away the layers of an onion, leaves not an essential core, but nothing. The group as a coherent entity with an identifiable standpoint, in this case the generic "black community" (or any given black community, for that matter), is a reification that at most expresses the success of some interest networks in articulating their interpretations and programs and asserting them in the name of the group. And the processes through which some interest positions succeed over others have less to do with their authenticity as representations of prior collective will than with their proponents' access to and ability to mobilize and deploy resources in order to defeat, neutralize, and pre-empt other outlooks and agendas and thereby to institutionalize their own as common sense.

What I have just described is the essence of politics. Yet it is a dimension of activity that is almost entirely absent from analyses and interpretations of politics among black Americans, and this oversight equally characterizes political scientists' academic study of black politics and radicals' strategic critiques. In both arenas inquiry into black politics systematically fails to take account of the operations of political processes among black people, within the black American population, and in discrete black communities.

This ironic circumstance is the outgrowth of features endemic to black political discourse in the segregation era. The most proximate source is the rhetorical frame of racial populism that became the signally resonant basis for internalist political critique in the black power era. As crystallized in Malcolm X's famous house Negro/field Negro comparison, this frame posits a tension between elite and masses as the central fault line in black political life. Characterizing black political stratification in this way has a superficially democratizing appearance because it proposes adherence to popular interests as the criterion of political legitimacy and because it alludes to political assertiveness emanating from the "masses." However, as I argue in chapter 2, the elite/mass model actually only reinforces the organizational logic of elite-driven pluralism—the logic of the systemically incorporated post-segregation black politics.

The concept "the masses" is in fact a homogenizing mystification; it is a category that has no specific referent in black institutional, organizational, or ideological life. Unlike workers, parents, the unemployed, welfare recipients, tenants, homeowners, lawyers, students, residents of a specific neighborhood, Methodists, or public employees, the term "the masses" does not refer to any particular social position or constituency. Nor is it likely that anyone consciously identifies simply, or even principally, as part of this undifferentiated mass. The category assumes a generic, abstract—and thus mute—referent. It therefore reproduces the nonparticipatory politics enacted by the mainstream black political elite. The masses do not speak; someone speaks for them.

In this respect, the category "the masses" is similar to the category "the underclass," and this similarity may account for some of the ease with which the latter notion has become hegemonic as a characterization of inner-city poor people—even among those who identify with left-critical or race-conscious critical stances within black political discourse. Although the image of the masses is romantically idealized and the classification "underclass" is fundamentally pejorative, the masses and the underclass are equally entities that exist only in the third person; no discernible constituency describes itself and rallies under either label. Each identity therefore must be spoken for by someone else. Each is construed as enacting politics only suggestively and by implication, not through direct, explicit civic participation.

The underclass is held to assert its political voice only substantively, in unconventional, often subterranean forms, such as existential rebelliousness and other ostensibly nonpolitical expressions of alienation, just as the masses' distinctive voice is supposedly expressed through extraordinary actions such as collective uprising and riot. The political content of either type of expression depends upon interpretive mediation, by those who possess special knowledge, to render it comprehensible to others as political action. Each population is understood to be a singular entity, and because each therefore is treated as having only corporate political agency, blanket interpretations of its aggregate will can seem reasonable.

In both cases the relation between the spoken-for population and its interpreters is ultimately custodial. The intimations of apocalyptic politics or jacquerie associated with the black power era's mystique of the masses obscure this relation by evoking popular insurgency. However, the jacquerie is always in the past or soon to come; in the politics at hand the masses and the underclass are indirect references, anonymous constituencies whose interests are articulated and brokered by others. To that extent, the underclass idea may be a conceptual extrapolation from the masses, an adaptation to a changed ideological context and a more draconian shift in the new regime of race relations management.

The image of the masses has supported a political practice centered on racial brokers' demands for government and corporate resources, figuring in as a specter of potentially cataclysmic forces that otherwise might erupt—as, for example, in the standard pre-Reaganite jeremiad threatening "a long, hot summer" if brokerage leaders' appeals were not met. At its most benign, this ploy was a useful tactic for increasing political leverage for a program of incrementally egalitarian redistribution; at its most venal, it was a cynical stratagem for extracting narrow payoffs. Unfortunately, radicals adopted the mythos of the masses as reality and targeted that nonexistent entity as their social base; the effect was to eliminate a possible restraint on those radical tendencies' flight into idealism because claiming such a base obviated two key practical tests of theories and strategies as explanations and mechanisms of mobilization: (1) whether they can persuade significant numbers of actual members of specific populations targeted for mobilization, and (2) whether they can guide action efficaciously. By contrast, the Reaganite right realized that the black masses existed only as a chimera and acted accordingly.

The underclass similarly embodies a threatening social force, though threatening in a different way. The underclass image represents the threat not of insurgency by an oppressed population with righteous grievances against injustice but of spreading and debilitating social pathology. As befits the changed ideological and policy environment, including the consolidation of the new black political class's role of managing racialized dispossession and inequality under conditions of retrenchment, the underclass appears as a fundamentally defective population whose dispossession stems most immediately from its own behavior. The nature of the threat it poses owes more to a language of contamination—crime and disease—than of jacquerie. Yet, even more than identifying and defusing the threat implied in the idea of the masses, dealing with the problem of an underclass depicted as almost ferally alien requires the black elite's intermediary role as socializing agents and role models.

The two mystifications' conceptual and functional symmetry could explain how so many of those professing left or populist affiliations could nonetheless, and apparently without qualms, embrace the underclass frame as a foundation for discussing inner-city poverty and inequality. From this perspective, it is only a rhetorical modification of the earlier, superficially more militant form of custodianship.

A long-standing commitment to a politics of racial custodianship is the deeper continuity from which the racial populism associated with the mythos of the masses derived. Its ultimate origins lie in a distinctive, class-based ideological orientation and language of politics that became hegemonic within black discourse as a direct result of disfranchisement at the turn of the twentieth century. This tendency's rise supported the institutionalization of the brokerage style that was the default form of black politics throughout the Jim Crow era and that, as I argue here, has continued to set the terms of mainstream black political debate.

By the 1880s a clearly articulated node that presumed elite priority in racial agenda setting was visible, though by no means hegemonic, in black political debate. This node's prominence grew as the national Republican party's retreat from support of black interests and the corollary ascension of white Redeemers to political power in the South after the mid-1870s altered the context of black political strategizing and threatened to curtail or nullify the gains made since Emancipation. This tendency, which converged on an ideology of racial uplift and noblesse oblige, was also steeped in the view—commonly articulated among upper-status people on both sides of the color line—that the better classes should lead the society. The black variant was propelled in particular by theories that the race's genteel and cultivated strata were best equipped to organize and guide the development of the remainder of the population.[20]

This tendency was never uncontested in black politics.[21] However, the black population's disfranchisement and expulsion from civic life in the South and the concomitant consolidation of a white supremacist order in the two decades bracketing the turn of the twentieth century altered the context of black public debate in four ways that biased the scope and participatory foundations of black political discourse sharply to favor the custodial and tutorial pretensions emanating from the race's elite strata. First, disfranchisement raised the cost of popular participation by eliminating the most accessible forms of political speech—voting and other aspects of electoral action. The effect, as in any polity, was to inflect black political discourse toward the perspectives and programs of those elements of the population with access to resources that could enable other kinds of expression—for example, newspaper publishing, business or other property ownership, and affiliation with institutions that provided visibility.

Second, the danger that any public expression of opposition to the white supremacist regime would provoke state-sanctioned retaliatory violence imposed an even greater potential cost and reinforced the voices of those who counseled accommodation to white supremacy, at least by silencing some of those who might have disagreed.

Third, the nature of the challenge posed by disfranchisement and the consolidation of the Jim Crow order exerted an understandable pressure toward a defensive and group-conscious orientation that also buttressed elite interpretations and programs. In a civic discourse otherwise biased toward elite views, the imperative of articulating a general group interest would necessarily reproduce that bias in defining collective objectives and shaping political strategies. Post-Emancipation black political activity had always strongly tended to be group conscious. The terms of discourse routinely focused, reasonably, on pursuing the good of the race, with debate—shaped most significantly through public forums such as Union Leagues and Loyal Leagues, local Republican party organizations, Colored Farmers Alliance locals, school boards and other government bodies, and lodge or church groups as well as the ballot box—centering precisely on the programmatic content of that good for specific communities and the individuals constituting them in specific circumstances. The totalistic nature of the white supremacist threat, which in principle affected all black people equally, buttressed the impetus to craft singular racial agendas.

Civic exclusion and the centripetal reaction to the tidal wave of white supremacist counterrevolution combined to install, as unexamined common sense, a political rhetoric that accepted synecdochic projection of the outlooks of the race's articulate elite strata as the collective mentality of the whole. The result was a default mode of politics in which individual "leaders" could determine and pursue agendas purportedly on the race's behalf without constraint by either prior processes of popular deliberation or subsequent accountability.

The segregation era's impact on issues of accountability and constituency is central to its fourth significant effect on the character of black political life. Not only did the segregationist regime hinder normal mechanisms of accountability, but, to the extent that a strategic vision stressing the elite's custodial and tutorial mission became dominant in black politics, concern with accountability to a popular constituency was easily made a nonissue. A leadership of the best men need not trouble itself with deliberatively based ratification and input from a population in need of tutelage and custodianship. This disposition, in fact, was one of the reasons that advocates of accommodationism were frequently willing almost blithely to accept disfranchisement. Many of them shared the view that the uncultivated should not vote and were willing to endorse disfranchisement on class grounds so long as it applied to whites as well. White Democrats often exploited black elites' belief in the possibility of interracial elite collaboration to gain acquiescence in disfranchisement schemes, disingenuously encouraging their hopes that electoral restriction was not simply a ruse for a principally racist agenda.

Although those blacks who argued for acceptance of disfranchisement were duped, it would be a mistake to dismiss them as Uncle Toms, notwithstanding that characterization's rhetorical appeal; nor should they be seen simply as sell-outs. Their expectations regarding alliance with upper-status whites stemmed most significantly not so much from self-hatred or moral deficiency as from a class-based, race-conscious conviction of their class's mission for racial stewardship and uplift. Insofar as it had philosophical underpinnings, this conviction was rooted in strains of the nineteenth century's theories of racial and cultural evolution. The discourse on which they and their strategic thinking converged was anchored on a teleology of racial destiny according to which a group's rank on the scale of civilization is measured by the level of cultivation attained by the best of its members, and the group's development is propelled by the leavening and tutelage of that elevated stratum. Far from denying racial consciousness, this view elevated racial responsibility to the grandest principle. Thus, subsequent scholars have occasionally characterized this view's prominent adherents — for example, Alexander Crummell or Booker T. Washington — as nationalist or protonationalist, though that characterization is problematic on historicist grounds.[22]

The case of Isaiah T. Montgomery, one of Mississippi's foremost apostles of racial uplift and most thoroughgoing accommodationists, illustrates the complex, historically specific features of the outlook that became predominant within black politics. Montgomery's case is suggestive as well of the constitutive role that outlook has played in shaping and constraining the content and horizon of black political thought and action, including its influence on scholars' subsequent characterizations of the nature and limits of possibility in black politics.

Isaiah T. Montgomery's father, Benjamin Thornton Montgomery, was a former slave who became one of Mississippi's most successful cotton planters. The elder Montgomery had been a slave of Jefferson Davis and his paternalistic, Owenite socialist brother, Joseph, and was a manager of their experimental, slave-run plantation at Davis Bend.[23] He eventually purchased the 4,000-acre Davis plantation and left it at his death in 1878 to his two sons, who operated the family's plantation holdings until the mid-1880s. Isaiah and his brother, William Thornton, then became central figures in another experiment, the creation of an all-black town at Mound Bayou.[24]

Isaiah became one of the wealthiest black Mississippians, a status all the more noteworthy because in the two decades before World War I Mississippi "seemed to lead all states in the development of Afro-American enterprise."[25] Like his father before him, Isaiah Montgomery thought little of suffrage for blacks, though he was an active participant in the state's Republican factional politics. In his view, racial advancement would come through racially solidaristic self-help and separate development. This was the essence of the Mound Bayou idea.

Montgomery exulted in race pride that Mound Bayou was a functioning, all-black town and boasted that "not a single white person resides or owns property within its limits." He saw the town as a monument to the race's accomplishment and a testament to its capabilities.[26] At the same time, he took accommodation to lengths that struck many of his contemporaries as extraordinary. He was the only black delegate to the 1890 state constitutional convention that disfranchised the black population and installed white supremacy. Not only was Montgomery a delegate; he even served on the key committee on elective franchise, appointment, and elections and actually voted for disfranchisement and endorsed the white supremacist regime from the convention floor, purporting to lay "the suffrage of 123,000 of my fellow-men at the feet of this convention" as "an olive branch of peace." Though he was not without black supporters, Montgomery's address and vote in no way reflected a consensus among black Mississippians, even within the elite, and he was widely reviled as a traitor.[27]

Understandably, McMillen wonders whether Montgomery's motives were sincere, whether his acquiescence in supporting the white supremacist juggernaut stemmed from an honest, if miscalculated, desire to make the best of a bad situation for blacks in Mississippi or from pursuit of narrower self-interest.[28] This is the issue on which debate about black accommodationism characteristically has pivoted in general. It is the central question driving the perennial controversy over the place of fin de siècle accommodationism's main symbol, Booker T. Washington.

Asking this question makes sense, especially because so much of interpretation and evaluation in both popular and scholarly discussion of black politics seems to hinge on it. It is crucial for judgment in a discourse that seeks to establish the place of particular leaders because it informs an assessment of the quality of individuals' leadership. However, concern with the quality of black leadership as the basis for primary interpretation and judgment is the artifact of precisely the elite-centered way of thinking about black politics that became hegemonic as a result of disfranchisement and the white supremacist consolidation.

If we imagine black political agents in the past as people much like ourselves, people who lived contingently and ambiguously within their history as it unfolded, concern with sincerity is both simpler and more complicated an issue than it might appear at first blush. From that perspective we might simply assume sincerity. Few people actually admit, even to themselves, venal or malevolent motives. And ideology, as a partial consciousness that imagines itself to be more general, exists to preserve sincerity by harmonizing potential tension between self-interest and other commitments. At one extreme is the rare individual who, under close scrutiny, may appear to be heroically selfless; at the other are some who will seem transparently and unambiguously impelled by personal gain above all else. Most, however, will fall in a vast gray area between those extremes. In such cases, debate about motives—however tempting intellectually and inescapable rhetorically—cannot be resolved conclusively.

Thinking of past political figures as operating, as we do, within contingent history also muddies the issue of the accuracy of their views regarding the limits of possibility. They were no better able to foretell which historical and political tendencies would triumph or exactly how the dominant tendencies would take shape in their time than we are in ours. Fin de siècle accommodationists' notions of what was politically possible and feasible derived from a particular sense of how the world worked. Prevailing beliefs that social development—in general and among Afro-Americans in particular—is properly and most effectively steered by enlightened upper classes disposed black accommodationists toward strategic goals and a politics that emphasized the importance of alliances with white elites as both desirable and necessary. This disposition biased perceptions of the horizon of possibility. Maintaining access to the goodwill and philanthropy of the "best" whites no doubt figured centrally in the calculus of feasibility. Similarly, and relatedly, concern not to jeopardize their own relatively well-off material circumstances and the small privileges that depended upon white largesse certainly played a role in shaping elite accommodationists' understanding of the boundaries of rational political strategy and action.

Accommodationism, therefore, appeared to be inevitable in the context of specific assumptions regarding proper social organization, appropriate goals, and the locus of effective political agency—assumptions that screened from view or preempted other possibilities. Because disfranchisement undercut processes of democratic political debate within black communities, we cannot really know how broadly that class-inflected common sense was shared among other strata of the black population. That it was challenged forcefully even within the black elite, however, certainly supports skepticism about its proponents' claims that the accommodationist course was the only one available.

The contention that accommodationism was the only realistic option also may underestimate the contingencies of the actual political circumstances by naively reading the exact forms of white supremacist politics that became dominant as evidence that no other form of politics could have existed. The range of options in black political life as white supremacy consolidated was very narrowly limited, without question, and I do not wish to exaggerate the extent to which there was space to maneuver. Nevertheless, recognizing how tightly constrained black options were and how powerful the white supremacist tide was does not justify the conclusion that nothing could have been at all different. Such a conclusion denies the fundamentally dynamic, processual nature of politics. More significantly for critical understanding of black politics, it also overlooks the active role of black political agency in shaping even the character of the white supremacist triumph.

Isaiah Montgomery is again instructive. His participation in the 1890 disfranchising constitutional convention clearly crossed the line from accommodation to complicity, notwithstanding however he may have understood his behavior, and his presence was instrumental for the white supremacist project. At the outset of the reactionary push in the 1890s enough sentiment persisted outside the South in support of black civil rights—and particularly in support of the Fifteenth Amendment—that white supremacists were typically careful to cloak their initiatives of civic exclusion in color-blind language for fear that being too explicit in their racial agenda could provoke federal intervention.[29] In that context, being able to point to black endorsements was at least marginally useful in salving the consciences of northern whites who might otherwise have felt their ethical sympathies and principles uncomfortably compromised. Support from prominent blacks thereby helped minimally to neutralize liberal whites' opposition. (Contemporary analogues can be seen in Reaganites' cynical use of Thomas Sowell and other black conservatives as insulation against charges of racism and in William Julius Wilson's role in legitimizing underclass ideology for Clinton-era liberals—who, like their counterparts a century earlier, would just as soon retreat from pursuit of racial justice—by giving a black, putatively liberal seal of approval to a fundamentally racialized explanation of inequality.) Not surprisingly, therefore, Montgomery was lauded for his capitulationist stance not only by Mississippi's white elite but also by much of national centrist and conservative opinion, including Democratic former president Grover Cleveland.[30]

Booker T. Washington's Atlanta Compromise address five years later prompted similar, even more elaborate enthusiasm, both from whites outside the South who were hopeful of eliminating race as an issue in national politics and from southern whites who happily projected his speech as evidence of blacks' support for white supremacy.[31] Washington's speech preceded by a year the infamous *Plessy v. Ferguson* decision, in which Justice Henry Billings Brown's majority opinion formalized what became the "separate but equal" doctrine in language quite similar to Washington's separate as the fingers, together as the hand metaphor. It would not be unreasonable to suspect that Washington's highly publicized address and his ensuing rise to prominence helped, again at least marginally, in creating the political and ideological climate that shaped the decision.

In raising this possibility I do not intend to argue that Washington should be held culpable for the *Plessy* ruling, any more than Montgomery should be held responsible for disfranchisement in Mississippi; both outcomes were driven by much more powerful and insistent forces. However, the claim, frequently advanced to defend the integrity or historical reputations of Washington or Montgomery, that blacks' accommodationist participation was purely a response to a fait accompli and played no active role in the white supremacist consolidation trivializes black political agency by assuming that blacks' actions could not af-

fect their institutional and ideological environment. The fact that white supremacists found conspicuous support from prestigious blacks helpful to their cause
implies that not having that support might have made their task that much more
difficult and that that additional increment of difficulty could have produced, at
a minimum, a differently enacted, perhaps less totalistic or superficially somewhat
more restrained, regime of white supremacy in the South. It does not require resorting to fantastic counterfactuals to envision a white supremacist victory that
was less thorough in expelling blacks from civic life and that therefore would
have had to craft different ways of coming to terms with even a moderately more
significant black presence in southern politics. A slight alteration in the balance
of political forces can produce incremental differences in governing arrangements
that, even if only of degree rather than kind, can have substantial consequences
for subsequent political opportunities.

The fact that disfranchisement's evisceration and class distortion of the black
public forum makes it impossible for us to determine how widely the accommodationist perspective was shared among black Americans is significant not because that uncertainty prevents us from establishing accommodationism's racial
authenticity. Not only, as I have argued here, is the idea of racial authenticity a
hopeless mystification, but even if it were possible to demonstrate majority, or
even consensual, support for accommodationist politics in the equivalent of black
public opinion, that by itself would not indicate its accuracy as a reading of political options at the time. The real significance of the narrowing of the black
public political forum is that in undercutting the mechanisms of democratic accountability, it absolved accommodationist elites of the need to subject their
strategies to popular discussion and debate.[32] That discussion would have included
the voices of those whose social positions probably would have led them to different calculations of the stakes involved in opting for any course. Because political reality is always contingent and fluid, all estimations of political feasibility
are inseparable from such differing calculations of the risks and opportunities
attendant on any given course of action at a given point in time. It is likely, therefore, that more open debate would have yielded substantially, if not radically,
different assessments of the limits of black political possibility.

Isaiah Montgomery's judgment of political necessity was influenced by his
larger views, views that made giving up the franchise seem not so great a cost
for the black population, and by his recognition that his fragile Mound Bayou experiment, as well as his personal standing, depended on alliances with the powerful
white proponents of disfranchisement. When Montgomery attempted to launch

the Mound Bayou Oil Mill and Manufacturing Company some years later, he sought financial backing from the American Bankers Association, the Illinois Central Railroad, and Julius Rosenwald, among other philanthropists and wealthy whites.[33] His sense of political rationality, like Washington's, had to have been colored by commitment to a racial uplift strategy predicated on the importance of access to such networks.

Other black people pursued very different kinds of strategy during the period between Hayes-Tilden and white supremacist consolidation. The Colored Farmers Alliance, linked with the Populist movement, claimed at its crest over 1,250,000 members.[34] The Knights of Labor had 3,000 members in the late 1880s in Montgomery's own Mississippi, a majority of them black, and some locals were even organized and operated on a racially integrated basis.[35] The Knights were active and had significant black membership through much of the South during the entirety of the organization's active existence, and Sterling D. Spero and Abram L. Harris consider reasonable an estimate that the Knights' black membership at one point totaled approximately 60,000.[36] In addition to the Knights, black people were involved during that period in labor and trade union activism all through the South.[37]

Elite figures such as Frederick Douglass, prominent journalist and publisher T. Thomas Fortune, and former Mississippi congressman and Republican official John R. Lynch endorsed this sort of political activity during the 1880s, even as the distinct node of conservative, self-help uplift ideology—the strain from which accommodationism emerged—was forming in petit bourgeois black political discourse. However, this support was tempered by their other pragmatic and material commitments to Republican party politics.[38] Douglass counseled against independent political action. Even as he acknowledged the importance of organizing and agitating on a class and economic basis, as early as the 1870s he discouraged the National Negro Labor Union from supporting an independent Labor party.[39]

For Douglass and others, reluctance to deviate from a politics based in the Republican party rested on the pragmatic argument that the GOP was the only dependable ally of black interests in national politics; they expressed fear that deserting the party would lead to unmitigated Democratic power in the South and perhaps nationally, an outcome that could only be dangerous for blacks. Yet their interpretation of the paramountcy of Republican partisanship also coincided with the articulation of a petit bourgeois racial politics that reflected the diminished expectations of the post-Reconstruction era. What came to be known as Black and Tan Republicanism pivoted on delivering a shrinking black vote to support the national ticket every four years in exchange for control of a limited set of patronage appointments.[40]

Particularly in the context of the narrowed black public forum, it is impossible to disentangle honestly pragmatic assessment and dependence on patronage politics as causes of elite aversion to independent political action. Either way, the petit bourgeois ideology of racial uplift reinforced the group custodianship that was Black and Tan Republicanism's foundation. Uplift, after all, presumed a mass population that was by definition not capable of steering its own programmatic course or mobilizing on its own behalf. Because its main resource was its claim to a connection to a bloc of black voters, patronage politics was most compatible with goals and organizational strategies that emphasized racial collectivity. Uplift ideology's foundations in the era's theories of racial development reinforced that practical, material bias by giving it an ontological rationality. On the premise that elevating the best men advanced the group as a whole, securing patronage appointments for elite blacks appeared to be a generic gain for the race. The potential for felicitous pursuit of a politics that took class interest as synecdochic for race interest was overwhelming.

Advocates of accommodationism, which was uplift ideology's most conservative expression, opposed trade unionism or labor-based political action for blacks almost by definition.[41] However, the class-inflected notions of race development on which uplift vision rested also undergirded similar views among many of the elite opponents of the conciliationist program of those like Washington or Montgomery.[42] Anna Julia Cooper, now heralded as an early black feminist, strikingly illustrates the connection between the black elite's racial theories, uplift ideology, and opposition to working-class political organization for blacks. Cooper interpreted the basis of American race conflict through the lens of prevailing historical, or neo-Lamarckian, race theories that emphasized racial differences in character or "ideals."[43]

She then argued that blacks' contribution to America derived from such racial traits, including "inborn respect for authority... inaptitude for rioting and anarchy... gentleness and cheerfulness as a laborer... which will prove indispensable and invaluable elements in a nation menaced as America is by anarchy, socialism, communism, and skepticism poured in with all the jailbirds from... Europe and Asia."[44] Later in the same text she confessed to a lack of sympathy for the workers suppressed in the 1892 Homestead, Pennsylvania, steel struggle, the eight-hour-day movement, or labor unions in general; she contended that her feelings arose from labor's ill-treatment of blacks, marshaling anecdotes and apocrypha to buttress her assertions, but at the same time she expressed strong nativist and anti-immigrant sentiments. Cooper also firmly maintained that philanthropy was to be the uplift enterprise's main source of material support.[45]

W. E. B. Du Bois, even as symbolic primus inter pares among militant foes of accommodationism, during this period unequivocally embraced the elite's uplift vision. Indeed, under his "Talented Tenth" rubric he theorized it more elaborately than most. Much of the keenness of Du Bois's early criticism of Washington, moreover, centered on the Tuskegeean's attempt to establish a personal monopoly among petit bourgeois race spokesmen. Similarly, the anti-Washington Niagara Movement proceeded from this class vision. The opening lines of its founding declaration praised black accomplishments in "the increase of intelligence, the buying of property, the checking of crime, and uplift in home life, the advance in literature and art, and the demonstration of constructive and executive ability in the conduct of great religious, economic and educational institutions." The statement went on to note the propriety of discrimination on the basis of "ignorance, disease or immorality," as distinct from that based on race.[46]

I have taken this excursion to the dawn of the segregation era to underscore the extent to which black political activity was differentiated prior to the white supremacist consolidation. Black people engaged, as individuals and as groups, in many different kinds of political action. Though black Americans' racial status always at least partly shaped the character of their political involvements, the goals of those involvements were by no means always exclusively, or even primarily, racial. Nor was their politics always enacted on behalf of a generically racial population. In addition to pursuing more broadly racial objectives, black farmers organized and acted as black farmers; planters acted on their interests as planters; dockworkers acted as dockworkers—even as they linked those activities to the larger goal of improving the race's condition.

The victory of the custodial approach to politics warranted by the ideology of racial uplift narrowed the scope of what was understood to be appropriate black political action to endeavors undertaken on behalf of or in the name of the race as an undifferentiated, corporate entity. This focus is exemplified in the common reference to "the Negro" as a collective subject.[47] Uplift ideology became hegemonic in black politics not because of inevitable historical forces or popular racial consensus but because its adherents' social position enabled them to establish that outlook's interpretive and strategic imperatives as the boundaries of legitimacy under prevailing political conditions. An intellectual consequence of that petit bourgeois hegemony was a forgetting: As the premises and practices of uplift ideology came to monopolize the effective substance of publicly visible black political discourse and action, they came to be seen as the only way of conceiving of black American politics.

The emergence of the study of black politics as an academic subfield reinforced this process of naturalization by formalizing its outcomes through a discourse that presumes black Americans to be a corporate racial body politically. This presumption requires anchoring conceptions of the black political universe to a strategic least common denominator of pursuit of racial advancement in general, thus rendering observable political differences as tactical, superficial (for example, owing to quirks of personality and individual character), or—if too great to be credibly minimized in that way—as reflecting deviant or inauthentic political commitments.

To be sure, a scholarly focus on activities consistent with the norm of advancing collective interests of the racial group has seemed appropriate not only because of petit bourgeois hegemony but also because institutionalized discrimination and explicitly racial exclusion have been such major factors in black American life, particularly during the field's formative period. Concern with countering racism and its effects has obviously figured centrally in black political practice and rhetoric; that it should be a central element in scholarly accounts of that practice and rhetoric is in one sense, therefore, only the expression of faithful representation of empirical realities. However, the field's foundation in a scholarly discourse that unreflectively takes the racial least common denominator as the conceptual orienting point for inquiry both artificially limits the content of black politics and distorts examination of its internal dynamics. Reducing black political differences to disagreements about tactics, for instance, supports the construction of procrustean, ahistorical typologies such as the variations on the theme of a dichotomy between tendencies advocating protest and those advocating accommodation (or Harold Cruse's recasting of the dichotomy as one between nationalism and integrationism) as the animating tension in black politics. As Judith Stein argues, with specific reference to August Meier's typology of black political thought as an oscillation between self-help and protest or between accommodation and militance, this presents an impoverished view of black political activity "by excluding actions which encompassed but transcended racial goals, and at the same time misrepresents the racial movements themselves because of the abstractions which lie at the base of the theory." Reliance on such an abstract and formalistic construction of black politics washes out significant substantive distinctions among kinds of political action. Again referring to Meier, Stein points out the conceptual inadequacy and potentially distorting effects of treating "legislators' attempts to pass civil rights bills, black laborers' entrance into unions, and social workers' negotiations to find jobs [as] equivalent acts."[48]

Early studies of black politics, such as Gosnell's *Negro Politicians* and Ralph Bunche's more engaged critical analyses during the 1930s and 1940s, demonstrate both the reasonableness of the field's thematization of the corporate racial subject and its ultimate inadequacy.[49] Gosnell provided a subtle and textured account of the intricacies of black political development in Chicago during the first three decades of the twentieth century. To Gosnell's left, Bunche laid out a comparably sophisticated view of the tendencies operating within black politics at the time. Both described the variety of organizational forms and patterns of alliance that shaped black politics.

Gosnell examined the relations between the structures of black electoral mobilization—chiefly churches, press, economic and professional groups, and fraternal and uplift/racial interest groups—and specific interest configurations in the larger local political system, arguing that those relations were partly constitutive of black politics insofar as they defined the substantive payoffs, material and symbolic, of political action and shaped issue positions among black elites and opinion leaders.[50] He indicated, for instance, that the general prevalence of antiblack racism in the local polity created a very narrow context of options from which an instrumental logic drew black politicians toward commitment to the dominant machine and business interests. He also noted the potentially contradictory implications of that logical alliance, as when Oscar DePriest, the first black person elected to Congress in the twentieth century, was forced in the second year of the Great Depression to retreat from his initial opposition (as a good Republican) to the federal provision of relief by his black constituents' extensive need for aid.[51] In Gosnell's view, mainstream black politicians "felt that it was necessary to go along with the white leaders in power in order that they might protect their own people against attacks on the Civil Rights Act and against intolerant movements."[52]

Gosnell recognized that a politics that was largely centered on obtaining the kinds of employment and appointments he described could not begin to be adequate as a material inducement for popular participation. He observed, though, that

the governmental jobs . . . have not only meant a livelihood for an important fraction but they have also brought prestige to the entire group. The presence in the city of a Negro ward superintendent, Negro principal clerks, Negroes in charge of branch libraries, Negro police lieutenants and sergeants, a Negro fire captain, a Negro school principal, Negro high-school teachers, and Negro postal foremen meant that the group was getting on. The occupation of these offices meant that the group was bearing some of the responsibilities of the government.[53]

This assessment was no doubt accurate. Even black people who did not themselves gain materially from the regime's distributive arrangements certainly viewed its partial and incremental benefits as symbolic accomplishments for the race at large. Such sentiments had a rational foundation in the objective limitations imposed on black aspiration by the environment of racial subordination. In a context defined by limited possibility for generalized material benefits, advances by individuals understandably came to represent successes for the group as a whole and could be regarded as steps along the way to more general benefits. Moreover, to the extent that racial subordination rested on ideological justifications alleging black incapacity, examples of black accomplishment took on significance as points of empirical refutation.

Nevertheless, the fact remains that the material benefits realized through the regime of racial politics that Gosnell describes were sharply skewed toward the stratum of upper-status blacks, who also propagated the outlook that imbued their material advances with broader symbolic meaning. Gosnell did not recognize the potentially complicating effect of that circumstance on his account of black politics because his a priori acceptance of the premise of a corporate racial subject provided no conceptual space for him to perceive fundamental distinctions between individual and group impacts. Seeing black politics as reducible to the generic "struggle of the Negro to get ahead," the least common denominator of racial advancement, encourages a naive view of the relation between the differential benefits of the prevailing regime of racial politics and black elites' arguments for its optimality.[54]

The hegemonic power of the presumption that there is a collective racial subject appears even more strikingly in Bunche's critical analysis of black politics. Bunche grounded his analysis of black politics during the 1930s and early 1940s on a rather doctrinaire Marxism. He was not blind to, or sanguine about, class stratification among blacks in general, and he was incisively critical of the petit bourgeois character of the programs of racial advocacy organizations. He also recognized the narrowness and inadequacy of a politics focused solely on eliminating discrimination and argued that its limitations reflected a petit bourgeois acquiescence to ruling-class interests.[55] Yet Bunche's analysis proceeded no less than Gosnell's from an undergirding conception of a corporate racial standpoint in politics. Indeed, the acuity of his judgment of racial advocacy organizations derived largely from his perception that their strategies poorly served the general group interest.

Bunche's Marxism, reflecting a common strain, accommodated this notion in an argument that the caste aspect of blacks' social position warranted a political strategy that would "defend and represent the basic interests of the Negro workers, of the Negro peasants, and of the Negro petty bourgeoisie, to the degree that the latter constitutes a progressive historical force."[56] His notion of the collective racial interest was purposively linked to a specific teleology, the march to socialist revolution, without which, he contended, the struggle for racial equality could not ultimately succeed. By the lights of that teleology, in principle (though not yet in fact) "the Negro proletariat constitutes historically the natural leadership of the Negro people in its social struggle in American society."[57] Therefore, even when Bunche characterized black Americans as a corporate entity—for example, the Negro people as a singular possessive—he did not construe that entity as an organic unit devoid of problematic differentiation or intrinsic tensions. His "Negro people" more closely approximated a coherent but internally stratified population whose different strata had different interests and agendas. Certain of those interests and agendas were consonant with the direction of the overarching teleology, and the strata identified with those interests constituted the "natural" or correct interests of the group.

For instance, a decade after his especially doctrinaire formulations in "Marxism and the 'Negro Question,'" Bunche expressed frustration with the National Negro Congress for operating on a "united front" principle. He objected that "the Congress has proceeded on the assumption that the common denominator of race is enough to weld together, in thought and action, such divergent segments of the Negro society as preachers and labor organizers, lodge officials and black workers, Negro businessmen, Negro radicals, professional politicians, professional men, domestic servants, black butchers, bakers and candlestick makers." Judging that approach to be immobilizing, he argued instead that a "Negro Congress with a strong labor bias and with its representation less diffuse and more homogeneous in its thinking could conceivably work out a clearer, more consistent and realistic program."[58]

Bunche was almost apologetic in his support of a politics of racial identity, noting:

> The white voter ballots according to his individual, sectional, and group
> interests. The Negro votes on the basis of identical interests, but the

social system of America dictates that he must give prior consideration to his racial group interests. So long as the dual social system persists in the United States, just so long must the Negro justifiably expect that political parties desiring his political support will devote specific attention to ways and means of Negro betterment in framing their platforms. The Negro finds himself in the uncomfortable position of decrying racial differentiation, while being compelled to demand it when important political policies are being formulated, in order to hold his ground in an uncongenial social milieu.[59]

Bunche considered black racial solidarity to be entirely a function of the "dual social system" and was emphatic and rigorous in his rejection of race-based social theory as well as of what we would now call racial essentialism.[60] Nevertheless, he constructed his critiques of black politics around the conventional notion of a collective racial subject. As his own statement indicates, his doing so was an expression of the reality of black life at the time, the centrality of explicitly and generically racial subordination as a fetter on black Americans across the board.

Bunche's attempt to articulate a popular, class-based critique within the political discourse oriented toward the idea of a corporate black interest throws into relief its interpretive shortcomings, most consequentially its reliance on a naturalistic rhetoric of racial authenticity as the standard of political legitimacy. His invocations of the collective subject sometimes hovered ambiguously between a formulation resting on the teleological assertion that the interests of the mass of Negro toilers, to borrow the parlance of the day, represented the true interests of the group and a formulation that seemed less mediated and thus more akin to the naturalized notion of corporate racial interest inherited from uplift ideology. However, even Bunche's more complex construction of group interest also fit uncontroversially within the discourse that cohered around the latter notion, which — in treating the racial interest as a given and not as the result of contestation or other contingent processes — inscribes elite race spokesmen as arbiters of group strategy.

Bunche surely would have objected to such a characterization. He certainly wanted no part of the belief on which the standard of racial authenticity ultimately rests: that racial identity confers a single, common sensibility. His notion of authenticity was concretely grounded and based on an analysis of Afro-American social structure; unlike others' notions, his was tied strategically to a long-term goal of broad social reorganization along very specific lines and did not claim to represent a universal racial consensus, and his notion of proper race leadership insisted on a major role for labor organizations.[61] Bunche astutely identified and challenged the limited class character of the main racial advocacy organizations' interpretations and programs; he drew attention to the programmatic and ideological significance of social differentiation and hierarchy among black Americans, which was an important intervention both analytically and politically. However, in positing a general racial interest that could be determined a priori—apart from processes of popular deliberation—his critique engaged strategic debate on terms that reproduced, probably unintentionally, the prevailing rhetoric of racial authenticity and thus the fundamentally custodial political discourse within which that rhetoric was, and remains, embedded.

Bunche's reading of the practical entailments of the "caste" system that he described combined with his particular teleological commitments to lead him to accept without hesitation a frame for critical inquiry and debate that centered on determining authentic spokesmanship for the racial group. The working class articulated the racial group's true interests because it was the segment of the population whose social position and perspective advanced the larger struggle for social transformation that was necessary to win racial equality. That interpretation was consistent with the exigencies of race-solidaristic politics at the time. Systematic racial exclusion and discrimination required broadly based responses that united as much of the black population as possible, and crafting such responses was understandably the default mode for black political debate. However, in unskeptically proposing the black proletariat as the agent of the entire racial group's true interests, Bunche tacitly accepted the most insidious foundations of the class-skewed ideology that he criticized.

As a result of his acquiescence to the rhetoric of authenticity, Bunche's critique did not confront the custodial model of political action that derived from and rationalized commitment to elite primacy in steering the affairs of the race. Nor was he attentive to the antidemocratic entailments of the presumption of corporate racial interest, which evaded potentially complicating questions of participation, legitimacy, and accountability by positing an organic unity as black Americans' natural state. And, of course, by operating within it he could not address the rhetoric of the authenticity of race spokesmanship as a mechanism facilitating those evasions. To that extent, Bunche's radicalism left intact the core of the ideology of racial uplift on which the black petite bourgeoisie rested its claims to political and cultural authority. Bunche did not explicitly ratify this discourse, but his historically reasonable acceptance of it at least instantiated, and arguably helped to establish, a pattern of radical social science discourse about black politics that strained against but did not fully transcend the petit bourgeois ideological hegemony.

During the post–World War II period, largely as an expression of the changing political climate I describe in chapers 2 and 3, the study of black politics began to coalesce as a conventional academic specialty. Robert E. Martin stands out for having provided an early institutional account of the sources and effects of increased black electoral participation and officehoolding. He described how the decades of black migration from the disfranchised South had culminateed in growth of black influence in national politics that buttressed the challenge to civic exclustion in Dixie.[62] Thereafter, however, reflecting the heightened awareness of black presence in national and big-city politics and the explosion of activist protest in the South, the subfield initially clustered around questions concerning the nature, dynamics, and composition of black political leadership.[63] It is instructive to note that despite often careful and nuanced case descriptions of leadership styles and much attention to construction of empirically based typologies, this scholarship generally bypassed or touched only superficially on questions of accountability and the actual processes of leadership selection.[64]

In part this lacuna resulted from the fact that the intensifying struggle against Jim Crow had strengthened programmatic solidarity within black politics, as was attested by the antisegregationist unanimity expressed in the 1944 anthology *What the Negro Wants*.[65] In that context, unless scholars were predisposed to pursue questions of accountability and legitimacy, there would be little reason for them to arise. In addition, the reputational method through which the case studies typically ascertained leadership was useful for identifying characteristics of those recognized as leaders and thus for describing how the politics of race advancement was enacted pragmatically at the level of local polities. This method by itself, however, did not prompt inquiry into issues bearing on the shaping of strategic consensus and the processes of legitimation within black politics because its focus was on describing the settled outcomes of those processes; nor did it facilitate critical examination of how different interests were weighted in defining the concrete substance of the racial agenda in particular circumstances. In effect this approach detached the idea of political leadership from participation and other group processes, and it presumed a simplistic identity between elite and nonelite interests and objectives.

These limitations on intellectual perception derived more from ideology than from methodology, however. As is indicated by Ladd's reduction of the function of black leadership to the promotion of generic, unproblematized group interests, the scholarly discourse that formed around inquiry into black political leadership unquestioningly reproduced the presumption of the black corporate political entity. It is telling that none of the main characterizations of black leadership considered either the possible existence — much less significance — of interest differentiation among black Americans or tension and ambiguity in the relation between the leaders and the led as factors shaping the dynamics of black leadership.[66] Perhaps most revealingly, this was true even of Oliver C. Cox, whose work and outlook were at least sympathetic to Marxism.

Cox's typology of black leadership began with the postulation of unitary racial interest: "Negroes, probably more than any other group of Americans, have an abiding common cause." He then defined black leadership as "those who, through their energy and insight, have become advocates of means and methods of dealing with this common cause and whose advocacy has been significantly accepted by the group."[67] Like Bunche, Cox viewed that cause as partly transcending race; he saw it instead as "an aspect of the wider phenomenon of political-class antagonism inseparably associated with capitalist culture. A principle involved in the process of democratic development is at the basis of the Negro's cause."[68] Again like Bunche, Cox saw this larger purpose as providing a foundation for making judgments regarding the efficacy of types of black leadership. He proposed that the truest leadership was the one that in charting a course for black people also advanced the historic "march toward democracy."[69] This led him to characterize protest leadership as "genuine," though "negative" in that it stopped short of challenging the basic social system, and radical leadership as both "genuine" and "positive" because "it is not only conscious of the source of the limitation of [blacks'] citizenship rights but also recognizes that the limitation itself is a function of the social system."[70]

Like Bunche and others before and since, Cox was motivated in part by a concern to theorize a coherent relation between black Americans' struggle against racial oppression and a Marxian strategy for more general social transformation. But his perception of class as a source of political tension did not extend to his analysis of black leadership. His account presumed the black population to be an inert entity, a singular mass to be mobilized by one or another strain of leader.

At the risk of repetitiveness, the bias in Cox's critique toward the presumption of corporate racial identity, as in the leadership studies generally, was a rational expression of the manifest realities of black politics at the time. On the one hand, regular mechanisms for the popular selection of leaders were rare, and on the other, the primacy and immediacy of the struggle against segregation imposed a practical coherence and commonality of purpose. The latter circumstance no doubt made the former all the less likely to arise as a matter for concern.

A need for formalized systems of participation is only likely to be perceived where substantial differences are apparent.[71] The hegemonic status of the outlook that defined the sphere of black political action narrowly, as the elite-driven politics of racial advancement, was also conducive to inattentiveness toward issues of participation, accountability, and legitimation. Social science reinforced this overdetermination because in establishing the terms of inquiry around an unquestioning acceptance of the prevailing model as the quintessential facts of black political life, scholarly discourse inscribed it as the natural truth of Afro-American politics. To that extent, the study *of* black politics has been a moment in the dialectical reproduction of petit bourgeois hegemony *in* black politics.

With the rise of black officialdom in the 1970s, Afro-Americanist scholarship in political science focused centrally on assessing the significance of the new, institutionally based black politics. This scholarship primarily examined such issues as the ways in which black public officials represent black political interests, the pressures operating on them to balance advancement of black concerns with other imperatives flowing from their formal positions and the alliances outside the race on which they depend, and the impact of systemic incorporation on black political styles.[72] In particular, Robert Smith provided an institutional account of the development of the new black officialdom from protest politics in the 1960s. Matthew Holden and Michael Preston very early explored the constraints that the autonomous imperatives of political institutions and entrenched patterns of political behavior in local polities placed on the capacities of the newly elected black mayors. Lenneal Henderson examined the effects of similar constraints on the growing cohort of nonelected public administrators. This current of scholarship began, albeit most often tentatively, to examine structural characteristics and tensions endemic to black politics. However, Martin Kilson was virtually alone in extending the analysis to take for granted political differentiation among black Americans—along class, ideological, and other lines—as a normal and predictable feature of systemic incorporation.

As black officeholding and governance became more established, scholars naturally enough began to consider its efficacy. Albert Karnig and Susan Welch, Peter Eisinger, and others sought to determine the policy impact of the new black officialdom. The overlap between the black politics specialty and the urban politics specialty grew, as scholars like William E. Nelson Jr., Rufus Browning, Dale Rogers Marshall, David Tabb, Clarence Stone, Larry Bennett, and James Button probed at the outcomes of the new minority politics.[73] Nelson, Stone, and Bennett were exceptional, however, in problematizing the differential distribution of the benefits of black officialdom within the black constituency. More typically, this issue did not arise. Instead, the main line of scholarly discourse assumed, as had been the norm in the field since Gosnell, that racial benefits delivered by black officials were indivisible, that even benefits to individuals—such as public procurement contracts or executive appointments—equally, if differently, benefited the black population as a whole.

That assumption was not without empirical basis. Black citizens by and large no doubt did regard gains made by black individuals, especially in the early years of post–segregation era black governance, as having larger racial significance. As in Gosnell's Chicago of the 1920s and 1930s, many people saw those individual benefits as symbols of generic racial accomplishment and a promise of more broadly disseminated concrete gains to come. The rhetoric of racial advancement that undergirded the rise of the new black political regime encouraged and reinforced such views. But scholars' acceptance of that ultimately elite-driven interpretation simply as transparent fact also contributed to its persuasiveness as ideology and as rationalization of class privilege. Even criticisms of the inadequacies and unrealized potential of black governance were couched in terms that presumed the existence of a coherent black community agenda and that most often absolved black officials of agency by stressing their powerlessness and dependence.[74] The presumption of corporate racial interest continued to shape the field's conceptual foundation.

Perhaps the most striking contemporary indication of that presumption's persisting force is that it frames recent scholarship explicitly concerned with examining black political differentiation. Studies by Katherine Tate and Michael Dawson inquire directly whether increased systemic integration and economic mobility since the 1970s have had a centrifugal impact on black political behavior and attitudes. Carol Swain, in a study centered on the quality of congressional representation of black interests, declares at the outset of her book that black Americans' political interests are "varied and complex." However, each author proceeds by assuming the primacy of corporate racial interests.[75]

Tate anchors her inquiry conceptually to an uninterrogated notion of "the black vote," or the "new black voter," as the baseline expression of black political activity.[76] This formulation, which, as I have noted above, has its origins in the elite brokerage regime of Black and Tan Republicanism at the dawn of the Jim Crow era, naturalizes the idea of a unitary racial voice. It biases interpretation toward assigning both logical and normative priority to high racial cohesion as the standard from which differentiation is the aberration. A politics centered on the idea of the black vote must be geared strategically toward defining the scope of political action in ways that facilitate mobilization around broad racial appeals. This in turn requires grounding the analytical universe of black politics on those programmatic and issue agendas that seem to have very broad or consensual black support—the program of generic racial advancement. To that extent, Tate's project verges on tautology: If the sphere of black politics is limited to areas of broad racial agreement, then interest differentiation within black politics will appear to be slight almost by definition. Although the range and number of practices and issues that compose that universe may vary at any given moment, the universe itself will always exhibit little differentiation on pertinent issues because its boundaries are stipulated so that group homogeneity is one of its essential features. Moreover, insofar as high racial cohesion is treated as a norm and an at least implicit goal, differentiation will appear as a problem to be explained and ultimately overcome. This logical problem's embeddedness in hegemonic ideology renders it invisible, but it is the source of conceptual difficulties in Tate's account.

Tate asks, "Are Blacks still race-conscious? Do Blacks have group interests, or have their policy views become more individualistic?"[77] Those questions set up false oppositions between race consciousness and political differentiation and between group and individual interests. Race consciousness can support many different, even conflicting, political programs, ranging across the ideological spectrum; therefore, the category is practically meaningless other than for demonstrating what the idea of "the black vote" already presupposes, the existence of a politics nominally centered on advancing the interests of the group in general. It would be very difficult, moreover, to imagine the disappearance of black race consciousness in the face of persisting racial stratification and resurgent antiblack rhetoric and political initiatives.

And the crucial question regarding group interests is not whether they exist; the notion of the black vote presumes their existence. The more important issues for making sense of black politics are how concrete group interests are determined, who determines them, and how those determinations, including the strategies and objectives they warrant, affect different elements of the black American population. Reducing black politics to the black vote hinders addressing these questions because its presumption of cohesiveness as a natural state overlooks the processes of interest formation to take their outcomes as given. This mindset also bypasses questions pertaining to the distribution of costs and benefits resulting from those outcomes, as well as consideration of possible alternative processes, strategies, and objectives.

Because it leaves no space for conceptualizing structural or institutional processes *within* black politics, that presumption of cohesiveness—the corporate racial interest—also leads analyses of differentiation to focus on aggregates of individual attitudes and opinions and the extent of their approximations to or divergence from putative group norms. This disposition may stem most immediately from the bias toward that sort of approach within the conventions of political science's larger American politics subfield. However, that line of inquiry also comports well with and reinforces the dominant tendency within Afro-Americanist discourse to naturalize formulations of group interests and agendas; the effect is to reify the group by screening out consideration of questions bearing on the internal and external dynamics of its constitution as a political entity. Here again the relation between ideological and intellectual commitments is dialectical, and that dialectic shapes the choice of approach and method for inquiry by informing the definition of problems and questions to be pursued. By vesting it with the appearance of a settled finding of social science, the interaction of unexamined ideology and approach to inquiry in this case buttresses the perception of black interests as given and unproblematic. At the same time, this convergence of ideological common sense and political science convention hampers Tate's ability to produce a coherent or textured account of the new black politics.

Finding continuities or incremental shifts on issue positions over time within a universe of black respondents does not tell us anything about the agenda-setting and opinion-leading dynamics operating within the new black politics; nor does comparing black and white attitudes, which substitutes conveying a sense of generic racial difference for describing politics among black Americans.[78] The limitations of Tate's approach and its encompassing mind-set show through clearly in the way that she seeks to address the relation of race and class in black politics.

She begins with the currently common move of juxtaposing race and class as alternative bases of political identification. Consonant with the underlying presumption of racial cohesion, that formulation implicitly denies the possibility that class dynamics may arise from and operate autonomously within black politics and the stratification systems of black communities. For example, Tate finds that among black Americans racial consciousness seems to vary by class and that "it is not the poor and working-class Blacks but the higher-status Blacks who possess the stronger racial consciousness and identities."[79] She observes that these findings contradict conventional social theoretical wisdom that "poor Blacks, particularly the urban poor, possess the strongest racial identities within the Black community."[80] Her attempts to locate possible explanations for this apparent anomaly focus on class status factors that could strengthen or weaken individuals' racial identity, which she takes as given.

She does not consider that what makes these findings seem anomalous could be the presumption of a singular, fixed racial identity that exists in greater or lesser degrees.[81] That presumption preempts the possibility that class-linked variations in expressed race consciousness indicate differences of kind as well as degree of racial consciousness and that those differences are linked to, among other factors, class-based ideological, institutional, and programmatic dynamics at least partly internal to black political life. The pattern that she finds could represent different ways of understanding racial identity and its political warrants, and those differences could reflect the different material stakes adhering to the idea of racial identity for different social positions. The experience of racial consciousness and the substantive political and economic entailments of racial identity of a black housing authority director, an inner-city public school principal, a real estate developer, or a corporate functionary will very probably differ from those of a resident of low-income public housing, a person underemployed without health care benefits in the low-wage consumer service sector, an industrial worker stalked by job insecurity and the threat of downsizing, a public sector line worker, a Deep South poultry plant worker, a college student besieged by aid and budget cuts, or a workfare assignee.

Tate's perspective does not provide for such differences. Instead, it yields only a standardized racial consciousness, measured largely in terms of aggregated issue positions and abstract attitudes, and deviations from it, also measured in terms of recorded attitudes and positions on issues already given as being of general racial significance. Nor does she consider the possibility that those issue positions and attitudes take shape within a discourse defined by agenda-setting elites and researchers. This is an account of black politics devoid of politics among black people.

Carol Swain explicitly engages the issue of determining black interests and the reality of black differentiation. However, she acknowledges differentiation only to subordinate it to a notion of collective group interests. She argues that

> the interests of blacks must vary in important ways; still, it would be a mistake to place more emphasis on the variations than on the commonalities. Broad patterns of objective circumstances and subjective orientations characterize American blacks, and striking differences continue to exist between black and white Americans.[82]

Swain relies largely on surveys of political attitudes and comparison of aggregate black and white socioeconomic conditions to construct an account that, notwithstanding her initial declarations, reproduces the premise of the corporate political entity. Her narrative distinguishes "objective" and "subjective" black interests. The former can be deduced from the extent of aggregate black socio-economic disadvantage relative to whites. The latter are discernible through identifying black/white differences in distribution of opinions on significant issues and a simple majoritarian approach to black opinions as expressed in the findings of survey research.[83]

Swain's characterization of objective interests seems reasonable enough. However, it implies a condition of racial parity as the goal of black aspiration and standard of equity, and that is a questionably modest ideal of egalitarianism or social justice. If black and white unemployment rates were equally high, for example, it is not clear that there would be no objective black interest in reducing unemployment. In addition, linking the determination of black interests to cross-racial comparison perpetuates the practice of defining black interests in terms of an exclusively racial agenda — even though many of the most pressing socioeconomic concerns of a great many black Americans are not purely or most immediately racial. Therefore, though she does not naturalize the category of racial interests, Swain's formulation presumes the restriction of black politics to the program of generic racial advancement.

Swain's reduction of what she calls "subjective black interests" to the findings of survey research also reinforces the premise of a black corporate political entity in at least two ways. First, as with Tate, her reliance on a simplistic notion of "the black public," defined by those survey findings, skirts fundamental questions concerning the processes of agenda setting and the opinion-leading role of black political elites, as well as questions about the context-defining roles of mass media and the interventions of researchers who themselves proceed unquestioningly from hegemonic assumptions about the scope and content of black politics. The attitudes and opinions recorded in those surveys probably do express a black public opinion, especially in the circular sense that public opinion generally is understood to mean what is expressed in such surveys. The surveys indicate how groups of black voters would probably line up on a range of given positions within given terms of debate in a particular political conjuncture. Treating those expressions as autonomous preferences, however, is problematic intellectually because doing so obscures their character as the products of political and ideological processes. Reifying those responses in that way also asserts a conservative force in political discourse by denying the fluidity and contingency of the terms of debate and positions held at a given moment; obscuring the ideological and political processes that shape those terms of debate — the dimension of power and hegemony — works to similar effect. Swain notes the role of interest groups in black politics, but she does not take account of their role in shaping the discursive field.

Second, Swain's reliance on a majoritarian standard for determining subjective black interests avoids the pitfall of naturalizing black interest only technically. Why should 50 percent plus any fraction of a percent be the threshold of racial authenticity? What does that standard say of the views of the possibly very large remainder? Even if the standard were a supermajority — say, two-thirds or even three-fourths — how could the one-third or one-fourth minority not be seen as also expressive of black interests? Swain finesses these questions by resorting to black/white comparison. But noting apparent racial differences in clustering of opinions on a range of issues does not indicate a corporate "black" point of view. In fact, Swain does not escape the presumptive rhetoric of racial authenticity, which underlies her discussion of black interests. She deploys it, apparently in service to her predilections in current politics, to suggest tension between rank-and-file black citizens, whom she casts as embracing a range of conservative social views, and the officially relatively liberal black political establishment.[84]

Michael Dawson's examination of the relative significance of race and class in black politics also proceeds from a formulation of corporate racial interest, though he attempts to ground it in a theory of pragmatic action. Because race is such a powerful determinant of the political and economic circumstances of black Americans of all strata, he argues, it has been practical for black citizens to employ a "black utility heuristic" in deciding their political views. What this means is that "as long as African Americans' life chances are powerfully shaped by race, it is efficient for individual African Americans to use their perceptions of the interests of African Americans as a group as a proxy for their own interests."[85]

This construct, however, fails to ground the idea of corporate interest. The black utility heuristic is a theoretical evasion; at bottom, it only stipulates the idea of group perspective at a one-step remove and does not thereby escape reifying and naturalizing it. Dawson's formulation begs critical questions as to how individuals form their perceptions of group interest: How do individuals determine that certain initiatives or conditions generate racial common effects? And, more significant, how do they ascertain which interpretations, issues, and strategies actually represent the interest of the collectivity rather than some more narrowly partisan or idiosyncratic agenda? He does not address such questions; in effect, he treats group interests as given and transparent to members of the group.

Dawson's avowed commitment to methodological individualism may obscure this problem—as it does with Tate and Swain—because it leaves him with no clearly articulated unit of analysis between individual and race.[86] Insofar as he attends to the region between individuals and the corporate racial body, his discussion both presumes group interest to be a coherent, out-there thing, rather than itself the product of political processes and contestation, and at least evokes the rhetoric of racial authenticity. He maintains that using group status as a proxy for individual status is efficient

> not only because a piece of legislation or a public policy could be analyzed relatively easily for its effect on the race but also because the information sources available in the black community—the media outlets, kinship networks, community and civil rights organizations, and especially the preeminent institution in the black community, the black church—would all reinforce the political salience of racial interests and would provide information about racial group status.[87]

Dawson bases this description on a retrospective characterization of the segregation era, when the politics of generic racial advancement had its clearest and solidest material foundation within the black American population. The straightforwardness that he imputes to the mediation between individual and group is certainly more plausible in an account of a context dominated by issues bearing on explicitly racial exclusion and subordination than in application to contemporary politics. Even then, however, such cut-and-dried racial questions did not exhaust the universe of black political concern and action; conflicting views existed with respect to specifics of strategic and tactical response, as well as larger, though still intraparadigmatic, interpretive and normative differences within the dominant group politics. And, as we have seen, the hegemonic status of that politics did not spring from nature or result from open, deliberative processes, and its program was not the pristine expression of a collective will. Most important, assuming a context that, even if only superficially, presents a best-case circumstance for a defense of Dawson's black utility heuristic is ultimately conceptual sleight of hand because doing so also sidesteps precisely the most crucial questions that his defense must address.

Because the black utility heuristic is based on an idealized model of unproblematic racial gemeinschaft in the segregation era, it is at least vulnerable to accommodating a rhetoric of racial authenticity. Construing the relation of race and class as a tension between group and individual identities reinforces this tendency. From that perspective, class interests can operate among blacks only through a departure from, if not rejection of, the interests of the racial group. Because Dawson presumes racial identity to be homogeneous or monadic, he can approach class differentiation only as a deviation from, rather than a constitutive element of, racial identity and consciousness.

In line with his formulation, Dawson suggests that increasing upward mobility (and, curiously, the so-called underclass's supposed isolation as well) could weaken race consciousness, partly by "weakening links between individual African Americans and the race as a whole."[88] He elaborates a view that is hardly distinguishable from a theory of racial authenticity:

> Consider two middle-class individuals, one with strong ties to family and other black community institutions, the other *with the same household or individual utility function* but with very weak ties to the black community. The individual with strong ties to family and community will be slower to deemphasize racial group interests than the individual with weak ties because of the greater impact of information from the black community for that person.[89]

He finds that, instead, upward mobility appears to this point to increase race consciousness and racial "common-fate" identity, and this finding supports what is in effect a validation of the politics of racial advancement, which remains the most legitimate and efficacious focus for black political activity.[90] He takes this finding as evidence that, because of linked-fate identification, the black middle class by and large remains connected to the racial interest and political agendas. This is tantamount to reducing assessment of the significance of class in black politics to a determination of whether or not individuals have "forgotten where they came from." Because of Dawson's reified notion of black interest, the possibility that prevailing forms of racial consciousness and identity might reflect class or other forces within black life cannot arise in his analysis. His approach to evaluating the significance of class among blacks never turns toward the dynamics of group interest formation. Like Swain, Dawson adduces evidence of persisting racial disparities, in particular between black and white middle classes, to support his claim that racial identity trumps class identity by creating the material basis for a primary community of interest among blacks.[91] But although the existence of disparity would arguably promote race consciousness and race-solidaristic perception, it does not automatically yield any particular strategic interpretation or response; it does not decree, that is, that race consciousness would take any particular form or content. This once again underscores questions concerning the political processes through which concrete notions of collective interest are shaped, who determines the boundaries of group activity, who participates in those processes, and who is advantaged and who disadvantaged by them—questions that have no place in Dawson's analysis.

Dawson reports that despite the power of race consciousness, "individuals' economic status plays a large role in shaping African-American public opinion in several issue domains" and that "affluent African Americans are much less likely to support economic redistribution than those with fewer resources [and] the most affluent African Americans hold views more consistent with those of the conservative white mainstream."[92] And he notes that upper-status blacks are more likely than other blacks to see themselves as having benefited from the politics of racial advancement.[93] Yet he does not consider the possibility that the "linked-fate" phenomenon that he observes may reflect not a mitigation of class consciousness but its expression as an ideology through which those very petit bourgeois strata enact the dominance of a particular definition of the scope and content of black political activity. His "group interest perspective" forecloses that possibility because it continues the pattern of reading politics *among* black people out of inquiry into black politics.

Dawson, Swain, and Tate stand out among students of Afro-American politics in that they attempt, in distinct but related ways, to problematize the issue of interest differentiation among blacks. Their concern with this issue is a response to a more broadly, if tentatively and inchoately, articulated suggestion in contemporary public discourse—usually propounded by conservatives in support of their own counternarratives of racial authenticity[94]—that systemic incorporation has destabilized conventional understandings of black political life. However, all three short-circuit inquiry from the outset by positing corporate racial interest as an unexamined background assumption that organizes their approaches conceptually and procedurally. In accepting that premise they perpetuate the restriction of black politics thematically to the domain of collective struggle against generic racial inequality and subordination. This in turn makes it unnecessary to acknowledge or examine, perhaps even impossible to notice, the autonomous political processes and structural, ideological, and institutional tensions that constitute the matrix of concrete black political action.

In thus insisting from the first that black politics be seen only as a corporate, group endeavor, it is as if these scholars raise the question of black differentiation only in order to refute it. The political sea change that has prompted questions about the presumption of corporate racial interest thereby calls forth active defense of it.[95] Ironically, as it purports to take a skeptical attitude toward the new black politics, this scholarship may be more explicitly and willfully engaged than its antecedents in reproducing ideological legitimations for the politics of generic racial advancement and in obscuring its class basis.

This characterization of the trajectory of scholarship on black politics is schematic and has no pretense to exhaustiveness. It nonetheless specifies a conceptual organizing principle that has underlain the subfield's discursive conventions throughout its history. Reconstruction of that history also highlights the dialectical character of the relation between the study and practice of black American politics. That relation is hardly unique to black politics, of course, though the precariousness of the black situation in the United States and the leading role of mainstream academic discourses in rationalizing racial injustice and inequality for most of this century have probably led Afro-Americanists to be more self-conscious and less diffident than others about it. The problem with the main lines of scholarly inquiry into black politics is not, therefore, that they have been partisan or engaged. It is that their partisanship has been unself-consciously fastened onto the racial vision of the black petite bourgeoisie — a singular class vision projected as the organic and transparent sensibility of the group as a whole.

This bias is problematic not only because it has produced accounts of black politics that are incomplete and static, devoid of political dynamics among black people, but also because its reductivist postulation of the corporate racial subject reinscribes essentialist presumptions regarding the black American population. Such constructions as "the Negro (or the black community) believes/wants . . ." originate in nineteenth-century race theory's notions of racial temperament and ideals and other formulations asserting in effect that blacks think with one mind. Both recent scholarship's insistent minimizing of the political significance of racial differentiation and the more general sanctification of racial unity as the substance of a political program in its own right are anchored in such formulations. Both also are active interventions that seek to impose those categories on an increasingly recalcitrant world of manifest black experience.

Although this scholarly orientation around the petite bourgeoisie's class vision of racial politics may have been pragmatically adequate to its intellectual and political objectives during the segregation era in which it emerged and evolved, it does not equip us well to make sense of the imperatives and possibilities that define current political conditions. The subfield's main discourse revolves around the dual objectives of defending a coherent and homogenized racial image and articulating putatively collective mentalities and aspirations. These objectives, and the deeply sedimented presuppositions on which they rest, direct the lens of critical investigation away from careful, skeptical scrutiny of interior features of black political life.[96] The field is therefore left without well-developed critical standards for judgment in black political debate, aside from a norm of racial authenticity.

However powerful it may have been rhetorically when universal group consensus seemed plausible in opposition to Jim Crow, the proposition that racial authenticity is a basis for intellectual and political judgment was always extremely problematic. Ideologically, it is an artifact of racial essentialism and presumes a given and objectively discernible mode of correct thought for the race. Practically, it begs questions of how authenticity is determined and who chooses its guardians. Because it focuses critical vision on ascriptive rather than substantive criteria, this standard does not make for clear, open political debate. Racial authenticity is a hollow notion that can be appropriated by nearly anyone to support or oppose any position, and it can be absurd and self-defeating. I have noted here and describe at greater length in chapters 2 and 4 how public officials and other functionaries of the new black elite's agenda were able in the 1970s to appropriate that notion and use it to delegitimize the radical critiques from which they coopted it.

At this point, the limitations of the rhetoric of authenticity should be abundantly clear. It may have been tempting to invoke that rhetoric as a shorthand explanation for opposition to Clarence Thomas, for instance, but that tack did nothing to expose his reactionary views and link him to them and their implications; nor did it stimulate popular discussion among black citizens of the substantive harm that his appointment could produce in specific areas of law and public policy. And Thomas was able to use that very rhetoric to gain advantage during the circus of his confirmation hearing. Moreover, throughout the Reagan/Bush/Clinton era the Republican right wing has appropriated it to legitimize black conservatives and their programs, often overlapping the right's similar appropriation of a radical-sounding populist antistatism, as well as to discredit advocates of civil rights and civil liberties.[97]

The bankruptcy of the notion of racial authenticity as a basis for political judgment is a thread that unravels the entire outlook that continues to shape both the study and practice of politics among black Americans. Without that notion the assumption of an a priori corporate group interest and program cannot be sustained. Practically, without the premise of a norm of authenticity, prevailing forms of political debate—which pivot on claims to represent the genuine interests of the racial collectivity—lose their fulcrum, and the corollary notions of generic race leadership also collapse. Intellectually, elimination of the notion of racial authenticity undermines the politics of generic racial advancement as a conceptual boundary for black politics and the crucial presumption of black Americans' default position as a corporate political entity. Without the standard of authenticity appeals to unity as a means to resolve conflicts or as an explanation of failure appear all the more clearly as the wish fulfillment and platitudes that they are.

Stripping away that complex of mystifications also removes layers of ideological evasion that have obscured the partial, class-skewed program that has dominated black politics for a century. What remains is a clear view that the dominant politics of generic racial advancement—though it has won genuinely popular victories and has had many beneficial consequences, especially during the antisegregation period—has always rested on a nonparticipatory, undemocratic foundation of elite custodianship and brokerage.

We need a different way of thinking about and doing politics among black Americans. I hesitate to proclaim a need for a *new* approach to black politics, partly because calls for new ideas are an academic marketing cliché, but also because I prefer to understand what I believe we need as a return to the path that black political development was on before the distortions of the Jim Crow era. The corrosive effects of the elite-brokerage politics did not come into existence only with the victories of the civil rights and black power movements; that politics is not simply obsolete, inappropriate for a new stage. Its contradictions were present all along, and the politics of racial advancement was organized as a class politics from the beginning. And it is not a foregone conclusion that a successful popular struggle against Jim Crow could have taken no other form.

Assuming a commitment to intellectual honesty and egalitarian ideals of social justice, we need an approach to black political activity that most of all recognizes the diversity of black life and concerns and that therefore cultivates popular, democratic participation and broad, open debate. Rejection of claims to racial authenticity and other forms of organicist mythology means that democratic and participatory values must be the cornerstone of credibility for the notion of black politics; group consensus must be constructed through active participation. Even then, it is important to realize that often there will be no universal racial consensus on key issues, that some conflicts derive from irreconcilable material differences. Unity is always on specific terms and in pursuit of specific objectives that probably favor some interests over others, and exhorting the black elite to commit "class suicide" on behalf of the race is at best naive idealism and at worst a romantic self-congratulation that provides a cover for imposing class hegemony through the back door.

We need to reconceptualize black political activity as a dynamic set of social relations and interests that converge on some issues as consequential for broad sectors of the black population and that diverge from others, based on other identities and interest aggregations. This is a black politics that does not pretend to exhaust all, or even necessarily the most important, aspects of all black people's political concerns and activity. It is a notion of black politics in which black people, as individuals and as groups, organize, form alliances, and enter coalitions freely on the basis of mutually constituted interests, crisscrossing racial boundaries as they find it pragmatically appropriate.

A democratic and popular politics of this sort also cannot tolerate models of "natural" or organic leadership. Acknowledging the autonomy of black individuals as the basis of group solidarity and the variety of black experience means that models of political association must be volitional. There can be no legitimate leadership that is not accountable to specific constituencies in clearly delineated ways. Claims to speak on behalf of some constituency should be received with skepticism unless the spoken-for have direct and accessible mechanisms at their disposal for ratifying or repudiating those claims. A credible, demystified black political leadership must be based on actual membership organizations and electorally accountable political institutions, not self-proclamation or recognition by third parties.

It may seem odd to argue for grounding a radical program for reorganization of black politics on what might be viewed as liberal formalism. However, this recommendation is a response to the century-long hegemony in which even radicals have adopted a form of politics and a program defined by petit bourgeois class interests as the natural expression of black Americans' collective political aspirations. Trivialization of the mechanisms of popular participation and political accountability has been a central element of the legitimation and reproduction of this politics since the initial articulation of the ideology of racial uplift in the decades after Hayes-Tilden. By contrast, the two moments of greatest political gains for black Americans were also the moments of most extensive popular participation and mobilization: the thirty-year period before the consolidation of the hegemonic form of black politics[98] and the high period of popular activism from the 1950s to early 1970s when that hegemony broke down temporarily in the face of popular insurgency. Encouraging popular participation is the only effective possibility for reinvigorating a progressive movement in black political life because people respond by organizing themselves when offered concrete visions that connect with their lives as they experience them, not to ideological abstractions or generic agendas that perfume narrow class programs.

Ironic though it may seem to many on the left, cultivating a liberal democratic, popular politics is also the clearest and likeliest way to redirect the focus of black political debate along more substantive lines by making its class content explicit. Only by acknowledging differentiation is it possible to discuss the issues of unequal impact of political strategies and unequal distribution of the costs and benefits of political action. Thus naturalistic or corporate racial justifications of inequality—including claims that a disproportionate distribution of material benefits to a few is compensated for by the alleged accrual of symbolic benefits to the many—should warrant skepticism. Ian Shapiro's argument that a disposition to question all hierarchies is a foundation of practical democracy is noteworthy in this regard. He observes that hierarchies

> will benefit some, harm others, and sometimes benefit some at the price of harming others. Hierarchies also tend to become hostage to the imperatives for their own maintenance, and these imperatives frequently involve the creation and propagation of fictions about either the nature or the arbitrariness of the hierarchy in question. Those who benefit from the existence of a hierarchy can be expected to try—more or less consciously—to obscure its hierarchical character through argument or to insist that it is rational or normal.[99]

In his view it should be incumbent on those who benefit from hierarchies to shoulder the burden of justifying them. The context for fulfilling this requirement must be a sphere of open political debate based on substantive, not ascriptive, criteria. There has rarely been such a sphere in black American political life in this century. Especially now, as the forces of reactionary counterattack are recomposing and mobilizing across the national political landscape and the objective basis for the politics of generic racial advancement recedes into the historical rearview mirror, we need to generate an approach to analyzing and enacting black politics that pivots on the fulcrum of Marx's famous heuristic: Who benefits? Who doesn't? Who loses? Politics can be created only by going to basics and building it from the bottom up, around the specific interests and concerns of specific groups of black individuals in specific places and specific social circumstances.

In the early 1960s Ralph Ellison lamented the disposition "to see segregation as an opaque steel jug with the Negroes inside waiting for some black messiah to come along and blow the cork."[100]

Ellison had in mind the argument of a white literary critic, but the metaphor applies equally well to a governing precept of the practice and study of black politics during much of the segregation era and since. The challenge for those of us who strive to advance emancipatory and egalitarian interests in black political life, as well as within the society at large, is to look within the jug, examine its varied contents, and pour them freely into the world.

1998

Part I

2. The "Black Revolution" and the Reconstitution of Domination

More than forty years ago Walter Benjamin pointed out that "mass reproduction is aided especially by the reproduction of masses."[1] This statement captures the central cultural dynamic of "late" capitalism. The triumph of the commodity form over every sphere of social existence has been made possible by a profound homogenization of work, play, aspirations, and self-definition among subject populations — a condition Marcuse has characterized as one-dimensionality.[2] Ironically, while U.S. radicals in the late 1960s fantasized about a "new man" in the abstract, capital was in the process of concretely putting the finishing touches on *its new individual.* Beneath the current black-female-student-chicano-gay-elderly-youth-disabled, ad nauseam, "struggles" lies a simple truth: There is no coherent opposition to the present administrative apparatus, at least not from the left.

Certainly, repression contributed significantly to the extermination of opposition, and there is a long record of systematic corporate and state terror, from the Palmer Raids to the FBI campaign against the Black Panthers. Likewise, co-optation of individuals and programs has blunted opposition to bourgeois hegemony throughout this century, and co-optative mechanisms have become inextricable parts of strategies of containment. However, repression and co-optation can never fully explain the failure of opposition, and an exclusive focus on such external factors diverts attention from possible sources of failure within the opposition itself, thus paving the way for reproduction of the pattern of failure. The opposition must investigate its own complicity if it is to become a credible alternative.

During the 1960s theoretical reflexiveness was difficult because of the intensity of activism. When sharply drawn political issues demanded unambiguous responses, reflection on unintended consequences seemed treasonous. Years later, coming to terms with what happened during that period is blocked by nostalgic glorification of fallen heroes and by a surrender that David Gross describes as the "ironic frame-of-mind."[3] Irony and nostalgia are two sides of the coin of resignation, the product of a cynical inwardness that makes retrospective critique seem tiresome or uncomfortable.[4]

At any rate, things have not moved in an emancipatory direction despite all claims that the protest of the 1960s has extended equalitarian democracy. In general, opportunities to determine one's destiny are no greater for most people now than before, and, more importantly, the critique of life-as-it-is has disappeared as a practical activity; that is, an ethical and political commitment to emancipation seems no longer legitimate, reasonable, or valid. The amnesic principle that imprisons the social past also subverts any hope, which ends up seeking refuge in the predominant forms of alienation.

This is also true in the black community. Black opposition has dissolved into celebration and wish fulfillment. Today's political criticism within the black community—both Marxist-Leninist and nationalist—lacks a base and is unlikely to attract substantial constituencies. This complete collapse of political opposition among blacks, however, is anomalous. From the 1955 Montgomery bus boycott to the 1972 African Liberation Day demonstration, there was almost constant political motion among blacks. Since the early 1970s there has been a thorough pacification, or else these antagonisms have been so depoliticized that they surface only in alienated forms. Moreover, few attempts have been made to explain the atrophy of opposition within the black community.[5] Theoretical reflexiveness is as rare behind W. E. B. Du Bois's veil as on the other side!

This critical failing is especially regrettable because black radical protests and the system's adjustments to them have served as catalysts in universalizing one-dimensionality and in moving into a new era of monopoly capitalism. In this new era, which Paul Piccone has called the age of "artificial negativity," traditional forms of opposition have been undermined by a new pattern of social management.[6] Now the social order legitimates itself by integrating potentially antagonistic forces into a logic of centralized administration. Once integrated, these forces regulate domination and prevent disruptive excess. Furthermore, when these internal regulatory mechanisms do not exist, the system must create them. To the extent that the black community has been pivotal in this new mode of administered domination, reconstruction of the trajectory of 1960s black activism can throw light on the current situation and the paradoxes it generates.

A common interpretation of the demise of black militance suggests that the waning of radical political activity is a result of the satisfaction of black aspirations. This satisfaction allegedly consists in (1) extension of the social welfare apparatus; (2) elimination of legally sanctioned racial barriers to social mobility, which in turn has allowed for (3) expansion of possibilities open to blacks within the existing social system; all of which have precipitated (4) a redefinition of "appropriate" black political strategy in line with these achievements.[7] This new strategy is grounded in a pluralist orientation that construes political issues solely in terms of competition over distribution of goods and services within the bounds of fixed system priorities. These four items constitute the "gains of the 1960s."[8] Intrinsic to this interpretation is the thesis that black political activity during the 1960s became radical because blacks had been excluded from society and politics and were therefore unable effectively to solve group problems through the "normal" political process. Extraordinary actions were thus required to pave the way for regular participation.

This interpretation is not entirely untenable. With passage of the 1964 and 1965 legislation, the program of the civil rights movement appeared to have been fulfilled. Soon, however, it became clear that the ideals of freedom and dignity had not been realized, and within a year, those ideals reasserted themselves in the demand for black power. A social program was elaborated, but again its underpinning ideals were not realized. The dilemma lay in translating abstract ideals into concrete political goals, and it is here also that the "gains of the 1960s" interpretation founders. It equates the ideals with the objectives of the programs in question.

To be sure, racial segregation has been eliminated in the South, thus removing a tremendous oppression from black life. Yet dismantlement of the system of racial segregation only removed a fetter restricting the possibility of emancipation. In this context, computation of the "gains of the 1960s" can begin only at the point where that extraordinary subjugation was eliminated. What, then, are those "gains" that followed the passage of civil rights legislation, and how have they affected black life?

In 1964, the last year before the Vietnam boom (which in addition to other ways reduced black unemployment through military service), black unemployment averaged 9.6 percent; the 1971 average was 9.9 percent.[9] Moreover, among the most vulnerable groups — women and youth — unemployment rates in business cycle periods not only were not reduced in the 1960s but by 1975 were nearly twice as high as in 1957.[10] Black median income did not improve significantly in relation to white family income in the decade after passage of civil rights legislation,[11] and between 1970 and 1974 black purchasing power actually declined.[12] Moreover, blacks were still far more likely to live in inadequate housing than whites, and black male life expectancy declined, both absolutely and relative to whites, from 1959 to 1961 and again to 1974.[13] Therefore, if the disappearance of black opposition is linked directly with the satisfaction of aspirations, the criteria of fulfillment cannot be drawn from the general level of material existence in the black community. The same can be said for categories such as "access to political decision making." Although the number of blacks elected or appointed to public office has risen by leaps and bounds since the middle 1960s, that increase has not demonstrably improved life in the black community.

The problem is one of focus. The "gains of the 1960s" thesis seems to hold only as long as the status of the "black community" is equated with that of certain specific strata. Although black life *as a whole* has not improved much beyond the elimination of racial segregation, in the 1970s certain strata within the black community actually have benefited. This development is a direct outcome of the 1960s activism—of the interplay of the "movement" and the integrative logic of administrative capitalism—and the "gains of the 1960s" interpretation cannot spell out what "satisfaction" is because it is itself the ideology of precisely those strata that have benefited from the events of the 1960s within the black community. These "leadership" strata tend to generalize their own interests, since their legitimacy and integrity are tied to a monolithic conceptualization of black life. Indeed, this conceptualization appeared in the unitarian mythology of late 1960s black nationalism. The representation of the black community as a collective subject neatly concealed the system of hierarchy that mediated the relation between the "leaders" and the "led."[14]

To analyze the genesis of the new elite is to analyze simultaneously the development of the new styles of domination in American society in general. Consequently, the following will focus on sources of the pacification of the 1970s and will expose the limitations of any oppositionist activity that proceeds uncritically from models of mass-organization politics that tend to capitulate to the predominant logic of domination.

Black resistance to oppression hardly began in Montgomery, Alabama, in 1955. Yet it was only then that opposition to racial subjugation assumed the form of a mass movement. Why was this so? Despite many allusions to the impact of decolonization in Africa, international experiences of blacks in World War II, and so on, the reasons that black activism exploded in the late 1950s have seldom been addressed systematically.[15] Although resistance before 1955 was undoubtedly reinforced by the anticolonial movements abroad, what was significant for post-1955 growth of civil rights activity were those forces reshaping the entire American social order. A historically thorough perspective on the development of black opposition requires an understanding of the Cold War era in which it took shape.

Although popularly symbolized by "brinkmanship," "the domino theory," fall-out shelters, and the atmosphere of terror engendered by Joseph McCarthy, the House Un-American Activities Committee (HUAC), and legions of meticulously anticommunist liberals, the Cold War was a much broader cultural phenomenon. Ultimately, it was a period of consolidation of the new mode of domination that had been developing for more than two decades. Piccone has noted that the Cold War era was the culmination of political and cultural adjustment to a dynamic of concentration that had attained hegemony over the American economy by the 1920s.[16] On the political front, the New Deal redefined the role of the state apparatus in terms of an aggressive, countercyclical intervention in the economy and everyday reality. At the same time, mass production required intensification of consumption. This requirement was met by the development and expansion of a manipulative culture industry and by the proliferation of an ideology of consumerism through mass communications and entertainment media.[17] Consumerism and the New Deal led to an intensification of the Taylorization of labor, which increasingly homogenized American life according to the dictates of bureaucratic-instrumental rationality. By the 1950s, Americanization had been institutionalized. Rigid political, intellectual, and cultural conformism (David Riesman's "other directedness") evidenced a social integration achieved through introjection and reproduction of the imperatives of the system of domination at the level of everyday life.[18]

Pressures toward homogenization exerted for decades at work, in schools, and through the culture industry had seriously reformulated cultural particularity among ethnic groups. What remained were residues of the lost cultures — empty mannerisms and ambivalent ethnic identities mobilizable for Democratic electoral politics.[19] Moreover, the pluralist model was available for integrating the already depoliticized labor movement. In this context, the ruthless elimination of explicit opposition through the witch-hunts was the coup de grace in a battle already largely won.

For various reasons, throughout this period, one region was bypassed in the monopolistic reorganization of American life and remained unintegrated into the new social order. At the end of World War II, the South remained the only internal frontier available for large-scale capital penetration. However, even though the South could entice industry with a docile workforce accustomed to low wages, full domestication of this region required certain basic adjustments.

For one thing, the castelike organization of southern society seriously inhibited development of a rational labor supply. Though much has been made of the utility of the segregated workforce as a depressant of general wage levels, maintenance of dual labor markets created a barrier to labor recruitment.[20] As a pariah caste blacks could not adequately become an industrial reserve army, since they were kept out of certain jobs. Consequently, in periods of rapid expansion the suppressed black labor pool could not be fully used, nor could blacks be mobilized as a potential strike-breaking force as readily as in other regions, since employment of blacks in traditionally "white" jobs could trigger widespread disruptions.

The dual labor system was irreconcilable with the principle of reducing *all* labor to "abstract labor."[21] Scientific management has sought to reduce work processes to homogeneous and interchangeable hand-and-eye motions, hoping eventully to eliminate specialized labor.[22] A workforce stratified on the basis of an economically irrational criterion such as race constitutes a serious impediment to realization of the ideal of a labor pool made up of equivalent units. (Consider further the wastefulness of having to provide two sets of toilets in the plants!) In addition, the existing system of black subjugation, grounded in brutality, was intrinsically unstable. The racial order that demanded constant terror for its maintenance raised at every instant the possibility of rebellion and to that extent endangered "rational" administration. Given this state of affairs, the corporate elite's support for an antisegregationist initiative makes sense.

The relation of the corporate liberal social agenda to civil rights protest, though, is not a causal one. True, the Supreme Court had been chipping away at legal segregation for nearly twenty years, and the 1954 *Brown* decision finally provided the spark for intensified black protest. Yet the eruption of resistance from southern blacks had its own roots. Hence, to claim that the civil rights movement was a bourgeois conspiracy would be to succumb to the order's myth of its own omnipotence. The important question is not whether sectors of the corporate elite orchestrated the civil rights movement but instead what elements within the civil rights movement were sufficiently compatible with the social agenda of corporate elites to prompt the latter to acquiesce to and encourage them. In order to answer this, it is necessary to identify both the social forces operative *within* the black community during segregation and those forces' engagement in civil rights activism. An analysis of the internal dynamic of the 1960s activism shows overlaps between the goals of the "New Deal Offensive" and the objectives of the "movement" (and, by extension, the black community).[23]

For the purposes of this analysis, the most salient aspects of the black community in the segregated South lie within the realm of management of racial subordination. Externally, the black population was managed by means of codified subordination, reinforced by customary dehumanization and the omnipresent specter of terror. The abominable details of this system are well known.[24] Furthermore, blacks were systematically excluded from formal participation in public life. By extracting tax revenues without returning public services or allowing blacks to participate in public policy formation, the local political system intensified the normal exploitation in the workplace. Public administration of the black community was carried out by whites. The daily indignity of the apartheid-like social organization was both a product of this political and administrative disfranchisement and a motor of its reproduction. Thus, the abstract ideal of freedom spawned within the civil rights movement took concrete form primarily in opposition to this relation.

Despite the black population's exclusion from public policy making, an internal stratum existed that performed notable, but limited, social management functions. This elite stratum comprised mainly low-level state functionaries, merchants and "professionals" servicing black markets, and the clergy. Though it failed to escape the general subordination, this indigenous elite succeeded, by virtue of its comparatively secure living standard and informal relations with significant whites, in avoiding the extremes of racial oppression. The importance of this stratum was that it stabilized and coordinated the adjustment of the black population to social policy imperatives formulated outside the black community.

Insofar as black public functionaries had assimilated bureaucratic rationality, the domination of fellow blacks was carried out in "doing one's job." For parts of the black elite such as the clergy, the ministerial practice of "easing community tensions" has always meant accommodation of black life to the existing forms of domination. Similarly, the independent merchants and professionals owed their relatively comfortable position within the black community to the special captive markets created by segregation. Moreover, in the role of "responsible Negro spokesmen," this sector was able to elicit considerable politesse, if not solicitousness, from "enlightened" members of the white elite. Interracial "cooperation" on policy matters was thus smoothly accomplished, and the "public interest" seemed to be met simply because opposition to white ruling-group initiatives had been effectively neutralized.

The activating factor in this management relation was a notion of "Negro leadership" (later "black" or even "Black" leadership) that was generated outside the black community. A bitter observation made from time to time by the radical fringe of the movement was that the social category "leaders" seemed to apply only to the black community. No "white leaders" were assumed to represent a singular white population; but certain blacks were declared to be opinion makers and carriers of the interests of an anonymous black population. These "leaders" legitimated their role through their ability to win occasional favors from powerful whites and through the status positions they already occupied in the black community.[25]

This mode of domination could not thoroughly pacify black life; only the transformation of the segregated order could begin to do that. Furthermore, the internal management strategy generated centrifugal pressures of its own. In addition to segregation, three other disruptive elements stand out within the black population in the 1950s: First, the emergence of the United States from World War II as the major world power projected American culture onto an international scene. Thus, the anticolonial movements that grew in Africa and Asia amid the crumbling French and British colonial empires had a significant impact on black resistance in this country.[26]

Second, the logic of one-dimensionality itself became a disruptive element. The homogenizing egalitarianism of the New Deal generated a sense of righteousness able to sustain a lengthy battle with southern segregation. The challenge to racial domination was justified in terms of the "American Dream" and an ideal of freedom expressed in a demand for full citizenship.[27] Thus, the same forces that since the 1880s had sought to integrate the various immigrant populations also generated an American national consciousness among blacks.

By the 1950s a sense of participation in a national society had taken root even in the South, fertilized by the mass culture industry (including black publications), schools, and a defensive Cold War ideology. In the face of this growing national consciousness, "separate but equal" existence was utterly intolerable to blacks. This is not to say that a perception rooted in the nation-state was universal among southern blacks in the 1950s, especially since the chief mechanisms of cultural adjustment—such as television, popular films, and compulsory schooling—had not fully invaded the black community. Yet mass culture and its corollary ideologies had extensively penetrated the private sphere of the black elite, the stratum from which systematic opposition arose.[28]

Third, the racial barrier limited social mobility for the black elite, relative to its white counterpart. Because of de facto proscription of black tenure in most professions, few possibilities existed for advancement. At the same time, as a result of population growth and rising college attendance, the number of people seeking to become members of the elite had increased beyond what a segregated society could accommodate.[29] In addition, upward mobility was being defined by the larger national culture in a way that further weakened the capability of the black elite to integrate its youth. Where ideology demanded nuclear physics and corporate management, black upward mobility rested with mortuary science and the Elks Lodge. This disjunction between ideals and possibilities delegitimized the elite's claim to brokerage and spokesmanship. With its role in question, the entrenched black elite was no longer able effectively to perform its internal management function and lost authority with its "recruits" and the black community in general. As a result, a social space was cleared within which dissatisfaction with segregation could thrive as systematic opposition.

From this social management perspective, sources of the Freedom Movement are identifiable within and on the periphery of the indigenous elite stratum. As soon as black opposition spilled beyond the boundaries of the black community, however, the internal management perspective became inadequate to understand further developments in the civil rights movement. When opposition to segregation became political rebellion, black protest required a response from white ruling elites. That response reflected congruence of the interests of blacks and corporate elites in reconstructing southern society and helped define the logic of subsequent black political activity. Both sets of interests might be met by rationalizing race relations in the South. The civil rights movement brought the two sets together.[30]

The alliance of corporate liberalism and black protest was evident in the aggressive endorsement of civil rights activity that was mobilized by the New Deal coalition. Major labor organizations and "enlightened" corporate elements immediately climbed aboard the freedom train through the "progressive" wing of the Democratic party and private foundations. Moreover, it was through its coverage of black resistance in the South that television developed and refined its remarkable capabilities for creating public opinion by means of "objective" news reportage (a talent that reached its acme years later with the expulsion of Richard Nixon from the presidency). However, television was not alone on the cultural front of the ideological struggle. *Life, Look,* the *Saturday Evening Post,* major nonsouthern newspapers, and other national publications featured an abundance of photo-essays that emphasized the degradation and brutalization of black life under Jim Crow.

Even popular cinema sought to thematize black life in line with civil rights consciousness, in films such as *The Defiant Ones* (1958), *All the Young Men* (1960), *Raisin in the Sun* (1961), *Band of Angels* (1957), and the instructively titled *Nothing but a Man* (1964). These and other films were marked by an effort to portray blacks with a measure of human depth and complexity previously absent from Hollywood productions. By 1957 even the great taboo of miscegenation was portrayed on the screen in *Island in the Sun,* and a decade later the cultural campaign had been so successful that this theme could be explored in the parlor rather than in back streets and resolved with a happy ending in *Guess Who's Coming to Dinner.* It is interesting that Dorothy Dandridge became the first black in a leading role to be nominated for an Academy Award for her role in *Carmen Jones* in 1954—the year of the *Brown* decision—and that the most productive periods of civil rights activism and of Sidney Poitier's film career coincided. Poitier's lead performance in the maudlin *Lilies of the Field* won him an Oscar in 1963, on the eve of the March on Washington and a year before passage of the landmark Civil Rights Act. Thus endorsed by the culture industry (which affronted white supremacy in the late 1950s by broadcasting an episode of the *Perry Como Show* in which comedienne Molly Goldberg kissed black ballplayer Ernie Banks), the civil rights movement was virtually assured success.

Though the civil rights coalition was made possible by the compatibility of the allies' interests in reorganizing the South, its success was facilitated by the ideals and ideologies generated in the protest. Even though there had been ties between black southern elites and corporate-liberal elements for a long time, if the civil rights program had raised fundamental questions regarding social structure, the corporate-elite response may have been suppression rather than support—especially given the Cold War context. Instead, from the very beginning the American establishment outside Dixie supported the abolition of segregation.[31] At any rate, it is clear that the civil rights ideology fit very well with the goals of monopoly capitalism. The civil rights movement appealed to egalitarianism and social rationality. On both counts segregation was found wanting, while nonracial features of the social order were left unquestioned.

The egalitarian argument was moral as well as constitutional. The moral argument was in the bourgeois tradition from the Reformation to the French Revolution. It claimed equal rights for all human beings as well as universal entitlement to equal life chances. This abstract and ahistorical moral imperative did not address the structural or systematic character of social relations and therefore could only denounce racial exclusion as an evil anomaly. The predominant form of social organization was accepted uncritically, and the moral imperative was predictably construed in terms of American constitutional law. Extension to blacks of equality before the law and equality of opportunity to participate in all areas of citizenship were projected as adequate to fulfill the promise of democracy in the backward South.

Coexisting with this egalitarian ideology was the civil rights movement's appeal to a functionalist conception of social rationality. To the extent that it blocked individual aspirations, segregation was seen as artificially restricting social growth and progress. Similarly, by raising artificial barriers, such as the constriction of blacks' consumer power through Jim Crow legislation and indirectly through low black wages, segregation impeded, so the argument went, the free functioning of the market. Consequently, segregation was seen as detrimental not only to the blacks who suffered under it but also to economic progress as such. Needless to say, the two lines of argument were met with approval by corporate liberals.[32]

It is apparent now that the egalitarian ideology coincided with corporate liberalism's cultural program of homogenization. The egalitarianism of civil rights demanded that any one unit of labor be equivalent to any other and that the Negro be thought of as "any other American." There is more than a little irony in the fact that the civil rights movement demanded for blacks the same "eradication of otherness" that had been forced upon immigrant populations. The demand hardly went unheard; through the blanket concept "integration" and the alliance with a corporate elite that was all too ready to help clarify issues and refine strategies and objectives, the abstract ideals of civil rights activism were concretized in a corporate-elite plan for pacification and reorganization.

The elimination of segregation in the South altered the specificity of both the South as a region and blacks as a group, and the rationality in whose name the movement had appealed paved the way for reconstruction of new modes of domination of black life. The movement had begun as a result of frustration within the black elite, and it ended with the achievement of autonomy and mobility among those elements. The civil rights and voting rights legislation officially defined new terms for the management of blacks and an expanded managerial role for the elite.

Although the civil rights movement did have a radical faction, that wing failed to develop a systematic critique of civil rights ideology or of the alliance with corporate liberalism. Moreover, the radicals—mainly within the Student Nonviolent Coordinating Committee (SNCC)—never fully repudiated the leadership ideology that reinforced the movement's character as an elite brokerage relation with powerful whites outside the South. Thus, the radicals helped isolate their own position by acquiescing to a conception of the black community as a passive recipient of political symbols and directives. When the dust settled, the black "mainstream" elements and their corporate allies—who together monopolized the symbols of legitimacy—proclaimed that freedom had been achieved, and the handful of radicals could only feel uneasy that voting rights and "social equality" were somehow insufficient.[33]

Outside the South, rebellion arose from different conditions. Racial segregation was not rigidly codified, and the management subsystems in the black community were correspondingly more fluidly integrated within the local adminis-trative apparatus. Yet structural, generational, and ideological pressures, broadly similar to those in the South, existed within the black elite in the northern, west-ern, and midwestern cities that had gained large black populations in the first half of the twentieth century. In nonsegregated urban contexts, formal political participation and democratized consumption had long since been achieved; there, the salient political issue was the extension of the administrative purview of the elite within the black community. The centrality of the administrative nexus in the "revolt of the cities" is evident from the ideological programs it generated.[34]

Black power came about as a call for indigenous control of economic and political institutions in the black community.[35] Because one of the early slogans of black power was a vague demand for "community control," the emancipatory character of the rebellion was open to considerably varied misinterpretation. More-over, the diversity and "militance" of its rhetoric encouraged extravagance in as-sessing the movement's depth. It soon became clear, however, that "community control" called not for direction of pertinent institutions — schools, hospitals, police, retail businesses, and so on — by their black constituents but for the ad-ministration of those institutions by alleged representatives in the name of a black community. Given an existing elite structure whose legitimacy had already been certified by federal social welfare agencies, the selection of "appropriate" repre-sentatives was predictable. Indeed, as Robert Allen has shown, the empowerment of this elite was actively assisted by corporate and state elements.[36] Thus, "black liberation" quickly turned into black "equity"; "community control" became sim-ply "black control"; and the Nixon "blackonomics" strategy was readily able to "co-opt" the most rebellious tendency of 1960s black activism. Ironically, black power's supersession of the civil rights program led to further consolidation of the management elite's hegemony within the black community. The black elite broadened its administrative control by accepting the inchoate black power agenda without criticism and instrumentally deploying it to gain leverage in reg-ular political processes. Black control was by no means equivalent to popular democratization.[37]

This state of affairs remained unclear even to black power's radical fringe. Such a failure of political perception cannot be written off as crass opportunism or as underdeveloped consciousness. Though not altogether false, explantions of this kind only beg the question. Indeed, black power radicalism, which absorbed most of the floundering left wing of the civil rights movement and generated subsequent "nationalist" tendencies, actually blurred the roots of the new wave of rebellion. As civil rights activism exhausted itself and as spontaneous uprisings proliferated among urban blacks, the civil rights radicals sought to generate an ideology capable of unifying and politicizing these uprisings. This effort, however, was based on two mystifications that implicitly rationalized the elite's control of the movement.

First, black power presupposed a mass-organizational model built on the assumption of a homogeneity of black political interests embodied in community leadership. It is this notion of "black community" that had blocked the development of a radical critique in the civil rights movement by contraposing an undifferentiated mass to a leadership stratum representing it. This understanding ruled out analysis of cleavages or particularities within the black population: "Community control" and "black control" became synonymous. The implications of this ideology have already been discussed: Having internalized the predominant elite-pluralist model of the organization of black life, the radical wing could not develop any critical perspective. Internal critique could not go beyond banal symbols of "blackness" and thus ended up stimulating demand for a new array of "revolutionary" consumer goods. Notwithstanding all its bombast, black power formulated racial politics within the ideological universe through which the containment of the black population was mediated.

Acceptance of this model not only prevented black power from transcending the social program of the indigenous administrative elite, but as Harold Cruse was aware at the time,[38] it also indicated the extent to which black power radicalism was itself a militant, rhetorically flamboyant statement of the elite's agenda — hence the radicals' chronic ambivalence over "black bourgeoisie," capitalism, socialism, and "black unity." Their mystification of the social structure of the black community was largely the result of a failure to come to terms with their own privileged relation to the corporate elite's program of social reconstruction. This state of affairs precipitated a still more profound mystification that illuminates the other side of black power rebellion: the reaction against massification.

The civil rights movement's demand for integration was superfluous outside the South, and black power was as much a reaction against integrationist ideology as against domination. Yet though militant black nationalism developed as a reaction to the assimilationist approach of the civil rights movement, it envisioned an obsolete, folkish model of black life. This yearning was hypostatized to the level of a vague "black culture" — a romantic retrieval of a vanishing black particularity. This vision of black culture, of course, was grounded in residual features of black rural life prior to migrations to the North. They were primarily cultural patterns that had once been enmeshed in a life-world knitted together by kinship, voluntary association, and production within a historical context of rural racial domination. As that life-world disintegrated in the face of urbanization and mass culture, black nationalism sought to reconstitute it.[39]

The nationalist elaboration of black power was naive both in that it was not sufficiently self-conscious and in that it mistook artifacts and idiosyncrasies of culture for its totality and froze them into an ahistorical rhetoric of authenticity. Two consequences followed: First, abstracted from its concrete historical context, black culture lost its dynamism and took on the commodity form (for example, red, black, and green flags; dashikis; Afro-Sheen; "blaxploitation" films; collections of bad poetry). Second, though ostensibly politicizing culture by defining it as an arena for conflict, black nationalism actually depoliticized the movement inasmuch as the reified nationalist framework could relate to the present only through a simplistic politics of unity.[40] Hence, it forfeited hegemony over political programs to the best organized element in the black community: the administrative elite. In this fashion, black culture became a means of legitimation of the elite's political hegemony.

"Black culture" posited a functionalist, perfectly integrated black social order that was then projected backward through history as the truth of black existence. The "natural" condition of harmony was said to have been disrupted only when divisiveness and conflict were introduced by alien forces. This myth delegitimated internal conflict and hindered critical dialogue within the black community. Correspondingly, the intellectual climate that came to pervade the movement was best summarized in the nationalists' exhortation to "think black," a latter-day version of "thinking with one's blood." Thus was the circle completed: The original abstract rationalism that had ignored existing social relations of domination in favor of a mythical, unitarian, social ideal turned into a militant and self-justifying irrationalism. Truth became a function of the speaker's "blackness"; that is, validity claims were to be resolved not through discourse but by the claimant's manipulation of certain banal symbols of legitimacy. The resultant situation greatly favored the well-organized and highly visible elite.[41]

The nationalist program also functioned as a mobilization myth. In defining a collective consciousness, the idealization of folkishness was simultaneously an exhortation to collectivized practice. "The folk," in its Afro-American manifestation as well as elsewhere,[42] was an ideological category of mass-organizational politics. The community was to be created and mobilized as a passively homogeneous mass, activated by a leadership elite.

Though the politicized notion of black culture was a negative response to the estrangement and anomie experienced in the urban North, as a "solution" it only affirmed the negation of genuine black particularity.[43] The prescription of cohesion in the form of a mass/leadership relation revealed the movement's tacit acceptance of the black management stratum's agenda. The negativity immanent in the cultural myth soon gave way to an opportunistic appeal to unity grounded on an unspecifiable "blackness" and a commodified idea of "soul." Black unity, elevated to an end in itself, became an ideology promoting consolidation of the management elite's expanded power over the black population. In practice, unity meant collective acceptance of a set of demands to be lobbied for by a leadership elite before the corporate and state apparatus. To that extent, "radical" black power reproduced on a more elaborate ideological basis the old pluralist brokerage politics. Similarly, this phony unity restricted possibilities for development of a black public sphere.

To be sure, the movement stimulated widespread and lively political debate in the black community. Although it hardly approached an "ideal speech situation," various individuals and constituencies were drawn into political discourse on a considerably more democratized basis than had previously been the case. Yet the rise of unitarian ideology, coupled with a mystified notion of "expertise," effectively reinscribed hierarchy within the newly expanded political arena.[44] At any rate, grassroots politics in the black community can be summarized as follows: The internal management elite claimed primacy in political discourse on the basis of its ability to project and realize a social program and then mobilized the unitarian ideal to delegitimize any divergent positions. On the other hand, the "revolutionary" opposition offered no alternative; within its ranks the ideology of expertise was never repudiated. The radicals had merely replaced the elite's pragmatism with a mandarin version of expertise founded on mastery of the holy texts of Kawaida nationalism, Nkrumahism, or "scientific socialism." By the time of the 1972 National Black Political Convention in Gary, Indiana, the mainstream elite strata were well on the way to becoming the sole effective voice in the black community. By the next convention, in 1974 in Little Rock, Arkansas—after the election of a second wave of black officials—their hegemony was total.[45]

By now the reasons for the demise of black opposition in the United States should be clear. The opposition's sources were formulated in terms of the predominant ideology and thereby were readily integrated as an affirmation of the validity of the system as a whole. The movement "failed" because it "succeeded," and its success can be measured by its impact on the administration of the social system. The protest against racial discrimination in employment and education was answered by the middle 1970s by state-sponsored democratization of access to management and other "professional" occupations. Direct, quantifiable racial discrimination remained a pressing public issue mainly for those whose livelihood depended on finding continuous instances of racial discrimination.[46] Still, equalization of access should not be interpreted simply as a concession; it also rationalized the recruitment of intermediate management personnel. In one sense the affirmative action effort can be viewed as a publicly subsidized state and corporate talent search.

Similarly, the protest against external administration of black life was met by an expansion in the scope of the black political and administrative apparatus. Through federal funding requirements of community representation, reapportionment of electoral jurisdictions, support for voter "education," and growth of the social welfare bureaucracy, the black elite was provided with broadened occupational opportunities and with official responsibility for administration of the black population. The rise of black officialdom beginning in the 1970s signals the realization of the reconstructed elite's social program and the consolidation of its hegemony over black life. No longer do preachers, funeral directors, and occasional politicos vie for the right to rationalize an externally generated agenda to the black community. Now black officials and professional political activists represent, interact among, and legitimate themselves before an attentive public of black functionaries in public and private sectors of the social management apparatus.[47] Even the ideological reproduction of the elite is assured: Not only mass-market journalists but black academics as well (through black publications, research institutes, and professional organizations) relentlessly sing the praises of the newly empowered elite.[48]

It was in the ideological sphere as well that the third major protest, that against massification of the black community, was resolved. Although authentic Afro-American particularity had been undermined by the standardizing imperatives of mass capitalism, the black nationalist reaction paved the way for the constitution of an artificial particularity.[49] Residual idiomatic and physical traits, bereft of distinctive content, were injected with racial stereotypes and the ordinary petit bourgeois weltanschauung to create the pretext for an apparently unique black existence. A thoroughly ideological construction of black uniqueness — which was projected universally in the mass market as black culture — fulfilled at least three major functions: First, as a marketing device it facilitated the huckstering of innumerable commodities designed to enhance, embellish, simulate, or glorify "blackness."[50] Second, artificial black particularity provided the basis for the myth of genuine black community and consequently legitimated the organization of the black population into an administrative unit — and, therefore, the black elite's claims to primacy. Finally, the otherness-without-negativity provided by the ideologized blackness can be seen as a potential antidote to the new contradictions generated by monopoly capitalism's bureaucratic rationality. By constituting an independently given sector of society responsive to administrative controls, the well-managed but recalcitrant black community justifies the existence of the administrative apparatus and legitimates existing forms of social integration.

In one sense, the decade-and-a-half of black activism was a phenomenon vastly more significant than black activists appreciated, while in another sense it was far less significant than has been claimed.[51] As an emancipatory project for the Afro-American population, the "movement"—especiailly after the abolishment of segregation—had little impact beyond strengthening the existing elite strata. Yet as part of a program of advanced capitalist reconstruction, black activism contributed to thawing the Cold War and outlined a model to replace it.

By the late 1960s the New Deal coalition was no longer able fully to integrate recalcitrant social strata such as the black population.[52] The New Deal coalition initiated the process of social homogenization and depoliticization that Herbert Marcuse described as "one-dimensionality." As Piccone observes, however, by the 1960s the transition to monopoly capitalism had been fully carried out, and the whole strategy had become counterproductive.[53] The drive toward homogenization and the total domination of the commodity form had deprived the system of the "otherness" required both to restrain the irrational tendencies of bureaucratic rationality and to locate lingering and potentially disruptive elements. Notwithstanding their vast differences, the ethnic "liberation struggles" and counterculture activism on the one side and the "hard hat" reaction on the other were two sides of the same rejection of homogenization. Not only did these various positions challenge the one-dimensional order, but their very existence betrayed the limitations of the administrative state.

The development of black activism from spontaneous protest through mass mobilization to system support assisted the development of a new mode of domination based on domesticating negativity by organizing spaces in which it could be expressed legitimately. Rather than suppressing opposition, the social management system now cultivates its own. The proliferation of government-generated reference groups in addition to ethnic ones (the old; the young; battered wives; the physically and mentally disabled; veterans; abused or gifted children) and the appearance of legions of "watchdog" agencies, reveal the extent to which the system manufactures and structures its own pacified opposition.[54]

This "artificial negativity" is in part a function of the overwhelming success of the process of massification operating since the depression and in part a response to it. Universal fragmentation of consciousness, with the corollary decline in the ability to think critically and the regimentation of an alienated everyday life set the stage for new forms of domination built into the very texture of organization.[55] In mass society, organized activity on a large scale requires hierarchization. Along with hierarchy, however, a new social management logic also comes into being (1) to protect existing privileges by delivering realizable, if inadequate, payoffs and (2) to legitimate administrative rationality as a valid and efficient model. To the extent that organization strives to ground itself on the mass, it is already integrated into the system of domination. The shibboleths that make up its specific platform make little difference. What is important is that the mass organizational form in pluralist politics reproduces the manipulative hierarchy and values typical of contemporary capitalism.[56]

Equally important for the existence of this social-managerial form is that the traditional modes of opposition to capitalism have not been able successfully to negotiate the transition from entrepreneurial to administrative capitalism. Thus, the left has not fully grasped the recent shifts in the structure of domination and continues to organize resistance along the very lines that reinforce the existing social order. As a consequence, the opposition finds itself perpetually outflanked. Unable to deliver the goods—political or otherwise—the left collapses before the cretinization of its own constituency. Once the mass model is accepted, cretinization soon follows, and from that point onward the opposition loses any genuine negativity. The civil rights and black power movements prefigured the coming of this new age; the feminist photocopy of the black journey on a road to nowhere was its farcical rerun.

The mass culture industry in this context maintains and reproduces the new synthesis of domination. Here, again, the history of the "black revolution" is instructive. In its most radical stage black power lived and spread as a media event. Stokely Carmichael and H. Rap Brown entertained nightly on network news, and after ordinary black "militancy" had lost its dramatic appeal the Black Panther party added props and uniforms to make radical politics entirely a show-business proposition. Although late-1960s black radicalism offered perhaps the most flamboyant examples of the peculiar relation of the mass media to the would-be opposition, that was only an extreme expression of a pattern at work since the early days of the civil rights movement.[57] Since then, political opposition has sought to propagandize its efforts through the mass media. Given the prevailing cretinization and the role of the culture industry in reproducing the fragmented, commodified consciousness, such a strategy, if pursued uncritically, could only reinforce the current modes of domination.[58]

That all forms of political opposition accepted the manipulative, mass organization model gave the strategy a natural, uncomplicated appearance and prevented the development of a critical approach. The consequence was the propagation of a model of politics that reinforced oversimplification, the reduction of ideals to banalized objects of immediate consumption — that is, the commodity form — and to an alienated, dehumanized hero-cultishness with "revolutionary" replacing either hero or villain. In short, opposition increasingly becomes a spectacle in a society organized around reduction of all existence to a series of spectacles.[59]

So monopoly capitalism has entered a new stage typified by the extension of the administrative apparatus throughout everyday life. In this context, genuine opposition is checkmated a priori by the legitimation and projection of a partial, fragmented criticism that can be enlisted in further streamlining the predominant rationality. In cases where existing bureaucratic structures need control mechanisms to prevent excesses, diffuse uneasiness with predominant institutions ends up artificially channeled into forms of negativity able to fulfill the needed internal control function. Always a problem for an opposition that seeks to sustain itself over time, under the new conditions of administered negativity, the one step backward required by organized opposition's need to broaden its constituency and conduct "positional warfare" becomes a one-way slide to affirmation of the social order. The logic of the transition to new forms of bourgeois hegemony requires adjustment of administrative rationality. The unrestrained drive to total integration is now mediated by peripheral, yet systemically controlled, loci of criticism; one-dimensionality itself has been "humanized" by the cultivation of commodified facsimiles of diversity.[60]

An important question remains: What of the possibilities for genuine opposition? The picture that I have painted seems exceedingly pessimistic. Yet this should not be understood to mean that opposition is futile. It *is* necessary, though, to examine closely the customary modes of opposition. The theory of artificial negativity historicizes the critique of the post–Cold War left and at the same time suggests some broad outlines for a reconceptualization of emancipatory strategy.

This examination of black radicalism in the wake of its integration offers a microcosmic view of the plight of the left as a whole. Having accepted an organizational model based on massification, the radicals were forced to compete with the elite on the latter's terms — an impossible proposition, since the elite had access to the cultural apparatus designed for mass mobilization. Moreover, even when opposition tried to reconstruct itself, it failed to generate systematic critique of its own strategy and was therefore unable to come to terms with shifts in the structure of capitalist social relations. Instead, it remained caught within a theoretical structure adequate for an earlier, preadministrative stage of capitalist development. Thus, the failure of mysticized black nationalism was reproduced in "ideological struggles" that reached their nadir in the 1978 dispute over whether Mao Tse-tung was really dead. Still, what of emancipatory possibilities? Certain general implications follow from the preceding analysis, but they become clear only through reflection on the forces currently driving the "really existing" American corporate liberalism.

Development into a sociopolitical order pacified through administration has been realized in the political sphere mainly through the integrative mechanism of a "pro-growth" coalition that has cemented linkages institutionally between national and local elites, as well as between representative elites from the various member constituencies in the coalition at both levels.[61] From the vantage point of global system logic the drive to administrative pacification reached its limits in the 1960s, as the homogenizing imperatives of mass culture were challenged by black nationalists and white counterculturists from one direction and rightist populism and white ethnic resurgence from another. Typical of such popular reactions, these challenges began with only the conceptual language of the prevailing social order in which to phrase their revolt, and before genuine alternatives could develop they were integrated into the social management apparatus as supportive appendages. They were thus reconstituted as regulators of rationality deficits in the administrative system. In this chapter I have traced the operation of that dynamic in the natural history of black activism.

At the level of practical political management, the growth politics model was undermined by its own contradictions. The strategy of maintaining social peace by ensuring incremental payoffs negotiated by recognized elites of potentially disruptive constituencies works only so long as the number of critical constituent groups is restricted. In this sense corporate liberalism, despite its superficial appearances and the effusions of political scientists, is exclusionistic and corporativistic rather than pluralistic.[62] Incorporation of activism in the 1960s forced open the circle of privileged constituencies to include first blacks and then a steady stream of other new claimants. The increasing volume of claims, in combination with other factors, pushed the costs of social control to a point that interfered with stable corporate profit making, the basis of the growth coalition in the first place.[63] By the early 1970s a process of gradual retrenchment had begun, largely under the aegis of the Nixon administration.

The Reaganite phenomenon of the 1980s in this regard represents an attempt to reconstitute a new growth coalition that eliminates both the claimant groups mobilized as a consequence of 1960s activism and the traditional labor component. Reganism appealed not only to racism, crude self-interest, and fantasies of international vigilantism but also—albeit disingenuously—to popular discontent with the bureaucratic regimentation and growing administration of social life.[64] A central justification for the program of retrenchment is that policies and programs aimed at new claimant groups have ensued primarily in creating unwarranted occupational opportunities for administrative elites.

Before such an argument, the post–civil rights era black elite—as the principal beneficiaries of activism—is virtually helpless. As a growing segment of the black population is increasingly marginalized into a generally optionless condition, consigned to deteriorating urban areas and destined at best to low-wage, dead-end subemployment, the black managerial elite is hard-pressed to defend its claims to status and function. At the same time, this stratum—whose existence is an artifact of the old coalition—appears to be incapable of generating any substantive critique of the inadequacies of the Democratic model of growth politics and is left only with bankrupt demands that its own privileges be secured in the reorganization. Indeed, signs are already visible that the elite's interest-group organizations are shifting their focus away from "state interventionist" to direct "corporate interventionist" strategies that uncouple from the old coalition's social welfare focus and reformulate black interests openly and exclusively in terms of securing leverage for upper-income, professional strata.[65]

So the wheels of corporate social reorganization turn, grinding beneath them the lives and hopes of the dispossessed and oiled by their misery. The legatees of activism, putative bearers of the principle of friction, simply cling to the wheels, hoping to go along for the ride no matter what the outcome.

Yet even if the current, draconian retrenchment is defeated, there will be little cause for celebration. Not only would a return to the old growth coalition be inadequate to meet the needs of large segments of American society, including a disproportionate element of the black population, but that coalition cannot be reinstated on its original basis. There is a sense, after all, in which Samuel Huntington's argument is sound. The partial success of 1960s activism in generating new status groups has intensified competition among noncorporate constituencies over the limited opportunities available for participation in the administrative distribution of privilege. Organized labor, feminist groups, and minority advocacy groups compete with one another in what they understand to be a zero-sum struggle for social and economic benefits. Added to these are the plethora of other interest configurations arising from the maturing, upwardly mobile post-war baby boom: urban revitalization, localism, environmentalism, and others characterized under the rubric of "new social movements."

Not only are the agendas of these "young urban professionals" ("yuppies") often in objective conflict, if not overt antagonism, with those of minorities and organized labor, but that stratum's neoprogressivist ideological orientation breeds fractiousness through its disposition toward the egoistic, single-issue activism of "citizen" initiatives. Despite the hyperpluralism that this orientation promotes, it often masquerades—as did its early-twentieth-century predecessor—as defense of the public interest.[66] However, beneath the hollow "new ideas" themes trumpeted by John Anderson in 1980 and Gary Hart in 1984 lies a neoliberal social agenda that at the national level would reinforce growth in the high-tech and information industries in which yuppies are concentrated and would accept the decline of the old industrial base, as Hart's opposition to the Chrysler bailout indicates. At the local level this agenda endorses a model of urban redevelopment that accelerates displacement of the poor under the guise of neighborhood renewal and advocates an expanding official role for neighborhood organizations in local policy making, which automatically advantages upper-income, better-endowed—and thus more easily mobilized—neighborhoods.[67] Moreover, the national neoliberal growth agenda promises to intensify local income stratification by exacerbating labor market segmentation; that model for growth generates for those outside language and symbol manipulating areas only service-sector or other poorly paid, optionless employment, and not much of that.[68] The prospect of recomposition of a growth agenda along these lines, therefore, does not portend a future for the general black population that is much different from that held out by Reaganism. Indeed, the neoliberal tendency identified with Gary Hart raises the specter of a Democratic consensus that—like Reagan's—excludes blacks and other minorities, as well as the AFL-CIO.[69]

In this context one has to strain to find emancipatory possibilities. The dangers that the present situation poses for the black population cannot even be conceptualized within the myopic and narrowly opportunistic pattern of discourse defined by the black political elite. A first step, therefore, must entail breaking this elite hegemony over ideas in the black community. The spoken-for must come to master political speech and to articulate their own interests, free of the intermediation of brokerage politicians and the antirational, antidemocratic conformism preached by charismatic authority. This mastery can develop only through a combination of unrelenting critique of the elite's program, as well as its authoritarian legitimations, and practical efforts to expand the discursive arena within the Afro-American population.[70]

The very success of the post–civil rights elite in imposing its agenda of administrative management has limited the terms of black political discourse to the options thrown up within the present arrangements of domination. Yet inadequate though they may be, those options at this point constitute the only meaningful terrain for political engagement. Creation of a sphere of black public debate on issues arising from the current tendencies in capitalist social reorganization — ranging from the ramifications of decisions about the allocation of public goods in a local political jurisdiction to national economic and social policy — is necessary to transcend the official black posture of quiet acceptance of any initiative that includes an affirmative action component. Stimulation of political controversy within the black community would lead to recognition of the diversity of interest configurations among blacks and is therefore a precondition to formulation of genuinely collective agendas, whose adherents may or may not be coterminous with the boundaries of racial identification. This ostensibly tepid call for the development of a political liberalism within the racial community offers, under the present circumstances, the only hope for combating the sacrifice of a growing share of the black population to permanent marginality in the American social order. The principles of "bourgeois democracy," on which the black elite has grounded its demands for participatory rights in the distributive queue of growth politics, must be applied against the hegemony of elite interests within the Afro-American group.

At stake in the short term is the specific character of the governing synthesis that ultimately replaces the New Deal coalition. The concrete form of those new arrangements, including the position of racial minorities in them, will be determined through political contention, and the black political elite — for reasons that I have indicated — cannot be relied upon to press the interests of a population that exists for it primarily as private capital. Beyond the immediate situation, the animation of a critical-democratic black political culture constitutes a necessary, though incremental, movement toward Afro-American participation in development of a more general critical dialogue that may produce the basis for a new oppositional politics — one capable of confronting squarely the irrational logic and mechanisms that constitute the mass capitalist order of domination.

The strategic proposal that I have sketched obviously provides no blueprint; it is modest and most contingent, and — even if implemented — it hardly guarantees social transformation. Its modesty only reflects the failure of oppositional forces to develop credible alternatives in the here-and-now. Acknowledgment of that failure, however, should not be misread as a pessimistic assessment; admission of failure expresses the distance between actually existing conditions and a goal that lives beyond the shortfall. Although contingent responses offer no sure exits from a bleak situation, contingency itself is the source of real hope, that which lies in recognition of the openness of history. Such hope, grounded in an unyielding vision of human emancipation, seeks its possibilities even in the darkest moments of the present; it is despair that hides its head from history and refuses to see the undesirable.[71]

1986

3. The Black Urban Regime
Structural Origins and Constraints

By the mid-1980s black regimes — black-led and black-dominated administrations backed by solid council majorities — governed thirteen U.S. cities with populations over 100,000, several of them among the nation's largest.[1] Popular accounts often herald accession of those regimes as fulfillment of grand democratic ideals. A more sophisticated, and more modest, view sees the black regime as a current point in an unfolding saga of urban ethnic succession. That view also entails an inference that black municipal governance signifies something more than office-holding. Black "succession" implies that the semi-Hobbesian democracy of "street-fighting" pluralism works now even for blacks, who therefore will finally join the long march of upward mobility along with other, allegedly earlier, "immigrant" groups. The first view is simply naive in its civics text–like exuberance. The second suffers from an ahistoricism that (1) glosses profound structural and institutional changes that have reshaped the urban context over the last two generations and (2) forgets that the strength of the racial element in American politics short-circuits neat comparisons with earlier instances of "ethnoracial transition."[2] Both take the rise of black regimes as reason to indulge a self-satisfied celebration of American political institutions and racial democracy. To be sure, black officials contribute to the perception that they represent larger purposes by presenting themselves as legatees of the civil rights movement.[3]

Certain other viewpoints counsel restraint of such celebrations. While genuflecting perfunctorily toward the rhetorical élan attending the first wave of black mayoral successes, Matthew Holden[4] and Michael Preston[5] stressed the limitations placed on mayoral capacities by political institutions and entrenched patterns of political behavior. More recent scholarship has examined consequences of those limitations by assessing black mayors' impact on budgetary allocations, including service delivery patterns and composition of public employment. Although the specific findings of that research have been mixed, the general conclusion seems to be that the presence of a black mayor or regime has some, but less than dramatic, racially redistributive effect on allocation of public resources.[6] However, black mayors have been unable to affect the high levels of poverty and unemployment that characterize the cities over which they preside. Benefits of racial redistribution have been concentrated among middle-class blacks, in part because the regimes adopt "corporate center" development strategies that generally contradict the reform platforms on which they are elected.[7] The key to apprehending the real significance of black urban governance lies in examining how and why regimes adhere to development strategies so much at odds with their electoral platforms.

To what complex of pressures does the black regime respond in choosing corporate center strategy? What is the nature of the tension expressed in Nelson's juxtaposition of the corporate and popular racial constituencies? What alternative courses, if any, might be pursued? These questions have seldom been addressed systematically in relation to black municipal governance. In what follows I shall respond to them by proposing a structurally and historically situated account of the black urban regime as a distinctive phenomenon. This account has two elements: (1) reconstruction of the demographic, socioeconomic, and ideological-political pressures that created the conditions for ascendancy of the black regime, and (2) examination of major structural constraints and issues that confront those regimes as they attempt to govern. In the latter connection I shall assess ways in which black regimes have generally reacted to those constraints and issues. In a concluding section I shall discuss possibilities for enhancing democratic interests—apropos of both practical politics and the discourse of political scientists—in the context of black urban governance.

Structural Origins of the Black Regime

Although individual perspicacity and organizational talent are probably the most pertinent factors determining election of a given regime, we can hardly believe that electoral political wisdom and aptitude came to urban black communities only in the late 1960s. Black control of the official institutions of municipal governance has been made possible by elaboration of a particular set of demographic, socioeconomic, and ideological pressures operative in the post–World War II urban arena.

Demographic Pressure

Most simply put, throughout the two decades following the war, the nonwhite share of big-city populations rose steadily. This increase was fed by three factors: (1) absolute increase of nonwhite population, largely by in-migration; (2) relative, and sometimes absolute, white decrease, mainly by out-migration; and (3) comparative fixity of municipal boundaries.[8] New migrants, largely black and Hispanic, flocked to the nation's major cities in quest of a better way of life. At the same time, spurred by federal housing policies that subsidized single-family, low-density housing, middle-class and stable working-class whites increasingly began relocating beyond municipal boundaries into the suburban standard metropolitan statistical area (SMSA). Consequently, by the latter 1960s, the prospect of black-majority cities had become an issue for national policy concern.

Whereas the pull factors drawing nonwhites to the central city are straightforward and familiar, the push factors nudging whites out are somewhat more complex. Moreover, the latter suggest a material as well as an attitudinal basis for the "white flight" syndrome. White exodus from central cities has been a response first of all to the ideology of upward mobility, buttressed by federal transportation and housing policies that stimulated suburban development in the postwar era.[9] For many, leaving the old in-city enclaves for modern, disconnected tract houses has been a symbol — albeit one largely articulated and propagated by private real estate development ideology — of arrival, a statement of self-improvement. Also, the mortgage subsidies provided by federal programs brought the relatively new "American dream" of home ownership within reach of a substantial portion of the population who would not otherwise have been able to afford it.[10] Moreover, white departure has been stimulated by nonwhite in-migration, in part for reasons that, although ultimately bigoted, are instrumentally rational. The clichéd fear of loss of property value has a factual basis. Property values do tend to fall when blacks enter a neighborhood because one element of property value in residential real estate markets is white exclusivity.[11]

Therefore whites who want to avoid living near blacks "pay more for otherwise similar housing in white neighborhoods than in integrated neighborhoods, pushing prices higher in the white interior than in the transition zone." Moreover, "white expectations about the future of neighborhoods in the transition zone depress prices for housing there."[12] We can thus see the tragic cycle. Whites flee with black encroachment. Real estate "values" fall, accelerating flight. As "values" fall, housing stock begins to deteriorate, prompting stable and middle-income blacks to follow fleeing whites, whose new neighborhoods lose their relative attractiveness once blacks move in. Moreover, federal housing policy played an active role in reinforcing this dynamic, often by building segregation into program priorities.[13]

This ironic situation has obvious revenue implications for the municipalities that anchor SMSAs. Suburban sprawl has meant relative and in some cases absolute reductions in municipal tax bases. In addition, the city finds itself in the position of providing services daily to hordes of suburban freeloaders. Nor is that the only harmful consequence of suburbanization for central municipalities. Gary Orfield provides a useful summary:

> Suburbanization not only redistributes taxable wealth, but also redistributes jobs and educational opportunities in ways that make them virtually inaccessible to minorities confined by residential segregation to parts of the central city and declining segments of the suburban ring. It greatly increases the physical scale of racial separation, particularly for children, since middle-class white families with children become rarities in many central cities. It overlaps the system of racial separation and inequality with a system of political and legal separation. Thus the best services, education, and access to new jobs are made available to affluent, virtually all-white communities that openly employ a full range of municipal powers to attract desirable jobs from the city while preventing low- and moderate income families, or renters of any kind, from moving into the communities. As a consequence, black and Hispanic political aspirations are concentrated very largely on municipal and educational institutions that lack the tax base to maintain existing levels of services, to say nothing of mounting vast new responses to the critical problems of these expanding minority communities.[14]

A simple solution to this problem would be for central municipalities to adopt programs of aggressive annexation. However, that response is impractical for a number of reasons. For one thing, given patterns of racial voting, elected officials and aspirants to officialdom in black-majority or near-majority cities are understandably loath to annex pockets of potentially antagonistic white voters.

The latter can, in any event, expect sufficient support in state legislatures to ward off unilateral annexations. Successful annexation appears to be strongly associated with both relatively low status differentiation between central city and suburbs and a relatively brief period of urban settlement.[15] Black regimes, as shown below, tend to hold power in older cities and in cities substantially differentiated from their SMSAs.

This means, of course, that the kind of city most likely to be governed by a black regime is also the kind of city most likely to suffer the regressive effects of suburbanization and least likely to have the option of mitigating them by means of expanding municipal boundaries.[16] However, though the proximate cause of this situation is, to paraphrase Orfield, the dialectic of suburbanization and ghettoization, its ultimate sources lie deeper, in the dynamics of changing urban and metropolitan economic function.

Socioeconomic Pressure

The modern American city has its roots in the logic of industrial production; so, in large measure, does the impetus of suburbanization. The heyday of urban growth coincided with the burst of industrial growth between the last quarter of the nineteenth century and the first quarter of the twentieth. By the 1920s, however, the processes of suburbanization had taken hold. Individuals had been moving farther away from the inner city for some time and for a variety of reasons,[17] but theretofore cities simply responded with periodic, often imperialistic annexations.[18] What was different after 1920 was that industry, particularly manufacturing, had begun to leave the city.[19] Two related developments made relocation outside the central city attractive. New mass production technologies increasingly required production processes — and therefore plants — to be laid out horizontally over larger parcels of land; this development favored location in suburban rings where land was cheaper than in central cities.[20] However, movement to the suburban ring was underway even before the proliferation of such mass production techniques. What especially made suburban relocation desirable was the search for more isolable, and thus more tractable, labor (and along the way perhaps reduced taxes).[21] This was an early manifestation of one of the corporation's most powerful assets in its relations with labor and government: the relative mobility of capital. It is not unusual in the history of capitalist development for labor's assertiveness to stimulate the forces of technical innovation as an instrument of managerial control.[22]

The defection of manufacturing production was the central event in launching the suburbanization dynamic in two respects. As Walker maintains, "Only with the dispersal of employment — of production and circulation activities as a whole" — was mass suburbanization possible even though residential decentralization had begun earlier; the location of industry grounded and accelerated the process.[23] More mundanely, but no less consequentially, newly suburbanized industrial elites gave the necessary muscle to well-off residents and other advocates of suburban independence to boost the home rule movement and thereby curtail central cities' powers to annex.[24] At the same time, downtown came to be recast as the locus for concentrating administrative business activity. "Downtown office space in the ten largest cities increased between 1920 and 1930 by 3,000 percent. Tall skyscrapers suddenly sprouted; by 1929 there were 295 buildings

21 stories or taller in the five largest cities alone."[25] Decentralization of plants to the suburbs, thanks to new communications technology, had made possible the separation of productive and administrative functions. The latter clustered downtown, creating the new central business district and completing what David Gordon describes as the transition from the "Industrial City" to the "Corporate City," which is built around several dispersive tendencies: (1) dispersion of manufacturing from the inner city through the metropolitan area and eventually beyond, (2) dispersion and segmentation of working-class housing, (3) dispersion of shopping centers from downtown, to be replaced by corporate institutions, and (4) intensified dispersion of middle- and upper-class housing.[26]

Reproduction of the corporate city, and thus of its centrifugal tendencies, became a principal project around which political entrepreneurs, corporate elites, and elites of other major interest configurations converged—growing from the New Deal experience—to improvise the distinctive American form of political-economic management that Alan Wolfe has called "counter-Keynesianism." As Wolfe succinctly puts it, "If Keynesianism implies the use of government to influence and direct decisions made in the private sector, then postwar macroeconomic planning could only be defined as counter-Keynesian: the use of the private sector to influence the scope and activities of government."[27]

Reproduction of the corporate city entailed reproduction of the principle of dispersion, by definition on a widening scale. This dynamic—aided and encouraged by federal and local governmental policy—not only created and exacerbated the now familiar problem of metropolitan fragmentation, which, of course, has contributed significantly to central-city deterioration; spurred by the tremendous postwar advances in communications technology (themselves often byproducts of the federally sponsored, "private" defense industry), the tendency toward decentralization of production has also proceeded even beyond the suburban fringe. By the end of the 1960s the corporate sector of the U.S. economy had begun, for a variety of reasons, systematically to deindustrialize, as investment in industrial production increasingly left the United States altogether in favor of more congenial climes where wage scales often fall in the sub–fifty cents per hour range.[28]

This economic dynamic combines with the demographic one discussed in the previous section to create a pattern of central cities that have become increasingly black and have offered rapidly declining opportunities for the kind of labor-intensive employment that supported earlier urban populations. Blacks in metropolitan areas are twice as likely as whites to live in central cities; they are more likely as well to reside in the largest metropolitan areas.[29] These tend also to be the oldest SMSAs and, in part because the processes of decentralization are more advanced in them, the most depressed.[30] Kathleen Bradbury, Anthony Downs, and K. Small found that whereas the black share of the population decreased by 0.4 percent in growing cities in growing SMSAs between 1960 and 1970, it increased by 7.8 percent in severely declining cities in declining SMSAs.[31]

At the same time that the central city's nonwhite population was growing and becoming ever more marginalized economically, the scope and character of urban politics were changing. The counter-Keynesian framework for local politics that developed in most cities after World War II, with its new concatenations of stakes and constituencies joined by a pro-growth imperative, eventually — but only after mass uprisings and "defiant" black political activity — articulated mechanisms to incorporate and channel forms of black systemic representation. That arrangement became the immediate context out of which black municipal governance emerged.

Ideological/Political Pressure

Three currents in the postwar urban political scene came together to set the stage for the rise of the black regime: (1) consolidation of a "pro-growth" framework as the driving imperative of and basis for allegiance in urban politics, (2) expansion of public service bureaucracies and their entry into the local political arena as interest configurations and constituencies, and (3) the development and spread of black activism. Of the three, the first is central in that the pro-growth agenda both increased public sector functions and employment and generated the specific issues in relation to which black activism was articulated.

John Mollenkopf has provided a cogent account of the sources and composition of pro-growth politics at the local level, and there is no need to rehearse all of its elements here. The guiding principle of the pro-growth framework has been aggregation of local interests to effect federally authorized local development projects. Toward that end, Mollenkopf observes:

> These pro-growth coalitions brought together a variety of constituencies into what Robert Salisbury has called "a new convergence of power." Among them were downtown business elites, ambitious political leaders seeking to modernize urban politics, middle class, good government reform groups, the professional city planners to whom they turned for advice, a powerful new stratum of public administrators, and private development interests, including developers, lenders, builders, and the construction trades.[32]

While each of the participating groups brought its particular interest (that is, developers and building trades unions wanted construction, planners and reformers wanted modernized, scientific government, politicians wanted identification with visible symbols of progress), the broader project of the agenda they served was completion of the functional transition from industrial to postindustrial, or corporate, city.

In addition to offering clear incentives for local participants the pro-growth framework held out at least two attractions at the national level: First, it provided the national Democratic party with a way to bring together its "disparate urban constituencies" and to unite them organizationally around a program of publicly underwritten local growth and development. Second, the pro-growth agenda became a significant part of national economic policy and provided a useful context for counter-Keynesian economic strategy in the postwar period. Mollenkopf estimates that "metropolitan physical development accounts for perhaps one-fifth of the GNP and perhaps one-fourth of its growth since World War II" and notes that government spending has contributed substantially to the magnitude and direction of those expenditures. Those considerable public expenditures have been directed toward reconstructing physical and institutional infrastructures along lines compatible with the functional requirements of the new corporate city. In the process the expanded governmental role naturally entailed an expansion of municipal functions and employment, a development that reinforced tendencies already operative in public bureaucracies.[33]

On the one hand, the growth of public employment, both absolutely and relatively, increased the significance of public employee unions as interest configurations in the local polity. This tendency was relatively more pronounced in older, larger cities, which had larger critical masses of public employees and experienced declines in non–public sector employment.[34] On the other hand, the expanded public role also contributed to the spread of professionalistic interests and ideologies in local politics. Professionalization has been driven by endemic forces in municipal service delivery, as in other spheres in American society, over most of this century.[35] With elaboration of the pro-growth framework professional and technical interests became embedded institutionally in local politics by virtue of the centrality of planning, engineering, and administrative functions in forming and realizing the growth agenda.[36] However, professionalization, as technique and as ideology, extended as well into the human service bureaucracies, which also grew in the postwar years.

At the same time, the general expansion of local public sector activity was tied in three ways to development of what Frances Fox Piven and Richard Cloward have called "defiant" urban black activism in the 1960s. First, urban renewal, which was a main programmatic vehicle for realizing the pro-growth agenda, became a focal point for black oppositional activity. The racial effects of urban renewal through the early 1960s are well known and best summarized in the phrase of the day, "Negro removal."[37] By the middle of the decade blacks had begun to react politically against the displacement and ghettoization that characterized the program. Second, growth of the local public sector increased the stakes of patronage politics, especially because of the relative success that blacks have had, along with women and other minorities, in governmental employment with respect to stability and upward mobility.[38] Finally, extension and professionalization of the local public sector added a new epicycle to urban politics (that is, the relationship between public agencies and their constituents or clients). As agencies professionalized, they sought greater autonomy in defining the terms and standards for their operations, especially in the human services. A result was increased tension between service providers and recipients.[39] As cities were simultaneously becoming blacker than the agencies, race was built into the texture of that politicized relationship.

Of the major urban constituencies of the national Democratic party, blacks had benefited least from the pro-growth framework. In fact several factors, including the racial component of real estate value, combined to make blacks victims rather than beneficiaries of pro-growth politics. The urban uprisings did not only signal discontent with the general quality of black life in cities and the insensitivity of institutions of social administration; they also indicated a need for additional mechanisms to cement black political loyalty. Both a sense of urgency produced by the uprisings (as well as by the energy recently set in motion through the civil rights movement) and the obdurateness of local governing coalitions that excluded black interests led to establishment of parallel linkages to create channels for black systemic representation. The federal program administration apparatus provided a linkage that bypassed entrenched local coalitions without destabilizing them.[40]

Successful incorporation of blacks into the pro-growth framework entailed two adjustments, one ideological and one programmatic. Ideologically, as Paul Peterson argues, municipal governments, because of their fundamental commitments to economic growth and revenue enhancement, naturally tend to reformulate potentially redistributive demands so that they articulate symbolic rather than redistributive goals.[41] Thus official black representation in decision-making processes became an alternative to alteration of growth-oriented patterns of resource allocation. Programmatically, however, though the demand for black representation was an alternative to broad-scale redistribution, accommodation of that more limited demand nonetheless required expanding the public sector pie to provide niches for minority functionaries in the social management apparatus.[42] Moreover, this strategy had longer-term implications.

Once black assertiveness was channeled into auxiliary linkage mechanisms of pro-growth politics, that is, what Michael Brown and Steven Erie call the public "social welfare economy," black political activity increasingly assimilated to familiar forms of urban ethnic pluralism. To that extent, as increasing black population in one city after another made it possible, in Carl Stokes's phrase, to "take City Hall," the process of "ethnoracial transition" was smoothed by the presence of a black leadership cohort that was already incorporated into the broader pro-growth coalition and accepted its imperatives.[43] In a study of black elected officials, for example, Peter Eisinger found that, especially in larger cities, the Community Action Program "provided an avenue to public service for a particular generation of young and relatively well-educated activists," and Albert Karnig and Susan Welch found black success in mayoral and city council aspirations to be associated with prior Model Cities program experience.[44] Sometimes the auxiliary linkages were more directly and immediately meaningful, as in the Ford Foundation's underwriting of a Congress on Racial Equality (CORE) voter registration project that enabled Stokes to win the Cleveland mayoral election on his second attempt.[45]

As I argue in chapter 2 of this volume, the interests of a growing professional-managerial stratum within the black community converged with those of pro-growth white elites to produce a new framework for black political activity in the post–civil rights movement era. That framework is largely a product of the several structural dynamics discussed here. Some scholars have seen this development as a natural progression from protest to mainstream political participation, which in that view had been the real or proper political objective all along. From that vantage point, election of a black regime realizes an element of a "modernizing" tendency in Afro-American politics.[46]

That interpretation is more or less true in general (particularly if its teleological connotations are discounted) and more or less laudable in given instances, and it discloses an important aspect of black political development. However, it does not account for three rather disturbing points. First, the dynamics that make possible the empowerment of black regimes are the same as those that produce the deepening marginalization and dispossession of a substantial segment of the urban black population. Second, the logic of pro-growth politics, in which black officialdom is incorporated, denies broad progressive redistribution as a policy option and thereby prohibits direct confrontation of the problem of dispossession among the black constituency. Third, the nature of the polities that black regimes govern is such that the relation between the main components of their electoral and governing coalitions is often zero-sum; gains for the predominantly black electoral constituency are experienced as losses by the corporate-led governing coalition, and vice versa. These conditions limit and shape the black regime's behavior in ways that I shall explain in the following sections.

Structural Constraints and Issues Facing the Black Regime

Clearly, the black regime does not inherit a tabula rasa. Indeed, for a regime that comes to power at the nodal point of long-term currents of ghettoization and deindustrialization and a collateral alignment of "systemic power,"[47] the environment for making policy decisions must appear nearly as confining as the geographical environment. The preceding discussion has identified dynamics that have structured the operating context of municipal regimes in cities of the general type most likely to experience transition to black rule. Now we will examine some of the more important ways that those dynamics constrain the behavior and optional field of the black regime in power. These constraints stem from three main sources: (1) the city's changing economic base and functions, (2) fiscal and revenue limitations, and (3) competition and conflict—both latent and overt—among the regime's constituencies.

Changing Economic Base

The black regime assumes power typically in a context of rapidly diminishing private sector employment opportunities for inner-city residents. Private economic activity continues to favor suburbs at the expense of anchoring municipalities; in fact, the processes of deconcentration are such that exurban areas beyond SMSAs have become increasingly attractive as production locations. George Sternlieb and J. W. Hughes, after noting that through the 1970s nonmetropolitan areas grew at a faster aggregate rate than SMSAs, observe that manufacturing firms, long the staple of the urban labor force, now show a locational preference for the rural South. There is, moreover, a portentous racial dimension to this preference; manufacturers seek the upcountry, "white South," where workers are more docile (blacks are seen as being less antiunion) and where problems of managing racial tension do not exist. Because residential and industrial movements are mutually reinforcing, the result is a general population shift toward exurbs as well.[48]

Not surprisingly, therefore, cities led by black regimes are among the most likely to have suffered both population and functional decreases. Of the eleven of the thirteen black-governed cities included in a ranking by population change, two scored as "stagnant," and nine were "severely declining"; moreover, six of the nine were located in growing SMSAs.[49] On a city-SMSA disparity index, all thirteen cities had negative scores (indicating an unfavorable comparative position for the central city), and all but two scored toward the extreme end of the disparity scale. On the city-SMSA divergence index, ten of the thirteen received negative scores, indicating a worsening trend.[50] Of the eleven listed, ten had experienced worsening city-SMSA per capita income ratios between 1960 and 1973, with the worst losses occurring in Sunbelt cities (Birmingham, Atlanta, and New Orleans).[51] Thus, by the time the black regimes came to power the cities they were to govern were already among the most depressed.

Perhaps the most striking indication can be seen on the Nathan and Adams "Central-City Hardship" index. Not only did all ten of the cities listed that are currently black-led show disadvantage (as did forty-three of the fifty-five central cities examined), eight of the cities that have black regimes were among the fourteen most disadvantaged. In a different, later ranking, Bradbury, Downs, and Small counted six of the black-led cities among the fourteen most "troubled."[52] Twelve of the thirteen had unfavorable "city distress" ratings (the thirteenth, Portsmouth, was at parity with its SMSA), and eight of them fell in the worst categories of distress.[53]

The components of both the "Central-City Hardship" index and those reflecting city-SMSA "distress," "decline," "disparity," and "divergence" have much to do with employment opportunity. The six elements of the Nathan and Adams index, for example, include three that directly concern employment: unemployment, income level, and poverty. The "city distress" index constructed by Bradbury, Downs, and Small has five components, of which two are unemployment rate in 1975 and percent of population poor in 1969. (Several of the other measures are arguably indirectly related to employment opportunity: for example, crowded housing, education, violent crime rate.) I have noted already that black-led cities are among the most likely to have lost manufacturing, wholesale, and retail jobs. However, even such employment as remains is not likely to do much for central-city residents.

Several of the black-led cities have realized increases in service sector employment and, consistent with the pro-growth scenario, have experienced expanding office economies.[54] However, neither development holds out particularly optimistic prospects for residents of depressed central cities. The "service sector" rubric actually conceals a dual labor market composed of a high-wage, professional component specializing in what have been called "advanced corporate services" and a low-wage, low-status, and dead-end consumer service component; the latter is filled largely by women and minorities.[55]

Of course, the increases in the advanced corporate services component are not likely to create much of a direct employment benefit for city residents, in part because they are not likely to have had the specialized training that much of that activity requires. Although central-city residents do gain some lower-level technical jobs in both private and public service sectors, the employment effects of expansion in that component, especially for better-paying jobs, generally cluster in the suburbs. Growth in the office economy does stimulate some growth in the low-wage service industries, in restaurants, hotels, and other facilities catering to the nonresident labor force and consumers of urban culture. The output from this activity is tied to the specific locale of its "production" and therefore accommodates a very small market. For that reason and because the typical service firm has relatively few employees this segment of the dual labor system cannot begin to compensate numerically — not to mention in wages and benefits — for employment possibilities lost to dispersion, deindustrialization, and capital flight.[56] Moreover, even low-wage service sector jobs are growing faster in the suburbs than in central cities.[57]

Robert Friedland observes that the low wages paid in the consumer service sector make traveling from central cities for such jobs uneconomic, and he notes that they usually are filled by "a secondary labor market of wives and children of employed suburban males, who (are) willing to accept low wages and [are] closer to work."[58] However, more complex market forces also may operate to limit reverse commutation for consumer service sector employment. For one thing, such jobs often are filled through word-of-mouth networks, especially during periods of slack labor supply; this amounts to a guildlike advantage for those living in suburban communities. For another, inner-city residents are likely to be penalized by what has been called "statistical discrimination" along racial lines.[59] Because inner-city nonwhites are assumed generally to have inferior skill levels and work habits, employers may prefer, when labor supply permits, to hire suburban whites for jobs that technically could be performed by either group. Operation of some such principle would explain the circumstance that when white suburban youth have access to more attractive sources of disposable income and eschew consumer service sector jobs, blacks and Hispanics with adequate "skills" and work habits materialize to replace them. Suspicion in this regard is strengthened by instances, which occurred in many areas beginning in the summer of 1986, when changes in the white suburban opportunity structure have resulted in shifts from nearly all-white to nearly all-minority crews in metropolitan fast-food restaurants and similar establishments. However, it is also possible that expansion of white options exhausts word-of-mouth networks and forces more active labor recruitment, which in turn reaches inner-city minorities.

In either case, however, what exists is akin to an employment filtering process. Unlike housing markets, though, this process is much more responsive to cyclical fluctuations. When employment options narrow, whites reenter the job spheres they had vacated and either ease the pressure on employers to recruit actively or reassert their statistical racial attractiveness or both. Thus seen, the inner-city minorities are in the familiar role of membership in the industrial reserve army: mobilized in periods of expansion to fill less desirable jobs in the consumer services sector and then cast out of the labor force when contraction makes those jobs relatively more desirable to whites.[60] This situation is in a way analogous to that of the "guest workers" in the more dynamic economies of western and central Europe. Suburbanites can exploit the advantages of having a nearby pool of underutilized labor while deflecting as many of the social and fiscal costs as possible onto other jurisdictions.

All of these conditions contribute to the high, chronic unemployment that prevails in central cities in general and in black-led cities in particular. In a comparison of changes in unemployment rates between central cities and suburbs in ten SMSAs between 1971 and 1976, cities currently governed by black regimes scored four of the five most significant instances of widening gap.[61] With unemployment and income inequality comes increased criminal activity,[62] which often enough victimizes participants in the office economy and other upper-income wayfarers into the central city. The rational response from a revenue- and image-conscious municipal administration is to mobilize police power to provide a cordon sanitaire to protect revenue-producing, upper-income consumers from potentially hostile — or at least worrisome — confrontation by an indigenous rabble. Thus Andrew Young's attempt to create a "vagrant-free" zone in downtown Atlanta is a mild, if gratuitous and odious, expression of a deeper logic.[63] The script for this scene was written when Great Britain marched into Calcutta and France sailed into Algiers, and it is replicated daily in the Third World. The irony here, as there, is that the black regime seems unable to generate remedies.

The economic forces that have produced this situation are national and international in scope, and to that extent they are largely beyond the effective influence of local government. The loci of pertinent decision making are elsewhere — Congress, the White House, corporate board rooms, international currency markets, the Federal Reserve Board, and so on. In that context the municipal regime has few systemic levers with which to press the interests of its dispossessed, marginalized citizens. Pursuit of economic growth on any terms looms as one of the few concrete options apparently open to local regimes, yet that orientation helps to reproduce the pro-growth framework that has reinforced and exacerbated the dispersion processes underlying much of urban social and economic marginalization. For the black regime this inherently contradictory condition is intensified because (1) the level of need is likely to be greater among its citizenry, (2) the dispossessed are a more central element of its electoral coalition, and (3) it is likely to govern in circumstances of greater fiscal stress.

Fiscal Constraints

There is little need to detail the character of the fiscal issues that face urban administrations. Instead, I shall simply highlight certain structurally embedded sources of the current relative fiscal straits and their particular implications for black regimes.

Municipal spending, like government spending at all levels, increased steadily over the two decades following the mid-1950s, with the greatest rates of increase occurring after the early 1960s.[64] At the local level four main factors generated the growth in spending. First, increasing municipal size and complexity, as well as the changing socioeconomic character of the urban population, naturally required city governments to take on new service functions and to expand on a per capita basis many services already provided. Second, the intrinsically expansionist tendencies of bureaucratic and professionalizing subcultures exerted pressures both toward upgrading the quality and level of service delivery and toward organizational hypertrophy. Third, the proliferation of "pluralist budgeting" integrated coalition building and conflict management into fiscal planning, thereby creating a situation in which "the dominant fiscal constraint is more likely to be one of meeting expenditure demands of key supporters and then redefining the revenue constraint in light of political commitments."[65] Finally, each of these tendencies was exacerbated by the pro-growth framework that added to municipal functions, reinforced the propulsion of technical interests, and made federal resources available to institutionalize the strategy of guaranteeing social peace through budget allocations.

On the other side of the ledger, population and tax-base loss and reductions in intergovernmental assistance combined with the relative fixity of prior expenditure commitments to send the specter of fiscal crisis haunting many cities. The cities governed by black regimes are among those most likely to be haunted.

The black-led cities are among the most likely to have experienced substantial losses of population, income, and employment.[66] In an examination by H. A. Garn and L. C. Ledebur of the 147 largest U.S. cities (excluding Washington, D.C.), 42 percent of the black-led cities ranked among those that had experienced "seriously adverse" income change between 1967 and 1972 (compared to 13 percent of the total); 25 percent had had "seriously adverse" job change (compared to 3 percent of the total); and 33 percent experienced "seriously adverse" unemployment rate change (compared to 16 percent of the total).[67] In their composite ranking of economic performance from most to least distressed, 25 percent of the black-led cites were among the worst-off 6 percent of the total; 58 percent were among the worst-off 18 percent; and 83 percent fell within the worst-off 38 percent.[68] At the same time rates of public spending increased more in the black-led cities. Of the thirty-seven central cities examined by Charles Schultze and his colleagues, the eight with black regimes had experienced an average per capita growth rate in government spending in the 1957–1970 period of 199 percent, compared to an average 158 percent increase among the remaining twenty-nine cities; in 1970 the cities now governed by black regimes received over 26 percent more than the others in per capita intergovernmental aid, which suggests that they were more likely to feel the strain of subsequent federal retrenchment.[69] Indeed, black-governed cities are among those for which federal aid was most significant as a percentage of total general revenue as of 1978.[70]

That the tendency toward fiscal stress is greater in the black-led cities is not most significant as a portent of imminent crisis or collapse; a more salient impact on municipal government is a narrowing of the latitude open to regimes both objectively (by limiting their ability to engage in pluralistic budgeting) and subjectively (by articulating the vernacular baseline of the local political culture in the direction of "fiscal conservatism" and more thorough subordination of policy agendas to market imperatives).[71]

When consciousness of fiscal limitation is prominent in the local political culture, as it is likely to be in black-governed cities, local governments are usually faced with an unpalatable choice. One option is retrenchment, which, as service reduction, affects most adversely those who lack resources to substitute in the private market for public services lost. Moreover, even when only "fat" is cut, some negative employment effect will probably be felt among the governing regime's electoral constituents. The other option is raising taxes, which business and financial interests oppose as "fiscally irresponsible" and harmful to the city's economic health. When those interests are relatively powerful, they "provide the city's politicians and public officials with a strong incentive to reach an accord with business and to pursue fiscal policies that are acceptable both to it and to participants in the public capital market."[72] For black regimes, because of the relations I explain in the following section, this political tension is more acute than for others in similar circumstances. Thus, for example, Maynard Jackson, who long had cherished his identification as an advocate of the interests of the disadvantaged, was moved to fire 2,000 black sanitation workers, among the city's lowest-paid employees, in a 1977 labor dispute even as he acknowledged the legitimacy of their needs.[73]

Competing Constituencies and Political Conflict

The black regime typically comes to power in a spirit of reform, surrounded by images of redress of long-standing inequities and breaking through walls of entrenched privilege.[74] It is symbolically identified with advancement of the interests of racial democracy, or as Ronald Walters once claimed of black politicians in general, "fulfilling the legacy of black power."[75] That symbolism, however, intensifies tensions on three terrains of political competition and conflict that the regime must somehow negotiate.

First, the election of the black regime destabilizes the "trench system" of ethnic and neighborhood interests that vie for shares of budget allocations, the terrain on which is decided who gets what, when, and how in the context of implementing a dominant policy agenda. The location of public facilities and public works projects (both desirable and undesirable) and patterns of concentrating public service delivery most visibly define the spatial dimension of this terrain. Another dimension — the allocation of jobs and other patronage — is only indirectly spatial, to the extent that ethnic or other group identity is overlapped by neighborhood identity.[76]

Paul Peterson observes that this is the terrain on which relatively unfettered pluralist processes operate; however, he also notes that introduction of a racial component "changes the character" of the trench system. Discussing the trench phenomenon in relation to what he refers to as the "politics of allocation," Peterson lays out the problem succinctly:

> Blacks themselves make redistributive demands as part of their claim for group recognition, and whites see even modest black allocational demands as redistributive in nature. What benefits blacks is perceived as damaging white interests — thus it does. Token integration of com-

munity institutions is perceived by whites as the first step in an inevitable process of total change, and in what becomes a self-fulfilling prophecy whites stop using that community resource.[77]

Peter Eisinger reports that whites perceived that the coming of black rule in Atlanta and Detroit somehow altered the "rules of the game" for local politics, though he contends that the transitions in those cities met less resistance than the earlier transition to Irish rule in Boston. However, the tension that Peterson attributes to a propensity of black demands to challenge inviolable, antiredistributive principles and that Eisinger enfolds within a more general theory of variations in response to status displacement is also an artifact of the pro-growth framework. It is, after all, only from that framework that Peterson's model derives. To the extent that the pro-growth consensus in most cities has assumed that blacks occupy at best a subordinate status within the supportive coalition, the prospect of election of a black regime does imply the possibility of a substantive adjustment of the pattern of public resource allocation within the trench system. Anxiety among white voters is a predictable result; moreover, local media typically fuel that anxiety by carefully scrutinizing the actions of black candidates and officials for instances of succumbing to the temptation to play racial favoritism. That whites' anxiety is itself a function of anticipated loss of their own racial favoritism apparently does not mitigate the tension.

In this terrain the black regime is especially vulnerable to charges of inequitable practices because from the beginning it faces hostility and skepticism from white trenches fearful that governance by blacks will also be governance for blacks only. Even from the initial stages of campaigning, black aspirants to office must constantly reassure white voters that their interests will not be ignored. Thus a pundit was led to observe that a black candidate who needs 95 percent of the black vote and 5 percent of the white vote will spend 95 percent of the time trying to secure the 5 percent and 5 percent of the time campaigning for the 95 percent!

Once in power, the black regime is very much constrained, probably more than others because of the unyielding scrutiny to which it is subject, by the pluralist canon of maintaining equity within the ethnic and neighborhood trench system. In fact, the black regime often seems to go overboard; for example, Kenneth Gibson was indicted on felony charges that resulted from his having provided a public sinecure for a superannuated member of the Italian regime that he had displaced.[78] However, neither altruism nor naiveté nor Uncle Tomism is the effective source of this behavior; rather, it represents the pragmatic attempt to demonstrate good faith to potentially hostile forces in the white trenches. When those forces cannot or will not be placated, as Harold Washington's experience in Chicago has shown, the regime's capacity to govern can be hindered severely. Such implacable hostility, in fact, was primarily responsible for the ouster of the Stokes regime after two terms in Cleveland.[79]

A second terrain on which the black regime faces the potential for considerable tension is its relationships with the different elements of its principal electoral constituency, although for the most part this tension has been far more potential than actual. Naturally, black expectations are raised by the election of a black regime, but the structural and ideological constraints outlined here limit the extent to which those expectations can be met. Black regimes generally have been successful in curbing police brutality, which often has been prominent among black constituents' concerns. Richard Hatcher in Gary, Lionel Wilson in Oakland, Kenneth Gibson in Newark, Maynard Jackson in Atlanta, and Coleman Young in Detroit were able to reduce significantly, if not eliminate altogether, the incidence of police terror.[80] (Ernest N. "Dutch" Morial and Sidney Barthelemy have been less successful in New Orleans, which ranks among the national leaders in citizen complaints against police.) Not surprisingly, black regimes have made substantial gains in black police employment, which contributes to the reduction in police brutality.[81] However, that is one of the few areas in which black regimes have been able to deliver payoffs that filter down through the entire black constituency.

In the other areas in which black regimes clearly generate racially redistributive effects — general municipal employment and contractual services — benefits cluster disproportionately among middle- and upper-strata blacks. Increased access to municipal contracts practically by definition advantages upper-income, upper-strata individuals almost exclusively. At the same time, Eisinger finds that black regimes do increase black representation in municipal employment, over and above the effects of the increased black proportion of city population, but that the greatest increases are in professional and administrative categories. That concentration occurs in part because upper-level positions are more likely to fall in unclassified service ranks, while most line and lower-level staff positions are likely to be covered by civil service rules and regulations, which constrain affirmative action efforts. However, even in the classified ranks the greatest gains seem to have been in managerial and professional positions.[82] Moreover, though Eisinger finds that black-led cities also may increase the income level of black employees generally, even this effect is limited by the fact that those cities are among the most likely to exact personnel reductions or freezes induced by fiscal straits, thereby countering the regime's redistributive use of public employment.[83]

The symbolic benefits ensuing from the election of a black regime may arguably constitute a public good for black constituents. If so, the potential for conflict resulting from the disproportionate concentration of material benefits may be lessened accordingly. In addition, the dominant practical discourse about and within black political activity posits the racial collectivity as its central agency and racial discrimination as its main analytical category. Within that discourse a benefit that accrues to any member of the group is a benefit to the entire group. This bias naturally obscures processes of intraracial stratification and impedes critical response to policy agendas that are intraracially regressive.[84] In local political cultures increasingly characterized by (1) diminishing expectations associated with retrenchment ideology, (2) a shrinking public realm, and (3) technicization of the framework for policy debate, the tension is all the more likely to be muted.[85] Nevertheless, the bandwagon response that Jesse Jackson's dubious claims in 1984 to represent the alienated black "masses" elicited from many black elected officials suggests that they indeed may perceive a need to insulate themselves against disaffection and populist assault in the black community. Sharpe James's 1986 defeat of four-term incumbent Gibson in Newark certainly indicates that such assaults are possible and can topple even ostensibly well-entrenched regimes.

The problem is not that black regimes are led by inept, uncaring, or mean-spirited elitists; in fact, black elected officials tend to be somewhat more attentive and liberal than their white counterparts in their attitudes about social welfare issues.[86] Nor is it necessarily the case that those regimes are so tightly hemmed in by absolute paucity of fiscal resources that they have no span for intervention; as we have seen, fiscal straits are defined within a configuration of ideological and programmatic priorities. It is within such a configuration that the policy relation between the regime and its electoral constituency is structured. The regime's operating context prohibits widespread redistribution, but it does provide space for meeting a more narrowly defined conception of black interest. Four factors ensure that the interests met are those of upper-income, upper-status blacks: (1) the conceptual bias in black political discourse against accounting for intraracial stratification, (2) the sociological circumstance that black officials themselves are members of upper-status communities and social networks and therefore are more likely to identify with upper-strata agendas,[87] (3) the pragmatic imperative to give priority to the most politically attentive constituents and most active supporters, and (4) the relatively low fiscal and political costs of defining black interests around incorporation into an existing elite allocation framework. Thus John Conyers and W. L. Wallace found that the racial advancement strategies most frequently advocated by black officials included increasing black-owned business (86 percent) and increasing black involvement in white businesses (71 percent).[88] Those are strategies most compatible with the larger configuration of systemic power in which the black regime operates. They are also among the most important means the regimes deploy to negotiate the third major terrain of conflict, the relation between electoral constituency and governing coalition.

The black regime comes to power within a local system already organized around the pro-growth framework. Indeed, the regime is itself most often an organic product of pro-growth politics, the culmination of a dynamic of incorporation that began as a response to protest in the 1960s. To the extent that this dynamic has assumed the pro-growth consensus as a backdrop, so does the kind of regime it produces. The regime forms and legitimizes itself (that is, establishes its credibility as a contender for power, builds the allegiances required for winning office and governing, and articulates its policy agenda) in a local political culture and system dominated hegemonically by the imperatives of the very "growth machine" that is the engine of black marginalization. That relation's practical consequences come into focus with consideration of the centripetal pressures that cement municipal governments into the pro-growth coalition. Dennis Judd and M. Collins explain the logic that creates and undergirds the hegemony of local pro-growth politics:

> The assumption is that investment leads to increased jobs and an increased tax base. This, in sum, raises the incomes for city residents and improves the public services which can be provided by city governments. Higher incomes lead to increased spending and consumption, which of course improves the general well-being of city residents. Better public services result in public improvements and neighborhood services such as police protection, education, streets, and so forth. This, in turn, results in a general improvement in the quality of neighborhood life. Increased spending and consumption creates a favorable business environment which, of course, encourages investment, and on around the cycle again.[89]

The logic of growth is propagated and reinforced by the actions of interested parties and percolates throughout the local polity. It comes to set the terms for discussion of public policy and, typically spearheaded by metropolitan newspapers and civic boosterism, becomes one of the community's central normative conventions about the ends of local politics and the basis of municipal well-being.[90] Local officials are no less likely than other citizens to adhere to that convention, and one who appears to break with it runs the risk of general repudiation as an irresponsible maverick. Dennis Kucinich's stormy tenure in Cleveland offers perhaps the most dramatic recent example of the potential dangers of deviating from the growth logic; as Todd Swanstrom observes in assessing the consequences of Kucinich's refusal to go along with a proposed tax-abatement giveaway, "control over the public's impression of the business climate is a potent weapon in growth politics."[91]

The importance of controlling public perception of the business climate implies the subordination of public policy to business interests and is an artifact of the growth logic's hegemony. Assumption of the priority of business interests in the polity is what allows the counter-Keynesian policy orientation to take hold at the local level.

In addition, at least two other factors dispose local regimes to accept the de facto cue-taking role assigned to them in the pro-growth framework. First, because of their command of information and other useful resources, business interests are likely to be especially attractive as partners in durable governing coalitions.[92] Second, business interests are attractive as partners not only to regimes in power but also to candidates seeking power; they can give valuable material and ideological assistance to candidates (and potential candidates) they support and can do considerable harm, particularly given the active agency of local media in pro-growth politics, to those they oppose. Thus, for a regime to come to power more often than not means that it already shares the outlook and has the imprimatur of pro-growth forces. Black regimes do not differ from others in this respect.

Coleman Young's accommodation to business interests in Detroit stands out both because of his candor in acknowledging its extent and because of the irony posed by his apparently left-activist background. He has, for example, quipped that there "is nothing wrong with Detroit that three or four factories can't solve" and has attempted whenever possible to act accordingly; he has shown little hesitation in giving priority to economic development interests over any others with which they might conflict.[93] However, Young's case is neither unique nor extreme. Atlanta's Andrew Young has been an even more flamboyant booster of business interests than his Detroit namesake; the former Southern Christian Leadership Conference (SCLC) activist has aligned himself with conservative Republicans on business issues and extols the merits of unrestrained development with an often ecclesiastical rhetoric that harkens back to the Gilded Age.[94] Washington, D.C.'s Marion Barry, another former civil rights activist, likewise has been disposed to give development interests free rein over his regime's policy agenda, with little regard to disadvantageous impact on other elements of his constituency. Kenneth Gibson and Sharpe James in Newark, Lionel Wilson in Oakland, "Dutch" Morial and Sidney Barthelemy in New Orleans, Wilson Goode in Philadelphia, and Richard Arrington in Birmingham have all come into office and governed on programs centered on making local government the handmaiden to private development interests.[95]

My point here is not really to imply that black regimes have "sold out" or betrayed a special racial obligation by their association with pro-growth politics. However, they are more likely than others to be beset with a chronic tension between satisfying the expectations of their governing and electoral constituencies. Their tension is greater not so much because they have an intrinsically greater moral obligation, though credible arguments to that effect might be made, but because (1) they govern in cities whose populations include relatively great proportions of those citizens most likely to be adversely affected by pro-growth politics, (2) those citizens are most likely to be black or Hispanic, and (3) the regimes tend to validate themselves to minority electoral constituents by invoking an image of progressive redistribution, whereas pro-growth politics is grounded on a more regressive principle.

To the extent that it fuels industrial deconcentration and the other dispersive tendencies described here, the pro-growth framework combines with sociological imperatives driving suburbanization (including the racial component of real estate value) at least to intensify black economic marginalization in central cities. The extent to which the "postindustrial" or corporate city has been effected at the expense of black citizens in general has already been noted, and the histories of cities with black regimes reveal a common pattern of displacement and ghettoization as products of the growth machine.[96] In addition, inner-city blacks suffer from pro-growth politics insofar as it reinforces the tendencies toward extreme labor market segmentation that characterize the postindustrial office economy. The regressive impact, furthermore, is heightened by the use of public resources to underwrite this kind of economic growth. The pro-growth logic rests on a trickle-down ideology that is faulty on two counts. First, even in the best-case scenario the benefits do not trickle very well, very far, or very efficiently. The big winners are the developers and locating firms who garner public subsidies and the suburbanites who take the relatively high-paying jobs created by the growth of the office economy. What trickles to a growing share of the electoral constituency are low-paying, consumer service sector jobs, and not very many of those per dollar investment. Moreover, growth may even increase certain material costs for city residents across the board.[97] Second, mounting evidence indicates that the array of subsidies that local governments offer to stimulate economic development may only needlessly underwrite development that would occur anyway. Local tax breaks and other fiscal inducements offered by municipalities appear to have little impact on business location and investment decisions, except perhaps insofar as they convey an ideological message concerning the city's "business climate."[98]

Therein lies the central contradiction facing the black regime: It is caught between the expectations of its principally black electoral constituency, which imply downward redistribution, and those of its governing coalition, which converge on the use of public policy as a mechanism for upward redistribution. This tension has been a part of pro-growth politics all along. It is neither accidental nor the product of some latter-day natural law that, as Peterson glibly declares, "it is the interests of the disadvantaged which consistently come into conflict with economically productive policies." Friedland expresses the critical essence of the situation succinctly: "The policies necessary to growth have high social costs while the policies necessary to social control cut into the revenues necessary to support growth."[99] However, this contradiction is sharper in black-governed cities, both because the disparity between the two poles is greater and because the current mood of fiscal conservatism and retrenchment inhibits use of the standard palliative device of compensatory public spending.

The black regimes have responded to this contradictory situation in two ways. They tend to cling dogmatically, even in the face of evidence to the contrary, to pro-growth trickle-down ideology, typically recycling the simplistic formula that growth leads to jobs, which lead to reduced inner-city unemployment. The defense of any specific project proceeds by citing the general cant, with an occasional admonition that the city is in effect the hostage of mobile wealth and therefore must allow private capital to loot the public treasury, unfair as that may be, in order to prove itself competitive in a dog-eat-dog world.[100] The other response entails defining black interests in such a way as to fit them into the given growth agenda and reinventing elements of the latter rhetorically as distinctively black preferences. In chapter 5 of this volume I examine how Maynard Jackson, when confronted by pressure to show his loyalty to the black community's concerns about a police issue and from the business elite (which simultaneously was pressuring him not to show "racial favoritism" in the police controversy) to take a stand on an airport-construction controversy, split the difference by arbitrarily and on specious grounds defining and arguing for one of the possible airport sites as the "black" choice. He was thereby able to reduce the pressure from both camps; however, it is instructive that though this reinvention was substantively meaningful to business concerns, it addressed black concerns only symbolically.[101]

These two responses, which are by no means mutually exclusive, are more effective now than they might have been several years ago because the programmatic discourse and thrust of pro-growth politics have become more technical and thus relatively less accessible to precisely those groups most likely to be adversely affected. As Judd notes:

> Most of the growth strategies of the 1980s have not been as divisive as the urban renewal clearance programs. Tax abatements, industrial development bonds, tax increment financing, enterprise zones, loan programs—all seem to be economic and not political in character. In most cases they involve quiet, behind-the-scenes transactions between a public authority and private institutions. Discussion of their merits and mechanisms usually proceed[s] in a market language—for example, their effect on interest rates or investment.[102]

The terms of general discourse in local politics likewise have been technicized in a way that helps to contain the tension between elite and electoral constituencies' interests. Jeffrey Henig observes that

> today's urban crisis . . . is discussed in terms of bond ratings, investment tax credits, infrastructure, business climate, and efficiency. To many Americans, these terms are unfamiliar and forbidding. The message they carry is that these are complicated matters, that decisions should be deferred to those with expertise.[103]

In this context, the racial symbolism that mediates the black regime's relation to its black electoral constituency may make it an especially attractive partner in the pro-growth coalition. The same racially evocative discourse that occasionally unsettles white elites can be instrumental in enlisting black support for pro-growth initiatives whose regressiveness otherwise might generate controversy and opposition. Focus on such issues as minority set-asides in effect pushes questions of the propriety and impact of the growth agenda into the background; at the same time, the regime can appeal rather effectively to obligations of race loyalty to bind constituent support for the growth-related projects it endorses, even those that are clearly regressive.

For similar reasons black regimes may be peculiarly well suited to implement the draconian retrenchment policies said to instill fiscal confidence. Andrew Young, for example, generated enough black support to pass a sales tax referendum engineered by the Atlanta business elite. Two previous efforts had failed under Maynard Jackson, one when Jackson refused to endorse the referendum for fear of reprisal from blacks. Young overcame that obstacle by waving the "bloody shirt" of his past as one of Martin Luther King Jr.'s lieutenants. "Dutch" Morial also convinced black voters to pass a sales tax referendum in New Orleans.[104] Gibson, Coleman Young, Goode, and others have effected substantial service and personnel reductions without protest. Indeed, cities governed by blacks seem to be particularly likely to experience significant retrenchment.[105]

It may be that black regimes are "cautious about any controversial policy initiatives... [because] the coalitions that elect them are usually so tenuous."[106] Those coalitions are tenuous because the relationship of their two principal components is or is very nearly zero-sum in many important policy areas. However, it is also the case that the black urban regimes are firmly rooted in the ideological and programmatic orientations of pro-growth politics. In each of the main areas in which the regime faces competing pressures within the local polity, its tendency is to respond in ways that preserve and privilege the growth agenda. Moreover, as the central city increasingly assumes the dual character of vibrant locale for a glitzy office economy and reservation for marginalized, dispossessed minorities, the black regime takes on a special ideological function. "Protecting development activities from popular pressures," in Clarence Stone's apt description, becomes an increasingly salient project as the uneven development of the city intensifies.[107]

Empowerment of a black regime contributes to that project in two unique ways, both of which derive from its ability to effect E. E. Schattschneider's famous "mobilization of bias" in the black community.[108] First, it provides a mechanism for incorporating upper-status, upwardly mobile blacks more autonomously (and thus more reliably) into the growth machine. This not only reduces the likelihood of disruption by the most vocal and attentive elements in the black community; when filtered through the discourse of symbolic racial collectivism, it also becomes a proxy for broader racial redistribution. Second, the dominance of that discourse allows the black regime to claim in effect that whatever stances it takes on growth-related issues are ipso facto expressions of generic black interests. Certainly the success of those devices depends on the magical power of the growth-jobs incantation, which Harvey Molotch describes as the "key ideological prop for the growth machine," and the generally obfuscating and immobilizing consequences of the technicization of local political debate.[109] Nevertheless, the promise held out by black regimes' special attributes is sufficiently attractive to prompt conservative business elites in such unlikely cities as Birmingham and New Orleans to support them and to endorse them enthusiastically over other possibilities.

Summary and Conclusions

It is now possible to pull together several threads of argument and thus draw some tentative conclusions about the character of the black urban regime. Moreover, once the black regime has been situated within its structural and historical contexts of origin and with respect to its immediate sphere of operation, we can discern at least an outline of expectations that reasonably can be held of it. One element of the concluding observations, therefore, consists of generalizations about (1) the apparent state of "really existing" black municipal governance in relation to (2) the scope and span of intervention likely to be possible in cities governed by black regimes, and (3) the kinds of standards that realistically might be brought to bear on evaluating these regimes' performances as agencies of social melioration.

The Black Regime and the Corporate City

The most consequential characteristic of the black urban regime is that it is an artifact of the changing socioeconomic functions and demographic composition of the central city. Specifically, it is a product of the following factors: (1) the economic dynamics that have constituted the transition from "industrial" to "corporate" city, (2) the long-term pattern of residential suburbanization and the attendant phenomenon of white flight, (3) the relative autonomy of local governments — chiefly a product of slack in the federal system and the home rule movement — that has enabled suburban jurisdictions to engage in zoning and other practices that in effect concentrate black metropolitan population growth in central cities, (4) consolidation of the pro-growth framework as the basis and medium for both binding political loyalty and directing local public policy, and (5) the rise of black political assertiveness in the 1950s and 1960s.

Because those regimes are artifacts of pro-growth politics, they tend to accept its imperatives as given and tend therefore both to underestimate the latitude open to them in their efforts to support economic development and to overestimate the extent to which fiscal straits hamper their capacities for deploying public policy in pursuit of redistributive goals. In fact, the fear of fiscal crisis may induce, or at least rationalize, the regimes' acceptance of a cue-taking role. Irene Rubin and R. Rubin have found that cities with higher property tax rates, lower median family income, larger number of families below the poverty line, and higher unemployment — all characteristics of both fiscally strained and black-governed cities — tend more than others to engage in municipally sponsored economic development activity.[110] As Swanstrom notes, though,

> even the most depressed industrial cities . . . are enjoying substantial growth in downtown service employment, which offers opportunities for redistributive reforms. Cities do not have to offer tax abatements to attract this investment; they can do just the opposite: Cities can tax this sector to provide funds to ameliorate the problems of uneven development such as neighborhood decay and a shortage of low-income housing.[111]

A regime's ability to exact concessions varies with the extent to which the city's attractiveness limits capital's relative mobility.[112] However, in many instances the desirability of being in a given central city and being able to draw on its agglomeration of financial, informational, and other support services gives the municipality enough leverage to enforce "linkage" policies that steer growth and capture a share of its proceeds for progressively redistributive purposes.[113] Nearly all of the big-city black regimes govern in cities that are advantageously situated as national or regional economic and administrative centers. Therefore those regimes should be capable of generating and enforcing measures aimed at channeling some of the proceeds of growth to address the needs of their electoral constituency. So far, however, none of the black regimes seems to have made genuine strides in that direction. Instead, they have only recycled the bankrupt growth-jobs formula, usually grafting on provisions for affirmative action and local small business development.[114] In fact, they tend to extrapolate immediately from their constituency's depressed economic condition to an urgency for strengthening standard public-private development partnerships, which are little more than mechanisms for co-opting public policy and resources for the risk management functions of private capital.[115]

Ironically, if the black regimes' failure to seek political leverage in development activity grows from an exaggerated sense of futility owing to the specter of fiscal stress, the development programs they endorse — as was the case with another supply-side economic strategy applied at the national level in the first Reagan term — may exacerbate stress by reducing revenues; in addition, development often actually increases service demand. Moreover, stress is a function of the relationship between potential revenues and expenditure commitments, and improving the "business climate" is only one — and a rather indirect and remote one at that—mechanism available for improving municipal revenue potential. That it is the primary option chosen by the black regimes is instructive.

Judd suggests that these regimes may be trapped in a structural dilemma: "They [want] to implement policies to promote their constituents' material interests, but they [face] declining local economies and tax bases, crumbling infrastructures, white flight, and deteriorating neighborhoods. . . . In response many of these mayors capitulated to the demands of the local corporate sector."[116] The problem with that view is that, in relying too much on Rod Bush's provocative but simplistic "quasi-neocolonial" interpretation, it overlooks the fact that other options may exist but have not been chosen.[117] A result is that the black regimes are depicted as entirely passive. They are thereby left out of consideration of the reproduction of the corporate city altogether, except insofar as they are seen as duped, coerced, or bought off—depending on the normative predilections attached to one or another group of politicians—by pro-growth interests. Thus the endemic characteristics of the regime remain opaque, and discussion of this new black goverance is imprisoned in a frame that is ultimately inadequate because it does not account for the regime's active agency.

Little evidence exists that black regimes have "capitulated" to "corporate sector demands" to implement the regressive pro-growth agenda; Bush acknowledges that it is not difficult to find black mayors who have "always been enthusiastic supporters of corporate intents."[118] No black regime has had to be forced into a showdown similar to the one that occurred in Cleveland under Kucinich. Maynard Jackson, in the incident to which Bush refers, was not pressured into firing sanitation workers; he did so voluntarily, even if unhappily, because the action seemed decreed by a specific logic of fiscal responsibility to which he adhered. Coleman Young was not pressured to generate a package of regressive fiscal incentives for the Poletown and Renaissance Center redevelopment projects, which shifted public resources to service corporate designs at the expense of working-class citizens; he proposed them without reservation because he accepted the pro-growth logic on which they are based.

That is the key to penetrating the character of the "really existing" black urban regime. Black regimes adhere to the pro-growth framework for the same reasons that other regimes do: It seems reasonable and proper ideologically; it conforms to a familiar sense of rationality; and it promises to deliver practical, empirical benefits. The regime does not step outside the framework or attempt to create leverage for redistribution because there is no need to do so; not only does "business climate" rhetoric apparently seem intrinsically reasonable, but the interests to which the regime is most attentive are included among the framework's beneficiaries.

In addition to the business community, which is the principal beneficiary, middle- and upper-middle-class blacks receive set-aside contracts, support for small business and private "neighborhood economic development" activity, and improved access to professional and administrative employment in both public and private sectors. Through the legerdemain of symbolic racial collectivism, those benefits are purported to represent general social and racial redistribution, which, buttressed by a rhetoric of race loyalty, either palliates or defuses countermobilization by the larger black electoral constituency that is disadvantaged by pro-growth politics.

The degree to which assumption of the growth-jobs logic engenders an exaggerated sense of helplessness before the prerogatives of private capital or reflects the extent to which the regime is simply the "executive committee" of private growth interests may differ from one regime to another. In any case the outcome is the same; the regime carries forward the pretense that providing a public safety net for private profiteering is in the long-term interest of those already marginalized people whose needs are sacrificed to make the netting. Thus, in 1984 the National Conference of Black Mayors, on the pretext of accommodating the developmental realpolitik, endorsed the Reaganite enterprise-zone stratagem, even though it is socially and economically regressive and is unlikely to stimulate any appreciable economic growth.[119]

Although those last remarks may appear somewhat harsh, my intention is not to deprecate black regimes. Nor is it particularly useful at this point to denounce them as class regimes, though they certainly embody the contingent class power of post–civil rights era black professional, managerial, and entrepreneurial strata. After all, the black regimes' class character is not really a shocking discovery; it is a natural outcropping of the class basis that for nearly a century has shaped black protest activity. Furthermore, those regimes do deliver payoffs to the general black constituency in some areas, such as police-community relations, and probably marginal improvement in the routine civility of client-serving bureaucracies. In any case, it does not appear plausible that a substantially more egalitarian regime could be elected in black-led cities at present, given requirements for campaign funding, the power of hegemonic ideologies and opinion-shaping media, and the absence of organized, popularly entrenched movements that might overcome those other obstacles. Nor is it likely, given experiences in Burlington, Vermont; Santa Monica, California; and elsewhere that such a regime, if it were to come to power, could expand its policy horizon radically.[120]

It is more appropriate in this context to ask whether the "really existing" black regime maximizes the options open to it, within its limited sphere, to press the interests of the rank-and-file black constituency. This is a modest standard that entails adoption of neither a reflexive opposition to economic growth nor an adversarial relationship with concrete business interests. It does mean that black regimes should be assessed with respect to their use of public authority to artic-ulate policy agendas that accommodate economic growth as much as possible to the needs of the municipality and its citizenry rather than vice versa. A prerequi-site for effective performance according to that standard is repudiation of the growth-jobs, trickle-down mystification. Once that is jettisoned, the regime should be expected to give its support to development projects on a more reasoned and conditional basis, one that reflects its public charge.

I have referred to discussions of several strategies adopted by municipali-ties to accommodate the growth imperative to social purposes. Local conditions vary, and no blueprints are possible; however, experiences in Hartford, Connecti-cut; Berkeley, California; and other cities suggest that municipal regimes are not inevitably the hostages of private economic activity. Moreover, black regimes generally may enjoy greater autonomy than others because of the loyalty of their black electoral support; a rebellious black regime, for example, would probably be less vulnerable to ideological assault from business elites than was Kucinich's, whose support among white "ethnics" declined in the face of a business propa-ganda campaign.[121] Given the characteristics of the cities they govern, black re-gimes should be among the most likely to seek to manage growth and its pro-ceeds for the ends of social justice and equality. In addition, other means besides elaborate planning mechanisms and direct or indirect taxation schemes are avail-able, though those are the most concrete and most immediately productive. Regimes can use the cultural authority of office to draw attention to unpalatable conditions that affect constituents but are beyond the scope of municipal control or formal influence. They can also take outrageous stands — for example, pass-ing unconstitutional tax ordinances — to dramatize existing inequities, thereby opening them to public awareness and debate and providing opportunities for political mobilization.[122] Along each of those dimensions of advocacy for justice and equity, the record of black regimes is poor. They are by and large only black versions of the pro-growth regimes that they have replaced, distinguished in part by the asymmetry of their campaign rhetoric and their practice of governance. They are in one sense even more attractive as junior members in the pro-growth coalition because of their peculiar skill at derailing opposition to development initiatives and cultivating the loyalty or acquiescence of the growth machine's victims. For that pattern to change will require greatly increased and informed pressure from the black electoral constituency, which in sum implies proliferation of public, policy-focused debate. I hope that this account can help to fuel that discourse.

Implications for Urban Theory and the Study of Afro-American Politics

This account of the black urban regime also throws into relief a problematic tendency current in the study of both black urban politics and Afro-American political activity more broadly. That tendency is important and troubling enough to warrant brief comment.

Recent, properly influential scholarly interpretations of different epicycles in Afro-American politics converge to imply a rather Panglossian view of the status of blacks in the American political system. This problem seems to be rooted in the structuralist and what might be called neopluralist biases of that scholarship.[123] The scholarship in question has produced important insights, is often engaging, and has contributed much to our understanding of its subject matter. However, that work is beset with a subtle but insidious flaw: failure to examine adequately the theoretical and public policy implications of black political strategies and agendas. As a result, those interpretations produce one-dimensional conclusions that are too neat and simplistically upbeat. Taken together, they authorize disturbingly superficial pictures of the dynamics and outcomes of black political activity in general and in cities in particular. This is not the place for a thorough review of that scholarship. Therefore, I shall limit myself to illustrating the problem I have identified as it appears in the work of Doug McAdam, Peter Eisinger, and Rufus Browning, Dale Rogers Marshall, and David Tabb, who present the most intellectually rigorous and useful, as well as the most influential, examples of this interpretive tendency.

McAdam, building through dialogue with a line of research on social movements initiated by Piven and Cloward, examines developments in the structural foundations of black protest activity over the period from 1930 to 1970.[124] His account argues in general very convincingly about the role of changes in the "structure of political opportunities," changes in blacks' "sense of political efficacy," and institutional articulation within the black community as important conditions influencing the rise of mass protest activity. Even though he flirts with structural determinism and occasionally succumbs to a questionable inference in order to fit the world to theory—for example, taking the decline in officially recorded lynchings as an indication of relaxation of the segregation system[125]—his study is the most important examination to date of the background influences that shaped the civil rights movement. The problem is that the heavy structural-functional bias of his interpretive lens glosses over the internal dynamics of the movement itself and sees a smooth consensus on objectives, at least until the black power era. His account is thus blinded to the struggle over ultimate goals and contending political visions that also shaped the movement and gave it its historical contingency. For that reason McAdam does not undertake any critical consideration of the substantive significance and implications of different elements of the movement's program; instead, he sees after 1966 only a "proliferation of issues," deviation from the "single issue of integration," and not the culmination of an internal debate of considerable duration concerning the movement's normative and programmatic trajectory. He contends glibly that those factors, along with abandonment of "limited-reform goals" contributed to the movement's decline because he makes no reasoned judgment concerning the efficacy of any of its goals.[126] His failure to link either programmatic differentiation within the movement or its substantive outcomes to any broader theory of power and stratification in American society renders his account utterly mute with respect to how we should apprehend the forms of black political activity that have become dominant since 1970. All he can say is that we might anticipate the occurrence of insurgency at some point because "institutional racism" remains entrenched.

The thrust of McAdam's interpretation is compatible, no doubt unintentionally, with the prevailing view that collapses the broad ideals and aspirations expressed in 1960s activism entirely into the incremental framework driving the regular systemic processes of interest-group politics. Their compatibility is visible in his critique of pluralist theory; he argues in effect for amending pluralist orthodoxy to include a systemically functional role for "noninstitutionalized," insurgent activity.[127] That notion converges on the naive evolutionary perspective that sees the role of 1960s activism simply as preparing for regular systemic participation, which is understood as the only truly proper and most efficient arena for articulation and pursuit of group interests. McAdam's account in this respect reinforces the tendency to focus black political objectives and to define black interests entirely in terms subordinate to entrenched system priorities, which are deeply implicated in the continuing disadvantagement and advancing marginalization among black citizens.

Eisinger's account of the transition to black rule and the impact of black mayors presents a somewhat clearer version of this problem. First of all, his comparisons of the transitions to black rule in Detroit and Atlanta with the Irish experience in Boston suffers from an ahistoricism that already shows the embedded flaw. Because he allows neither for the considerable changes that have occurred in the economic functions of central cities between the Boston case and the more recent ones nor the greatly changed set of actors and issues that constitute the local policy context, Eisinger's view is predisposed to see the black regime as the latest stage in a relatively uniform process of ethnic group succession in local politics. However, the contexts within which the black regime assumes power and governs greatly limit any such comparison's persuasiveness or usefulness. Black regimes take power in cities that are quite different from those in which earlier groups governed, and the needs of their constituents differ in relation to inherited system priorities. Eisinger's failure to acknowledge those differences leads him to suggest—after noting that "city governments . . . cannot fashion thorough, successful and speedy policies to deal with . . . poverty, discrimination, unemployment, housing, or the quality of life"—that electing "their own to city hall" may well have gotten blacks rolling along the upward mobility track already traversed by the comparable Irish.[128]

There is much in Eisinger's account that is sound and refreshing. His attempt to locate the black regime within a broader pattern of local ethnic group dominance brings discussion of black governance more centrally into the purview of the American politics field, and his focus on the regime's interaction with "displaced" elites illuminates certain constraining effects of political environment with much care and intelligence. However, in assuming a priori an identity between black interests and the racial agendas of black administrations, Eisinger eliminates any need to consider the operation of politics within the black community, and he renders himself blind to structurally induced intraracial tensions. This failing combines with his acceptance of pro-growth orthodoxy to underwrite an inverted argument that black regimes actually may "harness white economic power rather than vice versa."[129] Once he defines the affirmative action, minority set-aside agenda as the beginning and end of specifically black interests in development activity, then it does appear that blacks derive relatively great payoffs from pro-growth politics. There is no critical space for him to consider the impact of the growth machine on different elements of the black community and at the same time no space to consider the intraracial implications of the regime's agendas. As with McAdam, we have an account from the outside, one that cannot bring into focus the self-driving tensions in black politics.

Browning, Marshall, and Tabb bridge the gap between considerations of protest and electoral strategies in their study of minority political "incorporation" in ten Bay Area cities. In charting the relationships between political mobilization, response from other groups, organizational development and political experience, and size of minority population, they provide an impressively thorough explanation of the "steps that are necessary if excluded groups are to move toward political equality."[130] However, their notion of incorporation, though empirically sound and important, also has a darker theoretical dimension that surfaces only with consideration of the tension between black or Hispanic interests and the entrenched priorities that constitute the prevailing configuration of systemic power. In light of that tension, "incorporation" resonates with Peterson's observation that in local political systems potentially redistributive demands tend to be converted into symbolic ones. Thus incorporation may come at the price of making peace with the regressive policy framework that stimulates protest and mobilization in the first place.

The authors' choice of indicators of incorporation's policy impact sidesteps this critical issue. City employment, police review boards, minority contractors, and commission appointments, though certainly significant in their own right, are policy areas that have little bearing on the systemic inequality reproduced through the logic of pro-growth politics. Nor for that matter are patterns of federal program implementation much more instructive. Model Cities and Great Society programs facilitated mobilization, but toward what ultimate policy ends? Toward what uses are Community Development Block Grant (CDBG) allocations directed?

The three studies share a common disposition to conceptualize black politics one-dimensionally on an exclusion/inclusion axis. Though that perspective can organize very useful investigations of the nature of black political incorporation, as it does in different ways in each of these studies, it has serious limitations. It tends to assume uniform interests and agendas among blacks because incorporation itself is a universally shared value, insofar as incorporation is construed broadly as the antithesis of exclusion. It also tends toward an analytic exceptionalism that ironically reproduces an exclusionist bias within the study of black politics; to the extent that blacks are seen as excluded from the mainstream of American institutional processes, the latter are seen as relevant to blacks only as focal points in the struggle for inclusion. This view forgets that it is suffering the regressive impact of those processes that initially precipitates the demand for access.

In this sense a neopluralist bias is tacit in this scholarship; it picks up and responds to pluralism's original bracketing of race as an unhappy appendage of a system that allegedly worked well for everyone else—the ubiquitous "except for the Negroes" clause in pluralist studies in the 1950s and 1960s. This new scholarship has found ways, with the assistance of changes in the world, to dissolve the brackets. Noninstitutionalized activity, ethnoracial transition, and political incorporation all are accurate, important descriptions of what is occurring on one level in Afro-American politics. Moreover, those descriptions enhance our view of the changing urban political terrain. Despite being apparently well-intentioned politically, however, they are also intellectual devices for accommodating discussion of the political condition of blacks to a pluralist frame of reference that obscures the cumulatively redistributive outcomes of public policy in general and of the distinctive, pro-growth policy consensus into which blacks are incorporated in cities in particular. As a result they produce accounts that are incomplete and unsettling to the democratic temper.

Those problems can be overcome by grounding the exclusion/inclusion axis as an epicycle within broader configurations of systemic power and by bringing political dynamics within the black community into the foreground of analysis. I believe that at the urban level sharpening focus on differential impacts of policies and political agendas within the black community and examining the tensions between regimes' electoral and governing coalitions are useful avenues toward that end. In the event, I hope that I have suggested a useful orientation for more detailed case studies and aggregate analyses of black urban regimes.

Implications for Democracy in Urban Life

The most salient implications of the view of the black regime put forward here have to do with the need to compensate for the reinforcement and perpetuation of injustice produced through the federal system, either directly or by manipulation of slack. Most immediate is the need to offset federal and state policies that stimulate economic deconcentration and allow suburban jurisdictions to freeload on municipal services and cultural amenities while undergirding the Bantustanization of inner-city minority populations.

Metropolitan tax-base sharing is one technique that may offer a way to help balance two democratic values that appear to conflict in this case: equitable allocation of the costs of metropolitan life and representative government that is equitable along racial lines. Given the difficulty that blacks experience in electing representatives in non–black majority jurisdictions, simple annexation or metropolitan consolidation alternatives would generally sacrifice the value of equitable representation.[131] A nationally coordinated industrial policy aimed at smoothing out the imbalances of uneven regional development also seems to be called for, as does a national incomes policy that may both retard and help offset the disruptive effects of productive capital's mobility by bolstering the social wage.

In a similar vein, a concerted strategy of reindustrialization seems to be important for several reasons, including foreign policy. The vision of a postindustrial economy or "information economy" as the basis of the American future presumes an industrial foundation somewhere. To the extent that the information that drives our office economy is information about production or what to do with the proceeds of production, a strategy of concentrating a Ricardian advantage in postindustrial activity implies maintenance of the costly and dangerous so-called defense apparatus required to make certain that repressive regimes remain in power in Third World countries to ensure their comparative advantage in providing low-wage labor and minimally regulated production processes. Concern with humane and democratic interests must oppose that international division of labor. Moreover, the increased transnational mobility of capital has meant that suppression of wages and standards of living in the underdeveloped countries now reverberates into the advanced countries as well. So far in the United States the reverberation has been felt disproportionately by blacks and other minorities, who are pushed progressively further into the margins of the social order.

All the aforementioned suggestions of areas in which to focus strategy are well beyond the scope of effective municipal intervention. However, both individually and collectively—through lobbies such as the National Conference of Black Mayors, the U.S. Conference of Mayors, and the National League of Cities—regimes can push public discourse about these areas of concern and can agitate for reform. Within their domain, as I have indicated, it is possible to break with slavish adherence to pro-growth ideology and to assert public authority to limit the socially and culturally disruptive effects of development. It is also possible to insist that public resources be deployed on behalf of development in central cities in ways that optimize downward redistribution.

Should a truly democratic citizenry settle for anything less?

1988

4. Sources of Demobilization in the New Black Political Regime

Incorporation, Ideological Capitulation, and Radical Failure in the Post-Segregation Era

It is a commonplace move in current American political discourse to note the apparent irony that the exponential increases in black public officeholding since the early 1970s have been accompanied by a steady deterioration in the material circumstances of large segments of the inner-city black citizenry. Comment on that irony comes both from those on the left who would underscore the insufficiency of capturing public office and from those on the right who would either disparage the pursuit of public action on behalf of blacks and poor people in general or push more or less oblique claims about black incompetence. In the middle are liberal social scientists and journalists who, sometimes Candide-like, construe this inverse association as an anomaly, a puzzling deviation from the orthodox narrative of interest-group pluralism in American politics. The liberal and conservative tendencies especially — though the practice is by no means foreign to the left — are often elaborated through a rhetoric that juxtaposes black political power and white economic power, treating them almost as naturalized racial properties rather than as contingent products of social structure and political institutions. In this rhetoric noting the coincidence of black electoral success and worsening immiseration supports advocacy of an idealized notion of interracialism as an alternative to racially based political strategy.[1]

At the same time, a different anomaly bedevils those on the left who presume that oppression breeds *political* resistance, by which I mean resistance that constitutes an explicit challenge to power relations as they are enforced and mediated through the state apparatus and that is understood as such by those against whom it is aimed. The clearly observable intensification of oppression over the 1980s — seen in a worsening of material conditions, a narrowing of life options, increasingly institutionalized marginalization, and an expanding regime of social repression and police terror — has not produced serious oppositional political mobilization. This is the key problem for the articulation of a progressive black urban politics in the 1990s.

This problem's significance, indeed, is marked by the lengths to which commentators on the left have gone to deny its existence as a problem. The thrust of much of the interpretive tendency associated with the rubric of "cultural politics," after all, is to sidestep the issue by redefining people's routine compensatory existential practices — the everyday undertakings that enact versions of autonomy and dignity *within* the context of oppression — as politically meaningful "resistance," thus obliterating all distinction between active, public opposition and the sighs accompanying acquiescence. The effect is to avoid grappling with the troublesome reality of demobilization by simply christening it, Humpty Dumpty–like, as mobilization.[2]

Making sense of the anomaly requires examining critical characteristics of post-segregation era urban and black politics. Moreover, although the disparate fortunes of black officialdom and its constituents are not in any direct way causally linked, their relation does shed light on the problem of popular demobilization. In fact, this relation connects with each of the three features of the contemporary political landscape (in addition to well-discussed factors such as structural economic shift, enshrinement of the rhetoric of fiscal crisis, the domestic versions of the International Monetary Fund's regime of "structural adjustment" — all of which to some extent *presume* black demobilization for their success)[3] that I argue hinder progressive black mobilization: (1) political incorporation and its limits, (2) the hegemony of underclass discourse as a frame for discussing racial inequality and poverty, and (3) the left's failure to think carefully and critically about black politics and how it connects with the role of race in the American stratification system. In what follows I shall examine the ways that these three phenomena bear on mobilization. I shall then suggest approaches to strategic thinking that take them into account, focusing in particular on the crucial issues of program and identification of institutional levers and constituencies that might further mobilization on behalf of a progressive agenda.

The Limits of Incorporation

Systemic incorporation along four dimensions has been the most significant development in black urban politics since the 1960s, though certain of its most important consequences have drawn little attention.[4] First, enforcement of the Voting Rights Act has increased the efficacy of black electoral participation; invalidation of cruder forms of racial gerrymandering and biased electoral systems, as well as redress against intimidation, have made it generally easier for black voters to elect the candidates of their choice.[5]

Second, a corollary of that electoral efficacy, of course, has been the dramatic increase in black elected officials. Their existence has become a fact of life in American politcs and has shaped the modalities of race relations management.[6] Black elected officials tend overwhelmingly to operate within already existing governing coalitions at the local level and more generally within the imperatives of the Democratic party's internal politics, as well as with an eye to representing their electoral constituents. The logic of incumbency, moreover, is race-blind and favors reelection above all else. Not surprisingly, black officeholders tend to be disposed to articulate their black constituents' interests in ways that are compatible with those other commitments.

Third, black people have increasingly assumed administrative control of the institutions of urban governance, the public apparatus of social management. Housing authorities, welfare departments, school systems, even public safety departments are ever more likely to be run by black officials, and black functionaries are likely to be prominent at all levels within those organizations.[7] This means that those agencies (and their leadership) have their own attentive constituencies within the black electorate, radiating out into the family and friendship networks of agency personnel. It also means that a substratum of professional, often geographically mobile public functionaries with commitments to public management ideologies may now constitute a relatively autonomous interest configuration *within* black politics. This dimension of incorporation also short-circuits critiques of those agencies' operations that are crafted within the racially inflected language most familiar to black insurgency. A critique that pivots on racial legitimacy as a standard for evaluating institutional behavior cannot be effective—as a basis for either organizing opposition or stimulating critical public debate—in a situation in which blacks conspicuously run the institutions. Because they have their own black constituencies (who tend to be drawn generally from the most attentive and capacious elements of the black electorate) and greater access to resources for shaping public opinion, moreover, public officials have the advantage in any debate that rests simplistically on determining racial authenticity. Indeed, their claims to the positions they occupy in the state apparatus derive ultimately, to varying degrees of course, from the premise that their presence embodies racial interests.

A fourth and related dimension of incorporation is the integration of nongovernmental organizations (NGOs)—private civil rights and uplift organizations of various sorts — into a regime of quasi-corporatist race relations management driven by incrementalist, insider negotiation.[8] The tracings of this process could be seen rather dramatically at the national level during the Carter administration with the inclusion of Jesse Jackson's Operation PUSH (People United to Serve Humanity) and the National Urban League as line item accounts in Department of Labor budgets (though, in keeping with the current spirit of bipartisan largesse, I should note that Richard Nixon and Gerald Ford were only less formalistic in their practice in this regard). The boundaries between state agendas and elites and those of black NGOs, however, may even be more porous at the local level, where personnel commonly move back and forth from one payroll system to another and where close coordination with local interest groupings is more smoothly woven into the texture of everyday life. Not only are routine work-related contacts more common, but black public and private functionaries are likely to operate in shared social worlds apart from their professional lives.[9]

One effect has arguably been further to skew the black politically attentive public toward the new regime of race relations management. On the one hand, the generation of a professional world of public-private race relations engineers — practically by definition drawn from the most politically attentive elements of the black population — channels issue-articulation and agenda-formation processes in black politics *in general* in ways that reflect the regime's common sense. On the other hand, insofar as the NGOs and their elites carry the historical sediment of adversarial, protest politics, their integration into the new regime further ratifies its common sense and protocols as the only thinkable politics, as the totality of what politics *is.*

These trajectories of incorporation have yielded real benefits for the black citizenry. They have enhanced income and employment opportunity and have injected a greater measure of fairness into the distribution of public benefits in large and small ways. Black citizens have greater access now to the informal networks through which ordinary people use government to get things done — to find summer jobs for their children, obtain zoning variances and building permits, get people out of jail or avert arrest, remove neighborhood nuisances, site or renovate parks and libraries. Objectives that not very long ago required storming city council meetings — for example, getting streets paved, street lights or stop signs emplaced — can now be met through routine processes. Concerns that were the stuff of intense struggle and confrontation have in many cases been institutionalized in the normal functions of pertinent agencies.

These accomplishments are often dismissed in some quarters on the left as trivial and as evidence of co-optation. Certainly, such characterizations are true "in the last analysis," but we don't live and can't do effective politics "in the last analysis." For these accomplishments to function effectively as co-optation, for example, the fruits of incorporation cannot be so trivial for those who partake or expect to be able to partake of them. The inclination to dismiss them instead reflects problematic tendencies within the left to trivialize and simultaneously to demonize the exercise of public authority. This problem typically appears in the lack of concreteness and care taken to analyze the mundane operations of the political system, the microprocesses through which it legitimizes the prevailing political order by delivering palpable benefits to people, in the process propagating specific constructions of what reasonable expectations and limits are. As I shall argue later, so long as we leave that realm entirely in the hands of mainstream academics and functionaries, the left has little hope of being able to gain an audience in public debate. Nor, to speak directly to the issue at hand, can we make sense of the forces driving contemporary politics among black Americans.

The new regime of race relations management as realized through the four-pronged dynamic of incorporation that I have discussed has exerted a demobilizing effect on black politics precisely by virtue of its capacities for delivering benefits and, perhaps more important, for defining what benefits political action can legitimately be used to pursue. Ease in voting and in producing desired electoral outcomes legitimizes that form as the primary means of political participation, which naturally seems attractive compared to others that require more extensive and intensive commitment of attention and effort. One result is to narrow the operative conception of political engagement to one form, and the most passive one at that.

Incumbent public officials generically have an interest in dampening the possibilities for new or widespread mobilization — electoral or otherwise — because of its intrinsic volatility. Uncontrolled participation can produce unpleasant electoral surprises and, equally, can interfere with the reigning protocols through which public agencies define and discharge their functions. As popular participation narrows, the inertial logic of incumbency operates to constrict the field of political discourse. Incumbents respond to durable interests, and they seek predictability, continuity, and a shared common sense. This translates into a preference for a brokered "politics as usual" that limits the number and range of claims on the policy agenda. Such a politics preserves the thrust of inherited policy regimes and reinforces existing patterns of systemic advantage by limiting the boundaries of the politically reasonable.[10] The same is true for the insider-negotiation processes through which the NGOs now define their roles, and those organizations often earn their insider status in the first place by providing a convincing alternative to popular political mobilization.

Thus we can see that demobilization has been overdetermined by the normal workings of post-segregation era black politics. The failure of black radicals and of the left in general to produce appropriately sophisticated, pragmatically based critiques and alternatives that take these dynamics into account (which I discuss in greater detail later), in addition, eliminated the only possible source for the articulation of credible countervailing discourse and political practice. That failure, moreover, is implicated even more disturbingly in the second major current feeding demobilization during the 1980s and 1990s, the proliferation of underclass ideology and the legitimation of a new behaviorally focused, victim-blaming catechism—across the ideological spectrum and the veil of color—as the orthodox frame for discussing racial stratification and urban dispossession.

Underclass Rhetoric and the Disappearance of Politics

Fueled largely by sensationalist journalism and supposedly tough-minded, policy-oriented social scientists, underclass rhetoric became over the 1980s the main frame within which to discuss inner-city poverty and inequality. The pundits and the scholars, whose common sense the pundits provide, all define this "underclass" stratum's membership in slightly different ways; however, they all circle around a basic characterization that roots it among inner-city blacks and Hispanics, and they share a conveniently consensual assessment that the underclass—no matter how defined, that is, no matter which statistical fractions of demographic data are reified as behavioral groups—makes up about 20 percent of the impoverished population in inner cities.

I and others have criticized the underclass notion extensively elsewhere, on both normative and empirical grounds, and in chapter 6 in this volume I elaborate that critique extensively.[11] Simply put, it is a contemporary extrapolation from a Victorian petit bourgeois fantasy world, and it is almost invariably harnessed to arguments for reactionary and punitive social policy. Even at its best—that is, when it is connected with some agenda other than pure stigmatization and denial of public responsibility—this rhetoric is depoliticizing and thus demobilizing in at least three ways.

First, the underclass frame directs attention not to the political-economic dynamics that produce and reproduce dispossession and its entailments—that is, social structure—but focuses instead on behavioral characteristics alleged to exist among the victims of those dynamics. The result is to immerse discussion of inequality, poverty, and racial stratification in often overlapping rhetorics of individual or collective pathogenesis and knee-jerk moral evaluation. Conservatives bask in the simplicity of a political discourse that revolves around racialized stigmatization of people as good, bad, or defective.[12] However, even those versions propounded by liberals, like that offered by William Julius Wilson, which purport to provide structurally grounded accounts of inner-city inequality nonetheless describe the "underclass" in primarily behavioral terms. In such accounts "structure" appears as a reified, opaque background—a natural boundary, whose constraints are inexorable and beyond the possibility of human intervention, in a kind of "shit happens" ecological saga.[13]

In both conservative and putatively liberal versions, therefore, the underclass rhetoric reinforces tendencies to demobilization by situating debate about poverty and inequality not in the public realm of politics—which would warrant examination of the role of public action in the reproduction of an unequal distribution of material costs and benefits (for example, federal and local housing and redevelopment policies that feed ghettoization and favor suburbs over inner cities, that favor home owners over renters in the face of widespread and blatant racial discrimination in access to mortgages, direct and indirect subsidies for urban deindustrialization and disinvestment, systematic underfunding of public institutions serving inner cities, racial discrimination in law enforcement, and so on).[14] Rather, discussion fixates on the ostensibly private realm of individual values and behavior, pivoting specifically on images of male criminality and female slovenliness and compulsive, irresponsible sexuality. The specter of drugs is omnipresent as well, underscoring the composite image of a generically wanton, depraved Other and, of course, automatically justifying any extreme of repression and official brutality. Even when acknowledged as unfounded, an invocation of suspicion of the presence of drugs (and now, increasingly, gangs) exculpates arbitrary violation of civil liberties in inner cities and police brutality to the extent of homicide. One need not be Rodney King to complete and decipher the racist catch-22 embedded in the operative syllogism: Suspicion of drugs justifies any abrogation of civil rights and civil liberties; being black or Latino in inner cities constitutes adequate reason to suspect drug involvement; therefore . . .[15]

The underclass image is also profoundly gendered; with the exception of the clearly male category of violent crime and the gender-neutral one of drug abuse, the most commonly cited qualifications for underclass membership—female household-heading, teen childbearing, out-of-wedlock birth, and welfare dependency—all show up only in women. Christopher Jencks has actually delimited, just for the sake of clarity of course, a distinct "reproductive underclass," apparently untroubled by the eugenicist imagery his doing so evokes.[16]

Insofar as this focus opens to public policy at all, it tilts toward social and police repression, as in ubiquitous proposals for draconian "welfare reform" that seek only to codify the punitive moralism propelling the underclass narrative. That essentially racialized agenda is not likely to fuel broad political mobilization among black Americans, not in service to progressive agendas at any rate.

Second, the underclass rhetoric reinforces demobilization because of its very nature as a third-person discourse. As a rhetoric of stigmatization, it is by definition deployed *about* rather than *by* any real population. No one self-identifies as a member of the underclass. To that extent, as well as because the rhetoric presumes their incompetence, it is unthinkable to exhort the stigmatized population to undertake any concerted political action on their own behalf. In fact, the only calls to mobilize that derive from the underclass frame are inflected toward NIMBY ("not-in-my-backyard") politics (keeping out crime, as well as socially useful facilities, like homeless shelters and halfway houses, often deemed undesirable in embattled neighborhoods) or toward the black middle-class noblesse oblige associated with self-help ideology. Neither affords progressive possibilities, and neither is likely to generate much real mobilization—unless it does stimulate a black version of the kind of rightist, middle-class populism galvanized in the white Reagan-Perot-Buchanan ranks.

The underclass narrative's association with self-help ideology is in fact the third way that it undercuts popular political mobilization.[17] Because behavioral pathology appears in that narrative as at least the proximate source of poverty, inequality, and even contemporary racial discrimination, the programmatic responses that arise most naturally within its purview are those geared to correcting the supposed defects of the target population. This biases programmatic discussion toward bootstrap initiatives that claim moral rehabilitation of impoverished individuals and communities as part of their mission.

In this context two apparently different streams of neo-Jeffersonian romanticism—those associated respectively with the 1960s' New Left and Reaganism—converge on an orientation that eschews government action on principle in favor of voluntarist, "community-based" initiatives. The two streams share a general distrust of government's motives, as well as a presumption that localist, "grassroots" efforts are more efficacious, more authentically democratic and populist, and most of all more productive of civic virtue and personal transformation than those undertaken on a broader scale and by the state. This convergence of Reaganite and New Left antistatism is reflected dramatically in the "empowerment" rhetoric recycled from 1960s activism by the proponents of the

"New Paradigm" in the Kemp wing of the Republican party during the Bush administration.

Particularly when steeped in a language of "empowerment," this antistatist convergence overlaps current manifestations of a conservative, bootstrap tendency among black elites that stretches back at least through Booker T. Washington at the turn of the century. Indeed, it was the Reagan administration's evil genius to appeal to that tendency by shifting from a first-term tactic that projected combative black voices, like Thomas Sowell and Clarence Pendleton, to a more conciliatory style exemplified by Glenn Loury. Sowell and Pendleton relentlessly attacked entrenched race relations elites and black Democrats in the name of a mythical black silent majority. Needless to say, by alienating opinion leaders and appealing to no other really existing constituency, they made neither electoral nor ideological inroads into the politically attentive black citizenry.

In Reagan's second term the administration apparently opted for a different posture as a new group of its black supporters, led by Loury and Robert Woodson of the National Center for Neighborhood Enterprise, stepped into the spotlight. Although this wave of black Reaganites (Woodson especially) could also be pugnacious with adversaries, they were far more inclined than their predecessors to make overtures to the entrenched race relations elite. Those overtures, moreover, disarmed partisan skepticism by emphasizing a transcendent ideal, the black middle class's supposedly special responsibility for correcting the black underclass and the problems associated with it.[18] This message has both flattered black petit bourgeois sensibilities and meshed with, and no doubt also helped to solidify, the increasingly hegemonic view that nonpunitive government action on behalf of black and brown poor people is by definition ineffective and impolitic, if not misguided. Thus the stage was set for propagation of self-help ideology—at least vis-à-vis blacks—across the ideological spectrum.

Underwriting this version of self-help are three interlocked claims: (1) that black inner cities are beset by grave and self-regenerative problems of social breakdown and pathology that have undermined the possibility of normal civic life, (2) that these problems are beyond the reach of and in fact thwart direct public policy or positive state action, and (3) that they can be addressed only by private, voluntarist black action led by the responsible middle class. Over the late 1980s and early 1990s these three claims—each dubious enough on its own, all justified at most by appeal to lurid anecdotes, self-righteous prejudices, and cracker-barrel social theory—congealed into hegemonic wisdom. Black public figures supposedly identified with the left, like Jesse Jackson, Roger Wilkins, and

Cornel West, have become as devout proselytizers of this catechistic orthodoxy as are rightists like Woodson, Loury, and Clarence Thomas.[19]

The rise and consolidation of the Democratic Leadership Council (DLC) and the "New Liberalism" as dominant within the Democratic party no doubt reinforced and were reinforced by the black self-help bromides' elevation to the status of conventional wisdom. On the one hand, black self-help rhetoric historically has been associated with presumptions that blacks have no hope for allies in pursuit of racial justice through public policy, and the successful offensive of Democratic "centrists" and neoliberals—predicated in large part on flight from identification with both perceived black interests and downwardly redistributive social policy—certainly lends credence to the impression that the federal government is not a dependable ally of black objectives. Even New Liberal consciences Bill Bradley's and John Kerry's celebrated declamations for racial justice and tolerance were mainly, after brief statements against bigotry, extended characterizations of impoverished inner cities as savage hearts of darkness, saturated in self-destructive violence and pathology; the speeches, moreover, carried no particular warrant for action addressing inequality and its effects except calls for moral uplift. (That these frank endorsements of the principal tropes of contemporary racism are widely touted as courageous and sympathetic stands for racial decency indicates just how dominant the new racial orthodoxy has become.)[20]

On the other hand, black public figures' embrace of self-help rhetoric undoubtedly has emboldened the Democratic rightists; it both amounts to a capitulation before the DLC program *and* rationalizes the racial agenda driving retrenchment by giving it a stamp of liberal, race-conscious black authenticity, a form of insurance against charges of racism. Bradley, for instance, is reported to speak regularly with West to receive the line that he wants to hear on racial issues.[21]

In addition, despite its foundation on notions of grassroots activism, the self-help regime is best seen as community mobilization for political demobilization. Each attempt by a neighborhood or church group to scrounge around the philanthropic world and the interstices of the federal system for funds to build low-income housing or day care or neighborhood centers, to organize programs that compensate for inadequate school funding, public safety, or trash pickup, simultaneously concedes the point that black citizens cannot legitimately pursue those benefits through government. This is a very dangerous concession in an ideological context defined largely by a logic that, like that operative in the post-Reconstruction era of the last century, could extend to an almost genocidal expulsion of black citizens toward a Bantustanized periphery of the society. Already, respected New Liberal academic and Clinton administration adviser Paul Starr has called for rolling back the clock in American politics to the 1940s, in his view before race became an issue. And University of Chicago legal scholar Richard Epstein has recently published a book explicitly arguing for repeal of the 1964 Civil Rights Act. Like Starr, who proposes a strategy of black "separate development" administered by the equivalent of a Bureau of Negro Affairs, the prestigious historian Eugene Genovese has recently advocated political resegregation, citing blacks' allegedly special needs as justification.[22]

We cannot afford to concede the important ground of black people's equal proprietorship of public institutions with all other citizens; affirming the legitimacy of black Americans' demands on the state — on an equal basis with those who receive defense contracts, home ownership subsidies, investment tax credits, flood protection, and a host of other benefits from government — is also affirming black Americans' equal membership in the polity. The more ground we give on this front, the more the latter-day versions of the southern Redeemers and their allies will take. Frederick Douglass put it succinctly: "The limits of tyrants are prescribed by the endurance of those whom they oppress."

From this perspective the predominance of self-help rhetoric marks a capitulationist evasion whose dangers are obscured by its enshrinement of class prejudice and the soothing patter of class self-congratulation in an insipid discourse of "role models" and special middle-class tutelage as an antidote to impoverishment. That the self-help program is a strategic dead end is clear in the spectacle of the tremendous expense of effort poured, in communities all over the country, into Black Family Weekends, marches to Stop the Violence, proclamations of firearms-free or drug-free zones, failed attempts at economic development, gang or youth summits — which mainly produce platitudes and homilies and moments of orchestrated conviviality.

I by no means wish to disparage grassroots activism and community initiative in principle; the problem with self-help ideology is that it reifies community initiative, freighting it with an ideological burden that reduces to political quietism and a programmatic mission that it is ill equipped to fulfill. It is absurd to present neighborhood and church initiatives as appropriate responses to the effects of government-supported disinvestment; labor market segmentation; widespread and well-documented patterns of discrimination in employment and housing, as well as in the trajectory of direct and indirect public spending; and an all-out corporate assault on the social wage. It is, moreover, only with respect to social policy affecting poor minority citizens that such expectations seem reasonable; we do not imagine that the bloated defense budget or NASA's frivolities should be funded by selling chicken dinners at Fort Bragg, Electric Boat, Livermore Labs, or Cape Canaveral. To the contrary, self-help is attractive, as Gordon Lafer has argued persuasively about the related job training ideology, because of the qualities that destine it to fail; it appeals as an attempt to do social policy on the cheap, which amounts to little more than providing a pat response for public officials and private race relations engineers when asked what they are doing programmatically to address the oppressive conditions confronting inner-city poor people.[23]

In addition, it is particularly ironic that the self-help rhetoric has been endorsed by public officials. That endorsement amounts to an admission of failure, an acknowledgment that the problems afflicting their constituents are indeed beyond the scope of the institutional apparatus under their control, that black officials are in fact powerless to provide services to inner-city citizens effectively through those institutions. That admission should begin a discussion of what steps officials and constituents can take to exert pressure aimed at prying loose resources that would enable the proper functioning of public institutions; instead, recursion to self-help sidesteps that discussion, allowing public officials to pass the buck to their constituents by proclaiming the inadequacy or irrelevance of public institutions (while not plowing under the claims to status, prestige, and income commanded by virtue of institutional position). This is yet another way that self-help ideology feeds political demobilization.

A key to overcoming the demobilizing effects of self-help ideology, as well as those of underclass rhetoric more generally, lies in the stimulation of strategic debate—grounded in the relation between social conditions affecting the black population, public policy, and the larger political-economic tendencies to which it responds—within and about black political activity. This in turn requires attending to the complex dynamics of interest and ideological differentiation that operate *within* black politics, taking into account the who-gets-what-when-where-how dimension of politics as it appears among black political agents and interest configurations. In principle, the left should be intimately engaged in this project, which is the stock in trade of left political analysis. However, the absence of a sophisticated, left-critical discourse about and within black politics is, I shall argue, the third major hindrance to progressive black political mobilization.

The Left and Black Politics

As I argue in chapter 1, black activists' chronic failure to take account of the 1965 Voting Rights Act's consequences for Afro-American political life has been a crucial element in the atrophy of left-critical discourse within black politics.[24]

By outlawing official segregation and discriminatory restrictions on political participation, the Voting Rights Act and the 1964 Civil Rights Act rendered obsolete the least common denominator—opposition to Jim Crow—that for more than a half-century had given black political activity coherence and a pragmatic agenda plausibly understood to be shared uniformly among the black citizenry.[25] (This effect no doubt is a factor—along with the spread of self-help ideology and the aging of the population that can recall the ancien régime—driving contemporary nostalgia for the sense of community that supposedly flourished under segregation. Black politics did appear to be simpler, more coherent, and more cohesive then. That perception, however, was always more apparent than real; the coherence and cohesiveness were most of all artifacts of the imperatives of the Jim Crow system and the struggle against it. In black politics as elsewhere, what appears as political cohesiveness has been the assertion of one tendency over others coexisting and competing with it—in this case, first white elites' successful projection of Booker T. Washington's capitulationist program and then, for the half-century after Washington's death, the primacy of the focus on attacking codified segregation.) The Voting Rights Act, additionally, resulted in opening new possibilities, concrete objectives and incentives for political action, and new, more complex relations with mainstream political institutions, particularly government and the Democratic party at all levels. The dynamics of systemic incorporation that I have described here are the specific articulations of these new arrangements. They express the fulfillment of what had been a clearly central strategic principle of black politics at least since the founding of the Niagara Movement in 1905, the struggle for equal access to the regular mechanisms of political participation.

Passage of the Voting Rights Act, along with its subsequent enforcement, was the signal event marking that struggle's success; it also initiated a substantial reorientation of the character and practical objectives of black politics. In the decade after 1965 black political activity came increasingly to revolve around gaining, enhancing, or maintaining official representation in public institutions and the distribution of associated material and symbolic benefits. The greatest increases in black elective officeholding occurred during those years. That period also saw the rise of black urban governance, both in black-led municipal regimes and in growing black authority in the urban administrative apparatus—housing authorities and redevelopment agencies, welfare departments, school systems, and so forth. Naturally, these new opportunities and proximity to direct exercise of political power focused the mainstream of black strategic attention on electoral activity.

At the same time this shift exposed a long-standing tension in black political discourse between narrower and broader constructions of the practical agenda for realizing racially democratic interests. The narrower view has focused political objectives on singular pursuit of racial inclusion, either accepting the structure and performance of political and economic institutions as given or presuming that black representation is an adequate basis for correcting what might be unsatisfactory about them. The essence of this view was distilled, appropriately, in two pithy formulations in the late 1960s: the slogan demanding "black faces in previously all-white places" and the proposition that as an ideal black Americans should make up 12 percent of corporate executives, 12 percent of the unemployed, and 12 percent of everything in between.[26] The broader tendency is perhaps best seen as an ensemble of views joined by inclination toward structural critique. This tendency sees simple racial inclusion as inadequate and argues for tying political action to insurgent programs that seek either to transform existing institutions or to reject them altogether in favor of race nationalist or social revolutionary alternatives. It is, of course, the source of the oppositional impulse in black politics.[27]

The tension between these two views has been a recurring issue in black politics, overlapping and crosscutting — and, arguably, being mistaken for — other fault lines that appear more commonly in the historiography of black political debate (for example, the militant/moderate, protest/accommodationist, and integrationist/nationalist dichotomies).[28] In the 1960s, however, the combination of broad popular mobilization and heightened prospects for victory against legally enforced exclusion made this tension more prominent than at any prior time except during the 1930s and early 1940s, when Ralph Bunche and other Young Turks pushed sharp, Marxist-inspired critiques into the main lines of black debate.[29]

The processes of incorporation set in motion by the enforcement of voting rights and the rise of black officialdom created a new and unfamiliar context for expressing this tension and presented radicals with a difficult situation. On the one hand, incorporation was a major goal of the narrower inclusionist agenda, and evidence of progress therefore boosted that tendency's ideological momentum. Success, after all, breeds enthusiasm and adherence, and the emerging ranks of black elected officials and public managers were conspicuous signs of success. On the other hand, incorporation introduced an instrumental dimension without precedent in black political debate. Black accession to responsible positions in the apparatus of public management enabled for the first time — save for fleeting moments during Reconstruction — a discourse focused on the concrete, nuts-and-bolts exercise of public authority. This gave rise to a notion of political pragmatism that revolves around action within public institutions to redirect the distribution of costs and benefits incrementally to reflect black interests. And that is a notion that obviously gives an advantage in the struggle for hearts and minds to those with access to the mechanisms of distribution.

Three factors compel this pragmatic orientation toward incrementalism. First, the inclusionist program had developed largely as an insider politics, seeking legitimacy in part through emphasis on loyalty, particularly in the Cold War context, to prevailing political and economic arrangements except insofar as those were racially exclusionary. To that extent it has been predisposed to take existing systemic and institutional imperatives as given. Second, experience in War on Poverty and Great Society programs (most significantly Community Action and Model Cities agencies) socialized the pool of potential black officials into the public management system's entrenched protocols and operating logic, initiating them into the common sense of existing policy processes. This socialization spurred articulation of a rhetoric exalting the realpolitik and keying strategic consideration only to advancement of black representation among beneficiaries *within* existing policy and institutional regimes.[30] (This notion of political pragmatism not only reinforces incrementalism, it also requires a shifting construction of "black" interests to conform to options set in a received policy-and-issue framework. For instance, Mayor Maynard Jackson strained to define one of the alternatives in a developers' fight over siting a new Atlanta airport as the black choice, even though building a second airport at either location would have had no discernibly positive impact on black Atlantans; public support for the project on any site, moreover, would amount to a redistribution of fiscal resources away from the city's black population to developers and remote, generally hostile metropolitan economic interests.)[31] Finally, inclusionist politics affords no larger vision around which to orient a critical perspective on either the operations and general functions of political institutions or the general thrust of public policy. This characteristic, which might appear as political myopia, is rationalizable as pragmatic; in any event, it further reinforces incrementalism by screening out broader issues and concerns.

The hegemony of incrementalism has facilitated elaboration of a political discourse that sidesteps a critical problem at the core of post-segregation era black politics: the tension between black officials' institutional legitimation and their popular electoral legitimation. The institutions that black officials administer are driven by the imperatives of managing systemic racial subordination, but the expectations that they cultivate among their black constituents define the role of black administrative representation in those institutions as a de facto challenge to racial subordination. This contradiction has been exacerbated as the rightward turn in American politics has both eroded the fiscal capacities of public institutions serving inner-city minority populations (while rightist economic policies that intensify income polarization have increased service demand on those institutions) and redefined the constraining social policy framework in ever more punitive, repressive terms.[32]

So by the 1990s it was commonplace to see black housing authority directors' policy innovations run to advocating lockdowns and random police sweeps, black school superintendents discussing their duties principally through a rhetoric of discipline and order and calling for punishment of the parents of transgressors in their charge, black mayors and legislators locked into a victim-blaming interpretive frame that points to drug abuse and criminality as the only actionable social problems—and all falling back on the going bromides about family breakdown and moral crisis among their constituents to explain the inadequacy of the public services they deliver. This rhetoric also obscures their capitulation to business-led programs of regressive redistribution—tax breaks and other subsidies, as well as general subservience to development interests in planning and policy formulation—that contribute further to fiscal strain, thus justifying still further service cuts, which increase pressure for giving more to development interests to stimulate "growth" that supposedly will build the tax base and so on. From this perspective, Sharon Pratt Kelly's Washington, D.C., mayoralty is emblematic; her tenure has been distinguished only by repeated service and personnel cuts and her 1993 call for the National Guard to buttress municipal police efforts—even as the District of Columbia already has one of the highest police-to-citizen ratios in the United States. There could hardly be a more striking illustration of the extent to which minority public officials are the equivalent of Bantustan administrators. In this context, incrementalism serves as blinders, sword, and shield. It blocks alternative courses from view, delegitimizes criticism with incantations of realpolitik, and provides a Pontius Pilate defense of any action by characterizing officials as incapable of acting on their circumstances.[33]

It is possible that continued debate with the oppositional tendency in black politics could have mitigated the corrosive effects of incrementalist hegemony. Such debate might have broadened somewhat the perspective from which black officials themselves define pragmatic agendas. It may have stimulated among black citizens a practical, policy-oriented public discourse that would either have supported black officials in the articulation of bold initiatives or held them accountable to autonomously generated programmatic agendas and concerns or both.

Certainly, proponents of the narrower tendency had the upper hand in the contest for the direction of post-segregation black politics, if only by virtue of their ability to deliver payoffs on what they construed to be the stakes of political action. Nevertheless, into the early 1970s radicals, who were by and large veterans of black power community organizing, typically had credible claims to a grassroots political base—often institutionalized through the organizational spinoffs of antipoverty initiatives. Therefore, through that period at least mainstream black politicians felt a need to maintain communication and visible contact with radical activists. This was evident in black officials' attendance and participation at the 1970 Congress of African Peoples and the National Black Political Conventions at Gary, Indiana, in 1972 and Little Rock, Arkansas, in 1974, as well as lower-profile meetings of the National Black Assembly and in ongoing, albeit temporary, relationships struck at the local level. Candidates for office routinely sought radicals' campaign support, or at least felt obliged to go through the motions of seeking it.[34]

This "hundred flowers" period in black politics wilted and dissolved well before the end of the 1970s. Mainstream politicians asserted a monopoly on credible political strategy and, more fundamentally, on the idea of politics. Political action came to be isomorphic with the routine practices in which public officials engage. Radical critique either vanished through social amnesia or became dismissible as naive or quaint, like outmoded fashion. Radicals themselves either made peace with the new hegemony and pursued absorption into the public management system through employment in government and ancillary "community-based organizations" (the domestic NGOs), or they redoubled their ideological purity and sought to institutionalize their political marginalization in organizations of the faithful.

Few, I imagine, would dispute the argument that radicalism has been routed in post-segregation black politics. Some simply fit that fact into a naturalistic reading of the processes of incorporation: Radicalism automatically wanes as avenues open for regular political participation. Others, less sanguine about the outcome, concede incrementalist, petit bourgeois hegemony in electoral politics but claim that radicalism's social base has been not destroyed but only displaced to other domains—dormant mass anger, Louis Farrakhan's apparent popularity, rap music and other extrusions of youth culture, literary production, and the like—suggesting a need to reconceptualize politics to reflect the significance of such phenomena. Both sorts of response, however, evade giving an account of *how* the radical tendency was expunged from the black political mainstream, which is critically important for making sense of the limitations of inherited forms of black radicalism and, therefore, for the task of constructing a progressive black politics in the present.

Pointing to mainstream politicians' structurally advantageous position does not suffice to explain their success in propagating the narrower view of the stakes of black Americans' political activity. By definition, we should expect that radicals proceed from a relatively weaker institutional base than those associated with programs that presume the political status quo. What needs to be explained is how features of black radicalism itself short-circuited its critique of the narrower, inclusionist program and contributed to its own marginalization. I have approached this issue in chapter 2 in a somewhat different way, focusing more on the articulation of black power radicalism into concrete forms that were compatible with inclusionist, incrementalist politics and that fueled the new regime of race relations management.[35] I propose now to extend and refine that argument with a more textured account of the responses of black radicalism's different strands to ongoing incorporation during the decade or so after the Voting Rights Act.[36]

The oppositional tendency in post-segregation black politics was hampered by its origin in black power ideology. Radicals — all along the spectrum, ranging from cultural nationalist to Stalinoid Marxist — began from a stance that took the "black community" as the central configuration of political interest and the source of critical agency. This stance grew from black power rhetoric's emphasis on "community control" and its projection of the "community" as the touchstone of legitimacy and insurgent authenticity. This formulation is a presumptive claim for the existence of a racial population that is organically integrated and that operates as a collective subject in pursuit of unitary interests. That claim, which persists as a grounding principle in black strategic discourse, is problematic in two linked ways that bear on elaboration of a critical politics.

First, positing a black collectivity as an organic political agent preempts questions of interest differentiation. If the "community" operates with a single will and single (albeit perhaps internally variegated) agenda, then there is neither need nor basis for evaluating political programs or policies with respect to their impact on different elements of the black population. Any initiative enjoying conspicuous support from any group of black people can plausibly be said to reflect the community's preference or interest; the metaphorical organicism that drives the "black community" formulation presumes that what is good for one is good for all. Assuming a pandemically racial interest as the foundation of black politics, therefore, undercuts the capacity to orient Afro-American political strategy and critique around assessment of the distribution of costs and benefits *among* black Americans. Taking the organic racial community as the fundamental unit of black political life makes it difficult even to recognize that consequences of political action or public policy may differ for different segments of the black population because intraracial stratification is seen as ephemeral—an expression of idiosyncratic attitudes and personal style, not structured social relations.

Similarly, because the organic black community is construed as naturalistic, the notion precludes discussion of both criteria of political representation and the definition of constituencies. Those issues become matters for concern when the relevant polity is perceived to be made up of diverse and not necessarily compatible interests or when the relation between representatives and represented is seen as contingent and mediated rather than cellular or isomorphic.[37] By contrast, in the black community construct those who appear as leaders or spokespersons are not so much representatives as pure embodiments of collective aspirations. The relation between leaders and led appears to be unmediated, an identity; to that extent it is not a matter for concern and commands no particular attention. By the same token, in this view of black politics the constituency issue is resolved from the onset; there is one, generically racial constituency, as all members of the organic community are presumed to share equally in its objectives and the fruits of their realization. Again, apparent distinctions of social situation or position and function in the social division of labor are superficial from this perspective because the centripetal forces that form the racial community are prior to, and at least in principle more meaningful than, immediate social context.

As the stratum of black public officials emerged, black power radicalism's limitations became visible. Blacks' accession to prominence within the institutional apparatus of urban administration did not appreciably alter the mission or official practices of the institutions in their charge. Clearly, therefore, putting black faces in previously all-white places was not a sufficient program for those who identified with institutional transformation along populist lines or who otherwise rejected the status quo of race relations management. Yet because black power's communitarian premises reified group identity and could not accommodate structural differentiation among Afro-Americans, the only critical frame on which radicals could draw consensually was the language of racial authenticity. This reduced in turn to a rhetoric of good (those who were somehow "really" black) and bad (those who veered toward racial disloyalty) individuals.

By the end of the 1960s black power's inadequacy as a basis for concrete political judgment had begun to fuel radicals' self-conscious turn to the creation and adoption of "ideologies"—global political narratives encompassing alternative visions, norms, and strategic programs—that promised to provide definite standpoints for critical judgment and platforms for political mobilization. This development underwrote a logic of sectarianism that embedded a cleavage between Marxists and cultural nationalists as the pivotal tension in black oppositional politics. That tension, however, was enacted within a discursive field whose coherence derived in part from the ideological turn itself. That is, for both tendencies political action centered on propagation of mechanistic theories, typically reducible to a set of reified principles (for example, among nationalists the Seven Principles of the Nguzo Saba, for Marxists the "principles of scientific socialism"). From that perspective both Marxists and nationalists were inclined to disdain close critique of the practices then congealing around public officialdom, preferring instead to dismiss that domain as either ancillary to radical concerns or inauthentic. In both camps concern with the internal consistency of the global narrative drove the elaboration of ideological positions; the point was not to explain or comprehend dynamics current in mainstream political activity but to lay out a more visionary and authentic alternative. The relation consensually assumed to pertain between ideology and action was the hortatory juxtaposition of the ideal and actual rather than a more open-ended guidance for immediately practical interpretation and practice. To that extent, external criteria for validating competing accounts were relatively insignificant in the ideological discourse from the onset, and both nationalists and those claiming the Marxist rubric were wedded to an idealist frame of reference for political interpretation and debate—the latter all the more so the more emphatically they invoked the symbols of scientistic authority.

Ironically, the impetus propelling the ideological turn—the need to compensate for the inadequacies of black power's simplistic communitarianism—was thwarted by failure to break with the essential flaw, the stance positing the "black community" as the source of political legitimation and its attendant rhetoric of authenticity. Indeed, the turn to ideology may have reinforced propensities to rely on communitarian mystification because the flight into theoreticism made the need to claim connections with popular action all the more urgent.

The quandary faced by the oppositional politics that evolved from black power produced two main organizational responses: the National Black Political Assembly (NBPA) and the African Liberation Support Committee (ALSC).[38] The NBPA, which grew from the 1972 National Black Political Convention at Gary, was spearheaded by the cultural nationalist camp and was an attempt to unite activists and elected officials in support of a common, generically black agenda. Reflecting the view that there is a racial political interest that transcends other affiliations or commitments, the NBPA was organized on Imamu Amiri Baraka's principle of "unity without uniformity." ALSC was the outgrowth of an ad hoc African Liberation Day Coordinating Committee that had organized the first African Liberation Day national mobilization, also in 1972. Creation of ALSC reflected a concern to formalize a presence to act in support of African liberation movements, particularly in the Portuguese colonies, Rhodesia, South Africa, and South-West Africa. Like the NBPA, ALSC was in principle ecumenically black. ALSC differed, however, in its focus on popular mobilization; its agenda centered on mass political education and agitation, largely in concert with organizing an annual African Liberation Day demonstration, as well as fund-raising for annual allocations to designated liberation movements. To that extent ALSC was more an activist organization and was, as a consequence, somewhat less oriented to building formal relationships with mainstream politicians. Both organizations, though, represented radicals' desire to define a space for oppositional politics in the post-segregation context; both were attempts to create organizational bases that could institutionalize racially autonomous radicalism in the new Afro-American political culture and facilitate pursuit of practical agendas consonant with the ideological positions extrapolated from black power sensibility. There was also substantial overlap in radicals' participation in the two organizations.

In retrospect, the NBPA arguably confronted the new political situation more directly than did the more activist ALSC. The radicals associated with the NBPA recognized the significance of the developing stratum of public officials and their institutional resources. Officially, the organization's purpose — reflecting the ecumenically race-nationalist ideology — was to bring together radicals and mainstream politicians to craft a de facto division of labor for advancing the interests of the race. Unofficially, nationalist radicals hoped to provide mainstream politicians with an ideological orientation or at least to manipulate them to further propagation of nationalist consciousness. The nationalist activists were generally sanguine about their prospects, both because true belief led them to assume that adherence to nationalist views (even arcane and obviously concocted ones like the Seven Principles) was the natural state among black people and because Baraka's visible role in Kenneth Gibson's 1970 election to the Newark mayoralty suggested that they could be a potent political force.

The program of unity without uniformity presumed cultural nationalism's inattentiveness to concrete issues and public policy. The ideology's idealist character — its central focus on exhortation to accept an abstract "black value system" — was so remote from any particular programmatic warrant bearing on national or local policy that it could accommodate virtually any substantive position, so long as it was packaged as "race conscious." This underwrote strong tendencies to political quietism and opportunism. The main standard for judging politicians' and public officials' behavior had to do with whether they formally embraced the abstract nationalist creed, whether they made institutional resources available to nationalist groups, or both. Thus not only were alliances possible with all manner of political interests—including black Nixonite Republicans, typically with some version of the rationale "Yes, the Republicans are racist, but the Democrats are racist too. All white people are racist; we just need to use them to get what we can for black people." (This tendency reproduced a dangerous rhythm in black nationalism reaching back to Marcus Garvey's, and later Elijah Muhammad's, associations with the Ku Klux Klan.) The abstract ideology's disjunction from concrete political issues also elevated ignoring civic affairs to the level of political principle, an expression of ostensible political sophistication that conveniently left space for opportunist alliances, diminishing their substantive significance in the name of putatively higher purposes. Nationalist ideologues, for instance, dismissed anti–Vietnam War activism as a white issue and had no critique of the Nixon and Ford administrations' assault on social spending and the social wage from the standpoint of its implications for black politics, thereby glossing over the disturbing and contradictory character of a range of potential alliances.

Despite the élan drawn from Baraka's reputed role in Newark, moreover, NBPA nationalists' relation to black officials was ultimately parasitic. As the new stratum of officials consolidated its position in black urban politics, radicals increasingly sought to ingratiate themselves with those officials—their rhetoric of enforcing accountability notwithstanding—as a path to advancing nationalist ends. They looked either to ride on officials' coattails and take advantage of the latter's visibility and cachet by association or to gain funding, jobs, or comparable forms of legitimacy and access—for example, support for preschools, cultural centers, or other such initiatives; appointments to boards and commissions; patronage jobs; honorifics—within the institutional apparatus of black urban governance. In fact, the nationalist radicals' political strength was never so great as it appeared; even Baraka was trounced when he challenged Gibson by backing an opponent to the mayor's candidate in a city council race.

Indeed, after his Pauline conversion to Marxism-Leninism, Baraka helped to define the limits of "unity without uniformity." He was nearly purged from the NBPA on ideological grounds by a coalition of elected officials and nationalist activists, led by Hannah Atkins, an Oklahoma state senator, and Ron Daniels, a leader of midwestern nationalists. (Daniels, ironically, repackaged himself in the late 1980s to appeal to the left as really being what Jesse Jackson sought to be, still committed to an independent presidential candidacy—his own, of course.)[39] The NBPA simply faded out of existence over the later 1970s.

Although ALSC began as a sort of black united or popular front organization (there was always ambiguity about which type of front model should apply), within a year it had become the principal site for the struggle between Marxists and nationalists that was the consuming tension in 1970s Afro-American radicalism.[40] (Baraka's ideological conversion and expulsion from the NBPA, for example, happened within the frame of this struggle.) The proximate source of the conflict within ALSC, whose ranks had been divided between the two tendencies from the organization's inception, was a strategic debate over how to characterize the engine driving Euro-American domination and thus how to orient agitation and political education. Nationalists favored a simple and unmodified race line that isolated a Western pursuit of white world supremacy as the motive force of modern history; Marxists argued for embedding the account of Africa's subjugation in a global (though still as a rule racialized) theory of imperialism on a Leninist model. Despite the arcaneness of both nationalist and Marxist theoretical positions, this debate did have a practical foundation inasmuch as it was about an issue that had to be resolved to make effective agitation and mobilization possible. Almost immediately, however, the controversy opened into a more general one over whether ALSC itself needed to be grounded on a coherent ideology and, if so, what that ideology should be. The consequences of the ensuing "two-line struggle" reverberated through the remainder of the organization's existence.

The desire to vest ALSC with a definitive, abstract "ideology" reflected radicals' concern to generate a visible alternative to mainstream politicians' incrementalist rhetoric of incorporation. Beneath the overheated clash of catechistic narratives, therefore, lay a practical issue that only indirectly concerned Africa. Among both Marxists and nationalists were those who saw ALSC and the activity of organizing around support for African liberation movements as a vehicle for rekindling an indigenous popular black radicalism. But this impulse cut against the grain of one of the organization's founding objectives, building a black coalition, as broadly based as possible, to lobby and exert pressure on behalf of a least common denominator agenda of African liberation. (So, for instance, targeting those residual quarters of direct domination by whites helped to keep the focus of agitation neatly black and white, avoiding more complex, and therefore less emotionally resonant and potentially controversial, issues such as neocolonialism or the existence of oppressive black regimes.) Nonetheless, both camps joined the fight for ideological hegemony with zest; conducting political struggle on the abstract plane of contending global narratives—with little regard to their practical entailments, if any—glossed over the tension between the logic of ideological purification and that mandated by the consensual common front objective.

As with the NBPA experience, the ideological narratives' abstractness, their disconnectedness from the mundane realities of the post-segregation black political environment, helped to mediate that tension by providing space—and high-minded rationalizations—for opportunistic efforts to cultivate parasitic relations with black officials. Whether defined as building a mass, black anti-imperialist movement or inculcating racial consciousness and the "black value system," the larger ideological objective could justify suspending critique of really existing black officialdom on instrumental grounds—the usefulness of gaining access to the public schools to lecture on African liberation, the legitimating cachet of prominent officials' endorsement of annual events, perhaps even possibilities for sub rosa staff assistance from municipal agencies. Though such concessions to Realpolitik certainly were consistent with and appropriate for ALSC's popular front agenda, they also underscored the extent to which the radicals' flight to global ideology evaded precisely the terrain that radicalism most needed to map critically: the strategic and programmatic significance of black political incorporation and shifts in the political and ideological mechanisms of racial subordination in the United States.

Those drawn to ALSC because of its apparent potential for stimulating domestically focused radical activism were most likely to be in the organization's Marxist wing, but even that camp was split between a tendency that favored instrumentally withholding criticism of black officialdom and one that advocated direct confrontation and critique. (This cleavage generally overlapped another that separated supporters of national actions and those who argued for an emphasis on local organizing. The "local organizers" were more inclined toward an explicitly oppositional stance within black politics.) On the one hand, the instrumentalist logic had pragmatic force, given ALSC's commitments to ecumenical mobilization and an annual demonstration of numerical strength. On the other, proponents of an oppositional approach were hampered by their own unwieldy frame of "anti-imperialism," which came only obliquely to a critique of Afro-American political activity.

In part this problem stemmed from ALSC's having emerged from the pan-African ideological movement that had been a response to the problem of situating black power radicalism in a larger theory; pan-Africanism—along with Third Worldist rhetoric that defined black America as a "domestic colony"—was appealing among other reasons because it posited a universe in which black aspirations were not constrained by minority status. Indeed, one strand in ALSC's Marxist tendency was an import grafted by pan-Africanists after Portuguese African guerrilla leaders inveighed against their simplistic, idealist racialism and inattentiveness to class and political economy. The "Marxism" thus adopted was largely an extrinsic, formalistic overlay on a black power nationalist foundation. Its extrinsic origins, moreover, oriented it toward the global anti-imperialist perspective, from which it seemed a reasonable premise that drawing links to oppression in Africa could be a fruitful route for mobilizing domestically based critical politics. Other Marxist strands in ALSC were drawn largely from Maoist and similarly Third Worldist variants (thereby prompting nationalist poet Haki Madhubuti's angry quip at a pivotal ALSC conference that in his estimation Mao Tse-tung was "just another white boy") and were equally formulaic and distant from the textured dynamics forming the post-segregation political milieu.

Even with their best intentions, radicals in ALSC failed to connect with an effective social base. Efforts to create a popular constituency by perfecting and propagating one or another abstract ideology required that people disengage from their worlds of lived experience and undergo a process of ontological change not unlike conversion. Neither Marxists nor nationalists offered programs with demonstrable payoffs comparable to those promised by mainstream politicians; more important, neither radical camp provided concretely persuasive or inspiring critiques of mainstream agendas. To that extent, they held out nothing to compel the leap of faith for which they called. In those circumstances radicals were incapable of braking or modifying mainstream politicians' assertion of hegemony, and ALSC collapsed entirely into sectarian infighting. By 1977 all that remained was a squabble over the organization's carcass, as three factions simultaneously held competing "national" African Liberation Day demonstrations in Washington, D.C.

In both Marxist and nationalist camps the ideological turn was an imposition on—rather than a product of—the analysis of the forces animating black American politics. As a consequence, radicals were never moved to confront the ideal of effective political agency that they had brought forward from black power rhetoric: the reified notion of the "black community" and the language of racial authenticity attendant to it. Because the black community idea is a mystification, it gives no solid standpoint from which to situate policies or political programs; nearly everything benefits someone, and debate then must revolve around which beneficiaries (or losers) most genuinely embody the mystified racial community. This problem posed no difficulty for nationalists, who could simply adapt opportunistically to the new regime and define black authenticity to fit the needs of the moment. Marxists, though by no means immune to opportunism, strained to develop a critique, but their efforts were short-circuited by the pattern of mystification and evasion that denied them purchase on their really existing political environment.

So expired the autonomous black radicalism spawned in the 1960s. Paroxysms continued here and there. The Communist Workers party's 1979 shootout with the Ku Klux Klan in Greensboro, North Carolina, for instance, was the culmination of a sectarian spiral that reached back through ALSC to a pan-Africanist and black power activism rooted in dynamic labor and poor people's organizations. Individuals and networks adjusted to the new regime and attempted to advance progressive interests within it; some simply were incorporated. Nevertheless, by the time Jimmy Carter was elected president no signs of institutionalized opposition were visible in black political life except on a sectarian fringe; all traces of alternatives to the incrementalist program of black officialdom had been expunged from Afro-American civic discourse. In 1977, for example, Mayor Maynard Jackson was able to fire 2,000 striking Atlanta sanitation workers, nearly all of them black, without significant dissent; he won reelection in the same year with more than three-fourths of the vote.[41] The victory of the new regime was so complete that in the early 1980s liberal social scientists ratified it in Whiggish accounts that represented the contemporary status quo as the precise goal toward which the previous generation of black activism had unfolded smoothly, willfully, and ineluctably. This fundamentally Orwellian victor's narrative canonized as the only thinkable reality—the teleological fulfillment of black political aspiration—what was in fact the outcome of contingency and contestation, thus denying space for radical critique in both present and past.

The purblindness that has omitted post–black power radicalism from accounts of the transition "from protest to politics" partly reflects a perspective that derives from either prior commitment to incrementalist politics or premises that apprehend black political activity in relation to a simple inclusion/exclusion axis. From either vantage point it seems natural and automatic that the mainstream, incrementalist agenda would become hegemonic upon removal of the fetters restricting regular, systemically conventional forms of political participation. Omission occurs also, however, because the radical tendencies that emerged from black power sensibilities were purely endogenous to black politics. Consonant with their black power origins, radicals actively sought to maintain a racially exclusive universe of critical political discourse; they generally neither pursued interaction with whites nor were centrally concerned with interracialism as an issue. Therefore, those strains of autonomous black radicalism were largely invisible to white observers, who as a rule do not attend closely to the machinations internal to black politics.

Although whites' failure to discern endogenous tendencies among Afro-Americans extends across the political spectrum, it specifically has undermined the left's ability to generate an appropriate strategic approach to black political activity. In fact, at least since the Students for a Democratic Society's 1969 proclamation of the Black Panther party as the "vanguard of the black revolution," two problematic features have organized white left discourse about Afro-American politics: (1) a reluctance to see black political interests and activity as internally differentiated in ways that are grounded in social structure and (2) a converging focus on willingness to align with whites as the primary criterion for making judgments about individuals or currents in black politics. The first problem stems from and reinforces the familiar assumption of the existence of an organic "black community." In white strategic discourse this notion does not only have the same evasive and counterproductive qualities as it does in black political rhetoric; it also implies that black life is opaque to those outside it. Knowledge, therefore, appears to require identifying individuals or groups who reflect the authentic mood, sentiments, will, or preferences of the reified community. This impulse places a premium on articulate black spokespersons to act as emissaries to the white left. By definition, such emissaries — even if they adopt a different posture — satisfy the interracialism criterion, and the operative premises and biases leave no space for interrogating the claims to authenticity or popular legitimacy that underlie the role of racial emissary.

This circumstance led to the irony that in the 1980s — thanks in part to the consolidation of the Democratic Socialists of America, which provided a national forum — the institutional apparatus of the white left began designating and projecting one black figure after another as the voice of black radical activism, long after the last embers of organized oppositional activism (and thus any possible justification for a claim to being rooted in a real social base) had been expunged. Compounding that irony is the fact that the designated Star Black Voices are themselves biographically the products of the era of demobilization and have no links to mundane black political activity now or in the past. Their prominence originates entirely from visibility in and appeal to the networks of the white academic left.

In the absence of independent knowledge or nuanced insight regarding black politics, the assessment of claims to authenticity ultimately relies on the appeal that a given claimant's persona or stance offers to white auditors. Therefore, critical evaluation tends toward designation of good and bad, true and false black leaders. This failing has, in one venue after another — as, for example, in the case of former New York City mayor, David Dinkins—underwritten a cycle of exaggerated estimation of the progressive inclinations and commitments of ordinary black mainstream politicians followed by crashing disillusionment when they fail to live up to inflated expectations. This cycle does not only impede practical strategic analysis; it has also greased the skids of this generation's "god that failed" rightward political slide. Treatment of blacks as bearers of a deeper humanity and higher morality opens to a rhetoric of betrayal, and the imagery shifts to venality and immorality—thus synecdochically justifying resistance to black political aspirations.

The costly and dangerous entailments of the white left's approach to black politics reached a national apotheosis in the knee-jerk embrace of Jesse Jackson's campaign of self-promotion. As I have argued elsewhere, in 1984 Jackson, who had been a consummate insider for at least a decade, proclaimed himself an outsider, parlaying a well-publicized southern speaking tour into a Potemkin movement. He traded precisely on gullibility about the organic black community to project himself as the literal embodiment of a popular black insurgency.[42]

The left generally—black and white—accepted Jackson's propaganda on face value, in part because of simple wish fulfillment but in part also out of opportunistic attempts to ride on his coattails. For some (both white and black) this meant pursuit of status or leverage within mainstream political institutions—either elective office or a "seat at the table" in arenas of elite negotiation, such as the various levels within the Democratic party apparatus. Some, skeptical about Jackson's political predilections, hoped to steer him leftward or to use association with his celebrity to establish popular bases for their own programs. Each of those motives underscored the left's fundamental weakness (and thereby the questionable utility of a national electoral mobilization intended as a show of strength).

Black activists' hopes to co-opt Jackson's initiative, furthermore, demonstrated the persistence of radicals' naiveté regarding their ability to manipulate mainstream politicians to advance their own ends. Having established himself as the supposed champion of a Rainbow Coalition of the generically "locked out," between 1984 and 1988 Jackson abandoned his outsider posture and tightened his links with black regular Democrats. He had pried open a space for himself, momentarily at least, as primus inter pares in the national black political elite and had attained a quasi-official status in the Democratic hierarchy, both mainly on the strength of his claim to represent a popular black constituency. This claim was legitimized by the enthusiastic assent of his activist supporters, who sought through his cachet to *create* just such a constituency.

As it had for the NBPA and ALSC in the mid-1970s, this gambit backfired for the Rainbow Coalition activists. Radicals hardly succeeded in using Jackson to gain access to a popular base; instead, he used and discarded them. Whereas his 1984 campaign had affronted prominent black mainstream politicians, who saw him as trying to muscle his way into their domain and were discomfited by the rhetoric of grassroots insurgency, by 1988 they dominated the campaign organization, using identification with Jackson as a buttress to their incumbency and ambitions. In several states, including New York and New Jersey, conflicts erupted between regular Democratic politicians and insurgent activists for control of the Rainbow Coalition's organizational apparatus.[43] In each case Jackson anointed the regular Democrats. It also became increasingly clear that the Rainbow Coalition, Inc.—insofar as it would exist at all—would function only as had Operation PUSH and before that Operation Breadbasket, as a pure extension of Jackson's personal objectives. And once his insider status was secured, he curtailed even the pretense of support for building a popularly based political organization.

Skepticism in the white left about the Jackson phenomenon revolved primarily around the extent to which he would attempt to fashion a multiracial constituency. There was no significant effort to undertake critique of Jackson's essentially personalistic appeal to black voters or to make sense of his role in black politics. From this perspective, for instance, Jackson's move between 1984 and 1988 boosted his progressive credentials because of his elaborate, if pro forma and symbolic, multiracialist gestures in the latter campaign, even though those gestures were crafted to project his image as a responsible insider. As black activists colluded in Jackson's claim to embody collective racial aspirations, white leftists contrived to represent his receipt of an average of less than 10 percent of white votes in meaningful Democratic primaries as evidence of substantial cross-racial support.[44]

The combination of opportunism and evasive romanticism that blocked critical evaluation of Jackson's enterprise also left both black and white insurgents without effective response to its denouement. After all the symbolic rhetoric, photo-ops with striking workers, and canned leftist position papers, Jackson bargained at the Democratic National Convention for an airplane to use in campaigning for nominee Michael Dukakis and payoffs for cronies—benefits even skimpier and more narrowly personal than the ornamental fruits of his brokerage in 1984. Between 1988 and 1994 he provided ample evidence of his self-aggrandizing and conservative agenda: the launch of a talk show career, the quixotic definition of statehood for the District of Columbia as the most important civil rights issue of our time, the "Shadow Senator" farce, his pouting refusal to commit to or dissent from any candidate in the 1992 Democratic nominating process, and worst of all, his proclamation that black criminality is the central problem in contemporary Afro-American life (the opportunistically revised version of the "most important civil rights issue"). Yet none of this has prompted reevalaution, by either whites or blacks, of the political consequences of Jackson's rise to prominence and the left's reaction to it. It is worthwhile to consider why.

In both of his campaigns radicals endorsed Jackson's rhetoric of hope and inspiration as a way to sidestep grappling with empirically dubious claims about his impact on black voter registration and turnout and his candidacy's electoral coattail effects. Each time they slid back and forth instrumentally between representing the initiative as a serious electoral campaign and representing it as a social movement, thus avoiding consideration of the extent to which it satisfied the practical warrants of either activity. Construing it as a social movement helped to dismiss the fact that Jackson never had a chance to win the Democratic nomination, much less the presidency. Pointing to his electoral aspirations—and the imperative to aggregate as many votes as possible—preempted concern about opportunistic alliances and the tendency to present slogans rather than a coherent political program. The result was that practical questions regarding goals and purpose remained unclarified.

In the process these evasions obscured the possibility that despite his constant allegations that the Democratic party takes black voters for granted, Jackson's campaign facilitated just such an outcome. Especially in 1988, when it was clear from the beginning that Jackson would have nearly unanimous black support, the other contenders for the nomination made only perfunctory appeals to black voters during the primaries. Without Jackson's presence in the field at least some of the other candidates may have courted black Democrats, if only to gain a comparative electoral advantage in the South. With the black primary vote—and that of the party's left wing as well—conceded to Jackson, however, the others could simply avoid addressing black interests until the convention, at which point the eventual winner could broker some concessions to Jackson in the name of Afro-American and progressive concerns. And I have noted already how paltry those actual concessions were. If only one or two of the early contenders had chosen to pursue black support actively, the effect might have altered the terms of the Democratic debate during the primaries and beyond. The result might still have been a Dukakis candidacy, but a different debate may have produced a more liberal, more combative Dukakis.

In this regard also, Jackson's campaign may well have strengthened the party's rightist faction, formalized as the Democratic Leadership Council in the aftermath of Walter Mondale's defeat.[45] From the DLC's position Jackson's activities were doubly useful. On the one hand, they highlighted blacks' (and in 1988 the left's) symbolic visibility as a demanding interest group in the party; to that extent Jackson inadvertently gave verisimilitude to the DLC's claim that the party suffered from being too closely identified with black interests. On the other hand, by concentrating black and leftist energies and affect in support of a candidacy that was not really in contention for the nomination, Jackson eased the rightward drift in the terms of debate among the real contenders. The DLC ideologues had been pushing unremittingly in that direction since Mondale's loss, mainly by propagating an image of winning conservative, suburban whites as the key to success in national politics. By separating the mobilization of black and leftist voters from the contest among the group of candidates out of which the nominee would actually emerge, Jackson effectively narrowed the electorate for which candidates actually competed in a way that exaggerated the significance of the DLC's targeted constituency. This enhanced the tactical rationality of tailoring appeals to the supposedly disaffected white "middle class."

From this perspective, Jackson's 1988 candidacy may have worked in support of the rightist Democrats' larger agenda even though his presence derailed the prospects of DLC standard-bearer Al Gore. The Democratic right had devised the Super Tuesday format as a cluster of southern primaries offering early competition for a large bloc of delegates. The idea was that Super Tuesday could provide a conservative contender with a strong head start that would at best generate a bandwagon effect or at least authenticate a rightward shift in the debate. This strategy, though, presumed the modal southern Democrat to be a white, typically male conservative. Either it thereby reflected ideological wish fulfillment by overlooking the fact that blacks make up a larger share of Democratic voters in the South than elsewhere, or its proponents imagined that Gore would be able to neutralize more liberal candidates' attractiveness to black voters with an updated version of southern Democrats' fish-fry politics — mobilizing state party networks to call in chips from black Democratic officials, giving payoffs to opinion leaders, making saccharine gestures of racial magnanimity (visiting black colleges and churches, standing at Martin Luther King Jr.'s gravesite, and so on). In any event, by garnering huge black majorities, Jackson ran at or near the top of the Super Tuesday field, diminishing Gore's luster and keeping him from stepping out from the pack. Gore's campaign soon fizzled, but in establishing — with the Jackson forces unintended assistance — a national Democratic discourse geared to court-ing suburban whites, the DLC camp won a victory for the longer term.

In fact, the two Jackson campaigns were arguably purely beneficial for the Democratic right. Jackson's insurgency maximized black visibility yet posed no genuine threat programmatically because at the same time it demobilized blacks' participation in the debate over the party's future both substantively and strate-gically. It demobilized black Democrats substantively by defining their interests solely in relation to Jackson's personal fortunes and strategically by funneling black action through his insider's style of brokerage politics. By 1992 the right-ist narrative had become nearly hegemonic in the Democratic party and in the society at large, thanks principally to its continual, virtually unchallenged repe-tition as fact by sympathetic journalists and academics.

Of course, the Jackson insurgency did not generate the DLC camp, which would have sought to stigmatize blacks and the left anyway. The critical prob-lem, however, is that Jackson's radical supporters reproduced the pattern of op-portunism and abstract purism that has consistently evaded any tough-minded analysis of the practical forces driving American politics and black politics in particular. As a result, they were unable to respond frankly and forthrightly to Jackson's increasingly crude, personalistic maneuverings after 1988. In acquiesc-ing to a frame that designates Jackson ascriptively as the embodiment of pro-gressive interests, leftists and black activists sacrificed the political distance that would give them a critical foundation from which to assess his behavior. Jack-son's oscillation between platitudinous abstractions and political insiderism, moreover, only meshed with and reinforced the combination of formalistic ide-ology and unprincipled pursuit of alliances with mainstream elites that had plagued black radicalism and undercut its critical capacities throughout the post-segregation era.

Failure to make nuanced distinctions among individuals and tendencies in-side the Democratic party, furthermore, has vitiated radicals' strategic thinking about the implications of the rightist Democrats' offensive. In 1992 some radi-cals were incapacitated by Jackson's new posture of coy aloofness. Some looked for a new candidate to reprise Jackson's performance as heroic outsider, tilting at windmills with Ralph Nader, Larry Agran, Jerry Brown, or even Ron Daniels, and some simply rejected the process with sweeping denunciations.

Certainly, by the time the 1992 Democratic field was set, there was no real left option; Kerry, Clinton, and Paul Tsongas all operated entirely within the new rightist conventions, and even the short-lived Tom Harkin candidacy — perhaps the last gasp of the party's labor-left wing — was ambivalent in practice if not rhetoric about catering to the supposed skittishness of the white middle class. But one factor contributing to the lack of credible Democratic options in the first place was that radicals had failed to contest the rightist narrative directly and clearly on its merits. Instead, by filtering their critique through the logic of Jackson's personal ambitions, they situated opposition in airy shibboleths and on the insider's terrain of positional warfare over delegate selection and appointment procedures and other internal party rules. This tack neither effectively challenged the DLC's line in the public realm nor provided a basis for mobilizing new constituencies in support of a leftist alternative.

In addition, with respect to black politics, activists' lengthy subordination to Jackson's agenda had substituted for an articulation of a critical, programmatic response to the burgeoning rightist vision; it seemed easier to rely on the evocative power of Jackson as racial symbol. Radicals were generally immobilized by Jackson's brooding inaction in 1992 and lost vital time in reacting to the Clinton juggernaut. Even longtime activists with independent political bases convinced themselves that they could not act in advance of Jackson. Some had become so wedded to the idea of a black candidacy as the medium for black participation in presidential politics that they were prepared to accept even Boll Weevil Virginia Governor Douglas Wilder as the racial charger and lapsed into confused demoralization when his effort was stillborn.

In this environment no challenge appeared when Bill Clinton's well-organized and well-connected forces swept through, remonstrating with black political elites to support their candidate without questions because his nomination was a fait accompli. The Clinton campaign also exploited a long-standing problem in black political life: the tendency to conflate descriptive representation and representation of substantive interests. By defining representation among campaign leadership and prospective appointments as the key shorthand expression of openness to black concerns, Clinton and his black supporters manipulated this tendency—which Jackson's insistent personalism had ensconced as the coin of *militant* black critique—to avoid confronting the material implications of his rightist "New Democrat" agenda for black Americans.

Considering a counterfactual may highlight the limits of the Jackson phenomenon more clearly. What forms could an effective left-insurgent Democratic candidacy have taken? In the first place, it would have had to proceed from an institutional base within the party's left wing and from a coherent, well-articulated programmatic agenda—not the whim of a random individual. Any such insurgency most likely would have little chance of actually winning the nomination; its objectives would have to be to gain specific programmatic concessions, to exert a leftward pull on political debate, and perhaps to strengthen and build progressive networks within the party and outside. And those objectives require relative clarity of political vision and concreteness of strategy. The focus would have to be on advancing a specific program or critique rather than an individual. The candidate-centered bias in American electoral politics creates openings to co-optation for which an insurgent movement would have to compensate by fastening the candidacy as much as possible to a concrete, specific agenda.

An effective insurgency also would have required a different candidate. Probably no black candidate could draw enough white votes either to affect the rhetorical frames shaping debate in the primaries or to present a serious force of delegates at the convention. But Jackson was an especially poor standard-bearer. He has few particularly leftist inclinations, and his entire political career prior to 1984 had been characterized by a personalistic opportunism that virtually guaranteed that he would make a separate deal for himself at the expense of whatever larger initiative of which he was nominally a part.

The ease and thoroughness of the DLC's success is an entailment of the evasive pattern of abstraction and opportunism that has plagued black radicalism since the early 1970s. Choices made, positions and actions taken or not taken — whether or not they result in programmatic victories — contribute to the shaping of subsequent political possibilities. The limits of the pragmatically reasonable and thinkable are set through contestation. By not confronting issues bearing on governance in a direct and concrete way, the styles of radicalism that developed from black power sensibility have consistently skirted the terrain most crucially defining the boundaries of possibility — the institutional apparatus of public authority, the state in a broad sense. Radicals left attentiveness to that field to mainstream politicians and public officials, whose incrementalist orientation (and class commitments) could not generate leverage against the forces that have striven — with steadily increasing boldness and credibility since the Nixon presidency — to shrink the horizon for progressive political action. The absence of a powerfully critical, egalitarian response has combined with mainstream elites' insiderism to stymie the cultivation of popular black opposition to the rightward propulsion of national policy discourse. The result has been failure to counter effectively the offensive of retrenchment and reaction at each step along the way — from Carter's assault on downwardly redistributive social spending in favor of a military buildup to Reagan's all-out attack on civil rights and the "social safety net" to the rise of the Democratic right. The consequences, moreover, are accretive. Each failure to slow or force significant modifications of the rightist programmatic and ideological agenda further narrows the scope for subsequent opposition as the retrograde vision becomes increasingly hegemonic. So by the 1990s even putatively leftist black pundits had come to accept embedding discussion of poverty and inequality within the fundamentally racist and sexist underclass rhetoric as a sine qua non of legitimacy in respectable civic discourse.

The historical arc of black radicalism in the post-segregation era is thus drenched in a bitter irony. The effort to maintain a transcendent, alternative vision that could not be corrupted or restricted by mundane politics actually helped to sustain a climate that increasingly limited the compass of credible black and left options.[46] And this environment, of course, fuels demobilization.

In this situation radicalism has retreated ever more hermetically into the university, and the unaddressed tendency to wish fulfillment has reached new extremes, so that oppositional politics becomes little more than a pose livening up the march through the tenure ranks. The context of desperation and utter defeat enveloping activist politics outside the academy has not only reinforced the retreat to the campus; it has also removed practical fetters on the compensatory imagination guiding the creation of intentionally oppositional academic discourses. In this context the notion of radicalism is increasingly removed from critique and substantive action directed toward altering entrenched patterns of subordination and inequality mediated through public policy. As it is disconnected from positive social action, radical imagery is also cut loose from standards of success or failure; it becomes a mere stance, the intellectual equivalent of a photo-op.

The characteristics of this dynamic are mainly crystallized in the turn to a rhetoric pivoting on an idea of "cultural politics." The discourse of cultural politics does not differentiate between public, collective activity explicitly challenging patterns of political and socioeconomic hierarchy and the typically surreptitious, often privatistic practices of "everyday resistance"—the mechanisms through which subordinates construct moments of dignity and autonomy and enhance their options *within* relations of oppression without attacking them head on. The failure to make any such distinction—or making and then eliding it—dramatizes the fate that befalls black radicalism's separation of abstract theorizing from concrete political action when academic hermeticism eliminates the imperative to think about identifying and mobilizing a popular constituency. Participating in youth fads (from zoot suits in the 1940s to hip-hop today), maintaining fraternal organizations, vesting hopes in prayer or root doctors, and even quilt making thus become indistinguishable from slave revolts, activism in Reconstruction governments, the Montgomery bus boycott, grassroots campaigns for voter registration, and labor union or welfare rights agitation as politically meaningful forms of "resistance."[47]

It is instructive in this regard that the cultural politics discourse gained currency simultaneously with the legitimation of Jackson's emotive rhetoric as an appropriate language of radical political critique. Both seek to overcome the troubling facts of popular demobilization and the disappearance of a palpable constituency for a radical program without confronting them, by redefining politics to diminish concern with such matters. Both exalt faith in things unseen over goal-oriented, public political debate and action. For Jackson, his symbolic identity as an embodiment of progressive aspirations is the mystical ingredient that resolves strategic problems and contradictions in the present. Cultural politics discourse, the Straussianism of the Benetton generation, rests on the premises that *nothing* apparent is real and that hidden meanings, whose Aesopian codes are intrinsically and forever inaccessible except to those versed in the mysteries of an esoteric interpretation, define the true essence of social phenomena. Both Jackson and rhetorists of cultural politics presume a nominalist view of politics in which changing an interpretation is the substance of changing the world. Jackson calls a press conference a social movement; theorists of cultural politics relabel manifest acquiescence as rebellion. Unsurprisingly, therefore, both elevate the purely gestural over the combative and purposive, obscuring that stance's fundamentally quietistic character with a rhetorical fog.

Conclusion

The collapse of popularly based radicalism in the 1970s underlies the failure of a critical politics to develop as a significant force, even in response to the Reagan and Bush years' heavy-handed assault on the interests of racial equality. The demise of that autonomous radical strain has had important and extensive consequences. For instance, the absence of a populist activism has eliminated a constraint on the incrementalist, demobilizing tendencies of systemic incorporation. To that extent, it has distorted the development of what might have been, as some thought, a functional division of labor or, what was more likely, a creative tension between the new black public officialdom and attentive black constituencies. That tension could well have broadened processes of interest articulation and differentiation in black politics and brought them into the realm of public debate.

Contrary to the communitarian reflex on which Afro-American political discourse has pivoted for a generation, the stimulation of overt interest-group dynamics—organized on the basis of neighborhood, class, gender, occupation, or other aspects of social status, as well as crosscutting issue publics and other coalitional activity—could enrich democratic participation by encouraging controversy among black Americans over the concrete, tangible implications of policy issues. A sharply focused civic discourse grounded on the interplay of specific, clearly articulated interests could feed political mobilization, both electoral and otherwise, by highlighting the human impact of government action and the stakes of political activity in general. Elaboration of a political discourse based explicitly on a consideration of the differential allocation of costs and benefits of public policy within an attentive, relatively mobilizable polity could also increase public officials' accountability to the black constituencies they purportedly represent. The existence of such a lively context of public debate also contributes to civic education, which could further reinforce popular participation and democratic accountability.

From this perspective, it certainly seems possible that systemic incorporation might have occurred on terms that embedded more seriously progressive vision and momentum in black politics than has been the case. Either because electoral processes may have produced individuals independently more attuned to progressive black agendas or because of the need to respond to popular pressure, one outcome could have been a stratum of mainstream politicians and officials at least marginally more inclined to press aggressively against the left boundaries of dominant policy streams and to use the visibility of office as a bully pulpit from which to help shape the contours of black action and discourse in a leftward direction.

A sophisticated, sharp, and popularly grounded progressive black presence in the national Democratic coalition also could have exerted a more effectively countervailing force against the "retreat from McGovernism" narrative and program as they developed from Carter onward. A coherent black response along social democratic lines could have helped both to discredit the conservative Democrats' initiative on substantive grounds and to galvanize a broader, class-based counterattack. A revealing irony of the period, by contrast, is that for all their proclamations that Afro-Americans held a "core" position among Democratic voters, black political elites made no real attempts—excepting Jackson's personalistic pseudomobilization—to activate that base to join the contest for the party's future.

Of course, the foregoing is speculative, as is any consideration of what might have been. Nevertheless, this alternative scenario offers a plausible example of what contemporary black politics could be. The keys to the generation of such a politics, now as then, include breaking with the mystification of an organic black community. Recognition that all black people are not affected in the same ways by public policy and government practice is central to the construction of a civic discourse that revolves tough-mindedly around determining who benefits and who loses from public action. That focus in turn is a precondition for the development of practical debate over the particular relations that should pertain between representatives and represented; it similarly informs discussion of the more general issue of the concrete conditions specifying, and the mechanisms for realizing, ideals of social justice and equality.

Breaking with the communitarian mythology also means rejecting a first person/third person rhetoric concerning black Americans' relation to the institutions of public authority. The perception of black people as passive recipients of the actions of a government fundamentally alien to them reflected a material reasonableness during most of the Jim Crow era; it has been superseded by full enfranchisement and systemic incorporation since passage of the initial Voting Rights Act. In fact, as the history of black mobilization for governance during Reconstruction shows, the segregation era marked a shift—expressing the realities of systematic expulsion from civic life—from a presumption that the Thirteenth, Fourteenth, and Fifteenth Amendments authenticated Afro-Americans' claims to equal proprietorship of American political institutions. In positing a reified "we," however, the black community formulation sets up "America"—and, therefore, official institutions—as a "they" to which blacks relate most authentically as a collectivity, not as individual citizens.

This orientation has several disturbing features. It implies that black Americans hold a status similar to that of members of a protectorate, that their very membership (not simply their voices) in the polity—unlike that of other citizens—is not directly conferred on individuals but is collective and mediated through representatives of the group. It also diminishes black officials' accountability to their constituents. Communitarian mythology exaggerates identification with black functionaries at the expense of the institutional functions they perform. Corrupt officials, for instance, frequently elude opprobrium for their depredations by elevating their racial status over the public trust they have violated; this gambit works precisely to the extent that black people accept a narrative that constructs them as apart from the polity owning the institutional processes that have been corrupted. Even short of actual corruption, by exhorting black citizens to put racial membership at odds with and above civic proprietorship, this view undermines the principle of accountability for actual performance. Instead, its characterization of the imperatives driving public institutions as extrinsic to black life defines support for racially descriptive representation, rather than the substantive, institutional results of that representation, as the focal point of black concern. Presumption of Afro-Americans' third-person connection to public institutions also, consonant with the implication of mediated group membership, yields *within* black political life a weak attachment to the principles of individual protection established in the Bill of Rights; these principles become dismissible as racially inauthentic.

Finally, this view underwrites and gives rhetorical support to proponents of agendas of resegregation. Proposals that the black American population be organized officially into the equivalent of Bantustans have gained currency among respectable white scholars—occasionally with the exemption from messy Bill of Rights protections, based on blacks' supposed pragmatic sense that social exigencies value order over civil liberties, held out as a particular virtue of such arrangements.[48] Intrinsically rightist self-help ideology is a product of this resistant strain of the Jim Crow mind-set. More blatant are current attempts to rehabilitate Booker T. Washington—whose stature and program were pure artifacts of the segregationist regime—as a model race leader, as well as efforts to reproduce modified versions of his role for our time.[49] From Jesse Jackson and Al Sharpton to William Julius Wilson to Cornel West and Henry Louis Gates Jr. to Louis Farrakhan, the posture of being the authentic racial voice unaccountable to any black constituency necessarily reprises Washington's role as collective racial proxy designated by white elites.

With regard to specific foci for political action that could support progressive mobilization, it is critical to transcend a simplistic inclusion/exclusion axis for strategic thinking, with respect to both positive program and critical responses to dominant initiatives. This implies recognition that vigorous pursuit of an affirmative action and set-aside agenda is necessary but not sufficient for advancing the interests of racial democracy. Progressives' strategic political thinking in black politics should be based more than it is on public policy and government institutions, with specific attention given to the actual and potential effects of each on black Americans. Examples of pertinent issues and policy areas are the relation of government action to deindustrialization and its roots in global capitalist reorganization; the racially and intraracially differential impact of federal and local housing, transportation, redevelopment, and revenue (for example, the racially redistributive features of tax codes) policy; and the racist, draconian, and anti–civil libertarian programmatic rhetoric and presumptions undergirding the criminal justice system. Similarly important initiatives could include the fight against privatization of public services (which makes lines of accountability more diffuse and disproportionately lowers minority employment and income); the fight for equalization of school funding; the stimulation of open discussion, where ap-

propriate, of metropolitan tax-base sharing and the metropolitanization of functions on an equitable basis, in ways that ensure minority constituents' capacities
to participate effectively by electing representatives of their choice.

It is also important to keep in mind in this regard that the interests of constituents and incumbents are not always identical on issues like reapportionment
and packing of legislative districts. Progressives' mandate should be to expand
the electorate, an objective in which incumbents often have little interest. In addition, efforts to register new voters have begun to yield diminishing returns in
recent years, suggesting that conventional methods may have nearly exhausted
the population of the unregistered who might be added to the rolls with relative
ease. This circumstance has prompted voting rights advocates to push for changes
in voting law to facilitate reaching more-alienated and more-marginalized populations; it also has reinforced an increasing focus on revising electoral systems
and districts to enhance the effectiveness of the existing pool of minority voters.
Action on both those fronts is important, though resistance to both may be stiff-
ening in courts and legislatures. There are limits to which the engineering of jurisdictions and voting systems can be taken, particularly since at this point pro-
portional representation seems well beyond the scope of public imagination. And
the state legislative politics accompanying the reapportionment process as it bears
on this turn in the voting rights agenda has produced questionable alliances between urban minorities and suburban white Republicans who trade safe seats for
one another, a situation that does not clearly produce net gains — and may even
result in net political losses — for black constituents. As occasional cases like
Harold Washington's and David Dinkins's initial mayoral campaigns have shown,
however, aggressive political insurgencies based on popular agendas can substantially assist in reaching and mobilizing new voters. The same effect can derive from aggressive, popularly based campaigns against manifest evils such as
David Duke's two statewide Louisiana campaigns and similar contests against
racist reactionaries in Alabama and elsewhere.[50]

Another effect of dispensing with the communitarian mythological frame
would be an emphasis on the need to identify constituencies to be targeted and
cultivated. In a differentiated population, generic appeals to "black people" will
often ring hollow; even when things affect many distinct black social strata, they
are likely to do so in at least somewhat different ways, and sometimes impacts
on different strata will be diametrically opposed. Proponents of left agendas, therefore, need to be clear about the array of black interests and especially about which
of those are strategically critical.

In relation to a political strategy focused on issues of policy and governance, black academic radicals' romance of inner-city youth seems mistaken. Although politicizing young people is certainly important, making them the central point of strategic discourse amounts to leading from a position of weakness. They are among the most alienated and least connected segments of the black population, with the least practical understanding of how the world works, the thinnest commitments, the greatest volatility, and the most transient social status. Their energy and openness to experimentation only partially offset these limitations.

Current ruminations on the political significance of youth culture, in fact, forget that historically the relation between popular culture and politics has been just the reverse of present assumptions. In the 1960s, for instance, political content was attached to pop songs whose lyrics were at best ambiguous in that regard. "Respect," "A Change Is Gonna Come," "Big Boss Man," and others that became politically salient were appropriated and vested with political meanings by an active, dynamic, and contentious movement. Still others, like the Impressions' "Keep On Pushin'" and "Movin' On Up," *were inspired by* a climate of dynamic activism. Eventually, Marvin Gaye and even otherwise ordinary purveyors of rhythm and blues were occasionally moved to attack explicitly political themes, but not until fairly late in the day of activism. Not surprisingly, the flood of pop songs self-consciously inflected with black power rhetoric did not appear until well into the 1970s, after the insurgency had dissipated; the owl of the culture industry flies only at dusk, when no relevant market share is likely to take umbrage at the message.

A more efficacious strategy would center on segments of the population that are already politically attentive, people who presume efficacy in political action. To that extent, I submit, a more rational and effective course would be to undertake a struggle for the hearts and minds of the black working and lower middle classes who vote and attend to political affairs, especially union members; after all, the labor movement is the one domain where the working class, black or otherwise, is organized politically as a class. These are also in a way the most centrally placed strata of the Afro-American population. They overlap — through family, friendship and neighborhood networks, as well as in their own life courses — the ranks of the unemployed and recipients of those forms of public assistance designated for the poor. These are also the people who actively reproduce the character of black political discourse by trying to make sense of the world and constructing their own interests within the inadequate and self-defeating frames of underclass and self-help rhetoric, with which they are bombarded and on which they confer legitimacy by use in the absence of better alternatives. A crucial objective must be to provide such alternatives.

Similarly, a practical left agenda might profitably include the cultivation of such progressive or even guild consciousness as can be identified among the stratum of minority public functionaries and service providers. This is perhaps the most politically sophisticated element of the Afro-American population, the most knowledgeable regarding the real workings of political institutions. Yet they also by and large operate without an adequate alternative to the reactionary and victim-blaming frames that presently prevail. Many of them, of course, do so quite happily and will not be susceptible to left critique; the stratum is, after all, petit bourgeois. Some fraction of them, perhaps mainly among staff-level professionals, however, are committed to ideals of public service and use of government for progressively redistributive purposes. Their pragmatic understanding of government and policy processes could also significantly benefit the elaboration of a credible, systematic, and practicable left program. One approach to undercutting the effects of the current rightist hegemony among them, moreover, might be to attempt to organize coalitions of service providers and constituents of their institutions' services.[51] It should prove less difficult to reach alienated young people in an adult environment characterized by political debate and mobilization.

In any event, an approach of this sort provides the best possibility for transcending a simplistic politics that offers as critical touchstones only an abstract, disembodied racism or the victim-blaming self-help line. "Racism" has become too often an empty reification, an alternative to unraveling the complex, frequently indirect processes through which racial inequality is reproduced. Racial stratification is not enacted simply in the indignity of a black professor's inability to get a cab in Manhattan or being mistaken for a parking lot attendant; in discrimination in access to employment, business loans, mortgages and rental housing, or consumer discounts; nor even in the demonization of black and brown poor people, and the police terror routinely visited upon minority citizens. These problems—from the more petty to the more grave—must be attacked, of course. But racial inequality is also built into the "natural" logic of labor and real estate markets; it inheres, for example, in culturally constructed and politically enforced notions of the appropriate prices for different units of labor power (consider the relation between the retreat from social support and liberals' endorsement of self-help ideology for the poor, on the one hand, and the availability of "affordable" domestic labor for socially liberal yuppies on the other, as well as the racialized sophistries of "human capital" theory) and in the ways that parcels of land are valorized.[52] Racial inequality has been a central organizing premise of federal, state, and local public policy for at least a century, as housing, development, tax, defense, and social welfare policy making almost unfailingly have reflected its warrants.

The deeper structures of racial stratification are not accessible to the hortatory *and* demobilizing style of insider negotiation and communitarian mythology around which black political activity has been organized. What is required is the aggressive mobilization of black citizens to pursue specific interests in concert with the articulation of a larger programmatic agenda centered in the use of public power — the state apparatus — to realize and enforce concrete visions of social justice. This in turn requires resuscitation of a climate of popular debate in black politics, proceeding from an assumption of civic entitlement and ownership of the society's public institutions.

This is the combined opportunity and challenge presented by the successes of the civil rights movement; it has so far, as I have argued here, not been met in black politics. Especially now, as the forces of horrible reaction — both black and white[53] — gather steam once again precisely around such premises, it is vitally important to reject emphatically all explicit or tacit claims that black Americans are somehow citizens with an asterisk. Rejection must proceed not only by argument but most of all through the matter-of-fact acting out of black citizenship — through struggling, that is, to use and shape public institutions to advance black interests.

1995 and 1999

Part II

5. A Critique of Neoprogressivism in Theorizing about Local Development Policy
A Case from Atlanta

Local development policy is typically "promulgated through highly centralized decision-making processes involving prestigious businessmen and professionals," as Paul Peterson observes. "Conflict within the city," he notes further, "tends to be minimal, decision-making processes tend to be closed until the project is about to be consummated, local support is broad and continuous, and, if any group objects, that group is unlikely to gain much support."[1] That those processes are "closed" and "highly centralized" is not particularly inconsistent with democratic interests, in Peterson's view, because development — that is, any activity that enhances the municipality's revenue potential — is an interest of the city as a whole. In fact, it is fortunate that "local politics weakens the capacity for mass pressures" because by "keeping mass involvement at the local level to a minimum, serious pressures for policies contrary to the economic interests of cities are avoided."[2] Once popular intervention is circumvented, policy can be made through "informal channels" in which "the political resources that count are technical expertise, the power of persuasion, and the capacity to reason soundly."[3] Nor should we fret that this informalization and centralization of development policy either fuels inequitable concentrations of privilege or rationalizes the self-interested agendas of local power structures, for Peterson cautions:

> When developmental policies are considered, attempts to ascertain the power of one or another individual or group are probably pointless if not misleading. In this policy arena the city as a whole has an interest that needs to be protected and enhanced. Policies of benefit to the city contribute to the prosperity of all residents. Downtown business benefits, but so do laborers desiring higher wages, homeowners hoping house values will rise, the unemployed seeking new jobs, and politicians aiming for reelection. Those who seem to have "power" over de-

velopmental policies are those who do the most to secure these benefits for all members of the city.[4]

Therefore, the closed character of development-policy processes, even though its most proximate underpinnings are the structural and systemic factors that screen out avenues for popular participation, is an expression, he suggests, of the consensual basis on which development policy rests.[5] Indeed, "the frequency with which responsibility for developmental policy is granted to groups and entities outside the mainstream of local politics" itself illustrates the existence of a "consensual politics of development";[6] because development is a collective interest, its actualization via policy and program need not be subjected to public scrutiny and debate and is a matter for technical concern only.

Yet despite the fact that all the pieces fit neatly together, the picture rings somehow incomplete if not plainly false. To those students and citizens who have repeatedly seen development policy impose suffering and hardship on certain groups in the polity, notions of a consensual or collective city interest seem to be abstractions to a vantage point from which those very real victims blend into the background. Most often when he trumpets the unitary interest in development, Peterson himself seems not to notice those victims, although his tendency to choose the agentless passive voice at critical junctures in his account—for example, adverse popular pressures "are avoided"; responsibility "is granted to groups and entities outside the mainstream of local politics"—raises suspicions. However, in citing the virtues of minimizing popular involvement, he does acknowledge, almost in passing, that "it is the interests of the disadvantaged which consistently come into conflict with economically productive policies."[7] By denying the disadvantaged the opportunity to intervene, the local political system permits the articulation of development policy that realizes the interest of the city "as a whole."

When viewed through the lens of the historian of ideologies, Peterson's attempt to define a "city interest" exhibits a certain quaintness. It harks back to an earlier period when progressivist political science affirmed, perhaps more ingenuously than now, the prosperous burgher's self-congratulation by equating preservation and expansion of his prosperity and cultural preferences with the public interest; so also does Peterson's view that endorses systematically induced limitations on popular participation because they provide space for disinterested, public-regarding elites to make rational development policy in the interest of the whole. That view rings with echoes of the various "democratic distemper" theories and similar hoary rationalizations of entrenched privilege. Other students of urban politics have disputed Peterson's contention that development policy is free—even in principle—from the self-interested, conflictual processes that he would consign to the "allocational" realm. His analytical distinction of developmental and allocational policy processes, that is, collapses as it slouches toward the empirical world.[8]

A market-rationality model of local development activity breaks down in part because even in the most objectivistic view imaginable, it is unlikely that there will always be only one clear direction in which to realize the "city interest." When there are more than one course in contention, choices must be made, and the basis for choice inevitably includes not only calculations of abstract market rationality but also estimations of political feasibility. The latter of course entails, inter alia, accounting for which interests in the city can be mobilized on behalf of a given policy direction or given project and which must be isolated or neutralized. To that extent an allocational element is woven into the texture of development activity very early in the game, and that allocational element both undermines the premise that development policy is fashioned above the fray of political conflict and implies that development is indeed a coalitional activity. Therefore, what Peterson sees as a consensus might just as probably reflect only the hegemonic position of a durable coalition.[9] In that light, the "city interest" that exhausts itself in facilitating and realizing development might be simply an "interest" imposed by a dominant political-economic elite and may no more express intrinsic rationality than the divine right of kings truly expressed natural law.

This problem with Peterson's account grows in prominence with any increase in the proportion of the habitually "disadvantaged" among the city's population because by his own admission theirs are the interests that conflict most sharply with "economically productive" policy. The larger their cohort in the polity, the greater the strain on the premise that either a transcendent ideal or a de facto consensus legitimizes the pursuit of development as paramount for the city's policy agenda. Only an Orwellian logic can support an argument that a policy decision that imposes substantial net costs (ranging from physical displacement to the diversion of scarce budgetary resources) on a large segment of a city's population and that is made without its participation somehow expresses the municipal interest. (This reminds us of a Brazilian finance minister, General Garrastazu Medici, who in the late 1960s observed—proudly and with no sense of irony—after several years of his junta's draconian economic policy, that "the economy is doing fine; of course, the people aren't.") Yet precisely such a logic currently grounds most public discussion of urban development, and often it is applied, apparently as in Peterson's case, with the very best intentions.

Not only is that logic normatively unsatisfactory, but it cannot give an adequate response to a question that has very important implications for democracy and for political-economic equity in cities: How can local development policy proceed in a way that systematically disadvantages certain groups in the municipality but that at the same time produces little political challenge or conflict? To respond that discrete disadvantage melts away into collective advantage is a mystification; to respond that there is no conflict because there is consensus offers only the empty truism of tautology.

A path to more fruitful answers to that question, I believe, entails the illumination of the ways in which actual development coalitions legitimize policies, as well as policy courses, that have a broadly adverse popular impact. Because it is close to nature, as it were, this path avoids broad abstractions, such as the notion of a unitary city interest. Furthermore, it takes the existence of consensus as a starting point for the investigation of the political dynamics surrounding development policy rather than as a post factum defense for the premise of unitary interest or as a justification for the lack of popular accountability in development politics. Examination of the mechanisms through which coalitions are formed and consensus is created on behalf of a development agenda restores a sense of the political to the discussion of local development activity, a consequence that must by definition be salutary to political scientists. Moreover, that restoration speaks to the intellectual usefulness of one of the several approaches that presently vie for proprietorship of the rubric "political economy." Most of all, however, restoring the political reminds us that even within constraint in the urban polity a span for choice does exist and that how those choices are made and by whom says much about the character of democracy in our society.

In what follows, I shall examine an instance of coalition and consensus formation in a policy context characterized by a clear pattern that concentrates the benefits on certain groups and the costs on certain others — namely, Atlanta during the 1970s, during Maynard Jackson's regime. The centerpiece of this examination is the question: How did Mayor Jackson galvanize enough support and quiescence among the black electorate to cement blacks into the pro-development coalition despite the fact that the black community did not figure into the list of real beneficiaries? Answering that question, of course, requires attending to structural and ideological characteristics of the local political culture, as well as of its prevailing concatenation of political forces and interests, as they impinge on development policy. This focus can yield an account of the anomaly of systematic disadvantagement that does not produce challenge or conflict. In addition, the Jackson administration is an excellent case for purposes of illustration in at least two respects: It was a black administration, and it reigned in Atlanta.

In few settings are the disparities between developmental and popular interests likely to be sharper than in a municipality governed by a black administration. For at least three reasons those disparities are thrown into greatest relief when a black regime governs: First, as I demonstrate in chapter 3 in this volume, black administrations—by which I mean regimes that are led by blacks and that conform to Peter Eisinger's definition of "ethnoracial political transition"[10]—are more likely than not to come to power in cities characterized by general economic decline and comparatively high rates of economic privation among the citizenry.[11] Second, historically the social costs associated with development activity have been more likely to fall on blacks and other nonwhites than on other groups in the polity.[12] Third, because of the nature of its core electoral constituency, the black administration is more likely than others to associate itself with an aggressively egalitarian rhetoric; moreover, representatives of black regimes often have their roots in activist, protest politics and therefore embody an imagery of antagonism toward entrenched elites, even beyond the assertiveness that is typical of other displacing elites.[13]

While the black administration highlights the tension between electoral and development constituencies, Atlanta is perhaps the archetype of the hegemony of development elites in local politics. There is no need to rehearse the central place that Atlanta has held during three decades of debate among urbanists and power-structure theorists. In addition to being a much-studied city, it is also one whose political culture has long been characterized by a pandemic civic boosterism that champions unfettered development as the engine and emblem of progress.[14] The path of that engine, moreover, throughout the period of the "Atlanta miracle" has been such as to concentrate the costs of "progress" repeatedly on the city's quiescent black citizenry.[15] Empowerment of the Jackson regime in that context, as the symbol of a newly powerful black political voice, raised the clear specter of sharp potential conflict over development policy.

Maynard Jackson's first two terms (1974–1982) as Atlanta's mayor were shaped to a considerable degree by a stormy relationship with the city's "business community"—principally the leadership of the Metro Atlanta Chamber of Commerce and Central Atlanta Progress—a relationship that was at the same time predictable and anomalous. Jackson's administration was dogged throughout his tenure with charges of being either overtly antibusiness or at least suspiciously inattentive to the business community's needs and interests. At the same time, however, no major development initiative that was undertaken during those eight years failed to elicit his enthusiastic support. Despite the absence of any concrete evidence of antagonism, however, the charges persisted, recycled regularly through the editorial pages of the *Atlanta Constitution* (and the *Atlanta Journal,* its afternoon version), which can be described with little rhetorical excess as the Chamber of Commerce's chief ideological organ. In fact, Jackson's alleged hostility to business became a stigma from which his designated successor, Andrew Young, has striven mightily to absolve himself.[16]

In part, the perception that Jackson was not sufficiently responsive to business interests is simply an artifact of the process of "ethnoracial transition" and displacement. Business elites in Atlanta had governed the city directly for at least a generation, and both scholarship and local lore agree that City Hall and official governmental institutions were often less important as linkages in the public-policy process than were such private, voluntary associations as the Capital City Club, the Commerce Club, the Piedmont Driving Club, and of course the Chamber of Commerce itself.[17] It was not so much that political elites acquiesced to the desires of business elites or even that they shared the latter's interests and outlook. Rather, the political elites and the business elites were the same; the city's political leadership was designated by the business elite from within its own ranks, as is attested by the memoirs of Ivan Allen, the mayor who is most identified with the incorporation of racial progressivism into the city's sparkling New South image.[18] The election of any black mayor, therefore, would have increased the degree of inconvenience suffered by elites, if only by forcing them to venture into City Hall to conduct those of their affairs that involved the public sector. Having to accommodate those inconveniences combined with an overreaction to Jackson's early efforts "to do for blacks" to create an impression, however unfairly, that Jackson was hostile to business interests. Eisinger has observed that this reaction is a typical "response of a new minority uncertain of its position in the new order."[19]

Jackson's problems with those who spoke for the business community were also fueled by the latter's distaste for elements of Jackson's personality and political style. Ironically, the personal characteristics that members of the business elite found distasteful were closely related to those that had made Jackson more attractive to the voters than his more experienced black opponent, State Senator Leroy Johnson, in 1973. Jackson's initial mayoral candidacy was supported by an impressive list of business and community notables, including the chairmen of the boards of the Coca-Cola Company and two of the largest banks and John Portman, the Atlanta-based architect and developer, as well as the men who later would become the first two black presidents of the Chamber of Commerce.[20] Among those members of the business elite who accepted the inevitability of the transition to black political prominence (although acceptance was by no means unanimous),[21] Jackson was the preferred candidate partly because of his youthful, energetic demeanor, his articulateness, and his social polish.

As Mack Jones has observed, racial transition in Atlanta "coincided with the plans of the business and commercial elite [to build] a series of modern luxury hotels, a modern sports complex, a sprawling convention center, a new airport and/or expand the existing one, and a billion dollar rapid transit system."[22] Those capital projects were pieces of a development strategy that was aimed at exploiting the city's "natural" advantage as a regional transportation center by enhancing the city's attractiveness to the paperwork industry (finance, insurance, real estate, communications, and so on) and by competing more aggressively for the convention and trade-show market. This strategy entailed selling Atlanta as "the next great international city."[23] In that context the coming of black political power could be turned into a benefit, especially if its inevitability were acknowledged anyway, by incorporating it into the marketing image of the progressive "New York of the South," "cultural center of the Southeast," New South "international" city.[24] Jackson's smooth, urbane style certainly was better suited to such a campaign than was Johnson's; the state senator was more "down home" in both idiom and demeanor and therefore was more likely to evoke an image of an earlier New South, no longer in vogue — namely, the one that was associated with such unpleasantnesses as Jim Crow, Ku Kluxism, and subterranean instability.

The problem, however, was that the very qualities of urbanity, articulateness, and polish that made Jackson an attractive choice to be the city's first black mayor also, as has been the case ever since W. E. B. Du Bois, led him to succumb to the disagreeable habit of mind that in earlier days had been known as the assumption of "social equality." Therefore, Jackson was inclined to insist that his office of mayoralty be accorded the respect and deference to which it was formally entitled. This in turn meant that he was inclined to insist that his suitors come to City Hall to meet in his office and to ask for his support, rather than simply to inform him of their needs and assume his compliance. This posture was a shocking contrast to the long-standing norms of pubic-private interaction in Atlanta, and the added racial dimension to the shock led to charges that Jackson was "arrogant."[25] Similarly, his propensity to make his own patronage appointments and his attempts to give previously marginal groups representation in his administration fueled charges, which are commonly made against black (or populist) mayors, that he was a "poor administrator," that his regime suffered from "bad management" and "inept" appointments.[26]

Despite the rhetorical tempest, Jackson's record gives no reason to suspect that he ever would have considered breaking the long-standing public-private marriage that defined Atlanta's development policy. He unhesitatingly supported the implementation of the major development initiatives that his administration had inherited—such as the construction of the Metro Atlanta Rapid Transit Authority (MARTA) rapid-transit system, the Bedford-Pine Urban-Redevelopment Project (a slum clearance and redevelopment project in the urban-renewal mold), and airport expansion—and he was an avid proponent of the general framework for downtown development and revitalization. Indeed, even when Jackson sought, during his second term, to concentrate his energies on the problems of poverty and unemployment in Atlanta, his disposition was to define those problems in ways that conformed to the agendas of development interests. When, beginning in 1978 and continuing through the rest of his tenure, the annual Comprehensive Development Plan adopted unemployment as the city's principal concern, the administration's strategic thrust derived from the familiar premise that a rising tide lifts all boats. Thus, City Hall's intervention on behalf of the poor and the unemployed was centered in the economic development unit of the Department of Budget and Planning, the Mayor's Office of Economic Development, the economic development unit of the Bureau of Housing and Physical Development (BHPD) in the Department of Community and Human Development, and the newly formed public-private Atlanta Economic Development Corporation. Each of those agencies, except for the BHPD unit, had been formed specifically to anticipate and respond to the needs of large private developers. Not surprisingly, therefore, the Community Economic Development Strategy that they formulated to address the needs of the dispossessed recommended that greater proportions of Community Development Block Grant funds be shifted from the direct provision of social services to infrastructural and fiscal support for private development, both within and outside the Community Development Impact Area.[27]

Therein lies the means through which the Jackson administration reconciled the interests of the black citizenry with the business elite's development agenda—that is, by defining the latter as the essential context for fulfillment of the former. On no issue was Jackson's reliance on this approach more pronounced than on the controversy over airport expansion and construction.

Momentum for somehow expanding Atlanta's airport facilities preceded Jackson's mayoralty. In one form or another, the discussion of expansion dates from as early as 1968.[28] By 1973 a consensus had formed among the significant interests — the airlines, led by Delta, whose home base is Atlanta; the Federal Aviation Administration (FAA); city officials; local developers; and of course the Chamber of Commerce — that some measures needed to be taken soon to enlarge the airport's capacity. When Maynard Jackson was inaugurated in January 1974, the issue that confronted him was not whether some airport-development project should be undertaken but whether that project should be an expansion of capacity at the current airport site in Clayton County or the construction of a second airport.[29]

The airlines, which would have to approve any proposed expansion, for the most part were cautious about endorsing either of the options; they generally maintained a low profile in the debate, although Delta and Eastern dropped early hints that they might lean toward the construction of a second airport north of the city.[30] Developers, though, were not so much given to temporizing, and Tom Cousins — the developer of the Omni Complex and the World Congress Center in the old railroad gulch in the southwest central business district (CBD) — took the initiative by putting together a partnership to acquire a 48,000-acre tract approximately thirty-five miles northwest of the city in Paulding and Polk counties, with the understanding that part of the tract would be available as a possible airport site.[31] Less than two months later, in September 1973, the FAA gave encouragement to the proponents of a second airport by exhorting the city to begin the project within five years. However, the Paulding-Polk site was not the only contender; Sam Massell's administration had paid more than $5 million two years earlier for a 10,030-acre site in Dawson County to Atlanta's north; and a location in Henry County, to the city's south, was a third, albeit less favored, possibility.[32] The FAA and the Atlanta Regional Commission (ARC), the A-95 clearing house for the region, therefore undertook a study to determine the best location for a new airport, though, as we shall see, this study itself was to become a source of considerable controversy.

By the time Jackson assumed office, the environment of municipal governance included a consensus among significant elites that a major commitment of new public resources to Atlanta's airport capacity was a pressing item on the city's agenda, and the weight of opinion tilted toward the construction of a second airport to the north. Shortly before his inauguration the lame-duck Board of Aldermen took a two-phase option — a token $1 for the first three months and roughly $250,000 to secure the parcel for the next seven months — on 30,000 acres of Cousins's Paulding-Polk site. The new mayor was in the position, therefore, of having either to carve out his own position from within a very tightly constrained policy context or to break altogether from a nearly unanimous consensus of significant elites, among them many of his own supporters.

Though the concentration of elite support on behalf of airport construction would exert pressure on the mayor to "go with the flow," he was at the same time under pressure to deliver signs of good faith to his predominantly black electoral constituency. This pressure stemmed from at least two sources: First, like other black candidates in electoral contests auguring racial transition, Jackson had been packaged for black voters as a symbol of racial aspirations, a legatee of the civil rights movement. This symbolic aspect of his candidacy had become increasingly prominent as his opponent in the runoff, incumbent Sam Massell, opted for a scarcely veiled racist appeal to white voters to "save" the city from black rule.[33] A second source of pressure was more concrete. Police brutality had become so flagrant in the black community that Jackson had had to pledge that he would fire the incumbent chief of police, John Inman, to assure the heavy black turnout that Jackson needed in order to win. For reasons that need not be given in detail here,[34] however, Jackson found removing Chief Inman more difficult than he had anticipated; as a result, very early in his first term some of his less patient black constituents began publicly to question Jackson's commitment to the black electorate. In that environment the mayor needed to find some "black" position to take in regard to the airport issue, particularly as the controversy over alternative locations intensified.

Jackson found his "black" position in a strong endorsement of the principle of a second airport, coupled with an increasingly firm and vocal preference for the Henry County site on the southeastern fringe of the standard metropolitan statistical area (SMSA). This posture was shared by John Portman, who, like the mayor, argued that a northwestern location would exacerbate an already extant tendency toward an uneven concentration of development on the city's north side. This tendency, they observed, threatened to drain Atlanta's downtown toward the northern suburbs. For Portman this position became enmeshed with his running rivalry with Cousins, and it created considerable tension as their version of Maoists' "two-line struggle" spilled over into the politburo of Central Atlanta Progress.[35] For Jackson, advocacy of the Henry County location was also attractive because Atlanta's population distribution is such that blacks live primarily, if not overwhelmingly, in the city's southern quadrants. Even black suburbanization, which increased considerably during the 1970s and the early 1980s, has largely reproduced black enclaves in the southern half of Dekalb County and in nearby suburbs south of the city in Fulton County. On that basis, Mayor Jackson sought to tie black interests to the Henry County site by virtue of his claim that the construction of a second airport there would stimulate development on the city's south side and would thereby yield material benefits for Atlanta's black community.[36]

In fact, there was little reason to believe that a Henry County airport, which would have been nearly as far away from the city as the proposed north-side location, would have had any direct development impact on the communities in which black Atlantans lived. Nor would it have opened opportunities for black entrepreneurs that would not have been equally available at other sites. Indeed, ancillary development impact on black communities would have been most, but still not very, likely from the third option — namely, the expansion of capacity at the existing Clayton County location. However, when an unexpected turn of events returned that option to the agenda, the mayor vigorously opposed it.

To everyone's surprise, the preliminary report of the ARC's staff, which was completed in the spring of 1975 as the two lines on the second airport sharpened, indicated that there was no need for an additional airport after all. Instead, the draft recommended that the existing facilities be expanded and upgraded. Delta, which had long since become a vocal advocate of the Paulding-Polk site, attacked the report and, invoking support from the other airlines and from the Chamber of Commerce, urged discarding the recommendation and proceeding with construction plans. The city's finance commissioner, who was virtually autonomous under the new charter and was the chamber's principal representative in the municipal executive department, followed suit.[37] Shortly thereafter, the ARC overturned the staff report and recommended that a second airport be constructed northwest of the city. The decision to overturn the staff report apparently was influenced by lobbying from Mayor Jackson and his chief black ally on the city council.[38] Although the mayor expressed his continuing preference for a southeastern site, it seemed that he was committed first of all to the idea of a second airport. Then, two months later, shortly after City Hall had announced its intention to purchase the Paulding-Polk site for $9.5 million, the ARC reversed itself again and canceled its earlier recommendation of that site. The mayor decried this last reversal as a "setback for Atlanta" and reiterated his commitment to a second airport, even in the northwestern location.[39] Nevertheless, fed in part by antiairport protest from Paulding citizens' groups, the ARC's decision that recommendations concerning the second airport lay outside the commission's seven-county mandate effectively killed off the second-airport option by blocking access to federal funds. The airlines, as well, apparently got tired of the bickering and contented themselves with the construction of a huge new terminal close to the existing Clayton County location.

For his part, Mayor Jackson succeeded in defining the issues at stake in the airport construction controversy in a way that identified his black electoral constituency's interests with one pole of a debate over options within a development policy agenda that actually had little bearing on that constituency. To that extent he succeeded in neutralizing potential black opposition that might have been transferred from the parallel conflict over the reorganization of the city's Public Safety Department, a conflict that pitted the chamber-centered elite directly against the black community.[40] At the same time, he succeeded in assuring that elite that despite his combativeness over the right to control his own administrative public safety appointments, he could be counted on as a team player with respect to the chamber-endorsed development agenda and furthermore could help to cement black support. Finally, he succeeded even in the failure of the second-airport plan, because the decision to build a new terminal next to the existing one in the near-southern SMSA enabled him to claim a partial victory for his south-side preference. Those successes, though, were soon to be lost in the acrimony that resulted when the mayor sought to intervene in the development agenda by officially factoring a black-claimant status into the allocational component of the airport construction project.[41]

In concert with the city's new and widely noted Finley Ordinance (named for its author, Councilman Morris Finley), which laid out extensive guidelines to enforce minority participation in municipal contracts, Mayor Jackson announced that he would aggressively seek to involve minority-owned firms in all contractual phases of the airport construction project. This plan quickly came to be known by one of its components—the "joint venture" provision that called for nonminority contractors to form limited joint venture partnerships with minority-owned firms in order to receive special consideration in the competitive bidding process. That proposal generated almost unanimous opposition from the business elite. For months the *Constitution* railed editorially and otherwise against the administration's affirmative action and contract compliance efforts, particularly as they intersected the airport construction project. Awards and near-awards of a few dubious contracts to old cronies fueled the fires of opposition. The generally articulated oppositional line was that the construction of the new terminal was too important to be subjected to a "social experiment," no matter how noble. Somewhat more shrill voices charged "reverse racism" and unnatural governmental interference in the activities of firms.

As the lines of confrontation tightened, the mayor opted, first, to stand his ground by emphatically reiterating his rhetorical commitment to the joint venture strategy and to the principle of favoring firms that had substantial minority representation. Consequently, he found himself, upon entering the last year of his first term, under increasing attack from significant elements of the development coalition. Predictably, that attack led blacks to rally around both the mayor and the joint venture idea, but the black support turned out to be a double-edged sword.

By early 1976 a combination of the airlines' indirect threats to withhold financial support for construction and the business community's threats to back a strong candidate against Jackson in 1977 led the mayor to tilt toward compromise on his commitment to the joint venture program. Specifically, the compromise entailed (1) the softening of City Hall's official position on minority involvement, (2) the appointment of the business community's designee to supervise the entire airport construction project, and (3) the removal of the recalcitrant commissioner of administrative services, Emma Darnell, an aggressive black woman who had incurred the enmity of practically the entire business elite in her capacity as administrator of the joint venture–contract compliance program. In exchange, Mayor Jackson was assured the acceptance of the more modest version of his minority-contracting agenda and unanimous support in his bid for reelection.[42] Jackson's black supporters, however, displayed mixed emotions over his willingness to accept the compromise, especially because it required the dismissal of a black commissioner who was well known in the black community (technically she was not fired but was reorganized out of her job because her department was abolished). Charges circulated on the margins of the black political elite that Jackson had sold out to the "downtown power structure," and Darnell ran against Jackson in 1977. She received no significant support, though, and the mayor was reelected with 77 percent of the vote.

What can the Maynard Jackson experience tell us about the politics of local-development policy? First of all, although in both instances of controversy over airport construction Jackson accepted the business elite's development agenda, his attempts to meld blacks into the coalition met with drastically different responses. In the first instance his efforts were favorably received by the coalition because he simply chose sides in what essentially was a debate over what Peterson would call "allocational" issues. None of the three (or four, counting Dawson County) potential options was clearly preferable in technical terms. Therefore, the decision could be derived only through the tug of war between very particularistic interests. Certainly, the ARC's waffling back and forth on its "expert" recommendations does not give much comfort to those who would argue that such development-policy decisions are made on the basis of an impersonal, extrapolitical rationality. As mayor, Jackson had to take some position on the issue, and he chose one that was already a legitimate item in elite policy debate and that enabled him to express a claim, albeit only a symbolic one, on behalf of his black electoral constituency.

Jackson's effort to reinvent the south-side option as a black interest reflects a variant of Peterson's view of the translation of potentially redistributive demands into allocational or symbolic ones.[43] Jackson's success at reinvention suggests one of the mechanisms through which the black administration can mediate the tension between electoral and governing constituencies. By virtue of his representation of his position as the "black" position, he added an epicycle of racial self-defense to blacks' consideration of policy options; to that extent, Jackson shifted the basis for black response to policy debate away from substantive concern with the potential outcomes and toward protection of the racial image and status, as embodied in the idiosyncratic agenda of the black official. In this way it becomes possible for black officials to maintain support from both their black constituents and the development elites that systematically disadvantage them.

In the second instance, Jackson sought to reformulate the allocational element of the development agenda to include a niche for blacks. One point that stands out about this controversy is that it is sometimes very difficult to distinguish between the redistributive and allocational dimensions of public policy. In fact, the controversy centered precisely on whether the proposed minority-contracting program was redistributive or allocational. Jackson argued that it would have no impact on production timetables or on cost effectiveness and that it was only a matter of assuring that minorities received "parity" in budget allocations. His opponents contended that the program would produce delays, weaken investor and bidder confidence, and drive up costs and therefore that it was an inappropriate "social experiment"—that is, a redistributive program. To the extent that Jackson's proposal challenged an entrenched pattern of privilege with respect to allocation, it did in fact contain a redistributive component, at least insofar as the program implied a marginal redistribution of privileged access to public resources via the contract-award process. Nevertheless, if one abstracts from the self-interestedness of the discrete actors involved, the program's focus was on modifying the allocational dimension of a development-policy objective.

Another noteworthy characteristic of the second controversy is that Jackson's program incurred such uniform hostility in part because it represented an attempt to assert a version of black influence over the determination of the allocational rules of the game in the development-policy process. In Atlanta's political culture, such an assertion constituted a radical departure from business as usual and was therefore unacceptable to the business elites, even though the versions of black interests that were asserted accepted the developmentalist premises and agenda around which the business elite cohered. The problem was not that the black administration or the prospective black subcontractors or joint venture contractors were questionable as supporters of the agenda. The problem was simply that they were supposed to be cue-takers exclusively, even though their claimed representation of the aspirations of a popular black constituency no doubt raised some questions about their reliability. Eventually, however, even in Atlanta, the business elites recognized the virtues of the black administration's capacity to displace potential conflict by reinventing development agendas that had potentially disadvantageous outcomes for black constituents as campaigns for the defense of racial self-respect embodied in black officials. But that is the story of the Andrew Young administration.

What does all this say about the critique of Peterson with which this chapter began? Most important is that consensus around development policy derives from political processes that some interests are not allowed to have a voice in and that are largely defined and dominated by significant economic interests. Moreover, neat analytical distinctions between different posited policy types are difficult to sustain in places where matters rather approximate William James's "bloomin', buzzin' confusion." These two points, of course, do not speak well for a notion of unitary interest in development, which in practice is often little more than a cudgel with which to enforce an entrenched pattern of privilege.

1987

6. The "Underclass" as Myth and Symbol
The Poverty of Discourse about Poverty

In recent years the image of an urban "underclass" has become the central representation of poverty in American society. It has come also to shape much of public discussion — both academic and popular — and policy makers' agendas concerning racial democratization, cities, and social welfare. In less than a decade the notion has taken hold of the public imagination and has gone, across the ideological spectrum, from novel, sensational expression to deeply entrenched common sense. But what does it all mean? What is so compelling about the underclass image? What is its significance in American political life? And, finally, how should we talk, instead, about those who are stigmatized as "the underclass"?

These questions are fundamental for making sense of the image and its popularity, but they do not arise within the prevailing discourse about poverty. Indeed, the underclass idea rests on fuzzy and often very disturbing assumptions about poor people, poverty, and the world in which both are reproduced. Those assumptions amount to tacit — and sometimes explicit — claims regarding the defective nature of poor people's motivations, moral character, and behavior. They appeal to hoary prejudices of race, gender, and class that give the underclass image instant popularity and verisimilitude even though it is ambiguous and inconsistent on its own terms. In the end, underclass assumptions serve to take the focus away from (costly) demands for responsible government policies, blaming poor people, not societal choices, for another pat phrase, "persistent poverty."

A Concept Is Born

The attractiveness, as well as the apparent descriptive power, of the underclass concept is linked to the rightward shift over the 1980s in the terms of public debate about social welfare. Referring to that shift is practically a cliché at this point, but surprisingly little attention has been paid to the extent to which right-wing beliefs about poor people have come to suffuse even self-consciously liberal, technocratic policy discussion. Even erstwhile "friends of the poor" — that is, not simply more or less honest or disingenuous neoconservatives (or neoliberals—and how can we tell one from the other anyway?) like Charles Murray, Lawrence Mead, Nicholas Lemann, George Glider, Mickey Kaus, Thomas Sowell, Walter Williams, Robert Woodson, or Glenn Loury—assume the need to correct, or at least to take into account, poor people's defective tendencies as an essential limit on social policy. The reactionary, purely ideological foundation of the appeal of the underclass idea becomes clear on close examination.

Although the term has been around longer (*The Black Underclass* was published in 1980, for example, and the origination of the word itself has been attributed variously to Gunnar Myrdal, John Kenneth Galbraith and others),[1] it caught fire in popular and academic circles after Ken Auletta canonized it in 1982 in *The Underclass,*[2] a journalistic, mock-ethnographic essay originally serialized in *The New Yorker.* Auletta's underclass, unlike that of earlier references, was defined by its putative behavior. That focus—which harmonized well with the Reaganite ideological offensive—no doubt helped to propel it toward conventional wisdom. The underclass is appealing, though, entirely as a powerful metaphor; its resonance has far outpaced its empirical content, and it has thrived as a concept in search of its object. Nearly all who find the notion attractive agree that the underclass is mainly urban and largely nonwhite. They typically agree as well that it is a relatively small group, comprising approximately 10 to 20 percent of the poverty population. That percentage, however, operates as a sleight of hand, the invocation of the magical power of positivism's symbolic authority as an alternative to descriptive evidence. The number, glibly repeated by journalists and professional counters of poverty, has become the consensual estimate without any justificatory argument. In fact, descriptive efforts tend to assume that percentage and tailor empirical definitions to meet it as a target. The ultimate source of this estimate, instructively, may be Oscar Lewis, author of the "culture of poverty," an earlier generation's effort to ground a behavioral focus on poverty in the authority of social science. Lewis speculated that "about twenty percent of the population below the poverty line" fell into his poverty culture. But his speculation had no greater force than contemporary punditry. He characterized it as a belief and a "rough guess" and offered no supporting evidence or argument.[3]

Defining the Problem

Despite the general consensus on the size of the underclass no such clear agreement exists regarding who precisely constitutes this marked 10 to 20 percent of the poor. The criteria, and even the kinds of criteria, that qualify one for underclass membership vary—except, that is, for being black or Hispanic and urban—but as I shall show, only within a narrow context of victim-blaming presumptions about inner-city poor people. Specific formulations of the underclass's composition, therefore, speak eloquently of the pernicious orientation that frames public discussion about American poverty. Examining them shows just how bankrupt and purely ideological this notion is.

Auletta begins by joining "poverty" and "antisocial behavior" as equivalent qualifications for underclass status. He adduces the Victorian journalist, Henry Mayhew, to support a claim that "there is nothing new about such a class. There have always been pirates, beggars, vagrants, paupers, illiterates, street criminals and helplessly, hopelessly damaged individuals."[4] Having evoked the proper Victorian image, he then fleshes out his view of the stratum's composition:

> The underclass need not be poor—street criminals, for instance, usually are not. Which brings us to a second characteristic that usually distinguishes the underclass: *behavior.* Whatever the cause . . . most students of poverty believe that the underclass suffers from *behavioral* as well as income deficiencies. The underclass usually operates outside the generally accepted boundaries of society. They are often set apart by their "deviant" or antisocial behavior, by their bad habits, not just their poverty.[5]

Auletta muses that we might not want to include those who "actually earn a living in the underground economy" and maybe "add illegal or undocumented aliens," and he wonders whether "those with serious mental illness [should] be counted."[6] In a pinch, for a quick, quasi-empirical referent, however, he calls up the holy trinity of "welfare mothers, ex-convicts and drug addicts."[7]

Lawrence Mead's underclass includes all "those Americans who combine relatively low income with functioning problems such as difficulties in getting through school, obeying the law, working, and keeping their families together." To assist in finding them, he suggests we look for markers like "unstable family life marked by absent fathers, erratic parenting and low self-esteem and aspiration."[8]

Mickey Kaus and Nicholas Lemann propose explicitly racialized, culture-of-poverty constructions. For Kaus the underclass is the "black lower class" for whom "the work ethic has evaporated and the entrepreneurial drive is channeled into gangs and drug-pushing."[9] Culture figures prominently in Kaus's outlook. In addition to the culture of poverty, he asserts the existence of a "single-parent culture,"[10] a "welfare culture,"[11] a "culture of single motherhood,"[12] (presumably a more specific articulation from the single-parent culture), a "working, taxpaying culture,"[13] and a "work ethic culture."[14] Lemann never tells us exactly how we can identify a member of his underclass. In his nearest attempt at definition he simply announces that "blacks are splitting into a middle class and an under-class that seems likely never to make it."[15] He tells us that the underclass suffers from a "strongly self-defeating culture"[16] that has its roots in the sharecrop system and whose centerpiece seems to be out-of-wedlock birth. That is as precise as Lemann gets. He does, though, volunteer the information that this ghetto culture is "venerable" and "disorganized"[17] and that its members need tutelage in some equally vague "bourgeois values."[18]

Social Science Fictions

Instead of clarifying or correcting the impressionistic generalities and simple-minded prejudices spewed by journalists like Auletta, Kaus, and Lemann, social scientists have legitimated them with an aura of scientific verity, surrounding them in an authenticating mist of quantification. Within four months after publication of Kaus's and Lemann's articles, Richard Nathan, then of Princeton's prestigious Woodrow Wilson School, declared that it was time to shut off debate about the usefulness, empirical soundness, or implications of the underclass notion and that we should follow the media in using the term "as a shorthand expression for the concentration of economic and behavioral problems among racial minorities (mainly black and Hispanic) in large, older cities."[19] This underclass is "not just a function of being poor. It involves geography and behavior. It is a condition of alienated people living in communities in which antisocial activities are the norm— crime, prostitution, drugs, the lack of will and commitment to get an education or a regular job, long-term welfare, homelessness."[20] Isabel Sawhill, senior fellow at the Urban Institute, similarly proceeds from the authoritative imagery of "television and newspaper stories" that document the underclass's existence.[21] This underclass, she then tells us, can be found among "those who are chronically poor." But once again its behavior is its "most distinctive, most interesting, and most troubling" characteristic. Members of Sawhill's underclass exhibit behavior that is both "dysfunctional" and deviates from "existing laws and norms." She proclaims a set of homespun verities—beatified (without evidence of course) as "norms"—to be the consensual obligations that "society" demands of its members:

> First, children are expected to study hard and complete at least high school. Second, young people are expected to refrain from conceiving children until they have the personal and financial resources to support them; this usually means delaying childbearing until they have completed school and can draw a regular salary. Third, adults are ex-

pected to work at a steady job, unless they are disabled, or are supported by their spouse. Fourth, everyone is expected to obey the laws.[22]

Meeting these obligations, Sawhill announces, is an element of the American "social contract"; the underclass are those people—"too many" of them, in fact—"who are not fulfilling their end of the bargain."[23] Simply put—that is, without the garnish of cracker-barrel contractarianism—"the underclass is a subgroup of the American population that engages in behaviors at variance with those of mainstream populations";[24] or, as she has also described them, "people who engage in bad behavior or a set of bad behaviors."[25] The most important "somewhat indirect proxies" for deviant, dysfunctional, "underclass behavior" are, in her view, dropping out of school, female heading of families with children, welfare "dependency," and adult male unemployment or underemployment.[26] So important is behavior in identifying the underclass that it need not be embodied in human beings at all; the term, Sawhill and her coauthor Erol Ricketts decide, "describes the coincidence of a number of social ills including poverty, joblessness, crime, welfare dependency, fatherless families, and low levels of education or work-related skills."[27]

Where one stands on the liberal/conservative axis seems little to affect the appeal of the underclass concept. Kaus and Lemann probably think of themselves as liberals or neoliberals of some sort. Nathan is a moderate, statist Republican, and Sawhill probably considers herself a pragmatic liberal policy professional. Only Mead among the underclass pundits I have discussed would probably affirm his conservative identity without qualification. Even those avowing considerably greater liberalism have gravitated to the notion, however. Eleanor Holmes Norton, President Jimmy Carter's Equal Employment Opportunity Commission (EEOC) director and now congressional delegate from the District of Columbia, defines it as those who suffer from a "ghetto subculture," which she understands to be a "destructive ethos," "complicated, predatory, and self-perpetuating."[28] Though she does not explicate this subculture's components, she does inform us that family dissolution is its principal trace material, that it is incubated in female-headed households,[29] and that it is deficient in "hard work, education, respect for family," and other such "enduring values."[30]

William Julius Wilson gave the notion a ringing liberal imprimatur and even chastised the left for not being tough enough to face up to the underclass's existence as a "heterogeneous grouping of inner-city families and individuals whose behavior contrasts sharply with that of mainstream America."[31] Like Norton's, his underclass lives within a "ghetto-specific culture" whose identifiable characteristics are the well-known "tangle of pathology" litany: crime, drug abuse, teenaged pregnancy, out-of-wedlock birth, female-headed households, and welfare dependency.[32] David Ellwood identifies the "ghetto-poor"—his version of the underclass—as those who suffer from or live in areas dominated by "a frightening array of negative forces: deprivation, concentration, isolation, discrimination, poor education,... the movement of jobs away from central cities ... crime, drugs and alcohol, the underground economy, and welfare."[33] The "ghetto poor" are a "new underclass [who] live in the biggest cities yet seem to be in their own world. They seem to embrace values that the middle class cannot understand."[34]

These constructions fairly represent a cross section of attempts to define the underclass concept concretely. They also share certain features, despite the considerably different political and programmatic agendas to which they are connected. All zero in on inner-city blacks and Hispanics; all focus on behavior, values, and "culture"; and all in fact converge on an overlapping list of behavioral indicators. Yet they do not tell us very much about a distinct, discernible population. What exactly joins the various aggregations of people said to constitute the underclass? Why are street crime and teenage pregnancy signifiers of a common population? Does participation in an underground economy not suggest just the opposite of an evaporated work ethic? How exactly does out-of-wedlock birth become an instance of social pathology? If a thirty-five-year-old lawyer decides to have a baby without seal of approval from church or state or enduring male affiliation, we quite rightly do not consider her to be acting pathologically; we may even properly laud her independence and refusal to knuckle under to patriarchal conventions. Why does such a birth become pathological when it occurs in the maternity ward in Lincoln Hospital in the South Bronx, say, rather than within the pastel walls of an alternative birthing center? If the one woman's decision expresses pathology because she makes it in poverty, then we have fallen into a nonsensical tautology: She is poor because she is pathological and pathological because she is poor.

Victorian Echoes: Class and Culture

Part of the problem stems from reliance on psychologistic mystifications about class, attitudes, behavior, values, and culture. Indeed, underclass constructions revise the old nature/culture dichotomy, in which "culture" stood for the principle of human plasticity and adaptation—in the old Enlightenment view, the agency of progress. Instead, the underclass idea's power derives from its naturalization of "culture" as an independent force that undermines adaptability and retards progress. The notion—like other manifestations of culture-of-poverty ideology—

resuscitates the functionalist idea of cultural lag, itself a vestige of assumptions concerning the existence of racial temperaments.

In this regard, Auletta's decision to ground his definition on the authority of Henry Mayhew is instructive. The underclass image proceeds from a view of class in general that strikingly resembles Victorian convention. In that view class is not so much a category of social position as the reverse; social position flows naturally from the intrinsic qualities of class. In this light it is significant that Victorians often used "class" and "race" interchangeably; each category was seen as innate, imbued with a sense of immutability and independence from social relations that we nowadays would consider biological. Class and race essences generally were thought to include—in addition to distinctive physiognomy—values, attitudes, and behavior.

This premise of essentialized class natures is not exclusively an artifact of a naive past. It can be seen in contemporary American popular culture, as in the 1988 film *Big Business,* which featured Lily Tomlin and Bette Midler as two sets of identical twins—one impoverished West Virginians, the other Manhattan multimillionaires, who had been mistakenly matched at birth. Victorian holdovers—the assumption that class differentiation is most significantly a matter of differing behavior and attitudes and the naturalization of "culture" as a euphemism for "character"—account for much of the journalistic appeal of the idea of the underclass. Yet such holdovers are most clearly demonstrable among those scholars who self-consciously attempt, as Sawhill and her colleagues put it rather piously, "to clear away the theoretical and emotional underbrush surrounding the concept."[35] The Victorian resonances are highlighted through the rhetorical moves and chains of inference that those scholars employ as they seek to construct meticulous, apparently social scientific descriptions of an objectively existing underclass.

Freeze Frames: From Behavior to Values

The starting point for the construction of the underclass is a willingness to believe, an a priori receptiveness to journalistic, anecdotal claims that could, after all, provoke skepticism just as easily as reflexive acceptance. Next comes refinement of those porous claims through the stipulation of a list of specific, presumably empirical, descriptive characteristics. This process involves a number of discrete, ideological moves that, for instance, reify freeze-frame incidents in individual life trajectories under the static rubric "behavior." Someone who is unemployed or a drug abuser at the moment when that piece of her life is collected as a data point may not be a year or two later. Similarly, each of the categories proposed as an indicator of the underclass encompasses quite different sorts of individuals with quite various backgrounds and life situations — even in inner cities. When we learn that a woman gave birth in adolescence, for example, what exactly have we learned about her except that she happened to carry a pregnancy to term before her twentieth birthday? The incidence of certain occurrences (for example, birth, crime) or conditions (unemployment, female household-heading) by itself tells us nothing about the population under investigation except the statistical frequency with which those occurrences and conditions are distributed at a given moment — or a series of moments — among a universe of ongoing life processes. Construing them as definitive behavior snatches them out of that context of dynamic life processes and the webs of interaction within which they are shaped and take on meaning. Instead, analysts impose meanings on them from the outside by interpreting them through very specific social theoretical prejudices.

A central element of this move involves presumptions about the relationships between behavior and attitudes or values. Even if we grant that those freeze-frames should be understood as evidence of "behavior," they say nothing about attitudes or values. Yet assertions about the latter figure prominently in descriptions, despite lack of evidence. The a priori character of such assertions is obscured by their being nestled within statistically driven catalogues of "behavior." Analytical power emerges by cribbing off the authoritative aura of unrelated statistical narratives — as well as, of course, by exerting the will to believe.

Nathan, for example, might be able to adduce evidence supporting his contentions about the prevalence of crime, prostitution, drugs, long-term welfare, and homelessness, but "lack of will and commitment to get an education or a regular job" cannot be ascertained from the data at his disposal. On what does he base that inference? He avoids justifying it by slipping it into a list of categories for which he could marshal plausible evidence. Sawhill proceeds from her catalogue to suggest that once dysfunctional behaviors

> become commonplace, they are likely to become more acceptable.... Such a shift in social norms leads in turn to more bad behavior. To study hard, to defer childbearing, *to take a low-paid job* [emphasis added], to marry one's girlfriend — these are not what most members of the community expect one to do. Indeed, those who respect traditional norms may even be viewed as "chumps" or "losers."

Her sole explicit source for this scenario is "the common-sense intuition that people are locked into the ghetto not just by their lack of opportunities but also by cultural factors."[36] Ellwood too slides from a plausibly empirical statement about behavior to one about values, again relying on the standing of the former to support the latter. And he insulates this rhetorical sleight of hand with subjunctive verb construction: the ghetto poor "seem to be in their own world"; they "seem to embrace" alien values. Wilson alleges, albeit elliptically as ever, that the growth in his measures of pathology indicates that the underclass lacks a "sense of community, positive neighborhood identification, and explicit norms and sanctions against aberrant behavior."[37] He also deduces "norms and aspirations" from behavior.[38] How can we presume to know people's motivations without taking into account their self-understandings? Yet our students of the underclass act as if access to inner-city poor people's mental lives is exempt from that warrant.

Two related aspects of the underclass discourse circumvent the need for direct ethnographic justification. First, the notion comes with a ready-made explanatory system carried forward from earlier incarnations of culture-of-poverty theory and the normative apparatus of Chicago School sociological functionalism, with distinctive ideological inflections intact. Its explanatory frame pivots on the premise that a hierarchy of norms of social behavior exists and is objectively discernible. This hierarchy is based on propriety and functionality for maintenance of social order. Divergence from the prevailing norms is cause for concern because participation in the dominant normative structure is an essential condition for effective social integration. "Deviance" from those norms is associated with the development of "dysfunctional" or "pathological" patterns of organization and behavior, that is, patterns that impede integration and subvert moral order. From this vantage point deviance is, by definition, evidence of improper integration; therefore, behavior that "contrasts sharply with that of mainstream America" logically implies disorganized, pathological subgroup life and dysfunctional attitudes and values.

Second, members of a population characterized by widespread disorganization and pathology cannot be particularly transparent to themselves and are for that reason not well suited to making credible interpretations of their circumstances. Such a population can—perhaps should—be studied without reference to its members' self-understandings. The underclass theorists thus do not need to investigate attitudes and values directly; they can be read out from behavior.

Culture and Geography: Mapping the Underclass

This view is intrinsically circular and ideological, but its circularity is muted by another procedural mystification: reification of census tracts as meaningful units of social organization. The notion of "ghetto-specific culture" relies, at least among those who wish to avoid unattractively racial interpretations, on an argument that emphasizes the role of social isolation in the underclass. Wilson's formulation is that geographical isolation and concentration of the very poor sets off a dynamic of social disorganization that results in atrophy of the community's institutional structure and fuels the proliferation of various social pathologies.[39] This perspective disposes one toward a focus on communities or neighborhoods as analytic units inasmuch as it ties the underclass's existence to intranetwork dynamics, for example, in stressing socialization or demonstration effects and the role of social buffers. Genuine examination of those dynamics, however, would require the sort of thick, open-ended ethnographic inquiry whose absence I have already noted, though ethnography itself is no panacea.[40] Wilson sidesteps the need for direct investigation of poor people's lives by means of a subtle but critical elision: the stipulation of census tracts as proxies for neighborhoods.

But census tracts are not necessarily neighborhoods, in the sociological sense meaningful here. Their boundaries reflect technical imperatives associated with rational organization of data collection as well as homogeneity with respect to some pertinent material indicators. They do not, however, automatically represent units of overlapping networks of interaction. Analysis of aggregate socioeconomic and demographic characteristics culled from census tracts, moreover, does not in any way inform our understanding of either patterns of interaction or the character of norms, values, and aspirations operative within them. Nevertheless, the elision has become institutionalized in the poverty research industry, and debate occurs now only over which batches of indicators and what thresholds of them most satisfactorily mark an underclass area.[41]

These laundry lists of characteristics also entail a questionable extension of the category "behavior" to phenomena that very well might be only indirectly products of human agency. Female household-heading, for example, can result from a number of different circumstances entirely beyond the control of women whose lives are compressed under that label. The same applies to unemployment or underemployment, and even long-term status as a welfare recipient can stem completely from impersonal forces. Characterizing those phenomena as behavior reveals a zeal for validating the underclass concept, but doing so may also betray a fundamental inclination to seek the sources of poverty in the deficiencies of individuals. All versions of the underclass notion center on the behavior of its categorical members, even though liberals typically hedge that move with genuflections toward the ultimate weight of historical or structural forces. (The differences on that score, however, are not that great. Today's conservatives also frequently genuflect toward structural pressures and past oppression before enunciating one or another brand of tough-love remedy.) In fact, focusing on poor people's defects is hardly inconsistent with liberal conceptions; it is, after all, the foundation of all human capital ideology.

The Appeal of the Underclass: "They" Are Not [Like] "Us."

Why, though, does the underclass idea appeal so powerfully to people—including tough-minded scholars—even as they must struggle and perform elaborate, dubious maneuvers to define it? I suspect that the answer lies at the nexus of four factors, one sociological, the others ideological. Some of the notion's popularity is driven by the sociology of the policy research community. On the one hand, the technocratic discourse itself confers privileged status on constructions that depoliticize the frame for examining social problems. The underclass formulation is attractive in that light precisely because it does not exist as anyone's self-description. It is therefore absolutely devoid of agents or real constituents; it is purely a statistical artifact and to that extent exclusively the creation and property of its chroniclers. On the other hand, the poverty and social welfare policy business is an industry that operates with its own autonomous logic. "State of the art" research is expensive and requires large grants from government agencies and foundations. Getting grants depends on peer review processes and the politics of reputation. Less cynically, policy professionals function in a world of shared norms, conventions, and allegiances that can override other commitments; the community's belief structure also exalts this technicist mystique; that is, the social policy research community believes that careful search for consensually agreeable facts will produce consensus on policy. These circumstances overdetermine a tendency toward avoiding sharp criticisms of others' interpretations, as well as a tendency toward not venturing very far from conventional wisdom or the common sense of the moment or what passes for it. It is important to recognize that this is no less an ideological stance than any other, one whose internal contradictoriness Ellwood exemplifies strikingly. In *Poor Support* he repeatedly goes through a range of claims, concluding that we can not clearly resolve the conflict among them but going on to declaim some specific course of action. This practice amounts to asserting a privileged position in policy debate on the basis of expertise that is irrelevant by his own accounting.

Additionally, the underclass notion appeals to three distinct ideological dispositions. Most immediately, it resonates with the ahistorical individualism rampant in the Reagan-Bush era. As a corollary, it is attractive to many petit bourgeois blacks because it flatters their success by comparison and, through the insipid role model rhetoric, allows fawning over the allegedly special role of the middle class.

The idea of a behaviorally defined underclass also affirms an ensemble of racial and class prejudices that lurk beneath an apparently innocuous, certainly stupid tendency to reduce the social world to aggregates of good people and bad people. Simply, good people are people like "us," bad people are not, and the same behavior is assessed differently depending on the category into which the perpetrator falls. An eighteen-year-old drug courier with a monogrammed BMW is pathological; an arbitrageur who strays too far onto the wrong side of legality is too clever for his own good—the stuff of tragedy. Dependency on Aid to Families with Dependent Children (AFDC) breeds sloth and pathology; dependency on defense contracts, agricultural price supports, tax abatements, or Federal Housing Administration (FHA) loans does a patriotic service for the country, incubates family values, and so forth.

The point here is that the behavioral tendencies supposedly characterizing the underclass exist generally throughout the society. Drug use, divorce, educational underattainment, laziness, and empty consumerism exist no less in upper-status suburbs than in inner-city Bantustans. The difference lies not in the behavior but in the social position of those exhibiting it. Middle-class and upper-middle-class people have access to social resources—including the good will of social norms—that provide them safety nets along the way.

Instructively, Pete Hamill complains about underclass blacks' pathological habit of "wandering the streets at all hours."[42] Auletta finds a behavioral signal in his underclass subjects' walking five abreast down a Manhattan street, oblivious to their monopolizing the sidewalk.[43] By those standards the entire enrollment of Yale College qualifies for underclass membership.

Like Sawhill, Ellwood canonizes this way of thinking. He concocts a batch of platitudes and anoints them as "fundamental American values" by which we might fairly judge the poor.[44] True to form, he introduces them by announcing that he does not really know what they are. Not only are these "values" simple clichés—Autonomy of the Individual, Virtue of Work, Primacy of the Family, Desire for and Sense of Community—but his posture reveals the nasty core of the underclass imagery. What "we" demands compliance? Who defines the values? Are poor people not also Americans? Of course Ellwood's list is so airy it is unlikely that anyone would disavow it, but that is beside the point. The main problem is that his banal list, like Sawhill's cracker-barrel contract, presumes a first person–third person relationship in which some "we" lays down the laws of proper American behavior for some "they." Ellwood seems to think—unlike Sawhill—that he is being clever and faking right to go left; but he merely underscores the extent to which underclass thinking draws its force from its fundamental dehumanization and retrograde, ideological quarantining of inner-city poor people.

Gendered Dynamics

The underclass notion may receive the greatest ideological boost from its gendered imagery and relation to gender politics. As I noted in a critique of Wilson's *The Truly Disadvantaged,*[45] "family" is an intrinsically ideological category. The rhetoric of "disorganization," "disintegration," and "deterioration" reifies one type of living arrangement—the ideal type of the bourgeois nuclear family—as outside history, almost as though it were decreed by natural law. But—as I asked earlier—why exactly is out-of-wedlock birth pathological? Why is a female-headed household an indicator of disorganization and pathology? Does that stigma attach to all such households—even, say, that of a divorced executive who is a custodial mother? If not, what are the criteria for assigning it? The short answer is race and class bias inflected through a distinctively gendered view of the world.

The underclass carries with it images of drug-crazed, lawless black and Hispanic men and their baby-factory mothers and sisters. The companion image is the so-called "cycle of poverty," which focuses on women's living and reproductive practices as the transmission belt that drives the cycle. That focus permeates discussion of the underclass, and those who rely on it avoid confronting its antifeminist premises by running together female-headed households, out-of-wedlock birth, and teenage pregnancy into a single mantra. Those who want to impose female economic dependence on men under the pretext of restoring traditional family values, of course, perceive each of those three conditions equally as pathological. Some, like Wilson, claim that female household-heading is a problem not because it is intrinsically inferior but because such households are likelier than others to be poor.[46] Yet he does not just persist in describing female household-heading as pathological; his proposal for improving such households' conditions centers on making men "marriageable"—a strategy I have referred to as a "macroeconomic dating service."[47] Others push the specter of teenage pregnancy to the foreground in more or less transparent efforts to drown out objections to the obvious sexism behind stigmatizing female-headed households (which now are home to a majority of American children, by the way)[48] and apply a hierarchy of propriety to the conjugal arrangements within which women might give birth.

The three categories, however, are distinct. If one-parent households are especially linked to poverty, it is only because (1) the segmented labor market depresses women's earning capacity and (2) such households are overwhelmingly likely to be headed by women. Mary Jo Bane has found, moreover, that entry into a female-headed household is not particularly significant in generating poverty among black women because they are likely already to be poor before forming such a household.[49] The only pertinent issue, therefore, is how best to overcome gendered labor market and wage discrimination. Casting the issue instead as strengthening two-parent families is an ideological mystification that artificially ranks conjugal and other living arrangements in a way that is defensible neither theoretically nor empirically. People of course have the right to believe that husband-wife nuclear families are best and morally superior; they should not have the right to use public policy to impose that belief. How does one use policy to "strengthen families" other than by enhancing individuals' capacities to live in the world, that is, to increase the role of personal preference — in contrast to material compulsion — in people's decisions to form or continue intimate attachments? Anything else is either empty rhetoric or repressive moralism.

As for out-of-wedlock birth, insofar as it is not a subset either of the female-headed household concern or the teenage childbearing concern, it is simply nobody's business. "Teen pregnancy," though, is a more complicated issue, largely because of its power as a condensation symbol. It is the big trump in the underclass pundits' arsenal of pathologies. Kristin Luker's and Arline Geronimus's very important research, though, takes great strides in demystifying this issue.[50] Geronimus has been the object of bitter and almost conspiratorial attacks from elements within the poverty research industry, laying bare the fundamentally ideological commitments that ground the research community's conventions. Their work shows, first of all, that the actual object of public and policy concern — and record keeping — is not teenage pregnancy but teenage childbearing. The rhetorical focus on pregnancy both conveniently sidesteps the significance of restrictions on access to abortion for increases in adolescent fertility and trades on adult anxieties about youthful promiscuity to foment a tone of often hysterical urgency. Second, the issue itself dates only from the 1970s. Until then, teenage childbearing, far from indicating social pathology, was a broadly accepted norm in American life. Third, the concern is not even so much with teenage childbearing in general as when it occurs out of wedlock; to that extent the teen pregnancy issue is a subset of the out-of-wedlock birth issue. Moreover, despite much popular wisdom concerning an epidemic of black teen childbearing, actual rates of black teen fertility have declined steadily at least since 1970. Wilson, in acknowledging this fact, shows at the same time the ideological hold that the teen pregnancy image has. He maintains that we must be concerned nonetheless because adult black fertility has declined even more sharply, so teenagers account for a rising percentage of black births.[51] So what? There still is no "epidemic," which can only be an increase *within* the universe of teenagers; his response reflects an Orwellian attempt to hang on to an ideologically congenial thesis. Finally, Luker cites considerable evidence that teen childbearing does not seem to have the catastrophic, life-destroying consequences entailed by Sawhill's "common-sense intuition." Carrying a baby to term is not particularly likely to lead a girl to drop out of school. The reality is more likely the reverse: girls who have babies are most likely either to have dropped out or to have been failing in school already. Similarly, they do not seem to be particularly disadvantaged in later life in relation to their peers. They are, rather, likely to finish school and may wind up somewhat better off materially by their midtwenties than their peers who defer childbearing. This is presumably because (1) the younger mother has greater access to support from her own kin, in whose household system she is embedded, and (2) the older mother suffers, ironically, from being more likely to withdraw from the labor market to act out a nuclear family wife-and-mother role. When the nuclear union splits — as is the statistical norm — she lags behind in labor market experience.

Moynihan Revived: Family "Culture" and Blaming Women

In this light recent attempts from Wilson and others (including Senator Daniel Moynihan himself) to rehabilitate and sanitize the nefariously racist and sexist Moynihan Report take on a truly sinister and pernicious cast. Moynihan provides his own indictment. After proposing — just in time for the first big Vietnam buildup — that service in the military would be the best strategy for easing the appearance of unemployment and overcoming the effects of the tangle of pathology spawned through black family life, Moynihan gave forth with the following:

> There is another special quality about military service for Negro men:
> it is an utterly masculine world. Given the strains of the disorganized
> and matrifocal family life in which so many Negro youth come of age,
> the Armed Forces are a dramatic and desperately needed change: a
> world away from women, a world run by strong men of unquestioned
> authority, where discipline, if harsh, is nonetheless orderly and pre-
> dictable, and where rewards, if limited, are granted on the basis of
> performance.
>
> The theme of a current Army recruiting message states it as clearly
> as can be: "In the U.S. Army you get to know what it means to feel like

a man."[52]

If anything else needs to be said about the gendered character of underclass imagery, I should note that of the master list of empirical indicators of pathology, most—four of Wilson's six, for example—are observable only in women. We are, moreover, already seeing the policy fruit that this imagery bears. A judge in Kansas City has ordered children to use their absent fathers' names, presumably to strengthen obligation by establishing ownership.[53] A Kansas state legislator has argued—as had a *Philadelphia Inquirer* editorial—that impoverished women should be induced to accept Norplant birth control implants as a way to control welfare costs and recipient population.[54] State welfare departments have taken up marriage brokering, as in a Wisconsin plan to offer cash inducements for women who marry their way off AFDC and to cut benefits for "unwed teenage mothers." Even circumspect poverty specialists, for example, Gary Burtless of the Brookings Institution, empathize with the state's intentions, agreeing that "no one likes people having children out of wedlock."[55] (Wisconsin, we might recall, had already established a policy of cutting the welfare benefits of parents—naturally, overwhelmingly mothers—whose children exceed a designated limit of unauthorized school absences.)

These moves demonstrate unambiguously the repressive, antifeminist outlook lurking beneath the focus on family. It authorizes a moralistic rhetoric of parental (but really mainly maternal) responsibility reflecting a broader offensive—overlapping drug hysteria, labor market discrimination, antiabortionism, and a punitive, victim-blaming approach to poor people, which Katha Pollitt calls a "new assault on feminism." Pollitt notes in this regard that

> the focus on maternal behavior allows the government to appear to be concerned about babies without having to spend any money, change any priorities or challenge any vested interests. As with crime, as with poverty, a complicated, multifaceted problem is construed as a matter of freely chosen individual behavior. We have crime because we have lots of bad people, poverty because we have lots of lazy people (Republican version) or lots of pathological people (Democratic version) and tiny, sickly, impaired babies because we have lots of women who just don't give a damn.[56]

The offensive is inflected in ways that concentrate the punitive agenda along class and race lines. In addition to the presumption that only poor women are somehow culpable or defective for not being married, that inflection appears in differential susceptibility to punishment. Just as the antiabortionist program has left safety valves for upper-status women, other components of this new assault reserve their harshest treatment for poor and nonwhite women. Although women use illegal drugs during pregnancy at roughly the same levels across race and income categories, for example, black and poor women are ten times more likely to be turned in to authorities even when law mandates that pregnant drug users be reported.[57]

A lesson to be drawn from the reactionary substance of family imagery is that liberal attempts at cleverness that seek to co-opt "traditional values" are dangerously mistaken, if not worse. Marian Wright Edelman's attempt to build public support by stressing the needs and conditions of poor people as families inadvertently reinforces the practice of categorizing the poor on the basis of "family" characteristics.[58] Her stratagem overlooks the fact that the reified image of family is itself a principal vehicle for the stigmatization that she wishes to overcome.

Wilson and Ellwood are more troublesome in their efforts at cleverness. Each sets out to conciliate rightist presumptions on behalf of liberal policies. Wilson refers unabashedly to the liberal "hidden agenda" (though one wonders how hidden he expects it to be if he discusses it in a highly publicized book) that he intends his warmed-over culture-of-poverty interpretation to support. Ellwood is more problematic in that he not only actively embraces the categorization of poor people by family status, but he also caters to the implicitly racist presumption that the "ghetto poor" comprise yet another distinct population, outside the "normal" family system. Moreover, as I have noted, he accepts the premise that to merit support poor people must demonstrate that they fulfill an arbitrary set of cracker-barrel "obligations," a view that only reinforces the distinction of "deserving" and "undeserving" poor people. In each case the strategy has been too clever by half. Public response to each has focused on the author's affirmation of the reactionary frame, noting his liberal credentials as a further legitimization of the retrograde discourse (as in, "even liberal policy researchers agree...."). Meanwhile, the hidden policy agendas either remain hidden or are dismissed as impractical.

Alternative to the "Underclass"

How, then, should we talk about those who are stigmatized as the "underclass"? First, it is imperative to reject all assumptions that poor people are behaviorally or attitudinally different from the rest of American society. Some percentage of all Americans take drugs, fight in families, abuse or neglect children, and so forth. If the behavior exists across lines of class, race, and opportunity, then it cannot reasonably be held—that is, without some premise of generically different human natures—to be particularly implicated in producing poverty. If it does not cause poverty, therefore, we do not need to focus on it at all in the context of policy-oriented discussion about poverty.

We should also fight against lurid, evocative journalism that reproduces obnoxious class and racial prejudices (some of these accounts employ an imagery frighteningly evocative of genocidal rhetoric, as in the Chicago *Tribune* staff's book *The American Millstone*).[59] In addition we should be prepared to recognize the extent to which such prejudices infiltrate even ostensibly more careful, allegedly sympathetic depictions and expose them for what they are. Philip Kasinitz, for example, in a review of *The Truly Disadvantaged,* bemoans as mistaken the Chicago School's view of southern and eastern European immigrants as mired in social pathology but observes that that characterization applies correctly to contemporary inner-city blacks and Hispanics.[60] Similarly, Eleanor Holmes Norton alleges that World War II–era black migrants to cities were untutored victims of pathology whereas those who moved to cities in the World War I–era were not.[61] In both cases the real differentiation reduces simply to a matter of whose grandmother we want to label as pathological.

Affirmatively, we should insist on returning the focus in the discussion of the production and reproduction of poverty to an examination of its sources in the operations of the American political and economic system. Specifically, the discussion should focus on such phenomena, for example, as the logic of deindustrialization, models of urban redevelopment driven by real estate speculation, the general intensification of polarization of wealth, income, and opportunity in American society, the ways in which race and gender figure into those dynamics, and, not least, the role of public policy in reproducing and legitimating them.

Moreover, we should fight for policy changes that will open opportunity structures: support for improving access to jobs, housing, schooling, and real drug rehabilitation of the sorts available to the relatively well-off. A focus on behavior, after all, leads into blind alleys in policy terms. If we say that poor people are poor because of bad values, we let government off the hook, even though conscious government policy—for example, in the relation between support for metropolitan real estate speculation and increasing homelessness, malnutrition, and infant mortality—is directly implicated in causing poverty. Finally, with respect to the litany of moral repressiveness that seems to be obligatory these days, I want the record to show that I do not want to hear another word about drug or crime without hearing about decent jobs, adequate housing, and egalitarian education in the same breath.

7. The Allure of Malcolm X and the Changing Character of Black Politics

It is difficult to recall precisely when I first became aware of Malcolm X, but I was fourteen or fifteen, which would make it either 1961 or 1962. I was in the midst of negotiating adolescence in the life-world of a black New Orleans bounded by the regime of racial segregation, a boundary no doubt made all the more palpable by increasing contestation. Jim Crow had been eliminated on public transportation only a year or so before I started high school, so I had fresh memories of learning the ritual of making certain to sit behind — or to place on top of the seat in front of me — a movable "For Colored Patrons Only" sign. By adolescence, when I would have had to depend on my mastery of the ritual, the signs were gone. Holes for the signs remained on the seat tops, as did the unofficially enforced residues of segregation's racial etiquette, to remind one of what had changed and what had not.

My freshman year in high school began shortly after the highly publicized lynching of Mack Charles Parker in nearby Mississippi, where only four years earlier Emmett Till's murder had received even more attention. Adults made sure we knew of those horrible crimes and thus, among other things, of the dangers surrounding being in the presence of white women. The Greensboro sit-in occurred in February of that school year, and the Student Nonviolent Coordinating Committee (SNCC) was founded soon thereafter. At the same time, our civics teacher declaimed throughout the year on the splendor and superiority of the American way of life. Then, preparing us for a field trip, she reminded us of the imperative to use only Jim Crow facilities. (She could not imagine us overtly challenging the racial order; she feared only that some of our number might "pass.") She saw — or would admit — no contradiction. We were generally cognizant of these events, but only in the muted and diffuse way that adolescents experience the world outside teenage concerns. Mrs. Avery's admonition alone brought the segregated order to our shared consciousness, and provoked an inarticulate discomfiture.

Public school desegregation, however, began in my sophomore year, and the sociopolitical forces that channeled and constrained our adolescent pursuits erupted into everyday consciousness. (One of the selected elementary schools—named after Judah P. Benjamin, the Jewish Confederate official—was around the corner from my house, so I had to walk past barricades, police, and their dogs to get to my bus every morning. I also watched my neighborhood turn in a few months from evenly mixed by New Orleans standards—alternate blocks or half blocks, different sides of the same street—to very nearly all black.) Whites rioted endlessly and spewed venom all over the city. Our principal kept us in school an hour late to protect us and to keep us from fighting the marauding bands of white boys who roamed Canal Street—the center of the city—attacking black people. I recall the anger and frustration my friends and I felt at being kept in. We wanted, if only in the abstract, to go fight back.

The school crisis waxed and waned as an intrusion into our mundane lives. Toward the end of the year it was joined first by the Bay of Pigs invasion, which stood out because of the city's economic and cultural inflection toward the Caribbean basin, and then the Freedom Rides. New Orleans was the Freedom Riders' ultimate destination, and their bloody journey received enough news coverage to penetrate the parochial universe of youth.

By my junior year the direct action phase of the civil rights movement was in full swing. SNCC organizers were in the city, and the local National Association for the Advancement of Colored People (NAACP) youth group was recruiting pickets to demonstrate in front of stores on Canal Street, near my transfer point for the bus home. Both live and on television we regularly saw people—among them slightly older, more precocious members of our social world—being attacked and dragged roughly off to jail, singing and passively resisting all the while. We were awed by the demonstrators. As urban, adolescent males, all engaged in swaggering vaguely toward adulthood, we thought them crazy to take what they did, admired them, and were quietly enraged and humiliated by the treatment they received. Meek acceptance of being beaten and limply carted off carried, in our view, a taint of cowardice, no matter how modified. And the gleeful taunts and physical abuse from white bystanders seemed to reinforce that opinion, even while stoking our empathy with the demonstrators and hatred for their victimizers. (I do not remember any particular surge of animus toward the police in this regard. I suspect the reason is that their behavior was consistent with our normal experience of them. The police existed in our lives only as the embodiment of an absolute, hostile, and arbitrary authority, and they cultivated that role. The hypocrisy emblazoned on the parish court house—"The Impartial Administration of Justice Is the Foundation of Liberty"—was transparent even to distracted teens.)

This was the context in which I learned of Malcolm X, some time between the Bay of Pigs invasion and the Cuban Missile Crisis, when many of us fretted that nuclear war was imminent. I think the first reference to him was on television news, in a story raising the specter of dangerous "Black Muslims" and "black separatists." I recall my father remarking favorably, albeit with reservations, about Malcolm's criticisms of the civil rights establishment, the Kennedy administration, imperialism, and the pervasiveness of white supremacist ideology. I saw and heard more of Malcolm later, especially during the period between John Kennedy's assassination and his own. By 1968, like so many others in my cohort, I had been swept up into the movement and was looking for an organizational affiliation. The Socialist Workers party (SWP) attracted me, a few months prior to Martin Luther King Jr.'s assassination, in part because the SWP actively sought to identify itself with Malcolm, promising to bridge Marxism and the black power sensibility that seemed to be his legacy.

My purpose in taking this excursus into personal reflection is not to embrace the vogue of establishing authorial "positionality," which, I confess, most often strikes me as self-indulgent posturing. Rather, I draw on my own experience as part of a concern to situate Malcolm — and particularly the iconic appeal of the image of Malcolm — in historical context.

I realize that my circumstances were in meaningful ways idiosyncratic. Some of the events I have noted were, largely for familial reasons, more prominent in my consciousness than they probably were for many others in my age-set, even in the same social circle. Also, my familial environment and networks predisposed me to range toward the most politically attentive end of my high school cohort. The narrative I have presented, however, centers on phenomena that my peers generally noted in some degree — the large happenings that we discussed in current events classes and, occasionally at least, in informal conversations among ourselves, that we confronted conspicuously in our daily life — and our most broadly consensual reactions to them. I believe that it is fair to assume, therefore, that these occurrences and reactions typically formed part of the experiential backdrop of black, particularly male, urban youth in the early to middle 1960s. Outside the South, I suspect, the specific campaigns and symbols of the civil rights movement were likely to blend into a more remote, homogenized blur of things going on "down there," and some of them certainly were uniquely resonant in New Orleans. Nevertheless, they all are representative of the stream of events and dispositions in which young black (again, particularly male and urban) people at that time found the raw material for fashioning political consciousness and thus for assigning significance to Malcolm X.

The clock, moreover, hardly stopped in 1962. Malcolm became much more visible beyond the ranks of the political cognoscenti later, after the 1963 March on Washington, the Birmingham, Alabama, church bombing, and John Kennedy's assassination. In fact, he was most visible after he broke with Elijah Muhammad and the Nation of Islam. That was a period marked by the Harlem Uprising; Freedom Summer; the murders of Michael Schwerner, Andrew Goodman, and James Chaney; the sellout of the Mississippi Freedom Democratic party at the Democratic National Convention; the passage of the 1964 Civil Rights Act, which finally outlawed segregation in public accommodations; and the proclamation of the War on Poverty. Malcolm himself was killed just before the crest of the brutal struggle in Selma, Alabama, that resulted in passage of the 1965 Voting Rights Act.

Rehearsing this background helps to recall that both Malcolm and the construction of his image exist within specific circumstances in concrete history. That perspective is important for making sense of the recent "rediscovery" (though insofar as it is a generational matter, "discovery" is probably nearer the mark) that a colleague has dubbed "Malcolmania." It is first of all a reminder that the time in which Malcolm lived and the issues and problems that defined him as a public figure differ sharply from those confronting black Americans today. Keeping that distinction in mind, moreover, suggests that getting at the sources of Malcolm's current popularity requires examination of the ways in which politics among black Americans has altered since his death. Only then can we form an idea of what young people are responding to and doing now in identifying with him.

The main difference separating the two generations' attraction to Malcolm is that the Malcolm to whom my generation was drawn was alive. That difference is so obvious that its significance can easily be overlooked. However, the Malcolm X who engaged us was moving inside the history that we were living. He responded to it, tried to understand it, describe it, and shape its course. He was, as an image, a hologram produced by the same forces that made our immediate reality. In fact, Malcolm's appeal grew largely from the way that he counterpunched in very concrete terms against the changing elements of that reality — for example, in his responses to the Birmingham church bombing, the sanctimony surrounding the Kennedys, the civil rights movement's strategic reliance on the stereotype of the patient-suffering-slow-to-anger Negro. Malcolm emboldened us, or those of us whom he did, because he was an interlocutor with current orthodoxy, expressing forbidden thoughts hidden in the black silences of our time; he energized us by playing the dozens (a black narrative form of exposé, with humor) on the official narratives of race and power under which we strained.

Only a dead Malcolm X is available to young people today. He was killed five years before the birth of the typical member of the 1992 college graduating class. More important, though, is another sense in which their Malcolm is dead: He has no dynamic connection to the lived reality of the youth who invoke him. He is grafted onto their world of experience as a frozen icon to be revered, a reification of other people's memories. This Malcolm X does not encourage by providing a running critique of the prevalent narrative of oppression as it evolves. His voice is like that of a biblical figure or a computerized toy: a set of prepackaged utterances that can be accessed arbitrarily and that seem more or less pertinent depending on listeners' interpretive will. To that extent, today's Malcolm is marked for and by objectification.

That is the deeper truth beneath complaints about the penumbra of commodification surrounding Malcolm's new popularity. Malcolm's reduction to a logo on a baseball cap only reflects his prior reduction to a soothing object of contemplation, a talismanic image. Yes, it is ironic that Malcolm — whose appeal in life was linked in so many ways to being militantly *un*fashionable — has become a fashion statement. Those with older recollections of him understandably bristle at seeing Malcolm lined up alongside Black Bart Simpson in the urban trinketry outposts of the mass consumer market. That phenomenon, however, is less the real problem than it is a symptom. Malcolm's incorporation into the logic of merchandising was enabled by his already having been turned into a transcendent symbol, which is, at bottom, a decontextualized, hollow *thing.* Purists' old codger–like laments about the bowdlerization of Malcolm thus do not only miss the point; they are betrayed by their own self-righteousness. What is being bowdlerized is an already romanticized image, a hero larger than — and therefore outside of — life, an *object* of reverence.

Malcolm X is attractive to young people today in part because he was attractive to young people when he was alive. Those who are now drawn to Malcolm are therefore especially likely to take their elders' constructions of him and his significance as foundation for their own. What they have been given is a Malcolm X fabricated within an abstracted discourse of black "greatness," a discourse that lines up public figures like trading cards. (In this respect the Malcolm versus Martin cliché brings to mind the debate in the late 1960s over whether it was Hank Aaron or Willie Mays who was the best baseball player of all time or the debate in the 1950s pitting Mays against the White Hope, Mickey Mantle.) This notion of greatness even undermines the injunction to "learn from" Malcolm, which is a commonly proposed alternative to purely commercialized identification with him. Nothing can be learned from a decontextualized icon except timeless wisdom. And timeless wisdom is worse than useless for making sense of social life inside real history. It inevitably boils down either to tag phrases and slogans or to allegorically driven platitudes. The former function only as rhetorical parsley, an authenticating garnish ("As Malcolm said,..." and so on) in the patter of those who parrot them; the latter—for example, "when Malcolm (was in prison, went to Mecca, broke with Elijah Muhammad) he learned that..." et cetera—in addition replace thought and analysis with truisms and empty pieties. Both are ideally suited for inscription on buttons and T-shirts.

The current Malcolmania is not simply the product of clever marketing and merchandising. For many people, of course, the fad is just that, and the object could as easily be Black Bart or Michael Jordan. At the other end of the continuum are those who experience their embrace of the Malcolm imagery self-consciously as political behavior. Most probably fall someplace in between, in the big region where existential statement, political statement, and fashion statement swirl together into a more or less emphatic, but generally inchoate, attitude. Especially in these dispiriting times, though, the temptation is to read more coherence, strategy, and critique into the phenomenon than are warranted. Among those of us desperate for signs of political mobilization, it is all too easy to believe that Malcolm's apparent popularity either reflects or may crystallize a rising tide of activism. This temptation persists despite the existence of clear precedent to the contrary.

In the late 1960s and early 1970s the proliferation of black power tchotchke washed out the boundary between ideology and fad and exposed the inherent limitations of inferring outlook from either choices made among the artifacts of mass consumer culture or the vagaries of tonsorial and sartorial style. Anyone could cultivate an Afro, listen to the Last Poets, or wear a dashiki or a red, black, and green button, and doing so was in no way a reliable indication of any concrete views concerning political, social, or economic life. Individuals who consumed black power paraphernalia typically may have understood themselves to be endorsing or asserting a pro-black attitude through their choices. However, the symbols expressing that attitude—refracted as they were through the mass market's least common denominator—were so amorphous as to accommodate any sort of substantive belief or practice. As a popular recruiting slogan of the time put it, "You can be black and Navy too."

Black power consumerism (as distinguished from black power ideology), however, developed in an environment defined by political activism; it was parasitic, therefore, on a rhetoric of black assertiveness that presumed the centrality of ideological programs and strategic agendas. To that extent, the consumerist construction of radical black identity was regularly criticized as superficial, an inadequate proxy for concerted political thought and action. Of course, the ideologies and strategies on whose behalf critics disparaged the equation of commodities and consciousness were usually themselves neither free from mystification nor pragmatically acute as radical politics. Nevertheless, the critics nearly all insisted that claims to serious commitment or sophisticated analysis be judged in relation to an objective of changing social conditions affecting black people. And that view entailed an orientation to strategic thinking that paid at least instrumental attention to the institutions and processes of public authority. That inflection was encouraged, of course, by material inducements generated through War on Poverty and Great Society programs (for example, Community Action or Model Cities funding) as well as the energy created around the rise of black public officialdom. The key fact remains, though, that radical black consciousness in the 1960s and 1970s was at least partly a discourse about and intersecting with public power—from protests against police behavior and displacement for urban renewal to demands for community control, welfare rights, and tenants' rights. Even pan-Africanists and cultural nationalists, whose ideologies supported quietistic withdrawal from American politics, consistently sought to align themselves with black public officials (with the National Black Political Convention in Gary, Indiana, in 1972, the National Black Assembly, and the 1970 Congress of African Peoples as the most prominent examples) and to mobilize around contesting the exercise of public authority in the black community.

My point is not to romanticize that period as a golden age of black radicalism. On the contrary, the forces critical of black power consumerism, despite their genuflections to the need for practical action and concrete program, tended less toward coherent critique than to the kind of self-righteous denunciations of impiety or impurity we now hear from codgers (and wanna-be codgers) concerned to protect the sanctity of Malcolm's image. Nor were those forces ever dominant in Afro-American political or ideological life. Although the previous decade had been a time of fairly open-ended struggle for the hearts and minds of black America, by the middle of the 1970s radicalism had been generally marginalized. Primacy in articulating the discourse of black consciousness had been won by mainstream politicians, the centrist civil rights establishment, and the purveyors of sitcoms and blaxploitation films. (Watching children act out a perception of their authentic blackness derived from Jimmy "J. J." Walker on *Good Times*—"DY-NO-MIIITE!"—chastened at least some of us grappling with the slippery problem of crafting a critical politics tied to notions of cultural authenticity.)

Radicalism's defeat, moreover, resulted in part from internal tendencies. Because black power activism's sole critical category was race, radicals were generally unprepared to respond when the new, mainstream black political elite gained momentum in the late 1960s and began to consolidate a new kind of racially assertive but still accommodationist politics. The rising stratum of black officeholders and public managers advanced a model of racial empowerment defining incremental adjustment of the routine operations of institutions in their charge — for example, increasing minority personnel ratios, opening access to minority competitors for public contracting, fine-tuning mechanisms to reduce potential conflict arising in human service delivery, appointment of more black officials — and other forms of insider action as the only legitimate political goals. This definition drastically narrowed the horizon of political activity by denying the efficacy of all strategies geared to challenging entrenched policy priorities. The model also directly endorsed demobilization of the black citizenry by limiting the scope of legitimate participation to ratifying agendas set by elites; in this view voting on command becomes the standard of active participation, and simple acquiescence replaces engagement. A radical discourse that presumed uncomplicated uniformity of purpose in an organic "black community" was short-circuited by this outcome of the demand for community control; black power sensibility could neither anticipate nor effectively criticize the appearance of a cohort of (more or less decent and humane, more or less venal and reactionary — but all militantly race-conscious) Bantustan administrators as a stratum-for-itself. This problem was only compounded by the main civil rights organizations' incorporation into public management processes. The Urban League, the NAACP, Operation PUSH (People United to Serve Humanity), and the Southern Christian Leadership Conference (SCLC) all found their way into public budgets and the inner circles of policy implementation and thereby legitimized accommodationist, insider politics as the proper legacy of protest activism. The new elite gained ground rapidly, aided by the greater access to material and ideological resources that insider status confers and the related capacity to promise, and deliver, immediate benefits. As that occurred, radicalism increasingly took refuge in ideological purification.

In this context, the turn to ideology over the decade following the 1966 proclamation of black power aimed not so much to make sense of what was going on politically as to avoid confronting it by constructing alternative narratives in which mundane politics was ephemeral. Those narratives — chiefly Kawaida nationalism, pan-Africanism, and increasingly esoteric brands of axiomatic Marxism-Leninism — were also intended to define a black political agenda different from and more authentic than mainstream black accommodationism. They sought fundamentally, however, to preempt rather than to challenge the new political elite's vision. To that extent, the turn to ideology was an evasive maneuver, as even its form suggests.

The search for a guiding ideology usually began with uncoupling from the really existing situation to work out, in the abstract, an internally consistent cosmology, whose propagation then became the basis for attracting adherents. Ideology's relation to current practice was thus inevitably arcane and rested on a logic of imaginative rationalization that was vulnerable to the worst extremes of opportunism. After all, any specific action might be linked to one of the Seven Principles of the Nguzo Saba, might contribute to the millennial emancipation of Africa, might be historically correct for the appropriate stage of a class struggle that had no empirical referents. This notion of ideology was formulaic and even in its allegedly Marxist variants shared as much with religion as with politics. More significantly, in positing the "real" concerns — inculcation of a "black value system," liberation and unification of Africa, a resuscitated Comintern version of socialist revolution — as lying on a different plane from the agendas projected by elite politicians, radicals in effect conceded the latter's dominance by refusing to engage them head-on.

By the 1980s the mainstream elite was hegemonic in Afro-American politics and political discourse. Popular mobilization had dissipated, radical activism was a memory, and the ideological affiliations of the late 1960s and early 1970s existed mainly as relics. Not even the growing threat of the Reagan-Bush assault on black Americans could rekindle an assertive, popular political movement. The earlier failure to formulate a critical response to the post-segregation era's mainstream accommodationism had culminated in an inability to develop an effective language or practice of political opposition. Indeed, as the hegemonic national political discourse has moved ever more in a conservative, victim-blaming direction, the black elite has moved along with it. We have seen the steady expansion of a rhetoric of special black middle-class responsibility for impoverished Afro-Americans, calls for moral rearmament, and complaints about pathology, social disorganization, and self-defeating behavior — all tied together by a quasi-nationalist insistence on "self-help." As in the society at large, this rhetoric is not merely the province of avowed conservatives. Black liberals, even leftists, and of course nationalists of all stripes have embraced this line even as it becomes this era's common sense.

Also beginning in the 1980s, the invention of a youth-centered hip-hop culture, whose iconic markers allegedly constitute an immanent form of social criticism, has once again blurred the lines between ideology and style, political action and consumer preference. This time the tendency to read critical consciousness into fashion and fad is even less restrained than a generation earlier. Certain features of the Reagan-Bush-hip-hop era combine particularly to obscure the faultiness of conflating political outlook and identification with a consumer taste community. On the one hand, the relatively low level of political mobilization among black Americans (and its corollary, the absence of a dynamic political movement) has removed a pragmatic constraint on the ways people think and talk about alternative politics, at the same time that the official narratives have come to seem suffocatingly inadequate. On the other hand, the influence of a "cultural politics" discourse—an outgrowth of the structuralist and poststructuralist trends in radical social theorizing—denies the possibility of a problem in this regard by defining identification with a "taste community" as intrinsically political behavior, of equal status with purposive contests over state action.

This is the context in which the rediscovery of Malcolm X has occurred. To be sure, much of the ubiquity of X trinkets can be attributed to the snowball effects of Spike Lee's marketing campaign. Lee's concerted efforts and talent as a hypester—fueled by and fueling his own iconic presence—no doubt explain much of the greater visibility that this phenomenon has enjoyed in relation to the era's previous inner-city youth fads, for example, Africa medallions in the late 1980s and coonskin or Confederate battle caps (so much for immanently revolutionary consciousness) a few years earlier. It is also probably easier to produce Malcolmania knockoffs; all it takes is sticking X appliqués onto existing merchandise. Even when those factors are taken into account, though, there is almost certainly a residuum of autonomous attraction to Malcolm's image. And, in any case, the marketing blitz clearly has stimulated interest, which in turn has taken on a life of its own. So the main questions persist: Why does the Malcolm image have so much resonance now? What can its popularity tell us about our situation? Is there any way to look to Malcolm X for practical commentary on the present?

Those questions stand out especially when we consider that all of the most significant tendencies in post-segregation era black politics matured after his death. Malcolm was killed nearly six months before the Watts uprising, nearly a year and a half before Willie Ricks and Stokely Carmichael introduced the black power slogan on the Meredith march in 1966, two years before Ron Karenga invented Kwanzaa. Malcolm was dead more than two years before the election of the first black big-city mayor, more than a year before the establishment of the Model Cities program that became a principal training ground for black urban managers. (And he died months before the first major escalation of the Vietnam War, almost three years before the Tet offensive.)

By the time black power consumerism took hold, Malcolm had been dead for long enough to have been turned into a beatific symbol invoked as an emblem of righteousness rather than as a guide to action. "Niggers loved to hear Malcolm rap, but they didn't love Malcolm," declaimed the ever didactic Last Poets in "Niggers Are Scared of Revolution." In fact, during the 1970s Malcolm was already being rediscovered in fabulous terms, as *The Autobiography of Malcolm X* became a frequently assigned text — characteristically as a bildungsroman — in college and high school black studies courses.

In the early 1980s, things changed. A story making the rounds among black academics during that period had a perplexed student asking a professor earnestly, "Who was this Malcolm the Tenth?" The story reflected recognition of a generational passage; it was the signal of the first cohort to approach maturity with no clear memories of 1960s activism or the specific injustices it fought. The average first-year college student in 1980 had been at most three years old when Malcolm was murdered and was barely into school when the movement began to decompose. Also, the national ideological climate shifted toward out-of-hand dismissal of that activism as a benighted, outmoded style like long hair. Young black people were no less inclined than others to distinguish themselves from their elders in the terms provided by mass culture, and they had also grown up with perceptions of the 1960s acquired through *Laugh-In* and B movies. (A little-remarked feature of the blaxploitation genre was its standard depiction of "militants" as incompetent, naive, and "out-of-touch" with "real," apolitical blackness.) Even those who had read *The Autobiography of Malcolm X* as the disconnected story of a great, perhaps tragic, personality were no more knowledgeable than others in this respect.

As the popularity of the tale of the perplexed undergraduate attests, many in the older generation were alarmed by young people's dismissive ignorance. I confess to having been stopped in my tracks in a New Haven laundry upon seeing my first black teen in a Confederate battle cap, complete with stars and bars on top. (My query confirmed the obvious; he had not a clue about the Civil War or the Confederacy, much less either's relation to his choice in haberdashery.) Stories like these gained velocity, so that by the middle of the decade they combined to support an almost ritualistic lament that "our young people don't know anything about (our, their own) history." Embedded in this lament was a call for remedial action.

Unfortunately, the easiest, most immediately available alternative was one familiar from a decade of Black History Month ads and public service announcements, the compendium of Black Contributions and Accomplishments and Great Black Historical Figures. This approach, sort of a hybrid Homeric narrative and

Afrocentric version of *Jeopardy!*, bears traces of a pattern — reaching back through the turn of the century — of subordinating historical analysis to the project of vindicating the race's image. It is itself profoundly ahistorical and was one of the reasons that young people were so poorly informed in the first place. Television crews' trips to inner-city schools around Martin Luther King Jr.'s birthday annually exposed its limitations. In response to variants of the question "What do you know about Martin Luther King?" students — kindergarten through twelfth grade — invariably returned answers with the same structure: A long time ago black people didn't have any freedom, and then Martin Luther King came, and they got their freedom. (As a product of Catholic education under the regime of Pius XII, this is a form of call-and-response I knew only too well; the *Baltimore Catechism* is not a good model for understanding anything, least of all history.)

Those who had formed their political consciousness in the 1960s were somewhere between settled adulthood and middle age when they encountered this shift in the youth population. Therefore, the latter's apparent passivity and lack of appreciation for an epic past rang an especially discordant note against an older generation's slide toward nostalgic reflection on its own youth, a mood illustrated in (and encouraged by) the oldies' music boom during those years. Such nostalgia naturally feeds on invidious comparisons with "today's" youth, whose folkways thus appear increasingly opaque and irrational. The concern with historical amnesia and political inertness in this way flowed into stereotypical anxieties about the younger generation's deficiencies, which in turn commingled with the burgeoning "underclass" ideology that traded on images of widespread "cultural pathology" among inner-city black and Hispanic youth. The trope of black pathology has also blended with nationalist psychobabble about the need to repair supposedly damaged self-respect by teaching black people about "themselves." So a parade of racial self-esteem experts, who themselves had grown up with — depending on their ages — pink suits, konks, and the Cadets ("Stranded in the Jungle"); twelve-inch Afros, bell-bottom pants, and Archie Bell and the Drells; or pimp hats, new-style konks, platform shoes, and Bootsy's Rubber Band; came forward to pronounce on side-turned baseball caps, Gumby haircuts, and rap music as evidence of a rampant nihilism threatening to destroy the black social fabric. (Oh, I know, "but this is different because . . .")

In these circumstances it is not difficult to imagine how the desire to improve young people's civic education was — with notable exceptions, such as the *Eyes on the Prize* series — absorbed by an increasingly prominent fixation on finding "role models," a black manifestation of the decade's trickle-down ideology. But a focus on role models distorts history toward the search for heroes.

Similarly, linking examination of the past to a therapeutic project destroys a sense of history as process and reduces it to a field of static, decontextualized parables. Both traits suffuse the prevailing constructions of Malcolm X, and, as I have noted, they yield an objectified image primed for commercial exploitation.

This generational dynamic was overlapped by the instability arising from Reaganism's matter-of-fact break with the established model of race relations management. Not only was the Reagan agenda forthrightly hostile to black interests, but it also explicitly rejected and set out to discredit the conventional practice of insider negotiation with black political elites. Prominent black elected officials and civil rights technicians complained repeatedly during Ronald Reagan's first term that the administration had not made overtures toward the black leadership establishment and was in fact refusing access. The administration and its allies responded by challenging the mainstream political elite's legitimacy as representatives of racial interests and pursued an overt strategy of creating an alternative "voice" of pro-Reaganite blacks.

These developments exacerbated tensions at the core of the post-segregation era's style of political accommodationism, and the Reaganite strategy exposed and manipulated the points at which the new black political elite is most vulnerable. The pattern of race relations engineering that had congealed over the 1970s pivots, in its logical essence, on a quid pro quo: black retreat from a politics based on popular mobilization and potentially disruptive protest activism in exchange for a regime that guarantees regular, if only incremental or symbolic, payoffs. Central to this arrangement is a very delicate balancing act by the new Bantustan administrators. On the one hand, they must secure black acquiescence to the regime and its terms of governance. Realizing this objective has meant, in practice, channeling black political participation into support for the regime, in part by defining any other course as illegitimate and in part by successfully representing the payoffs generated as both significant and optimal. Because incremental or symbolic payoffs are hardly adequate to overcome systemic disadvantage and inequality, though, they must be buttressed by a justifying rhetoric of steady, even if very gradual, progress. On the other hand, the black political elite's capacities for generating payoffs rest ultimately on the specter of disruptive, popular mobilization, to which the regime of incrementalist race relations engineering is presented as a preferable alternative. Well into the 1970s, for example, arguments for meliorative initiatives regularly evoked the fear of a "long, hot summer" that might result from failure to pursue the desired course.

Over time, the new regime's success has made the prospect of disruptive mobilization ever more remote. Incumbent leadership is incumbent leadership regardless of race or electoral status, and incumbents generally prefer to minimize the size of the attentive public in order to maximize their loyal supporters' relative strength. Black elected officials, like other elected officials, are not particularly interested in increasing voter registration or turnout once they have carved out electoral bases that will dependably reelect them. Infusions of new voters both increase the cost and effort of campaigning and introduce a potentially volatile element into the electorate. Similarly, civil rights organizations operate most comfortably with a strategy of insider advocacy. This strategy is incompatible with popular mobilization because its principal audience is policy-making elites, and it is embedded in a technicistic discourse that requires insider knowledge. The insider advocacy strategy reorients these organizations as professional agencies of race relations administration. As a result, they function both as an independent brokerage elite and as auxiliary branches of public management. Both functions are averse to popular mobilization, and for similar reasons. Commitment to a professionalistic ideology that mystifies expertise reinforces class prejudice and defense of privilege. Also, the incremental and symbolic nature of the payoffs in this arrangement exerts a further pressure toward demobilization. It is just as well for those who do not benefit from the payoffs to be alienated or inattentive; otherwise, they might become actively dissatisfied and uncontrollably disruptive politically.

The successful institutionalization of post-segregation era elite-brokerage politics, therefore, has undercut the principal leverage (other than the ability to deliver a large bloc of Democratic voters) that the new black political elite has in negotiating payoffs. The Reaganite right exploited this contradiction. In staking out a position expressly antagonistic to blacks and in challenging the black establishment's legitimacy, the Reagan administration in effect called the tacit bluff and dared the political elite to mobilize popular opposition. In the parlance of bid whist, the Reaganites called for trumps and caught black leadership with a void.

Recognition that Reaganism was a qualitative departure from politics as usual settled in only slowly. Even Richard Nixon, after all, had not completely broken with the elite-brokerage model; despite its willingness to court white ressentiment rhetorically, the Nixon administration did not stonewall the black political establishment in the way that the Reagan administration did. Indeed, the transition from agitation to technical administration as the substance of civil rights advocacy occurred mainly under Nixon. I suspect that the Nixon-Ford precedent may have led to discounting the manifest hostility of Reagan's rhetoric. Some probably treated even his inflammatory policy agenda as a grandstand play, imagining that he would, like Nixon, slouch toward the center.

In any event, the dawning truth of the Reagan agenda precipitated anxious groping for a proper response. But lack of commitment to a larger vision of social, political, and economic organization, a related entrapment within an incrementalist discourse suddenly without pragmatic basis, and a flickering hope that the apparent was not real combined to undermine those efforts, rendering them contradictory and strangely anticlimactic. Statements whose structure and context implied the indictment and militant demand characteristic of protest politics were tepid in their actual complaints, tentative and indirect in their accusations, and likely to dribble off into bland calls for improved communication.

The 1983 March on Washington for Jobs and Freedom exemplifies the extent of the problem. The march was packaged by its organizers largely as a nostalgic event—a gathering to commemorate the famous civil rights march on the same site twenty years earlier. This focus muted the counterattack on Reagan by mixing it with a celebration of past glories. Moreover, in attempting opportunistically to draw energy from nostalgia, it in effect acknowledged the inadequacy of the black political elite's purchase on the current situation. Insofar as the turn to nostalgia was not opportunistic, it reflected the persistence of the evasive tendency in post-segregation era black politics. Constructing a supposedly simpler, clearer time in the past and then projecting it as a model for the present is, when all is said and done, a move that yearns for a different reality in lieu of engaging the one that actually confronts us.

Totemic nostalgia for civil rights activism converged with the ongoing reconstruction of Martin Luther King Jr. as singular embodiment of the movement. The intensification of a campaign to declare King's birthday a national holiday both reflected and drove this convergence. The attempt to define the holiday issue as the central racial concern also indicates how desperate and pathetically inadequate the black leadership stratum was in the face of the Reagan juggernaut. Anxiety about Reaganism grew among black Americans generally, as could be seen in a surge in voting that sharply narrowed the racial gap in voter turnout in 1982. And a backdrop blended of King idolatry and yearning for the civil rights movement's apparent clarity gave rise to a view that the black political elite's palpable failure stemmed from the absence of a comparable leader in the present. (Never mind that compression of civil rights activism into King's persona was a myth that became orthodoxy only in the 1980s.) Then, riding on the wave of pertinent symbolism condensed by the 1983 march, Jesse Jackson stepped forward to present himself as heir to King's fictitious legacy.

Jackson had been campaigning since the early 1970s to be appointed National Black Leader, a job description for which historically there had never been appreciable demand from putative constituents. Significantly, the one period during which there had been anyone approximating a singular race spokesperson was during what remains the worst time in Afro-American history since Emancipation. Booker T. Washington asserted greater influence over initiatives regarding black Americans than any individual before or since, and his preeminence corresponded almost identically with the years during which the gains of Reconstruction were largely overturned and black people were driven to the margins of American life. The relation, moreover, was not coincidental. Washington, whose agenda was by no means consensually accepted by Afro-Americans, was denominated National Black Leader by the dominant white political, economic, and philanthropic interests precisely because he preached accommodation to their program of black marginalization. To be sure, because Afro-Americans have had no referendum or other forum for legitimizing claims to be a national leader, the support of white opinion makers has been key for all aspirants to such Race Leader status. From Marcus Garvey to Elijah Muhammad to Louis Farrakhan to Jesse Jackson—all have reproduced the ironic strategy of seeking to become the Black Leader by means of white acclamation.

Jackson's quest has shown another ironic characteristic of the National Black Leader status today. Race Leaders work best if they are already dead when appointed. Through two campaigns for the Democratic presidential nomination Jackson produced few benefits besides his own aggrandizement—no shift in public policy, no institutionalized movement, not even a concrete agenda (except, again, Jackson's aggrandizement) around which to mobilize. At the same time, the rightist program has become increasingly hegemonic and has tightened steadily around the lives and aspirations of the most vulnerable strata in the black population. Under these circumstances, a doggerel rhetoric of hope, calls for self-esteem, platitudes about caring for the unfortunate, and promises of oceanic identification with the Leader's prowess could be expected to lose appeal after eight years.

Jackson exploited nostalgic yearning during the summer and fall of 1983 by staging a Potemkin grassroots movement, a speaking tour through the South, centered on churches and the occasional campus and ostensibly connected to a voter registration drive. Mass-mediated projections of the tour evoked images of civil rights activism's heroic phase and enshrined Jackson's claim to be an activist-outsider with a mobilized popular base. (Public acceptance of his self-representation as an outsider is in a way an equal opportunity spur of a line of political gullibility running from Jimmy Carter in 1976 to Jerry Brown and H. Ross Perot in 1992 and Pat Buchanan in 1996—the consummate insider as outsider, Pericles dressed up as Cincinnatus. Jackson had been incorporated into the inner circles of elite race relations management by the early 1970s. His presidential endorsement had been sought since 1972, when he flirted with Richard Nixon, and, as head of Operation PUSH, he had for about as long been negotiating covenants with major corporations and administering substantial public grants and contracts.) Jackson parlayed the persona thus created and the stirrings of germinal black impatience with incumbent leadership, along with calls to racial patriotism, to generate heavy black voting for himself in the 1984 Democratic primaries.

Local activists and fringe politicos sought to use the visibility surrounding Jackson's bid to advance their own objectives. The campaign's newsworthiness promised to enhance individual and organizational name recognition, and the motion around the candidacy opened possibilities for greater leverage vis-à-vis entrenched elites. Black elected officials in particular had come around to supporting Jackson only slowly. Some were already committed to Walter Mondale. Some questioned or opposed the idea of a black candidacy on pragmatic grounds. Some were open to a candidacy in principle but resented Jackson's presumptuousness in putting himself forward. However motivated, their reluctance to join what soon became a bandwagon appeared to make them vulnerable to insurgents. But marginalized activists' and aspiring politicians' enthusiastic embrace of Jackson was not merely strategic; the Jackson phenomenon's cathartic aspect appealed to them as well as to others. All these factors underwrote a wishful scenario in which Jesse Jackson, reborn as noble outsider and self-proclaimed "moral force" in American politics, would embody and authorize a redemptive movement— and maybe even become president, or at least a presidential nominee.

Between 1984 and 1988, however, Jackson moved his image back inside. He operated not so much as a lightning rod for black insurgents as symbolic first among equals and as authenticating touchstone for the black establishment. The most regular of black regular Democrats— for instance, David Dinkins—jumped to the forefront of Jackson motion at the local level. Jackson assured the national Democratic leadership that he most of all wanted to be a member of the inner circles of the party; he could be trusted, therefore, not to support activity that would actually violate the existing regime of race relations management. Simple familiarity also made Jackson's new persona part of normal politics. As his status thus became normalized, the potential costs of identification with him receded toward zero for mainstream black politicians. The stage was set for them to position themselves as principal manipulators (and beneficiaries) of the symbolism that many activists had hoped would galvanize an insurgent opposition. Moreover, when establishment and activist factions squared off for control of local organizations, as in New Jersey, Jackson gave the nod of legitimacy to the former. (This disposition reflected both the practical advantage of supporting the claimants who have greater resources and Jackson's fundamental commitment to the stratum of black insiders, a commitment that later led him even to defend Marion Barry.) As had happened with black power, mainstream elites co-opted the putative symbols of insurgency. In this case, moreover, the co-optation occurred more smoothly. It was facilitated by Jackson's presence as exclusive arbiter of the main symbol—himself—and by the relative absence of contestation of elite hegemony over the terms of black political debate.

Jackson's 1988 campaign presumed that he had proven his status as National Black Leader in 1984, and he did seem to have united insiders and outsiders consensually under the umbrella of his candidacy. So uncontested was his claim to be the Black Leader that the campaign focused most concertedly on demonstrating his broader appeal as spokesman for the generically "locked out." When the dust settled, though, Jackson had been able to draw only about 10 percent of the white vote. And he had won no concessions from the party or the nominee except the use of an airplane for his efforts on behalf of Michael Dukakis in the race against George Bush. The official script of hope, excitement, enthusiasm, and so on attendant on Jackson's 1988 effort obscured at least two of its dangerous characteristics. Jackson's success in forging consensual black identification with his candidacy effected the most radical narrowing of the focus of Afro-American political action to date. He managed more thoroughly than in 1984 to squeeze the totality of recognized black concern with presidential politics into his demand for personal "respect" from the Democratic party leadership and, eventually, its standard-bearer. That the payoff was so skimpy only adds insult to injury.

Similarly, Jackson's custodianship of black voting power allowed the other Democratic candidates to avoid directly courting black voters during the primary season. Instead, it was entirely reasonable for them to concede the black primary vote to Jackson. The eventual nominee then would be free to cut a separate deal with the Black Leader and would thus be able to benefit from black electoral support without being stigmatized as the blacks' candidate. Jackson's candidacy, therefore, probably made it easier for the white candidates to act out the belief—formalized in the party by the Democratic Leadership Council (DLC), formed in 1985 after Mondale's defeat—that the party had fallen onto hard times in presidential politics because it was too closely identified with minorities, labor, and other "special interests."

This perspective puts new light on the love feast shared in 1988 by Jackson and Bert Lance, who had always been associated with the party's conservative, southern white wing. Jackson's visibility aided the DLC's agenda both by keeping the specter of racial polarization in the limelight and by giving the other candidates space to refine a pattern of debate that excluded explicit concern with issues bearing on specifically Afro-American interests. When Jackson succeeded in becoming the symbolic embodiment of black interests in the campaign, he also helped those forces seeking to marginalize blacks among the agenda-setting constituencies in the Democratic party.

After two emotional campaigns and incessant maneuvering and posturing between them, Jackson apparently had no further moves to make. Despite his contention that his candidacy was necessary to stop white Democrats from taking black voters for granted, he had contributed to producing just the opposite effect. In positioning himself as National Black Leader, he has also claimed the status of singular broker of a black population whose interests and concerns are isomorphic with his own. In the process he has helped to diminish black Americans' autonomous significance in the party by insisting that their preferences be channeled through him. Insofar as satisfying him can be construed as satisfying black Americans, Jackson has seriously reduced the level of black demand on the party and the political system. At the turn of the century, making a private railroad car available so that Booker T. Washington could avoid the indignities of Jim Crow was less costly than protecting black people's civil rights; in the same way, giving Jesse Jackson an airplane for campaigning and recognition in inner circles (in his phrase, "a seat at the table") is more convenient than trying to craft a political agenda that actually safeguards and advances social justice and racial equality.

So on the verge of becoming a black Harold Stassen, Jackson decided not to run in 1992. The damage, though, had already been done. Political and economic conditions have steadily continued to deteriorate within the Afro-American population, and demoralization seems ever more pronounced. Even activists who had steered by their own lights for decades before Jackson's rise to prominence find themselves hamstrung conceptually and programmatically, trapped by a narrative that requires Jackson as Black Leader to provide a basis and direction for action. Politics seems not to offer avenues for response, ironically, in part because the National Black Leader myth, particularly as realized in the Jackson phenomenon, has cut political action loose from its moorings in practical activity and reconfigured it as existential drama. This is the setting in which Malcolm X has been rediscovered.

It is perhaps instructive that Malcolmania has come at the same time as Jackson's attempt to embody the Black Leader myth appears to be running out of steam. Suspicion that he and Malcolm contend for the same iconic and affective space is reinforced by popular culture; Public Enemy's "Bring the Noise," for example, moves between the two in its imagery. A living Leader is handicapped by having at some point to produce real outcomes. Jackson has taken smoke and mirrors about as far as they can go, and he may now be on the verge of exemplifying how gossamer thin is the line between icon and cliché. Malcolm, as I have noted, is exempt from any test of efficacy based on current practice; unlike Jackson, he quite literally can do no wrong. In trying to move into the role previously assigned to King, Jackson seems to have overlooked an essential point: King had to die before attaining the status of iconic Leader. One can in fact only secure it in retrospect, as a posthumous garland. To that extent, Malcolm is much better suited to the position than Jackson. Illustratively, Spike Lee may hold Jackson in high regard, but he ended *Do the Right Thing* with supposedly hortatory quotations from Malcolm and King, whose images recur throughout the film.

I do not mean to be either callous or pointlessly irreverent in stressing the all-too-obvious fact that King and Malcolm are dead. I do so only in service to a less obvious point. The King, Jackson, and Malcolm iconologies that have spread during the Reagan-Bush era—as well as the mythos of the singular Black Leader that connects them—are most meaningfully expressions of the tendency toward evasiveness that has undermined the development of critical vision in black politics in the post-segregation era. Yes, the turn to Malcolm in part reflects deepening frustration with material conditions and Jackson's failure, but more important, it reproduces the vicarious, or even apolitical, approach to politics that undergirded the earlier romanticizations of King and Jackson.

Three weeks before the 1992 Illinois primaries I attended an all-day public forum on Malcolm X in Chicago. (An earlier one on a similar format had been held in New York.) The organizers had in mind that the gathering and discussions would shed light on the serious issues confronting Afro-Americans today. Speakers generally applauded young people for their interest in Malcolm X but also challenged them to dig beneath the X and Afrocentric fashion items to apprehend and emulate Malcolm's "real" essence. Tacitly or explicitly, this challenge presumed that proper orientation toward Malcolm would usefully inform contemporary action. During the entire day, however, there was only one direct reference to current political issues and events, and all the discussions proceeded as if the institutions of public authority were peripheral, if not entirely alien, to Afro-American concern.

Old warhorses often have remained stuck in rituals of opposition that do not take account of important shifts—inspired by consequences of the Voting Rights

Act—in the institutional and ideological environment of racial subordination over the 1970s and 1980s. Those old rituals cannot help make sense of the rise of black governance's complex meanings. For example, even construed as Bantustan administration, black control of public institutions creates black constituencies for those institutions by democratizing access to the spoils and perquisites of government. If only by virtue of increasing the likelihood of their sharing social networks with pertinent functionaries, black government increases black citizens' access to zoning variances, summer jobs in municipal agencies, waivers on code enforcement, breaks in the criminal justice system, special parks and recreation services, and a host of other nonroutine benefits, as well as public contracts. But this improved access does not trickle uniformly through the black citizenry, and black control of those agencies whose principal function is the management of the dispossessed does not alter their ultimately repressive function. Black control also does not alter the way those agencies socialize their personnel; few speak less sympathetically of black poor people than black service providers in housing authorities, welfare departments, and school systems. Neither generic black power radicalism nor its more elaborate descendants (most prominently now, for example, Afrocentricity) can provide categories that capture these or comparable subtleties associated with the construction of political meaning in the post-segregation era. Nor can they productively conceptualize the subtle ways that social position, point of view, and political interest interact within the Afro-American population.

That the old rituals cannot account for the dynamics that have shaped the environment within which contemporary black politics has developed just makes bad matters worse. They induce blindness to the import of such factors as the intricate logics of reorganization at work in domestic and global political economy since World War II: the consolidation of a domestic political model—joining national and local levels—that cements interest-group loyalties and legitimizes state power through participation in a regime of public stimulation of private economic growth; the subsidiary role of defense spending, transportation, and urban redevelopment policy in recomposing regional and metropolitan demographic, economic, and political organization. The result is a radicalism that gives away some of the most important conceptual ground to defenders of the status quo. This is a radicalism that cannot effectively challenge questionable reifications such as the dichotomy between manufacturing sector and service sector jobs, the representation of deindustrialization as if it were natural law, or the series of mystifications that run through imagery surrounding the terms "high-tech" and "skill" and their bearing on debates about education, training, unemployment, and income inequality. There is nothing that understanding the "real" Malcolm X — an impossibility in any event — could do to clarify or to help formulate positions regarding any of those phenomena, neither the internal nor the external forces shaping black political life. Invoking his image in these circumstances amounts to wishing away the complexities that face us. So, for instance, when Spike Lee (at the end of his epilogue to *Do the Right Thing*) denounces the regime of racial subordination represented by then New York mayor Ed Koch, he poses the trite juxtaposition of Malcolm and King, standing for violence and nonviolence, as the available alternatives. But that juxtaposition does not suggest what was substantively wrong with the Koch regime (hardly a difficult task, if Lee had but attended to it), hint at how governance of New York City might proceed more equitably, or even imply anything really concrete about mobilization for change. His statement is vague on all the questions central to the sort of call to arms he obviously intends it to be, the questions bearing on the who, what, when, where, and why of political action. Despite its hortatory form, Lee's injunction is pointlessly evocative. The reference to King and Malcolm is just filler, conveying a specious appearance of substance. The reference substitutes for analysis and critique of an obviously objectionable political situation; it is an evasion.

Lee's presentation of the violence/nonviolence dichotomy as a proper frame for organizing political response calls on style and emotional posture to do the work of critical argument, program, and strategy. In doing so, and especially by retailing the hackneyed Malcolm/King trope in the process, he links the defects of the old rituals of opposition to the particular form of political evasion that has developed during the Reagan-Bush era, the discourse of cultural politics. This discourse avoids the problem of black demobilization by redefining the sphere of political action to center on everyday practices of self-presentation and popular cultural expression. Repeating a move of the previous generation, it sidesteps the thorny issues surrounding Afro-Americans' relation to the exercise of public authority in the post-segregation era by dismissing the domain of official politics and governance as inauthentic and therefore not pertinent to radical concern.

As with the different manifestations of the earlier turn to ideology as well, the cultural politics discourse's main analytical weapon is taxonomy; its critical edge consists principally in reclassifying, or recoding, conventional understandings of apparently mundane practices. An important difference, however, is that the objective to which cultural politics' discourse harnesses taxonomic revision is much more celebratory than hortatory. In the other narratives of political evasion, reclassification of conventionally recognized phenomena (for example, the use of Swahili relabeling in Kawaida nationalism to impute racial authenticity, the domestic colony analogy, attempts to impose a map of reified class categories onto the black population) is directed toward winning adherents to a specific program of action; the thrust of countertaxonomy runs, therefore, to exhorting people to change their perceptions as a step toward redirecting or otherwise altering their behavior. The rhetoric of cultural politics, by contrast, exalts existing practices as intrinsically subversive and emancipatory; it neither calls to action nor proposes sharp changes in quotidian activity. From this standpoint it is the ultimate concession to the fact of political demobilization; it is a construction of radical opposition that naturalizes the demobilized state as outside the scope of intervention and limits itself to celebrating moments of resistance supposedly identifiable within fundamental acquiescence.

Because it rejects distinctions between style and substance, form and content, this new rhetoric of evasiveness gives an intellectual justification for conflating political commitment and consumer market preference. Similarly in focusing on the expressive dimension of action to the exclusion of the instrumental, it refuses to make any distinction between symbolic and purposive activity. In defining participation in popular culture as political action, this stance merges the avant-garde in fashion and ideological radicalism, thus vesting fad with strategic political significance. It consequently makes a fetish of youth as a social category (another failure to learn from the mistakes of the 1960s) and idealizes trends in inner-city fashion as emancipatory expression. These characteristics work to reduce politics to purely affective and symbolic endeavor. And that is a construction of politics in which appeal to icons readily takes the place of careful argument and critical analysis. The youth fetish is especially revealing in this regard.

To represent youth as a status group is to forget the inherently transitory character of that status. Treating youth as authentic bearers of the principle of opposition, moreover, confuses existential rebellion and political rebellion. The former can be pacified through mass marketing; the latter cannot. This romantic view also elides the problem that the coherence of youth as a group in American society derives mainly from its status as a market fraction. Consumption figures so prominently in youth culture because that is the main arena that exists for young people's autonomous action and, relatedly, because the category itself is a creation of the sales effort. Perhaps the most problematic aspect of the youth fetish in cultural politics discourse, though, is the premise that we should look to those who know the least about and have the least experience in the world for our salvation. (This premise even seemed ridiculous to me when I was in a position to benefit from it.)

The climate thus created nurtures the nightmarish absurdity in which rappers project themselves as political sages. Confused and depressingly ignorant performers such as KRS-One, Public Enemy, X-Clan, and Sister Souljah spew garbled compounds of half-truth, distortion, Afrocentric drivel, and cracker-barrel wisdom, as often as not shot through with reactionary prejudices, and claim pontifical authority on the basis of identity with the props of their stage and video performances. Interviews raise the disturbing possibility that many of these "raptivists," the purportedly authentic voices of politically astute youth, in their minds construe the scenes staged in their message videos as identical with actual political experience.

Malcolmania arises in this environment, as the image of Malcolm X, for reasons I and others have described, increasingly takes on a talismanic quality. But the Malcolm iconology does not simply support continued evasion of tough political questions; in addition, attempts to draw on Malcolm for guidance reproduce his inaccurate, simplistic reading of Afro-American history and reinforce inadequate and wrongheaded tendencies in the present. Few images from the 1960s, for example, have had such broad and lasting resonance as Malcolm's construction of the difference between the "house Negro" and the "field Negro." This construction gave an institutional foundation to the image of the Uncle Tom and has provided a powerful metaphor for characterizing class and ideological cleavage among black Americans. The fact is, though, that this metaphor is historically wrong, obfuscatory, and counterproductive.

Whether or not Malcolm meant the house Negro/field Negro antagonism to be an accurate description of a dominant historical pattern rather than simply a rhetorical device, the metaphor draws its force from the implication of sedimented tension and historical continuity. But the reality of slave acquiescence and resistance was much more complex and mediated. Nat Turner, Denmark Vesey, and Gabriel Prosser—leaders of the best-known slave revolts—all were house slaves. More important, the distinction itself was one imposed from outside the slave population. When they could, slaves were as likely as not to try to avoid assignment to work in the house; such work could be especially demeaning, and it represented a further erosion of the already exceedingly limited autonomy slaves could fashion for themselves. This is not a merely pedantic point; Malcolm's metaphor also implies an ontological claim about an original position of organic unity among Afro-Americans.

The field Negro in Malcolm's rendition stands not only for the "masses"; he (and the image is male) also represents authentic racial unity. The house Negro is therefore not simply wrong, or even just duped, but is also a race traitor. This construction presumes that unity of purpose is black Americans' "natural" condition and that disunity, as a result, must spring from treason or some comparably pathogenic force, such as brainwashing, personal ambition, or moral laxity. In addition to its historical falsity (which ironically reflects the prerevisionist portrayal of black slaves as a brutalized, undifferentiated mass huddled around a campfire) and its implicit intolerance of dissent, there are two things grievously wrong with this view: First, it reduces political differences to a matter of individual psychology and morality. This biases political criticism to allegations concerning personal virtue or mental health and disconnects it from examination of functional relation to structures of power and the autonomous effects of social position. Second, the tacit ontological premise of an originally organic unity establishes racial authenticity as a primary criterion for political judgment. The combined effect of these two problems is to sustain an impoverished form of debate that revolves around assessing whether individuals or positions are "really" black. This pattern of debate stands in the way of making sense of the dynamics propelling Afro-American political life and is, of course, a demagogue's dream.

Malcolm's injunction that black disagreements and problems should be resolved "in the closet" — that is, quietly among Afro-Americans themselves — at the same time acknowledges the reality of difference within the race and seeks to subordinate it to a naive vision of perfect unity. He repeatedly employed family imagery to appeal to a notion of unity that is not purposive but is instead an independent ethical, for the most part racially grounded, imperative. But any unity must exist on some terms, and Malcolm's dicta do not inform the articulation of those terms, especially not under post-segregation era conditions when no clear objective, such as the destruction of Jim Crow, leads toward consensus. Malcolm never developed a sophisticated or coherent strategy, even for his times; he certainly could not predict the changed conditions that would prevail after his death. Indeed, none of Malcolm's formulations can provide the basis for effective commentary on contemporary Afro-American politics.

Not surprisingly, Malcolm nevertheless is frequently invoked, particularly since the spread of Malcolmania, as a luminous product endorsement for one or another current political program. These are, moreover, often — but not exclusively — programs whose substance is in present circumstances reactionary. Self-reliance or self-help is one such case. In current political debate self-reliance is a code for a Booker T. Washington–style forfeiture of the right to make claims on public authority. In this vein black conservatives such as Clarence Thomas or Tony Brown are at least as likely to annex Malcolm's authority as are nationalists, who prefer not to be thought of as conservative.

Malcolm's image is also attractive to those concerned to advance the cause of black men. His appeal to some degree has always had a distinctively male inflection. The alternative that he posed to the civil rights movement's passive resistance was bound up with constructions of masculine assertiveness in at least two ways: On the one hand, as I have noted, he appealed to the urban male sensibility that associated failure to fight back with cowardliness. On the other hand, he embodied a sort of Afro-American version of republican manhood; he projected civic virtue, respect for and protection of home and hearth (including women), and the patriarchal vision that defines public life as a masculine realm. He spoke often of manhood rights. It is no accident, therefore, that Ossie Davis's eulogy was steeped in masculine imagery; that imagery had a great deal to do with what Malcolm meant to black men.

Malcolm's image as vicarious redeemer of the suppressed prerogatives of black manhood received a boost from, of all sources, Daniel Moynihan's nefarious report *The Negro Family: A Case for National Action.* Nationalists and other petit bourgeois black sexists began incorporating Moynihan's charges concerning the existence of a debilitating black matriarchy that crushed male spirit and arrested masculine development. By 1972 this line underwrote opposition to Shirley Chisholm's entry into presidential primaries on the ground that she usurped a male prerogative. Worry about the dangers of excessive feminine influence was already an old chestnut. At the turn of the century many scholars fretted that the upper classes would slide into degeneracy because of the "feminization" of their men. The trope is rooted in the gendered dichotomy of nature and culture. Moynihan extended it to blacks (who already had a special place in the nature/culture dichotomy, of course).

The Moynihan line was attractive because it gave a race-conscious foundation to black sexism, though most of its proponents would never acknowledge their ideological debt to him. (For his part, Malcolm remained at best an unexamined, paternalistic sexist to his death, and his paternalism bordered on misogyny in its insistence on female subservience.) Beginning in the 1980s we have seen the stirrings of another wave of antifeminist backlash from black men. Under the guise of rhetoric alleging the "crisis of the black male" and proclaiming black men to be an "endangered species," calls for male assertiveness and discussion of men's special needs have returned. From William Julius Wilson to Glenn Loury to entertainers and athletes a popular consensus is forming, across the ideological spectrum, that black men need gender-inflected help.

Role-model rhetoric meshes with this concern and authorizes practices such as sending male buppies into inner-city schools and neighborhoods to propagate "authentic" (and respectable) models of black manhood. Malcolm has been enlisted in these efforts as a version of the ideal black man. His image very well may be etched onto the club used to try to beat black women toward the background so that damaged black manhood may be repaired, or to drive them—by making the currently existing alternatives still more horrible and repressive—into economic dependence on men through marriage.

Because Malcolm has no agency at all, he is now even more a hologram of social forces than he was for my generation. The inchoate, often apparently inconsistent trajectory of his thought makes him an especially plastic symbol in the present context. It is all too tempting to play the what-Malcolm-would-do-if-he-were-alive game, but the temptation should be avoided because the only honest response is that we can have no idea. Part of what was so exciting about Malcolm, in retrospect anyway, was that he was moving so quickly, experimenting with ideas, trying to get a handle on the history he was living. Recognizing that he never did does not demean him, but it does underscore the reality that though we all certainly have our own favorite scenarios, no one can have any hint of where he would have wound up politically. If he had not been killed when he was, what developed as black power radicalism may have taken a somewhat different form and so, therefore, would the responses it generated. Yet even imagining that everything would have happened as it did, it is still impossible to say what course Malcolm would have taken. One irony in the present appropriation of his image does stand out, however. Despite Malcolm's own ambivalence about his status as a race spokesman and the legitimacy of black leadership as a category (and notwithstanding his rhetoric about unity), Malcolm made his reputation by attacking entrenched elites and challenging their attempts to constrain popular action and the vox populi. Now he is canonized as an icon, an instrument of an agenda that is just the opposite of popular mobilization.

It seems to me that the best way to think of the best of Malcolm is that he was just like the rest of us: a regular person saddled with imperfect knowledge, human frailties, and conflicting imperatives but nonetheless trying to make sense of his very specific history, trying unsuccessfully to transcend it, and struggling to push it in a humane direction. We can learn most from his failures and limitations because they speak most clearly both of the character of his time and of the sorts of perils we must guard against in our own. He was no prince; there are no princes, only people like ourselves who strive to influence their own history. To the extent that we believe otherwise, we turn Malcolm into a postage stamp and reproduce the evasive reflex that has deformed critical black political action for a generation.

1992

Notes

1. The Jug and Its Content

1. Martin Kilson, "The New Black Political Class," in *Dilemmas of the Black Middle Class,* ed. Joseph Washington (Philadelphia: Washington, 1980), and Kilson, "From Civil Rights to Party Politics: The Black Political Transition," *Current History* 67 (November 1974): 193–99.

2. Rufus P. Browning, Dale Rogers Marshall, and David H. Tabb, *Protest Is Not Enough: The Struggle of Blacks and Hispanics for Equality in Urban Politics* (Berkeley: University of California Press, 1984). Browning, Marshall, and Tabb define incorporation as a reflection of "the extent to which group interests are effectively represented in policy making. [They] measure the political incorporation of black and Hispanic minorities by assessing the extent to which they were represented in coalitions that dominated city policy making on minority-related issues" (25). See also the theoretical overviews and case studies in Browning, Marshall, and Tabb, eds., *Racial Politics in American Cities,* 2nd ed. (White Plains, NY: Longman, 1997). I discuss the demobilizing effects of incorporation on black activist politics in chapter 4 of this volume.

3. Floyd Hunter, *Community Power Structure* (Chapel Hill: University of North Carolina Press, 1953). Also see Hunter, *Community Power Succession: Atlanta's Policy Makers Revisited* (Chapel Hill: University of North Carolina Press, 1980); Mack H. Jones, "Black Political Empowerment in Atlanta: Myth and Reality," *Annals of the American Academy of Political and Social Science* 439 (September 1978): 90–117; Clarence Stone, *Economic Growth and Neighborhood Discontent* (Chapel Hill: University of North Carolina Press, 1976), and Stone, *Regime Politics: Governing Atlanta, 1946–1988* (Lawrence: University of Kansas Press, 1989); Malcolm Suber, "The Internal Black Politics of Atlanta, Georgia, 1944–1969: An Analytic Study of Black Political Leadership and Organization" (M.A. thesis, Atlanta University, Atlanta, Georgia, 1975); Claude W. Barnes Jr., "Political Power and Economic Dependence: An Analysis of Atlanta's Black Urban Regime" (Ph.D. diss., Clark-Atlanta University, Atlanta, Georgia, 1991), and Barnes, "Black Mecca Reconsidered: An Analysis of Atlanta's Post–Civil Rights Political Economy," in *African Americans and the New Policy Consensus: Retreat of the Liberal State?,* ed. Marilyn E. Lashley and Melanie Njeri Jackson (Westport, CT: Greenwood, 1994); see as well Peter Eisinger, *The Politics of Displacement: Racial and Ethnic Transition in Three American*

Cities (New York: Academic Press, 1980). Richard A. Keiser notes that the regime of dependent incorporation that the biracial coalition assumed nevertheless produced real benefits for black Atlantans. And although the concessions won in that regime were typically symbolic and class-skewed, some — such as the employment of black police officers and lighting for streets in black residential and commercial areas — had direct effects among the black population more generally. Keiser insists, rightly, that the perceptions of black Atlantans at the time should weigh heavily in our assessment of the significance of those tangible and symbolic concessions; see Keiser, *Subordination or Empowerment? African-American Leadership and the Struggle for Urban Political Power* (New York and Oxford: Oxford University Press, 1997), 135–36. We must take those perceptions into account to guard against simplistic interpretations that reduce to narratives of selling out or that underestimate black agency. At the same time, it is also important to retain a sense of the narrowly circumscribed arena within which benefits were attainable through the cooperative regime and the rudimentary character of the incremental benefits actually attained; these limitations stand out particularly in relation both to the scope of the concessions to white supremacy and white elite prerogative that were required as a precondition for black participation in the coalition and to the magnitude of the racial inequality and injustice that defined the local political-economic order. In this vein, it is important as well to consider the role of black political agency — the ideological and institutional imperatives shaping black elite conceptions of political rationality — in establishing and reinforcing the regime as it was constituted, and thus the active role of black elite participants in defining the horizons of black political action. I address this last issue, and the significance and implications of its absence as a line of inquiry among students of black politics, at greater length later in this chapter.

4. See Stone's discussion of the NPUs in *Regime Politics*, 86–87, 189–91. Stone focuses on the NPUs' ultimately unfulfilled promise as vehicles for citizen participation rather than their role in shaping grassroots black politics. However, his analysis emphasizes the importance of the Planning Bureau's central control of the NPU process and of CAP's agenda-setting dominance for undermining the NPUs' democratic possibilities. Ironically, the fact that the NPUs were prohibited from engaging in their own electoral action may have made them especially vulnerable to serving as stepping stones for individuals desiring to launch electoral careers. Becoming active in the NPU quickly became an easy first step to visibility, name recognition, and elite contacts.

5. Hannah Pitkin, *The Concept of Representation* (Berkeley: University of California Press, 1967), 60–91. The key feature of Pitkin's formulation in this regard is that descriptive representation "depends on the representative's characteristics, on what he [*sic*] *is* or is *like*, on being something rather than doing something" (61).

6. Jones, "Black Political Empowerment," 115; Stone, *Regime Politics*, 93, 163. Stone stresses the role of the black clergy in preempting opposition to Jackson's strikebreaking.

7. The "Seven Principles" of cultural nationalism, evocatively encoded in Swahili terms, are *Umoja* (unity), *Ujamaa* ("cooperative" economics), *Kujichagulia* (self-deter-

mination, though not necessarily linked to political objectives), *Ujima* (collective work and responsibility or building and maintaining group businesses), *Nia* (purpose), *Kuumba* (creativity), and *Imani* (faith in one's teacher, in the people, and in the "struggle"); see Imamu Amiri Baraka (LeRoi Jones), *Kawaida Studies: The New Nationalism* (Chicago: Institute for Positive Education Press, 1972), 9–10, and Jennifer Jordan's critical examination of cultural nationalism in "Cultural Nationalism in the 1960s: Politics and Poetry," in *Race, Politics, and Culture: Critical Essays on the Radicalism of the 1960s,* ed. Adolph Reed Jr. (Westport, CT: Greenwood, 1986). On the eight points of pan-Africanism, see Ideological Research Staff of Malcolm X Liberation University, *Understanding the African Struggle* (Greensboro, NC: The "X" Press, 1971). I discuss the mechanistic foundation of post–black power radicalism's Marxist turn in Adolph Reed Jr., "Scientistic Socialism: Notes on the New Afro-American Magic Marxism," *Endarch* 1 (Fall 1974): 21–39. Robert C. Smith discusses the problems of commitment to an abstract ideal of unity as a principle and a utopian politics that beset at least the nationalist strain of this radicalism; see his *We Have No Leaders: African Americans in the Post–Civil Rights Era* (Albany: SUNY Press, 1996), esp. 75–78.

8. Alex Willingham was among the very few, and was definitely the most incisive, to note this problem of black radicalism at the time; see his "Ideology and Politics: Their Status in Afro-American Social Theory," *Endarch* 1 (Spring 1975): 4–23, reprinted in Reed, *Race, Politics, and Culture.*

9. Adolph Reed Jr., "Narcissistic Politics in Atlanta," *Telos,* Summer 1981: 97–105. Preston H. Smith examines the continuity of self-help ideology as a conservative force within several strains in black politics in " 'Self-Help,' Black Conservatives, and the Reemergence of Black Privatism," in *Without Justice for All: The New Liberalism and Our Retreat from Racial Equality,* ed. Adolph Reed Jr. (Boulder, CO: Westview, 1999).

10. Frances Fox Piven and Richard A. Cloward, *Regulating the Poor: The Functions of Public Welfare* (New York: Pantheon, 1971).

11. Frances Fox Piven and Richard A. Cloward, *The Politics of Turmoil: Race, Poverty, and the Urban Crisis* (New York: Pantheon, 1974), and Robert L. Allen, *Black Awakening in Capitalist America: An Analytic History* (Garden City, NY: Doubleday, 1969).

12. Other significant sources of this critique of the liberal state included two books by Alan Wolfe, *The Limits of Legitimacy: Political Contradictions of Contemporary Capitalism* (New York: Free Press, 1977), and *America's Impasse: The Rise and Fall of the Politics of Growth* (New York: Pantheon, 1981), as well as discursive communities centered around journals such as *Kapitalistate, Radical America, Socialist Revolution,* and *Telos.* Michael K. Brown and Steven P. Erie, "Blacks and the Legacy of the Great Society: The Economic and Political Impact of Federal Social Policy," *Public Policy,* Summer 1981: 299–330, described the elaboration of a public social welfare economy as a partial — and consequential — accommodation of black political insurgency.

13. One such formulation is "Although black life *as a whole* has not improved much beyond the elimination of racial segregation, in the 1970s certain strata within the black

community actually have benefited." The chapter goes to some length to argue this claim on empirical grounds.

14. Jürgen Habermas, *Legitimation Crisis* (Boston: Beacon, 1975), 70–72.

15. See, for instance, Raymond Williams, *The Country and the City* (New York: Oxford, 1973); E. J. Hobsbawm and T. O. Ranger, eds., *The Invention of Tradition* (Cambridge: Cambridge University Press, 1983); Eric R. Wolf, *Europe and the People without History* (Berkeley: University of California Press, 1983); William Roseberry, *Anthropologies and Histories: Essays in Culture, History, and Political Economy* (New Brunswick, NJ, and London: Rutgers University Press, 1989); William Roseberry and Jay O'Brien, introduction to *Golden Ages, Dark Ages: Imagining the Past in Anthropology and History,* ed. Jay O'Brien and William Roseberry (Berkeley: University of California, 1991); Robert J. Gordon, *The Bushman Myth: The Making of a Namibian Underclass* (Boulder, CO: Westview, 1992); Leroy Vail, ed., *The Creation of Tribalism in Southern Africa* (Berkeley and Los Angeles: University of California Press, 1989); and Micaela di Leonardo, *Exotics at Home: Anthropologies, Others, American Modernity* (Chicago: University of Chicago Press, 1998).

16. I examine this issue at length in Adolph Reed Jr., *W. E. B. Du Bois and American Political Thought: Fabianism and the Color Line* (New York: Oxford, 1997), 109–20.

17. George W. Stocking Jr., *Victorian Anthropology* (New York: Free Press, 1987), esp. 233–37. Stocking carefully reconstructs this approach's emergence from several currents in eighteenth- and early-nineteenth-century scholarly and intellectual milieus.

18. For discussions of modernization theory's essentializing and ahistorical views of culture—including its mystified presumptions of "natural economy"—see Colin Leys, *The Rise and Fall of Development Theory* (Bloomington: University of Indiana Press, 1996), esp. 65–66; Roseberry and O'Brien, introduction, 2–3; Roseberry, *Anthropologies and Histories,* 200–202; Wolf, *Europe and the People without History,* 12–13.

19. Habermas pursues this sharp distinction actively; it is a cardinal premise of his theory of contemporary industrial capitalist societies' tendencies to generate crises of legitimacy and motivation, which arise from the displacement of "nature-like" and "unquestionable" structures of meaning by the processes of bourgeois rationalization without adequate normative replacement (*Legitimation Crisis,* 70–80). He argues that the imperatives of capitalist political and economic stratification short-circuit possibilities for the articulation of alternative forms of discursively constituted meaning that could perform the legitimating and motivating functions of traditional systems. He therefore embraces a critical political perspective that distinguishes his project from modernization theory; however, though he may disagree with modernization theorists' ultimate evaluation of the circumstance they describe (e.g., as laid out in Gabriel Almond and Sidney Verba, *The Civic Culture: Political Attitudes and Democracy in Five Nations* [Boston: Little, Brown, 1965]), he endorses a similar view of the relation between traditional and modern institutions.

20. For discussions of this strain in black American thought, see August Meier, *Negro Thought in America, 1880–1915: Racial Ideologies in the Age of Booker T. Washing-*

ton (Ann Arbor: University of Michigan Press, 1963), esp. 3–82; Judith Stein, " 'Of Mr. Booker T. Washington and Others': The Political Economy of Racism in the United States," *Science and Society* 38 (Winter 1974/75): 433–63; William S. Toll, *The Resurgence of Race: Black Social Theory from Reconstruction to the Pan-African Conferences* (Philadelphia: Temple University, 1979); Wilson J. Moses, *The Golden Age of Black Nationalism, 1850–1925* (New York and Oxford: Oxford University Press, 1988); Reed, *W. E. B. Du Bois and American Political Thought*; Kevin Gaines, *Uplifting the Race: Black Leadership, Politics, and Culture in the Twentieth Century* (Chapel Hill: University of North Carolina Press, 1996); and Michele Mitchell, "Adjusting the Race: Gender, Sexuality, and the Question of African-American Destiny, 1870–1930" (Ph.D. diss., Northwestern University, Evanston, Illinois, 1998).

21. For instance, see Stein, " 'Of Mr. Booker T. Washington and Others' "; James Anderson, *The Education of Blacks in the South, 1860–1935* (Chapel Hill: University of North Carolina Press, 1988); Neil McMillen, *Dark Journey: Black Mississippians in the Age of Jim Crow* (Urbana and Chicago: University of Illinois Press, 1989); Clarence A. Bacote, "The Negro in Georgia Politics, 1880–1908" (Ph.D. diss., University of Chicago, 1955); Louis R. Harlan, *Booker T. Washington: The Making of a Black Leader, 1856–1901* (New York and London: Oxford University Press, 1972), 224–27.

22. See, for instance, Meier, *Negro Thought,* 42–58; John H. Bracey Jr., August Meier, and Elliott Rudwick, eds., *Black Nationalism in America* (Indianapolis, IN, and New York: Bobbs-Merrill, 1970). Harold Cruse provocatively declared Booker T. Washington to be the ideological progenitor of black power nationalism in *Rebellion or Revolution* (New York: Morrow, 1968), 193–258. Building on Wilson Moses's examination of the conservative, "civilizationist" commitments that underlay this strain in black political discourse, Dean Robinson argues that more conceptual difficulties are created than resolved by construing its adherents as nationalist. As Robinson argues, the ensemble of political views and presuppositions embraced by the fin de siècle accommodationists differs so markedly from those we characteristically associate with black nationalism after Marcus Garvey that the use of the same label posits a dubious continuity and clouds perception of the actual content of the earlier cohort's concerns; see Dean Robinson, *Black Nationalism in American Political Thought* (New York and Cambridge: Cambridge University Press, forthcoming).

23. The Davises had attempted to establish what Foner describes as a "model slave community, with blacks far better fed and housed than elsewhere in the state and permitted an extraordinary degree of self-government, including a slave jury system that enforced plantation discipline." The Davis brothers' experiment was ended by the war, which provided the slaves the opportunity to take the plantation over and run it entirely on their own. Their success in doing so prompted General Ulysses S. Grant in 1863 to promote Davis Bend as a model for post-Emancipation life; see Eric Foner, *Reconstruction: America's Unfinished Revolution, 1863–1877* (New York: Harper and Row, 1988), 58–59. The Davis Bend experiment and the Montgomery family's history are discussed most exten-

sively in Janet Hermann, *The Pursuit of a Dream* (New York and Oxford: Oxford University Press, 1981).

24. McMillen, *Dark Journey*, 116.

25. Ibid., 177. McMillen also notes that Mississippi blacks in addition were central officeholders in Booker T. Washington's National Negro Business League "and in such subsidiary organizations as the National Negro Bankers' Association, the National Negro Bar Association, the National Negro Retail Merchants Association, and the National Association of Negro Insurance Men" (178). Hermann describes the opulent lifestyle the Montgomerys enjoyed, noting that it rivaled that of the wealthiest and most highly cultivated white planters; *Pursuit of a Dream*, 164–75, 241–42.

26. McMillen, *Dark Journey*, 186; Hermann, *Pursuit of a Dream*, 227.

27. McMillen, *Dark Journey*, 50; Hermann, *Pursuit of a Dream*, 230–32.

28. McMillen, *Dark Journey*, 51.

29. Ibid., 41–44; J. Morgan Kousser, *The Shaping of Southern Politics: Suffrage Restriction and the Establishment of the One-Party South, 1880–1910* (New Haven and London: Yale University Press, 1974), 45–62. Stanley P. Hirshson details the gradual and ambivalent character of the national Republican party's retreat from the protection of black civil rights after the Hayes-Tilden compromise in *Farewell to the Bloody Shirt: Northern Republicans and the Southern Negro, 1877–1893* (New York: Quadrangle, 1968). In North Carolina blacks continued to hold office and were active in local politics until the turn of the century. Moreover, Republican-Populist Fusion victories in that state in the mid-1890s, which were largely dependent on black votes, supported an interracial governing coalition the likes of which would not be seen again in the South until the 1970s; see Helen G. Edmonds, *The Negro and Fusion Politics in North Carolina, 1894–1901* (Chapel Hill: University of North Carolina Press, 1951); and Glenda Elizabeth Gilmore, *Gender and Jim Crow: Women and the Politics of White Supremacy in North Carolina, 1896–1920* (Chapel Hill: University of North Carolina Press, 1996).

30. McMillen, *Dark Journey*, 50.

31. Harlan, *Booker T. Washington*, 227–28; Robert W. Rydell, *All the World's a Fair* (Chicago: University of Chicago Press, 1984), 74–75.

32. Revealingly, Houston A. Baker Jr. praises the closure of the regime of democratic participation in postbellum black politics, which he disparages as a frustratingly undefined period when the mass of black citizens suffered being "buffeted on all sides by strategies, plans, hopes, and movements, organized by any number of popular, or local, black spokespersons." He lauds Washington's rise for eliminating this putative confusion; see his *Modernism and the Harlem Renaissance* (Chicago and London: University of Chicago Press, 1987), 15.

33. Hermann, *Pursuit of a Dream*, 231–32; 239. When Montgomery faced disgrace for mishandling funds as a collector of government monies (a Theodore Roosevelt patronage appointment), he tried to mobilize his network of powerful patrons in his effort to save face. Those whose aid he sought, as well as those whose financial support he so-

licited for Mound Bayou, indicate the kinds of relationships most meaningful to prominent accommodationist politicians: their relationship to the constituencies to which they were actually accountable; see *Pursuit of a Dream*, 234–35.

34. C. Vann Woodward, *Origins of the New South, 1877–1913* (Baton Rouge: Louisiana State University Press, 1951), 192; Jack H. Bloom, *Class, Race, and the Civil Rights Movement* (Bloomington: University of Indiana Press, 1987), 41.

35. McMillen, *Dark Journey*, 164–65. It is important to note that whether local organizations were racially integrated was not likely to be as salient an issue during that period as it would become later, when commitment to organizational interracialism assumed greater symbolic meaning as an indicator of whites' reliability as allies.

36. Woodward, *Origins of the New South*, 229–30; Leon Fink, *Workingmen's Democracy: The Knights of Labor and American Politics* (Urbana and Chicago: University of Illinois Press, 1983), 169–72; Daniel Letwin, *The Challenge of Interracial Unionism: Alabama Coal Miners, 1878–1921* (Chapel Hill: University of North Carolina Press, 1998), 75–80; Sterling D. Spero and Abram L. Harris, *The Black Worker* (1931; reprint, New York: Atheneum, 1968), 42.

37. For a flavor of the extent of this activism see Spero and Harris, *The Black Worker*; Letwin, *The Challenge of Interracial Unionism*; Eric Arnesen, *Waterfront Workers of New Orleans: Race, Class, and Politics, 1863–1923* (New York and Oxford: Oxford University Press, 1991), and "'What's on the Black Worker's Mind?': African-American Workers and the Union Tradition," *Gulf Coast Historical Review* 10 (Fall 1994): esp. 7–12; Peter Rachleff, *Black Labor in Richmond, 1865–1890* (Urbana and Chicago: University of Illinois Press, 1989); Stein, "'Of Mr. Booker T. Washington and Others.'" The case of New Orleans dock workers is a particularly interesting instance of black workers' enacting a relatively successful race-conscious strategy of carefully negotiated class alliance with white counterparts. Clarence A. Bacote reports that the Populists enjoyed considerable black support in Georgia through the early 1890s, noting that twenty-four black delegates, from eleven different counties, participated in the party's 1894 state convention and that blacks voted in substantial numbers — perhaps even a majority — for the Populist gubernatorial candidate in that year's election; Bacote, "The Negro in Georgia Politics." See also Edmonds, *The Negro and Fusion Politics*, and Gilmore, *Gender and Jim Crow*.

38. Meier, *Negro Thought*, 46–47; August Meier and Elliott M. Rudwick, "Attitudes of Negro Leaders toward the Labor Movement from the Civil War to World War I," in *The Negro and the American Labor Movement*, ed. Julius Jacobson (Garden City, NY: Doubleday, 1968), 27–48; McMillen, *Dark Journey*, 165, 373n; Stein, "'Of Mr. Booker T. Washington and Others,'" 434–35. Fortune apparently continued to support labor union activity, even after he became an ally of Washington and retreated from the radicalism he had displayed in the late 1880s around the Knights and presumably through his association later in life with Garvey, though, as Meier and Rudwick note, the main focus of his politics after the 1890s was more conventionally petit bourgeois; see Meier and Rudwick, "Attitudes of Negro Leaders," 37. Fortune is an especially interesting figure in this regard

in that his simultaneous commitments to labor organization and the ideal of a racial group economy may help to map the evolution of those two strains in black political ideology from the republican, free-labor discourse that seemed the dominant intellectual frame of black politics before Hayes-Tilden. Lynch also held to his support of labor union activity, though he was never tempted by labor radicalism. See T. Thomas Fortune, *Black and White: Land, Labor, and Politics in the South* (1884; reprint, New York: Arno, 1968); Emma Lou Thornbrough, *T. Thomas Fortune: Militant Journalist* (Chicago: University of Chicago Press, 1972), 81–82, 158; John R. Lynch, *Reminiscences of an Active Life: The Autobiography of John Roy Lynch* (Chicago: University of Chicago Press, 1970), 476–78. Lynch actually invoked republican principles to oppose labor's organization of class-based political parties.

39. Stein, " 'Of Mr. Booker T. Washington and Others,' " 431.

40. Stein, " 'Of Mr. Booker T. Washington and Others,' " 432; McMillen, *Dark Journey,* 57–65.

41. Harlan, *Booker T. Washington,* 91.

42. Gaines, *Uplifting the Race,* 94–96.

43. Anna Julia Cooper, *A Voice from the South* (1892; reprint, New York and Oxford: Oxford University Press, 1988), 151–66.

44. Ibid., 173.

45. Ibid., 252–57. For discussions of Cooper's and other elite blacks' antilabor and nativist views see Gaines, *Uplifting the Race,* 145–48; and Kenneth W. Warren, *Black and White Strangers: Race and American Literary Realism* (Chicago: University of Chicago Press, 1993), 68–69.

46. "The Niagara Movement Platform: 'We Do Not Hesitate to Complain . . . Loudly and Insistently,' " reprinted in *Black Protest Thought in the Twentieth Century,* 2nd ed., ed. August Meier, Elliott Rudwick, and Francis L. Broderick (Indianapolis, IN: Bobbs-Merrill, 1970), 59–61; W. E. B. Du Bois, "The Talented Tenth," in *The Negro Problem,* multiauthor collection (1903; reprint, New York: Arno, 1969); Du Bois, "Of Mr. Booker T. Washington and Others," in *The Souls of Black Folk* (Chicago: McClurg, 1903).

47. Even attempts to reflect strategic and programmatic variety have tended to presume the possibility of — and to seek — the racial least common denominator implied in this usage, as is indicated in the titles of key anthologies of black thought during the segregation era: Alain Locke, ed., *The New Negro: An Interpretation* (1925; reprint, New York: Atheneum, 1968); Rayford W. Logan, ed., *What the Negro Wants* (Chapel Hill: University of North Carolina Press, 1944); and Robert Penn Warren, ed., *Who Speaks for the Negro?* (New York: Random House, 1966). The genesis of the Logan volume highlights an aspect of the contradictory character of this project. The idea for the volume originated not with Logan but with two white racial liberals at the University of North Carolina, W. T. Couch and Guy B. Johnson, who approached Logan to compile and edit the collection. According to Jonathan Scott Holloway, who describes the controversy, Couch at least was motivated by a desire to respond to Gunnar Myrdal's *An American Dilemma: The*

Negro Problem and Modern Democracy, which also appeared in 1944. Serious disagreements developed between Logan and Couch and Johnson over ideological balance in the volume, with the latter two hoping that leavening with conservatives would temper the volume's antisegregationist tilt. (Ironically, Logan initially considered excluding radicals such as Doxey Wilkerson but was persuaded by Couch and Johnson to adhere to a format of one-third radicals, one-third liberals, and one-third conservatives.) When the conservatives did not write as expected, Couch balked and threatened not to publish the volume. See Jonathan Scott Holloway, "The Black Intellectual and the 'Crisis Canon' in the Twentieth Century," unpublished; also see Kenneth Robert Janken, *Rayford W. Logan and the Dilemma of the African American Intellectual* (Amherst: University of Massachusetts Press, 1993), 145–66. This episode captures the plausible foundation of the impulse to imagine a corporate black politics; after all, it is reasonable to expect that blacks would share almost universally an opposition to white supremacy and Jim Crow. It also illustrates the problem that the impulse itself is implicated in a style of politics that centered less on mobilizing collective black action than on communicating with white elites.

48. Stein, " 'Of Mr. Booker T. Washington and Others,' " 424. "Although these three initiatives, perhaps, formally sought integration, the basis of the actions and their relationships with other forces in society were very different. Similarly, the formation of the Colored Farmers Alliance and the creation of black professional organizations shared formal attributes of nationalism. But defining them solely in this way distorts the dynamics of the organizations — their class origins, the future course of their actions, and their impact on the social order" (ibid.).

49. Harold F. Gosnell, *Negro Politicians: The Rise of Negro Politics in Chicago* (1935; reprint, Chicago: University of Chicago Press, 1967); Ralph Bunche, *The Political Status of the Negro in the Age of FDR* (1940; reprint, Chicago: University of Chicago Press, 1973), and "A Critical Analysis of the Tactics and Programs of Minority Groups," "The Problems of Organizations Devoted to the Improvement of the Status of the American Negro," and "The Negro in the Political Life of the U.S.," all reprinted in *Ralph J. Bunche: Selected Speeches and Writings,* ed. Charles P. Henry (Ann Arbor: University of Michigan Press, 1995). On Bunche, also see Jonathan Scott Holloway, *Confronting the Veil* (Chapel Hill: University of North Carolina Press, forthcoming).

50. Gosnell, *Negro Politicians,* 93–114. Among the material payoffs of black electoral participation were first of all jobs and appointments, which Gosnell details (196–318).

51. Ibid., 371–72. Gosnell also discusses black legislators' opposition to the trade union agenda, including the eight-hour day for women.

52. Ibid., 372.

53. Ibid., 368.

54. Ibid., 11.

55. Bunche, "Tactics and Programs of Minority Groups," 52, and "Problems of Organizations," 74–80. A flavor of Bunche's Marxism can be gleaned from his 1935 essay "Marxism and the 'Negro Question,' " also reprinted in Henry, *Ralph J. Bunche,* 35–45.

56. Bunche, "Marxism and the 'Negro Question,' " 45. He contended that because of "the characteristic caste status of the Negro people in American society, the Negro petty bourgeoisie is destined to play a far more significant and progressive social role in the struggle of the Negro people for emancipation and in the general social struggle than is the white bourgeoisie in the analogous situation. As a significant factor in the life and development of the Negro race, petty bourgeoisie is second only to the Negro proletariat" (40). Consistent with an orthodoxy of the time, Bunche maintained that the racial caste system was "the only form of an uncompleted bourgeois revolution in the United States today. In that respect it is similar to the liberation of subject nations of colonies" (43). This sort of interpretation, particularly the colonial analogy, would become a conceptual linchpin of post–black power radicals' efforts to craft variants of a Third Worldist Marxism or Marxist-nationalist hybrids. Bunche, however, insisted that black Americans were not a colonial people or a true "national minority" and emphatically opposed demands for black self-determination (36–37).

57. Ibid., 42.

58. Bunche, "Problems of Organizations," 80.

59. Bunche, *Political Status of the Negro,* 104–5.

60. His most extensive critique of racial thinking, including the idea of race itself, is in Ralph J. Bunche, *A World View of Race* (Washington, DC: Associates in Negro Folk Education, 1936).

61. See, for example, Bunche, "Problems of Organizations," 82–83.

62. Robert E. Martin, "The Relative Political Status of the Negro in the United States," *Journal of Negro Education* 22 (Summer 1953): 363–79. Henry Lee Moon also examined the growth and significance of the black vote in national politics in particular; see his *Balance of Power: The Negro Vote* (Garden City, NY: Doubleday, 1948).

63. Representative examples of this scholarship include Everett Carll Ladd Jr., *Negro Political Leadership in the South* (Ithaca, NY: Cornell University Press, 1966); M. Elaine Burgess, *Negro Leadership in a Southern City* (Chapel Hill: University of North Carolina Press, 1962); James Q. Wilson, *Negro Politics: The Search for Leadership* (Glencoe, IL: Free Press, 1960); Daniel C. Thompson, *The Negro Leadership Class* (Englewood Cliffs, NJ: Prentice-Hall, 1963); Donald R. Matthews and James W. Prothro, *Negroes and the New Southern Politics* (New York: Harcourt Brace, 1966); Oliver C. Cox, "Leadership among Negroes in the United States," in *Studies in Leadership,* ed. Alvin W. Gouldner. (New York: Harper and Brothers, 1950); Jack L. Walker, "Protest and Negotiation: A Case Study of Negro Leadership in Atlanta, Georgia," *Midwest Journal of Political Science* 7 (May 1963): 99–124; and Tillman C. Cothran and William Phillips Jr., "Negro Leadership in a Crisis Situation," *Phylon* 22 (Winter 1961): 107–18.

64. Ladd, in distinguishing between black leaders selected by whites and those selected by blacks, was among the few to approach the issue of leadership selection as a problematic issue. However, he did not follow up the implications of that distinction by considering whether and how both in-group and out-group selectees can be seen as black political leaders; see *Negro Political Leadership,* 113–16.

65. See note 47, this chapter.

66. "Ethnic group leadership is, by definition, concerned with promoting the interests of the ethnic group. . . . Negro leadership in the United States has been and remains issue leadership, and the one issue that matters is race advancement" (Ladd, *Negro Political Leadership,* 114–15). Thompson defined the black leader as "one who for some period of time identifies overtly with the Negro's effort to achieve stated social goals" (*Negro Leadership Class,* 5). Burgess, a sociologist, was purely reputational in her formulation of leadership, defining a leader as "an individual whose behavior affects the patterning of behavior within the community at a given time" (*Negro Leadership,* 77). Matthews and Prothro, while noting that it is less reliable than officeholding as a barometer of political leadership, were forced by the realities of black exclusion also to opt for a simply reputational criterion: "In view of these special difficulties, *we shall regard those people most frequently thought of as leaders by Negro citizens as being their leaders*" (emphasis in original; *Negroes and the New Southern Politics,* 178). Wilson also relied on purely reputational means for ascribing leadership and explicitly eschewed attempting any more-substantive definition (*Negro Politics,* 10). He constructed his list of leaders, in contrast to Burgess and others, more by culling names from the public record than from snowball interviews; however, he seemed not to notice that that approach begs questions concerning the interests participating in determining which individuals would be recognized and projected.

67. Cox, "Leadership among Negroes," 228.

68. Ibid., 229.

69. Ibid., 269.

70. Ibid., 271.

71. Following Drake and Cayton, Susan Herbst examines the contests from the 1930s through the early 1960s for honorary mayor of Bronzeville in Chicago. These elections, sponsored by local black newspapers, fell somewhere between pure popularity contests and selections of men (one woman was elected, in 1959) held to represent community aspirations and values. Herbst notes that some holders of the title sought to use it to pursue ends linked to the politics of racial advancement, though the title was understood to be nonideological and devoid of politics; see Susan Herbst, *Politics at the Margin: Historical Studies of Public Expression outside the Mainstream* (New York and Cambridge: Cambridge University Press, 1994), 71–95; and St. Clair Drake and Horace R. Cayton, *Black Metropolis: A Study of Negro Life in a Northern City* (New York: Harcourt, Brace, 1944), 383. In any event, the enthusiastic response to the Bronzeville mayoralty contests suggests at least a willingness to take advantage of opportunities to participate in selecting leaders. At the same time, though, the contest itself attests to the hegemony of the elite politics of racial advancement. The field of candidates was limited in principle to nonideological "race men"; elections were candidate-centered and heavily favored prominent businessmen and professionals, and the prohibition on political programs actually reinforced the naturalization of conventional petit bourgeois ideas of racial uplift as a noncontroversial black agenda. In addition, the fact that the office carried no institutional power or resources

militated against linking candidacies to durable poitical alliances or membership-based organizations. According to Herbst, *The Defender* newspaper's leadership saw the contest as a way to create back-channel leverage to City Hall, but the overarching context for that objective remained the elite politics of race advancement.

72. See, for example, Matthew Holden, "Black Politicians in the Time of the 'New' Urban Politics," *Review of Black Political Economy* 2 (Fall 1971): 56–71; Michael B. Preston, "Limitations of Black Urban Power: The Case of Black Mayors," in *The New Urban Politics,* ed. Robert Lineberry and Louis Masotti (Boston: Ballinger, 1976); Leonard Cole, *Blacks in Power: A Comparative Study of Black and White Elected Officials* (Princeton: Princeton University Press, 1976); "Symposium: Minorities in Public Administration," *Public Administration Review* 34 (November/December 1974): 519–63; Lenneal J. Henderson, *Administrative Advocacy: Black Administrators in Urban Bureaucracy* (Palo Alto, CA: R and E Associates, 1979); E. J. Keller, "The Impact of Black Mayors on Urban Policy," *Annals of the American Academy of Political and Social Science* 439 (September 1978): 40–52; William E. Nelson and Philip J. Meranto, *Electing Black Mayors: Political Action in the Black Community* (Columbus: Ohio State University Press, 1977); Albert Karnig and Susan Welch, *Black Representation and Urban Policy* (Chicago: University of Chicago Press, 1980); Bette Woody, *Managing Urban Crises: The New Black Leadership and the Politics of Resource Allocation* (Westport, CT: Greenwood, 1982); Peter Eisinger, "Black Mayors and the Politics of Racial Economic Advancement," in *Readings in Urban Politics: Past, Present, and Future,* ed. Harlan Hahn and Charles Levine (New York: Longman, 1984); Willingham, "Ideology and Politics"; Robert C. Smith, "Black Power and the Transformation from Protest to Politics," *Political Science Quarterly* 96 (Fall 1981): 431–43; Michael B. Preston, Lenneal J. Henderson, and Paul L. Puryear, eds., *The New Black Politics: The Search for Political Power* (New York: Longman, 1987); Charles E. Jones, "An Overview of the Congressional Black Caucus: 1970–1985," in *Readings in American Political Issues,* ed. Franklin D. Jones and Michael O. Adams (Dubuque, IA: Kendall/Hunt, 1987); Earl Picard, "New Black Economic Development Strategy," *Telos,* Summer 1984: 53–64; and Martin L. Kilson, "Political Change in the Negro Ghetto, 1900–1940s," in *Key Issues in the Afro-American Experience,* ed. Nathan Huggins, Martin L. Kilson, and Daniel Fox (New York: Harcourt Brace, 1971), vol. 2; Kilson, "The New Black Political Class" and "From Civil Rights to Politics"; Adolph L. Reed Jr., *The Jesse Jackson Phenomenon: The Crisis of Purpose in Afro-American Politics* (New Haven, CT, and London: Yale University Press, 1986).

73. William E. Nelson Jr., "Cleveland: The Evolution of Black Political Power," in Preston, Henderson, and Puryear, *The New Black Politics*; Browning, Marshall, and Tabb, *Protest Is Not Enough*; Stone, *Regime Politics*; Larry Bennett, "Harold Washington and the Black Urban Regime," *Urban Affairs Quarterly* 28 (March 1993): 423–40; James Button, *Blacks and Social Change: Impact of the Civil Rights Movement in Southern Communities* (Princeton: Princeton University, 1989); also see chapters 2 and 5 in this volume, as well as Dennis R. Judd, "Electoral Coalitions, Minority Mayors, and the Contra-

dictions of the Municipal Policy Agenda," in *Cities in Stress,* ed. Marc Gottdiener (Beverly Hills, CA: Sage, 1986); and Picard, "New Black Economic Development Strategy."

74. Jones's "Black Political Empowerment" is an instance of the former tendency, though not the latter. Ironically, leftists may have tended more than others toward implicitly absolving black officials of responsibility for their actions by emphasizing their powerlessness; see, e.g., Rod Bush, ed., *The New Black Vote: Politics and Power in Four American Cities* (San Francisco: Synthesis, 1984).

75. Katherine Tate, *From Protest to Politics: The New Black Voters in American Elections* (Cambridge, MA, and London: Harvard University Press, 1994); Michael C. Dawson, *Behind the Mule: Race and Class in African-American Politics* (Princeton: Princeton University Press, 1994); Carol M. Swain, *Black Faces, Black Interests: The Representation of African Americans in Congress* (Cambridge, MA, and London: Harvard University Press, 1995).

76. Tate, *From Protest to Politics,* 9.

77. Ibid., 18.

78. Ibid., 20–49.

79. Ibid., 25. She notes that one study found that "more than 60 percent of self-identified middle-class Blacks . . . stated that they felt closer to their racial group than their class group. In contrast, a mere 5 percent of self-identified poor and working class Blacks preferred their racial group over their class group." She also found a positive relation between education and race consciousness, noting that "college-educated Blacks, in particular, possessed the strongest racial common-fate identities." Yet she also finds that those who "identify with the middle, upper-middle and upper classes were less likely to identify strongly with the race" (28). This contradictory finding could result from limitations of the 1984 National Black Election Study, from which it and the education finding are derived. Dawson notes that existing surveys of black Americans are not equipped to capture complexities of class structure and relations; see Dawson, *Behind the Mule,* 75.

80. Tate, *From Protest to Politics,* 27.

81. Ibid., 90–92.

82. Swain, *Black Faces, Black Interests,* 7.

83. Ibid., 10–13.

84. Ibid., esp. 10–14. Swain's claim that 60 percent of black voters supported Clarence Thomas's appointment to the U.S. Supreme Court illustrates the limitation of relying on such data as evidence of firmly held views. Claims of polls reporting majority black support for Thomas often were exaggerated; that support evaporated when respondents were informed of Thomas's views. And no matter what polls at the time might have shown, Thomas has hardly enjoyed substantial black support since his elevation to the Court.

85. Dawson, *Behind the Mule,* 61.

86. Ibid., 11–12, 47, 75–79. On the other hand, other contemporary scholars who employ more institutional approaches are no less likely to presume and defend the principle of corporate racial interest; see, for example, Smith, *We Have No Leaders,* and Keiser,

Subordination or Empowerment? Keiser actively argues for seeing black Americans as a corporate political entity even while acknowledging the existence of significant intraracial stratification and differential policy impacts; he rests this argument on a notion of group political empowerment, which he defines as "the incremental growth of group political power" (9). The main problem with this defense, however, is that Keiser proposes no account of how power is exercised by the group as a collectivity and no convincing argument that we should accept on face value petit bourgeois politicians' claims that the agendas they pursue represent the most that can be won for the race; he simply assumes that racially descriptive representation and membership in a governing coalition suffice as evidence of empowerment of the racial group as a whole within the pertinent polity. Though he is not a political scientist and not immersed in the disciplinary study of black politics, Manning Marable's *Black Leadership* (New York: Columbia University Press, 1998) also illustrates the pervasiveness of the tendency to naturalize the premise of generic racial interest. Even as an ostensible leftist, Marable embraces a notion of black leadership that requires no systematic consideration of questions of representativeness or accountability to specific constituencies.

Curiously, Dawson himself has noted the "shortage of sophisticated treatments of the internal political dynamics of African-American communities and populations," though it is revealing that he and his coauthor characterize this as "the internal political experience of *the* black community" (my emphasis); see Michael C. Dawson and Ernest J. Wilson III, "Paradigms and Paradoxes: Political Science and African-American Politics," in *Political Science: Looking to the Future,* vol. 1: *The Theory and Practice of Political Science,* ed. William Crotty (Evanston, IL: Northwestern University Press, 1991), 194. Moreover, opting for an approach centered on attitude and opinion surveys does not necessarily preclude attention to historical, structural, and processual dimensions of politics; see, for an especially intelligent use of such an approach, Edward Carmines and James Stimson, *Issue Evolution: Race and the Transformation of American Politics* (Princeton: Princeton University Press, 1989).

87. Dawson, *Behind the Mule,* 11.

88. Ibid., 80.

89. Ibid., 67.

90. Ibid., 67, 87–88, 211–12. "The future of African-American politics may well depend on how the racial and economic environment of twenty-first century America dictates which African Americans perceive that their fates remain linked" (212).

91. Ibid., 15–34. Black/white comparison is the standard in contemporary academic discussion of the black middle class, which hardly ever addresses issues such as the systemic features and entailments of social stratification and hierarchy among blacks. Discussion of the role of upper strata within black social life typically centers on questions of problems of racial identity, as with Dawson, or on role modeling and other forms of noblesse oblige; see, for instance, Bart Landry, *The New Black Middle Class* (Berkeley: University of California Press, 1987); Charles V. Willie, ed., *The Caste and Class Controversy* (Bayside, NY: General Hall, 1979), and *Caste and Class Controversy on Race and*

Poverty: Round Two of the Willie/Wilson Debate, 2nd ed. (Dix Hills, NY: General Hall, 1989).

92. Dawson, *Behind the Mule,* 205; also see 181–99.

93. Ibid., 83.

94. Preston Smith discusses at length this rhetoric and the ideological agenda in which it is embedded; see his " 'Self-Help,' Black Conservatives, and the Reemergence of Black Privatism"; Robert Woodson, Clarence Thomas, and the next–most recent incarnation of the recently reborn Glenn Loury are among the most prominent, and tendentious, exemplars of this rightist appropriation of the rhetoric of racial authenticity to challenge the legitimacy of the black liberal political establishment. Also see Willie Legette, "The Crisis of the Black Male: A New Ideology in Black Politics," in Reed, *Without Justice for All.*

95. Indeed, it may be that an understandable desire to meet the right-wing attack with which that questioning is usually associated partly motivates scholars like Tate and Dawson to vindicate the premises of the politics of racial advancement and thus contributes to the short-circuiting of their critiques. In any case, the fact that the intellectual challenge to the rhetoric of racial authenticity and presumptive corporate group interest originates most conspicuously from the sophistries and political disingenuousness of conservative ideologues has not helped the quality of the debate.

96. This orientation is not idiosyncratic to the field of black politics. The institutionalization of black studies in niches within mainline academic disiplines — itself a phenomenon of the post-segregation political context — has shown that this mind-set is pandemic in black intellectual life. Afro-Americanist scholarship in literary studies, psychology, and anthropology is dominated by it, and it is a prominent node threatening dominance in the field of Afro-American history. Black studies discourse in sociology appears grounded on an ambivalent amalgam of this racial vindicationism and the discipline's fetishized discourse of inner-city social pathology.

97. See Smith, " 'Self-Help,' Black Conservatives, and the Reemergence of Black Privatism." In the theater of organic grassroots spokesmanship, right-wing ideologues increasingly adduce poll data allegedly showing substantial rank-and-file black social conservatism and mobilize testimonials from black ministers and former welfare recipients to give a patina of racial legitimacy to items of the rightist agenda such as school prayer, tuition vouchers, welfare "reform," and capital punishment.

98. As an illustration of the extent of popular political participation during Reconstruction, an inventory of black officeholding reveals that the nearly 1,500 black men who held elective office between roughly 1865 and 1877 included scores of blacksmiths, farmers, barbers, coopers, carpenters, butchers, laborers, shoemakers, tailors, a baker, a basket maker, cabinet makers, harness makers, a machinist, an upholsterer, a teamster, servants, wheelwrights, millers, millwrights, mechanics, an oysterman, and a tanner, in all well outnumbering the healthy complement of planters, teachers, ministers, and lawyers; see Eric Foner, ed., *Freedom's Lawmakers: A Directory of Black Officeholders during Reconstruction* (New York and Oxford: Oxford University Press, 1993), 253–61. The pattern of popular activism that this distribution of officeholding suggests further under-

scores the ideological character of the custodial rhetoric of uplift around which petit bourgeois interests were consolidated as the center of black politics.

99. Ian Shapiro, *Democracy's Place* (Ithaca, NY, and London: Cornell University Press, 1996), 124. Shapiro points out that he does not claim "that all social hierarchies should be eliminated but rather that there are good reasons to be nervous about them. Escapable hierarchies can be alleged to be inescapable, oppression can be shrouded in the language of agreement, unnecessary hierarchies can be declared essential to the pursuit of common goals, and fixed hierarchies can be shrouded in myths about their alterability. Accordingly, although many particular hierarchies might in the end be conceded to be justified, this concession should truly *be* in the end and *after* the defender of hierarchy has shouldered a substantial burden of persuasion" (125–26).

100. Ralph Ellison, *Shadow and Act* (New York: Random House, 1964), 116.

2. The "Black Revolution" and the Reconstitution of Domination

1. Walter Benjamin, "The Work of Art in the Age of Mechanical Reproduction," in *Illuminations* (New York: Beacon, 1968), 251.

2. Herbert Marcuse, *One-Dimensional Man: Studies in the Ideology of Advanced Industrial Society* (Boston: Beacon, 1964).

3. David Gross, "Irony and the 'Disorders of the Soul,'" *Telos*, Winter, 1977/78: 167.

4. Possible sources of the left's failure to interpret its past meaningfully are also discussed by Christopher Lasch, "The Narcissist Society," *New York Review of Books* 23 (30 September 1976): 5ff.; Russell Jacoby, "The Politics of Objectivity: Notes on the U.S. Left," *Telos*, Winter, 1977/78: 74–88, and *Social Amnesia: A Critique of Conformist Psychology from Adler to Laing* (Boston: Little, Brown, 1975), 101–18; Andrew Feenberg, "Paths to Failure: The Dialectics of Organization and Ideology in the New Left," in *Race, Politics, and Culture: Critical Essays on the Radicalism of the 1960s*, ed. Adolph Reed Jr. (Westport, CT: Greenwood, 1986); and David Gross, "Culture, Politics, and 'Lifestyle' in the 1960s," in Reed, *Race, Politics, and Culture*.

5. The work of Alex Willingham is the most consistent and noteworthy exception. See, e.g., his "Ideology and Politics: Their Status in Afro-American Social Theory," in Reed, *Race, Politics, and Culture*, and "California Dreaming: Eldridge Cleaver's Epithet to the Activism of the Sixties," *Endarch* 1 (Winter 1976): 1–23.

6. Paul Piccone, "Beyond Critical Theory" (mimeographed), and "The Crisis of One-Dimensionality," *Telos*, Spring 1978: 43–54. See also Tim Luke, "Culture and Politics in the Age of Artificial Negativity," *Telos*, Spring 1978: 55–72.

7. See, e.g., Thomas R. Brooks, *Walls Come Tumbling Down: A History of the Civil Rights Movement, 1940–1970* (Englewood Cliffs, NJ: Prentice-Hall, 1974), 290ff.; Eddie N. Williams, *From Protest to Politics: The Legacy of Martin Luther King, Jr.* (Washington DC: Joint Center for Political Studies, n.d.); and Robert Smith, "Black Power and the Transformation from Protest to Politics," *Political Science Quarterly* 96 (Fall 1981): 431–43.

8. This slogan first rose to prominence on the back of the black elite's voluble reaction to the *University of California Regents v. Bakke* case, which is said to portend the reversal of those alleged "gains." One interpretation of these gains is found in Richard Freeman, "Black Economic Progress since 1964," *Public Interest,* Summer 1978: 52–68.

9. Dorothy K. Newman, Nancy Amidei, Barbara Carter, Dawn Day, William Kruvant, and Jack Russell, *Protest, Politics, and Prosperity: Black Americans and White Institutions, 1940–1975* (New York: Pantheon, 1978), 64. Since 1971, of course, unemployment among blacks has averaged more than 10 percent.

10. Ibid., 66.

11. Bureau of the Census, U.S. Department of Commerce, *The Social and Economic Status of the Black Population in the United States: 1974* (Washington, DC: GPO, 1975), 25.

12. Barbara Jones, "Black Family Income: Patterns, Sources, and Trends" (paper presented at the annual meetings of the National Economic Association, American Economic Association, Atlantic City, New Jersey, September 1976), 2.

13. Bureau of the Census, *Social and Economic Status,* 123, 137.

14. That the leadership elite projects its interests over the entire black population is neither unique nor necessarily suggestive of insidious motives; however, it is just in the extent to which the elite's hegemony develops unconsciously that it is most important as a problem for emancipatory action; cf. Alvin W. Gouldner's critique of intellectuals and intelligentsia, "Prologue to a Theory of Revolutionary Intellectuals," *Telos,* Winter 1975/76: 3–36, and *The Dialectic of Ideology and Technology: The Origins, Grammar, and Future of Ideology* (New York: Seabury, 1976), 247–48 passim. More recently Gouldner attempted to elaborate a systematic theory of the place of intellectuals in the modern world that concludes that they function as a "flawed universal class"—a thesis that does not augur well for the emancipatory content of his theory—in *The Future of Intellectuals and the Rise of the New Class: A Frame of Reference, Theses, Conjectures, Arguments, and an Historical Perspective on the Role of Intellectuals and Intelligentsia in the International Class Context of the Modern Era* (New York: Seabury, 1979). See also the critique of Gouldner's thesis in Michael Walzer's thoughtful review essay "The New Masters," *New York Review of Books* 27 (30 March 1980): 37ff.

15. John Hope Franklin does not raise the question in his standard volume, *From Slavery to Freedom: A History of Negro Americans,* 3rd ed. (New York: Random House, 1969); nor, surprisingly, does Harold Cruse's *The Crisis of the Negro Intellectual: From Its Origins to the Present* (New York: Morrow, 1967), which is a benchmark contribution to a reflexive approach to black political activity. That Cruse and Franklin fail to raise the question is perhaps because both—reflecting an aspect of the conventional wisdom—see an unbroken, if not cumulative, legacy of black activism in the twentieth century. Franklin sees the civil rights movement simply as the culmination of a century or more of protest. Cruse, in establishing the continuities of the poles of integrationism and nationalism, projects them back and forth from Frederick Douglass and Martin Delany to black power, glossing over significant historical differences in the process. In *The Making of Black*

Revolutionaries (New York: Macmillan, 1972), James Forman is so consumed by the movement's chronology and organizational unfoldings that he is unable to subordinate it to history. His account of the 1950s focuses on his personal awakening. Louis Lomax, *The Negro Revolt,* rev. ed. (New York: Harper and Row, 1971); Lewis Killian, *The Impossible Revolution? Black Power and the American Dream* (New York: Random House, 1968); and the two period volumes by Lerone Bennett Jr., *The Negro Mood* (New York: Penguin, 1964) and *Before the Mayflower: A History of the Negro in America, 1619–1964,* rev. ed. (Baltimore: Penguin, 1969), all raise the question only to answer casually or to beg the question further. An all-too-common shortcoming exemplified by each of the writers cited and extending throughout the study of black political activity is a tendency to abstract black life from the currents of American history. The resulting scenarios of black existence suffer from superficiality. By the end of the 1970s some social scientists had begun to seek after the structural origins of black mass protest, but their accounts do not adequately consider political dynamics operating within the black community.

16. Piccone, "Crisis of One-Dimensionality," 45–46; Piccone, "Beyond Critical Theory," 6.

17. John Alt observes that "the problem of legitimating industrial reorganization was solved through a new social practice and ideology structured around the pursuit of money, material comfort and a higher standard of living through consumerism. Mass consumption, as the necessary corollary of Taylorized mass production, was itself offered as the ultimate justification for the rationalization of labor" ("Beyond Class: The Decline of Industrial Labor and Leisure," *Telos,* Summer 1976: 71). Stuart Ewen identifies the Cold War period as the apotheosis of consumerism, whose enshrinement during those years was aided by the continued spread of popular journalism and the "mass marketing of television . . . which carried the consumer imagery into the back corners of home life" (*Captains of Consciousness: Advertising and the Social Roots of the Consumer Culture* [New York: McGraw-Hill, 1976], 206–15).

18. Cf. David Riesman (with Nathan Glazer and Reuel Denney), *The Lonely Crowd: A Study of the Changing American Character,* abr. ed. (New Haven: Yale University Press, 1961), 19–22; and Jules Henry's perceptive and telling study of the period, *Culture against Man* (New York: Random House, 1963). Marcuse went so far as to suggest that even the concept of introjection may not capture the extent to which the one-dimensional order is reproduced in the individual on the ground that "introjection implies the existence of an inner dimension distinguished from and even antagonistic to the external exigencies—an individual consciousness and an individual unconscious apart from public opinion and behavior. . . . [However, mass] production and mass distribution claim the entire individual. . . . The manifold processes of introjection seem to be ossified in almost mechanical reactions. The result is not adjustment but mimesis: an immediate identification of the individual with *his* society and, through it, with the society as a whole" (*One-Dimensional Man,* 10).

19. The point is not that ethnicity has lost its power as a basis for self-identification or associational activity. What has been obliterated, however, is the distinctiveness of the institutional forms that were the source of group consciousness in the first place. W. Lloyd Warner and Leo Srole proudly acknowledge the centrality of the prevailing order in the determination of ethnic consciousness: "The forces which are most potent both in forming and changing the ethnic groups emanate from the institutions of the dominant American social system" (W. Lloyd Warner and Leo Srole, *The Social Systems of American Ethnic Groups* [New Haven: Yale University Press, 1945], 283–84). Stuart Ewen and Elizabeth Ewen observe that the dynamic of homogenization began with integration into the system of wage labor, which "created great fissures and, ultimately, gaps in people's lives. Money...rendered much of the way in which non-industrial peoples understood themselves, and the reproduction of their daily lives, useless. The money system itself was a widely disseminated mass medium which ripped the structure of peoples' needs from their customary roots, and by necessity transplanted these needs in a soil nourished by the 'rationality' of corporate industry and the retail marketplace" ("Americanization and Consumption," *Telos,* 37 Fall 1978: 47). Traditional ethnic ways of life hardly stood a chance under conditions in which the terms of survival were also those of massification! See also Maurice R. Stein, *The Eclipse of Community: An Interpretation of American Studies* (New York: Harper and Row, 1960); Gross, "Culture, Politics, and 'Lifestyle' in the 1960s."

20. See, e.g., John V. Van Sickle, *Planning for the South: An Inquiry into the Economics of Regionalism* (Nashville, TN: Vanderbilt University Press, 1943), 68–71; Gene Roberts Jr., "The Waste of Negro Talent in a Southern State," in *Freedom Now: The Civil Rights Struggle in America,* ed. Alan F. Westin (New York: Crowell, 1964); and Eli Ginzberg, "Segregation and Manpower Waste," *Phylon* 21 (December 1960): 311–16.

21. Harry Braverman, in *Labor and Monopoly Capital: The Degradation of Work in the Twentieth Century* (New York: Monthly Review, 1974), notes the ironic circumstance that capital has appropriated as a conscious ideal Marx's "abstraction from the concrete forms of labor" (181–82). In the logic of monopoly capitalism — characterized in part by constant reduction of labor's share of the overall costs of production and increasing sensitivity to optimizing profits over time in a stable production environment (cf. Andreas Papandreou, *Paternalistic Capitalism* [Minneapolis: University of Minnesota Press, 1972], especially 80–89) — the short-term benefits likely to accrue from a dual industrial labor market need not be expected to hold any great attractiveness.

22. Braverman, *Labor and Monopoly Capital,* 319 passim. Also see David Noble, *America by Design: Science, Technology, and the Rise of Corporate Capitalism* (New York: Knopf, 1977), 82, 257–320.

23. A clarification is needed concerning the use of the constructs "black community" and "black activism." Racial segregation and the movement against it were southern phenomena. Black power "nationalism" was essentially a northern phenomenon for which legally sanctioned racial exclusion was not an immediate issue. Although the two historical

currents of rebellion were closely related, they nevertheless were distinct. Consequently, they must be considered separately.

24. See, e.g., Charles S. Johnson, *Patterns of Negro Segregation* (New York: Harper, 1943), and *Growing Up in the Black Belt* (Washington, DC: American Council on Education, 1941); C. Vann Woodward, *The Strange Career of Jim Crow* (New York: Oxford University Press, 1966); Wilbur J. Cash, *The Mind of the South* (New York: Random House, 1941); Robert Penn Warren, *Segregation: The Inner Conflict in the South* (New York: Modern Library, 1956); John Dollard, *Caste and Class in a Southern Town* (New Haven: Yale University Press, 1937); James W. Vander Zanden, *Race Relations in Transition* (New York: Random House, 1955); George B. Tindall, *The Emergence of the New South: 1913–1945* (Baton Rouge: Louisiana State University Press, 1967); Arthur Raper, *Preface to Peasantry: A Tale of Two Black Belt Countries* (Chapel Hill: University of North Carolina Press, 1936), and *The Tragedy of Lynching* (Chapel Hill: University of North Carolina Press, 1933); William L. Patterson, *We Charge Genocide* (New York: International, 1951); Martin Luther King Jr., *Why We Can't Wait* (New York: Signet, 1964); Mayo Selz and C. Horace Hamilton, "The Rural Negro Population of the South in Transition," *Phylon* 24 (June 1963): 160–71; Thomas Patten Jr., "Industrial Integration of the Negro," *Phylon* 24 (December 1963): 334; Donald Dewey, "Negro Employment in Southern Industry," *Journal of Political Economy* 60 (August 1952): 279–93; and Herbert R. Northrup et al., eds., *Negro Employment in Southern Industry: A Study of Racial Policies in Five Industries* (Philadelphia: Wharton School of Finance, 1970). (The discussion here of the South draws freely from these sources.)

25. Certainly, the bizarre notion of "black leadership" was not an invention of the postwar era. That strategy of pacification had been the primary nonterroristic means for subduing black opposition since Booker T. Washington's network of alliances with corporate progressives and New South Bourbon Democrats. Moreover, the notion of a leadership stratum that was supposed to speak for a monolithic black community became the ideological model and political ideal for 1960s radicalism — especially in its "nationalist" variants. Johnson (*Patterns of Negro Segregation*, 65ff.) discusses stratification among blacks under segregation and white responses to the different strata. Perspectives on the phenomenon of black leadership in this context can be gleaned from Tillman C. Cothran and William Phillips Jr., "Negro Leadership in a Crisis Situation," *Phylon* 22 (Winter 1961): 107–18; Everett Carll Ladd Jr., *Negro Political Leadership in the South* (Ithaca, NY: Cornell University Press, 1966); Jack Walker, "Protest and Negotiation: A Case Study of Negro Leadership in Atlanta, Georgia," *Midwest Journal of Politics* 7 (May 1963): 99–124; Daniel C. Thompson, *The Negro Leadership Class* (Englewood Cliffs, NJ: Prentice-Hall, 1963); Floyd Hunter, *Community Power Structure* (Chapel Hill: University of North Carolina Press, 1953); and M. Elaine Burgess, *Negro Leadership in a Southern City* (Chapel Hill: University of North Carolina Press, 1962).

26. King's fascination with satyagraha suggests (although it exaggerates) the influence that decolonization abroad had on the development of civil rights opposition. See David L. Lewis, *King: A Critical Biography* (Baltimore: Penguin, 1970), 100–103; and Martin Luther King Jr., "Letter from Birmingham Jail," in King, *Why We Can't Wait,* 76–95.

27. Lomax, *The Negro Revolt,* 21 passim; Martin Luther King Jr., "I Have a Dream," in *Speeches by the Leaders: The March on Washington for Jobs and Freedom* (New York, n.d.); Whitney Young, *To Be Equal* (New York: McGraw-Hill, 1964); and Samuel DuBois Cook, "The American Liberal Democratic Tradition, the Black Revolution, and Martin Luther King, Jr.," in *The Political Philosophy of Martin Luther King, Jr.*, ed. Hanes Walton (Westport, CT: Greenwood, 1971), xiii–xxxviii.

28. This does not mean that *Life* magazine and *Father Knows Best* taught blacks to "dream the dream of freedom." Rather, the integrative logic of massification exacerbated disruptive tendencies already present within the black elite.

29. Enrollment in black colleges increased nearly sixfold between 1928 and 1961 and doubled between 1941 and 1950 alone, on the threshold of the civil rights movement. Doug McAdam, *Political Process and the Development of Black Insurgency, 1930–1970* (Chicago: University of Chicago Press, 1982), 101–2.

30. Concepts such as "duplicity" and "co-optation" are inadequate to shed light on why corporate and liberal interests actively supported the civil rights movement. Interpretations so derived cannot fully explain programs and strategies that originated in the black community. They suggest that naive and trusting blacks, committed to an ideal of global emancipation, allowed themselves to be led away from this ideal by bourgeois wolves in sheep's clothing. This kind of "false consciousness" thesis is theoretically unacceptable. Consciousness is false not so much because it is a lie enforced from outside but because it does not comprehend its historical one-sidedness.

31. Of course, suppression was the reaction of certain elements, most notably within the state apparatus, whose bureaucratized priorities urged suppression of any disruptive presence in the society. Howard Zinn, *SNCC: The New Abolitionists* (Boston: Beacon, 1965), as well as Forman, shows that the federal apparatus, which developed a reputation at the grass roots as the patron saint of equality, was at best lukewarm toward black demands for enforcement of constitutional rights and often set out to suppress tendencies and particular persons in the movement. Nevertheless, the movement was not suppressed, and not simply because it forced its will upon history. That bit of romantic backslapping has as little credence as the contention that the antiwar movement ended the Vietnam War. The state was hardly mobilized against civil rights activism; the Supreme Court had legitimized the movement before it even began. See also Cleveland Sellers (with Robert Terrell), *The River of No Return: The Autobiography of a Black Militant and the Life and Death of SNCC* (New York: Morrow, 1973). Clayborne Carson details, though without remarking on the ironic outcomes of the dynamic, the systematic attempts by the Kennedy

administration and private foundations to steer the civil rights movement toward enfolding itself in the national Democratic agenda. He carefully reconstructs the portentous tension this attempt generated in the movement. See his *In Struggle: SNCC and the Black Awakening of the 1960s* (Cambridge: Harvard University Press, 1981), 35–39 passim.

32. John F. Kennedy picked up the line and ran it as if it were his own; see his "Message to Congress," 88th Cong., 1st sess., *Congressional Record* (February 28, 1963), vol. 109, pt. 3.

33. It was out of this milieu of muddled uneasiness that the Reverend Willie Ricks gave the world the slogan "black power!" on the Meredith march in 1966. A taste of the radicals' frustration at the time can be gotten from Julius Lester, *Look Out, Whitey! Black Power's Gon' Get Your Mama* (New York: Dial, 1968). In some respects Lester's account, though more dated, has greater value for understanding this period than either Forman's or Sellers's because *Look Out, Whitey!* is written from within black power rather than retrospectively from the vantage point of new ideologies and old involvements that need to be protected. See also Stokely Carmichael, "Who Is Qualified?," in *Stokely Speaks: Black Power Back to Pan-Africanism* (New York: Random House, 1971). Carson's account in *In Struggle* meticulously rehearses the internal ideological and programmatic tensions and debates within SNCC during this period.

34. This is not to suggest, however, that events inside and outside the South were totally unrelated. As a practical matter, Democratic willingness to accommodate southern activism may have been influenced by blacks' increasing prominence within the urban constituencies of the party's electoral base in the Northeast and Midwest after 1932. In this context—especially after black defections from the national Democratic ticket in 1956 and erosion of white electoral support in the South after 1948—the party was given a pragmatic incentive to acknowledge a civil rights agenda. Arguments to this effect are developed in Frances Fox Piven and Richard A. Cloward, *Poor People's Movements: Why They Succeed, How They Fail* (New York: Pantheon, 1977), 214ff.; McAdam, *Political Process,* 81–86; and Woodward, *The Strange Career of Jim Crow,* 129.

35. See, for example, Stokely Carmichael, "Power and Racism," in Carmichael, *Stokely Speaks.* This essay is perhaps the first attempt to articulate a systematic concept of the notion "black power."

36. Robert L. Allen, *Black Awakening in Capitalist America: An Analytical History* (Garden City, NY: Doubleday, 1969), 129–92. Allen's interpretation, however, cannot move beyond this descriptive point because he accepts a simplistic notion of co-optation to explain the black corporate-elite nexus. Julius Lester charged by 1968 that the "principal beneficiaries of Black Power have been the black middle class" (*Revolutionary Notes* [New York: Baron, 1969], 106).

37. Piven and Cloward observe astutely that black power assisted in the pacification of activism by "providing a justification for the leadership stratum (and a growing black midlle class more generally) to move aggressively to take advantage of . . . new opportunities" opened by the movement (*Poor People's Movements,* 253).

38. Cruse, *Crisis of the Negro Intellectual,* 544–65.

39. Jennifer Jordan notes this "nostalgic" character of 1960s culturalism and its grounding in the black elite in her "Cultural Nationalism in the Sixties: Politics and Poetry," in Reed, *Race, Politics, and Culture.* In the most systematic and thorough critical reconstruction of black cultural nationalism to date, Jordan identifies two core nationalist tendencies: one Afro-American preservationist, the other African retrievalist. Presumably, Ron Karenga is to be seen as a bridge between those tendencies with his commitment to "creation, recreation and circulation of African American culture" ("From the Quotable Karenga," in *The Black Power Revolt,* ed. Floyd Barbour [Boston: Porter Sargent, 1968], 162).

40. Cf. Imamu Amiri Baraka (LeRoi Jones), "Toward the Creation of Political Institutions for All African Peoples," *Black World* 21 (October 1972): 54–78. "Unity will be the only method, it is part of the black value system because it is only with unity that we will get political power" (Imamu Amiri Baraka [LeRoi Jones] *Raise, Race, Rays, Raze* [New York: Random House, 1971], 109).

41. The legacy of this ultimately depoliticizing pattern of discourse can be seen in Jesse Jackson's 1984 presidential campaign, in which criticism of Jackson's effort was denounced as heresy or race treason.

42. George Mosse examines the theoretical components and historical significance of folkish ideology as a response to mass society in *The Crisis of German Ideology: Intellectual Origins of the Third Reich* (New York: Schocken, 1964), 13–30.

43. The fascination shared by most of the nationalists with the prospects of consciously creating a culture revealed both the loss of a genuine cultural base and the extent of their acceptance of manipulation as a strategy (cf. Karenga's "seven criteria for culture," "From the Quotable Karenga," 166). The farther away the nationalists chose to go to find their cultural referents, the more clearly they demonstrated the passage of a self-motivated, spontaneous black existence from the arena of American history. The ultimate extension of escapism came with the growth of pan-Africanism as an ideology; that turn — at least in its most aggressive manifestations — conceded as a first step the inauthenticity of all black American life. See Carmichael, *Stokely Speaks,* 175–227; and Ideological Research Staff of Malcom X Liberation University, *Understanding the African Struggle* (Greensboro, NC: The "X" Press, 1971).

44. In this regard expertise translates into superficial articulateness and ability to negotiate within the social management apparatus.

45. After Little Rock, Ronald Walters was able to boast that the black elected officials had become the vanguard political force in the black community; "The Black Politician: Fulfilling the Legacy of Black Power," *Current History* 67 (November 1974): 200ff. Baraka, a former chairman and a central organizer of the National Black Assembly, was very nearly expelled from the assembly in 1975 by a force of elected officials put off by his newfound "Marxism." Note, however, that even he had to admit the activists' marginality and weakness compared to the mainstream elite as early as 1970 at the Congress of African

Peoples; Imamu Amiri Baraka (LeRoi Jones), ed., *African Congress: A Documentary of the First Modern Pan-African Congress* (New York: Morrow, 1972), 99.

46. This is not to say that blacks are no longer oppressed, nor that the oppression no longer has racial characteristics. Nor still is it possible to agree with Wilson's claim that race is receding as a factor in the organization of American society; as Harold Barnette notes, the integration of affirmative action programs into the social management apparatus suggests race's continuing significance; see William Julius Wilson, *The Declining Significance of Race: Blacks and Changing American Institutions* (Chicago: University of Chicago Press, 1978), and Barnette's review of Wilson in *Southern Exposure* 7 (Spring 1979): 121–22. With legitimation and absorption of antiracism by the social management system, race has assumed a more pervasively explicit, officially institutionalized function than ever before in American life. Moreover, this function is often life-sustaining; controlling discrimination has become a career specialty, complete with "professional," "paraprofessional," and "subprofessional" gradations in public and private bureaucracies. However, "racial discrimination" fails as a primary basis from which to interpret or address black oppression.

"Racism" is bound to an "equality of opportunity" ideology that can express only the interests of the elite strata among the black population; equality of access to the meaningless, fragmented, and degrading jobs that make up the bulk of work, for example, hardly is the stuff of "black liberation" and is ultimately a retrograde social demand. It is not an accident, therefore, that the only major battle produced by the struggle against racism in the 1970s was the anti-Bakke movement, whose sole objective was protection of upwardly mobile blacks' access to pursuit of professional employment status.

Racism makes its appearance in black political discourse as an opaque reification grafted onto otherwise acceptable institutions. Small wonder that it is the only issue the black elite can find to contend with! Not only does racism carry the elite's sole critique of U.S. society, but the claim that racism creates a bond of equivalent victimization among blacks is one of the sources of the elite's legitimation. It is interesting to recall in this context that "racism" became the orthodox explanation of black oppression when the Kerner Commission anointed it as the fundamental source of the 1964–1967 urban uprisings; see its *Report of the National Advisory Commission on Civil Disorders* (New York: Bantam, 1968), 203. This document goes far toward articulating the outlines of what became the new strategy for management of the black population.

47. The most significant shift in the occupational structure of the black population in the decade after the 1964 Civil Rights Act was a relative expansion of its elite component. Between 1964 and 1974 the percentage of minority males classified as "professional and technical" workers increased by half; the percentage classified as nonfarm, salaried "managers and administrators" quadrupled over that period. Similar increases were realized by minority females. See Bureau of the Census, *Social and Economic Status*, 73–74. James A. Hefner and Alice E. Kidder discuss these developments, which they laud as constitutive

of a new era of black opportunity, even though they express concern — appropriate to an upwardly mobile stratum — that the rate of progress could be increased; see their "Racial Integration in Southern Management Positions," *Phylon* 33 (June 1972): 193–200.

Moreover, whereas in the 1960–1970 period the proportions of black low-income families decreased and high-income families increased at roughly the same impressive rate, between 1970–1979 the shares of families in both categories increased. In 1970, 30.6 percent of black families earned in the low-income range, and 35.2 percent were high income. In 1979, 32.5 percent were low income and 38.6 percent high income, while the middle-income component fell from 34.2 percent in 1970 to 28.9 percent in 1979. Between 1979 and 1982 the low-income category rose steadily to 37.8 percent, the high-income category dropped to just over 35 percent in 1981 and stabilized at that level, and middle-income families continued to decline, reaching 26.9 percent in 1982. Distribution of wealth by asset category is equally instructive. While proportions of total black wealth represented by equity in homes (the largest single category) and vehicles and in financial assets declined slightly between 1967 and 1979, equity in rental or other property more than doubled, from 12 percent to 25 percent of the total; see William P. O'Hare, *Wealth and Economic Status: A Perspective on Racial Equality* (Washington, DC: Joint Center for Political Studies, 1983), 18, 25.

An indication of the social management apparatus's centrality for this expansion in the black elite can be gleaned from consideration of the growth of the public sector as an avenue for black middle-class employment. Though government has consistently been more significant for black employment than white, between 1960 and 1970 the proportion of black males in managerial or professional jobs who were employed in the government sector doubled from 18.2 percent to 37.1 percent. Black females, whose professional opportunities had been more severely restricted to the public sector, realized more modest gains, from 57.9 percent to 63.3 percent. Despite a stabilization and slight tailing off, by 1980 nearly a third of black professional males and more than half of black professional females were employed in government; see Martin D. Carnoy, Derek Shearer, and Russell Rumberger, *A New Social Contract: The Economy and Government after Reagan* (New York: Harper and Row, 1983), 133–34.

This is the context in which the Reaganite assault on public spending is most directly racial in its thrust. Indeed, the mobilization of Thomas Sowell, Walter Williams, and other ideologues of black neoconservatism by the Reaganite forces is instructive. Sowell and the others seek to justify Reagan's reversal of racial palliatives and "entitlement" programs largely by pointing to the disproportionate benefits bestowed by those programs on middle-class black functionaries. For critical discussion of this phenomenon see Jerry G. Watts, "The Case of the Black Conservative," *Dissent,* Summer 1982: 301–13; and Alex Willingham, "The Place of the New Black Conservatives in Black Social Thought" (unpublished).

48. The celebration of the new elite is not, as once was the case, restricted to black media. Stephen Birmingham has testified to their presence and allowed them to expose

their personal habits in his characteristically gossipy style of pop journalism in *Certain People: America's Black Elite* (Boston: Little, Brown, 1977). The *New York Times Sunday Magazine* has at least twice lionized the beautiful black stratum of the 1970s; see Peter Ross Range, "Making It in Atlanta: Capital of 'Black is Bountiful,'" *New York Times Sunday Magazine,* April 7, 1974; and William Brashler, "The Black Middle Class: Making It," *New York Times Sunday Magazine,* December 3, 1978. Despite occasional injections of "balance," each of these brassy accounts tends to accept and project the elite's mystical view of itself and exaggerates its breadth and force in society. However, that the *Times* would even care to make the statement made by these two articles suggests minimally that the elite has been integrated into the corporate marketing strategy on an equal basis.

49. This distinction between "authentic" and "artificial" particularity is similar to Jürgen Habermas's distinction between "living" and "objectivistically prepared and strategically employed" cultural traditions. A cultural particularity is "authentic" insofar as it (1) reproduces itself within the institutional environment that apparently delimits the group, that is, outside the social administrative system, and (2) is not mobilized by the mass culture industry; cf. Jürgen Habermas, *Legitimation Crisis* (Boston: Beacon, 1975), 70–72. Therefore, in this usage, "authentic" particularity relates not to any notion of ethnic genuineness but to the oppositional impetus posited in a group's existence. This oppositional quality derives from the otherness that characterizes the autonomously reproductive, unintegrated group's relation to the mass capitalist social order and that necessarily (1) demonstrates the possibility of a form of social life alternative to that decreed by the logic of administration and (2) poses a practical negation of the order's claims to cultural hegemony. As the group is integrated into the material and cognitive frameworks of the prevailing order, the sense of alternate possibility is lost, and the negativity that had mediated the group's relation to mass capitalism is overcome in favor of a nontranscendent, system-legitimizing, and systemically authorized pluralism—which becomes the basis for what I have described as "artificial" particularity. Authenticity thus is a category of emancipatory interest rather than ethnographic integrity.

50. Jordan, in her "Cultural Nationalism in the Sixties," even contends that radical culturalism was most susceptible among all the 1960s' oppositional forms to the logic of commodification because of its tendency to reduce identity to the artifact.

51. Compare, e.g., S. E. Anderson, "Black Students: Racial Consciousness and the Class Struggle, 1960–1976," *Black Scholar* 8 (January/February 1977): 35–43; Muhammad Ahmad, "On the Black Student Movement: 1960–1970," *Black Scholar* 9 (May/June 1978): 2–11; and James Boggs and Grace Lee Boggs, *Revolution and Evolution in the Twentieth Century* (New York: Monthly Review, 1974), 174ff.

52. The coalition's bankruptcy was demonstrated by the defections from its electoral constituency to Nixon's "silent majority" in 1968 and by its wholesale collapse in the face of McGovernite and Republican challenges in 1972. Unable to end the Vietnam War and adjust to a new era of imperialism or to address the concerns of such postscarcity-era advocacy centers as the student and ecology movements, the productivist liberal-labor

forces who had controlled the Democratic party for a generation also found it impossible to establish a common discursive arena with the ethnic and feminist consciousness movements of the 1960s.

53. Paul Piccone, "Future of Capitalism," in Reed, *Race, Politics, and Culture,* and "The Changing Function of Critical Theory," *New German Critique* (Fall 1977): 35–36.

54. Habermas calls these "quasi-groups" and maintains that they perform the additional function of absorbing the "secondary effects of the averted economic crisis" (*Legitimation Crisis,* 39).

55. Russell Jacoby, "A Falling Rate of Intelligence?" *Telos,* Spring 1976: 141–46; Stanley Aronowitz, "Mass Culture and the Eclipse of Reason: The Implications for Pedagogy," *College English* 38 (April 1977): 768–74, and Aronowitz, *False Promises: The Shaping of American Working Class Consciousness* (New York: McGraw-Hill, 1973).

56. This integrative bias in mass movements is clear from Piven's and Cloward's accounts in *Poor People's Movements.* Their interpretation, however, emphasizes the structural determinants of protest movements to an extent that seems not to allow the possibility of transcendence.

57. Todd Gitlin carefully reconstructs the dialectic of mutually reinforcing interaction between the mass media and the New Left in general, including black power radicals, in *The Whole World Is Watching! Mass Media in the Making and Unmaking of the New Left* (Berkeley: University of California Press, 1980). Also see Carson, *In Struggle.*

58. Julius Lester was one who saw the prominence of a media cult in the movement (*Revolutionary Notes,* 176–180). On the peculiar media-inspired style of the Black Panthers, see Earl Anthony, *Picking Up the Gun* (New York: Pyramid, 1970).

59. "The spectacle presents itself as an enormous unalterable and inaccessible actuality. It says nothing more than 'that which appears is good, that which is good appears.' The attitude which it demands in principle is this passive acceptance, which in fact it has already obtained by its manner of appearing without reply, by its monopoly of appearance" (Guy Debord, *Society of the Spectacle* [Detroit: Black and Red, 1970], para. 12).

60. A shift in advertising style captures contemporary life: During the national telecast of the 1978 Miss Black America pageant, General Motors, a sponsor of the broadcast, featured a commercial in which a utility man at a plant listed the attractions of his job. Among them were pay, fringe benefits, security, opportunity to perform various tasks (a function solely of his particular position), congenial supervision, and a *good union*! In the metaphor of a colleague who is one of a vanishing breed of baseball fans, the bourgeoisie has a shutout going with two away in the bottom of the ninth.

61. For examination of the genesis of this growth coalition and its constituents and practices, see Alan Wolfe, *America's Impasse: The Rise and Fall of the Politics of Growth* (Boston: South End, 1981); and John H. Mollenkopf, *The Contested City* (Princeton: Princeton University Press, 1983).

62. R. Jeffrey Lustig develops this point in *Corporate Liberalism: The Origins of Modern American Political Theory, 1890–1920* (Berkeley: University of California Press,

1982). Samuel Huntington speaks explicitly of this characteristic of the American order and bemoans the disruptive qualities of the "democratic distemper" in *American Politics: The Promise of Disharmony* (Cambridge: Harvard University Press, 1981), and in his chapter on the United States in *The Crisis of Democracy: Report on the Governability of Democracies to the Trilateral Commission,* ed. Michel J. Crozier, Samuel P. Huntington, and Joji Watanuki (New York: New York University Press, 1975). Lustig notes that the model of social management in which growth politics is embedded actually antedates the New Deal.

63. The various elements that combined to erode the efficacy of what they refer to as the "postwar corporate system" are described in Samuel Bowles, David M. Gordon, and Thomas E. Weisskopf, *Beyond the Wasteland: A Democratic Alternative to Economic Decline* (New York: Random House, 1983), 79–97. Barry Bluestone and Bennett Harrison emphasize the role of shortsighted corporate management strategies and capital flight in undermining the growth coalition's usefulness; see their *The Deindustrialization of America: Plant Closings, Community Abandonment, and the Dismantling of Basic Industry* (New York: Basic, 1982).

64. Kevin P. Phillips examines this aspect of Reagan's base in *Post-Conservative America: People, Politics, and Ideology in a Time of Crisis* (New York: Random House, 1982), esp. 193–204.

65. Earl Picard, "The New Black Economic Development Strategy," *Telos,* Summer 1984: 53–64. Picard develops this argument through a study of the current programs of the National Association for the Advancement of Colored People (NAACP) and Jesse Jackson's Operation PUSH (People United to Serve Humanity).

66. For a careful examination of the narcissistic style of new middle-class politics and a refutation of the inherited wisdom that increased education and income produce a "public-regarding" ethos, see Clarence N. Stone, "Conflict in the Emerging Post-Industrial Community" (paper given at the American Political Science Association annual meeting, Denver, Colorado, 1982). Stone charts the coordinates of conflict through an examination of the narrowly self-interested politics of the mobile middle class in Montgomery County, Maryland, a largely upper-income jurisdiction in the Washington, D.C., metropolitan area. With its skills for organization and manipulation of language and image, this "yuppie" element is naturally suited to the formation of political agendas along interest-group lines.

67. See, e.g., Mollenkopf, *The Contested City,* 261–66. The organizational and ideological mechanisms through which these advantages are realized in the natural workings of the political system are discussed in Clarence N. Stone, "Systemic Power in Community Decision Making," *American Political Science Review* 74 (December 1980): esp. 983–84; and David Harvey, *Social Justice and the City* (Baltimore: Johns Hopkins University Press, 1973), 82–86. See also J. John Palen and Bruce London, eds., *Gentrification, Displacement, and Neighborhood Revitalization* (Albany: SUNY Press, 1984).

68. For critiques of neoliberal, high-tech development strategies see Carnoy, Shearer, and Rumberger, *A New Social Contract,* 150–59; and Bluestone and Harrison, *The Deindustrialization of America,* 210–30. Systematic statements of neoliberal reindustrialization strategy include Lester Thurow, *The Zero-Sum Society* (New York: Penguin, 1980); Robert Reich, *The Next American Frontier* (New York: Times Books, 1983); and Felix Rohatyn, *The Twenty Year Century* (New York: Random House, 1983).

69. It is instructive that the postwar baby boomers voted more consistently for Reagan than did any other age cohort in 1980. One view of this group's distinctive political style is proposed in Carter A. Eskew, "Baby-Boom Voters," *New York Times,* July 15, 1984.

70. A major focus of this project must be the secularization of the discussion of the black political situation. Certain elements in the left buttress the foes of democratic discourse in the black community by propagating a view that blacks — unlike other groups in the American polity — are moved to action only through the intervention of charismatic spokesmen who embody collective aspirations personalistically, outside of any discursive processes. Black religiosity is adduced to validate this authoritarian politics of cathartic folkishness, and these leftists opportunistically endorse the confounding of church and state in the black community even as they fret over the protofascist characteristics of the "moral majority." See, e.g., Andrew Kopkind, "Black Power in the Age of Jackson," *The Nation,* November 26, 1983; and Cornel West, *Prophesy Deliverance! An Afro-American Revolutionary Christianity* (Philadelphia: Westminister, 1982). I have developed critiques of these views in a review of West's book in *Telos,* Summer 1984: 211–18, and in *The Jesse Jackson Phenomenon: The Crisis of Purpose in Afro-American Politics* (New Haven: Yale University Press, 1986).

71. "The main thing is that utopian conscience and knowledge, through the pain it suffers in facts, grows wise, yet does not grow to full wisdom. It is *rectified* — but never *refuted* — by the mere power of that which, at any particular time, is. On the contrary it confutes and judges the existent if it is failing, and failing inhumanly; indeed, first and foremost it provides the *standard* to measure such facticity precisely as departure from the Right" (Ernst Bloch, *A Philosophy of the Future* [New York: Seabury, 1970], 91).

3. The Black Urban Regime

This chapter has been improved by criticisms, comments, suggestions, and reassurances from several individuals at various stages of its production. Among those whose efforts should be noted are Claude Barnes, Demetrios Caraley, Ester Fuchs, Jennifer Hochschild, Dennis Judd, Willie Legette, John Hull Mollenkopf, David Plotke, Stephen Skowronek, Michael Peter Smith, Clarence Stone, Linda Williams, Rhonda Williams, and Kathryn Yatrakis.

1. Joint Center for Political Studies, *Black Elected Officials: A National Roster* (Washington, DC: Joint Center for Political Studies, 1986), 1. Those cities are Chicago; Philadelphia; Detroit; Washington, D.C.; New Orleans; Atlanta; Newark, New Jersey;

Oakland, California; Birmingham, Alabama; Richmond, Virginia; Gary, Indiana; Hartford, Connecticut; and Portsmouth, Virginia. Seven other regimes govern in cites between 50,000 and 100,000 in population. All of them, e.g., East St. Louis, Illinois; East Orange, New Jersey; and Mount Vernon, New York; are small cities adjacent to a major central city. This definition of the black urban regime does not include the administrations of black mayors who lead administrations and govern coalitions in which blacks are not the dominant or principal group—e.g., Tom Bradley in Los Angeles.

2. Peter K. Eisinger, *The Politics of Displacement: Racial and Ethnic Transition in Three American Cities* (New York: Academic Press, 1980).

3. See contributions by Richard Hatcher and Kenneth Gibson in *African Congress: A Documentary of the First Modern Pan-African Congress,* ed. Imamu Amiri Baraka (New York: William Morrow, 1972).

4. Matthew Holden, "Black Politicians in the Time of the 'New' Urban Politics," *Review of Black Political Economy* 2 (Fall 1971): 56–71.

5. Michael Preston, "Limitations of Black Urban Power: The Case of Black Mayors," in *The New Urban Politics,* ed. Robert Lineberry and Louis Masotti (Boston: Ballinger, 1976).

6. Sharon Watson, "Do Mayors Matter? The Role of Leadership in Urban Policy" (unpublished paper presented at the American Political Science Association conference, 1980); Albert Karnig and Susan Welch, *Black Representation and Urban Policy* (Chicago: University of Chicago Press, 1980); Peter K. Eisinger, "Black Employment in Municipal Jobs: The Impact of Black Political Power," *American Political Science Review* 76 (June 1982): 380–92, *Black Employment in City Government, 1973–1980* (Washington, DC: Joint Center for Political Studies, 1983), and "Black Mayors and the Politics of Racial Economic Advancement," in *Readings in Urban Politics: Past, Present, and Future,* 2nd ed., ed. Harlan Hahn and Charles H. Levine (New York: Longman, 1984); and Edward J. Keller, "The Impact of Black Mayors on Urban Policy," *Annals, American Academy of Political and Social Science* 439 (September 1978): 40–52.

7. William E. Nelson Jr., "Cleveland: The Evolution of Black Political Power," in *The New Black Politics: The Search for Political Power,* 2nd ed., ed. Michael Preston, Lenneal Henderson, and Paul Puryear (New York: Longman, 1987).

8. Charles Tilly, "Race and Migration to the American City," in *The Metropolitan Enigma,* ed. James Q. Wilson (Garden City, NY: Doubleday, 1968); Kathleen A. Bradbury, Anthony Downs, and K. Small, *Urban Decline and the Future of American Cities* (Washington, DC: Brookings Institution, 1982), 133–38.

9. Patrick J. Ashton, "The Political Economy of Suburban Development," in *Marxism and the Metropolis,* ed. William Tabb and Larry Sawers (New York: Oxford University, 1978), 73–74.

10. Ashton, "Political Economy"; Arthur P. Solomon, "The Emerging Metropolis," in *The Prospective City,* ed. A. P. Solomon (Cambridge: MIT, 1980); and Dennis R. Judd,

The Politics of American Cities: Private Power and Public Policy (Boston: Little, Brown, 1979), 171–74.

11. Anthony Downs, *Neighborhoods and Urban Development* (Washington, DC: Brookings Institution, 1981), 51; Gary Orfield, "Ghettoization and Its Alternatives," in *The New Urban Reality*, ed. Paul Peterson (Washington, DC: Brookings Institution, 1985); and Joe T. Darden, "The Significance of Race and Class in Residential Segregation," *Journal of Urban Affairs* 8 (Winter 1986): 49–55. Orfield concludes that "economics cannot begin to explain the present extreme pattern of separation" (169) because he uses "economics" somewhat narrowly to refer to dynamics of segregation by income. That conclusion, therefore, is not necessarily inconsistent with the view that a racial element is embedded in the "natural" operation of residential real estate markets.

12. Downs, *Neighborhoods and Urban Development*, 91–93; David O'Brien and J. Lange, "Racial Composition and Neighborhood Evaluation," *Journal of Urban Affairs* 8 (Summer 1986): 43–61.

13. Thomas Pettigrew, "Racial Change and the Intrametropolitan Distribution of Black Americans," in Solomon, *The Prospective City*.

14. Orfield, "Ghettoization and Its Alternatives," 163–64; see also Kenneth Newton, "American Urban Politics: Social Class, Political Structure, and Public Goods," *Urban Affairs Quarterly* 11 (December 1975): 261–64; Anne B. Schlay and Peter H. Rossi, "Putting Politics into Urban Ecology: Estimating the Net Effects of Zoning," in *Urban Policy Analysis: Directions for Future Research*, ed. Terry N. Clark (Beverly Hills, CA: Sage, 1981); R. S. Harrison, "The Effects of Exclusionary Zoning and Residential Segregation on Urban-Service Distributions," in *The Politics of Urban Public Services*, ed. Richard C. Rich (Lexington, MA: D. C. Heath, 1982); R. Babcock, "Exclusionary Zoning: A Code Phrase for a Notable Legal Struggle," in *The Urbanization of the Suburbs*, ed. Louis Masotti and J. Hadden (Beverly Hills, CA: Sage, 1973); and Judd, *Politics of American Cities*, 171–88.

15. Thomas R. Dye, "Urban Political Integration: Conditions Associated with Annexation in American Cities," *Midwest Journal of Political Science* 8 (November 1964): 430–46; J. T. Black, "The Changing Economic Role of Central Cities and Suburbs" in Solomon, *The Prospective City*, 97–98; Bradbury, Downs, and Small, *Urban Decline*, 51–55; W. H. Oakland, "Central Cities: Fiscal Plight and Prospects for Reform," in *Current Issues in Urban Economics*, ed. P. Mieskowski and M. Straszheim (Baltimore: Johns Hopkins University Press, 1979), 325.

16. An apparent exception is Atlanta, where it appears that a city-county consolidation may be on the horizon. However, it is not clear whether (1) consolidation actually will occur or (2) what the net revenue implications — after factoring in the costs of extending municipal services to the remainder of the county — of consolidation would be. The county is already predominantly black, which makes the plan credible to several black officials, but projections done in 1975 by Atlanta's Department of Budget and Planning

and Department of Finance, which assumed a best-case scenario for consolidation, showed the city incurring a net revenue loss until the twenty-first century; see Adolph Reed Jr., "Annexation and Consolidation Options for Atlanta: An Evaluative Report" (unpublished staff paper, Department of Budget and Planning, City of Atlanta, 1975).

17. Samuel Bass Warner, *Streetcar Suburbs* (Cambridge, MA: Harvard, 1978); and Henry C. Binford, *The First Suburbs: Residential Communities on the Boston Periphery, 1815–1860* (Chicago: University of Chicago Press, 1985).

18. Ashton, "Political Economy," 67.

19. David M. Gordon, "Class Struggle and the Stages of American Urban Development," in *The Rise of Sunbelt Cities*, ed. D. C. Perry and A. J. Watkins (Beverly Hills, CA: Sage, 1977), 74–75.

20. John Kain, "The Distribution and Movement of Jobs and Industry," in Wilson, *The Metropolitan Enigma*.

21. Gordon, "Class Struggle," 75–77; Richard A. Walker, "A Theory of Suburbanization: Capitalism and the Construction of Urban Space in the U.S.," in *Urbanization and Urban Planning in Capitalist Society*, ed. Michael Dear and A. Scott (London and New York: Methuen, 1981), 399–401.

22. Harry Braverman, *Labor and Monopoly Capital: The Degradation of Work in the Twentieth Century* (New York: Monthly Review, 1974).

23. Walker, "A Theory of Suburbanization," 399.

24. Ann Markusen, "Class and Urban Social Expenditure: A Marxist Theory of Metropolitan Government," in Tabb and Sawers, *Marxism and the Metropolis*, 100–101; and Ashton, "Political Economy," 71.

25. David M. Gordon, "Capitalist Development and the History of American Cities," in Tabb and Sawers, *Marxism and the Metropolis*, 51.

26. Gordon, "Capitalist Development," 54–55.

27. Alan Wolfe, *America's Impasse: The Rise and Fall of the Politics of Growth* (Boston: South End, 1981), 54.

28. Barry Bluestone and Bennett Harrison, *The Deindustrialization of America: Plant Closings, Community Abandonment, and the Dismantling of Basic Industry* (New York: Basic, 1982); Samuel Bowles, David M. Gordon, and Thomas E. Weisskopf, *Beyond the Wasteland: A Democratic Alternative to Economic Decline* (New York: Random House, 1983); and S. M. Miller and Donald Tomaskovic-Devey, *Recapitalizing America* (Boston and London: Routledge and Kegan Paul, 1983). This claim is a source of controversy among economists. One view contends that plant closings indicate "creative destruction," the flow of capital from less- to more-productive uses in the domestic economy; see H. C. Leroy, "The Free Market Approach," in *Deindustrialization and Plant Closure*, ed. P. D. Staudohar and H. E. Brown (Lexington, MA: D. C. Heath, 1987). On that view, what appears to be atrophy is actually a sign of economic health. Another view—focused on absolute changes in domestic manufacturing employment and comparison of aggregate output, investment, and employment trends in the United States and other industrialized

nations—questions whether deindustrialization is even occurring at all; see R. Z. Lawrence, "Is Deindustrialization a Myth?," also in Staudohar and Brown, *Deindustrialization and Plant Closure*. However, declines in actual manufacturing production employment indicate that domestic labor markets are deindustrializing; furthermore, increases in structural unemployment and the overall decline in real wages suggest that those labor markets cannot absorb the workers left jobless by capital's present mobility. That implies, in sum, that the social costs of capital restructuring—along regional and global lines—are concentrated in the ways that deindustrialization theorists argue: in urban areas, among blue-collar workers, in the Northeast and the North Central region, among minorities, and in labor-intensive industries; see Barry Bluestone, "In Support of the Deindustrialization Thesis," in Staudohar and Brown, *Deindustrialization and Plant Closure*; and R. L. Smith, "Interdependencies in Urban Economic Development: The Role of Multi-Establishment Corporations," in *Public Policy across States and Communities*, ed. Dennis R. Judd (Greenwich, CT: JAI, 1985), 214–17.

29. Pettigrew, "Racial Change," 62.

30. John Kasarda, "Urban Change and Minority Opportunities," in Peterson, *The New Urban Reality*, 46.

31. Bradbury, Downs, and Small, *Urban Decline*, 75.

32. John H. Mollenkopf, *The Contested City* (Princeton: Princeton University Press, 1983), 141.

33. Mollenkopf, *The Contested City*, 42–44.

34. Martin Shefter, *Political Crisis/Fiscal Crisis: The Collapse and Revival of New York City* (New York: Basic, 1985), 118–19; Mollenkopf, *The Contested City*, 33–34.

35. Douglas Yates, *The Ungovernable City: The Politics of Urban Problems and Policy Making* (Cambridge: MIT, 1977), 54–73; Burton J. Bledstein, *The Culture of Professionalism* (New York: Norton, 1976); Magali Sarfati Larson, *The Rise of Professionalism* (Berkeley: University of California, 1977); and Timothy W. Luke, "The Modern Service State: Public Power in America from the New Deal to the New Beginning," in *Race, Politics, and Culture: Critical Essays on the Radicalism of the 1960s*, ed. Adolph Reed Jr. (Westport, CT: Greenwood, 1986).

36. Wallace Sayre and H. Kaufman, *Governing New York City* (New York: Norton, 1960); Theodore Lowi, "Machine Politics—Old and New," *Public Interest* 9 (Fall 1967): 83–92; Robert Salisbury, "The New Convergence of Power," *Journal of Politics* (November 1964): 775–97; Scott Greer, "Bureaucratization of the Emerging City," in *Fiscal Retrenchment and Urban Policy*, ed. J. P. Blair and D. Nachmias (Beverly Hills, CA: Sage, 1979).

37. Martin Anderson, *The Federal Bulldozer: A Critical Analysis of Urban Renewal, 1949–1962* (Cambridge: MIT, 1964), 7–9; Norman Fainstein and Susan Fainstein, "New Haven: The Limits of the Local State," in Susan S. Fainstein, Norman I. Fainstein, Richard Child Hill, Dennis Judd, and Michael Peter Smith, *Restructuring the City: The Political Economy of Urban Development* (New York: Longman, 1983); Clarence N. Stone, *Economic Growth and Neighborhood Discontent: System-Bias in the Urban Renewal Program*

of Atlanta (Chapel Hill: University of North Carolina Press, 1976); Todd Swanstrom, *The Crisis of Growth Politics: Cleveland, Kucinich, and the Challenge of Urban Populism* (Philadelphia: Temple University Press, 1985), 37–55; Mollenkopf, *The Contested City*; Heywood T. Sanders, "Urban Renewal and the Revitalized City: A Reconsideration of Recent History," in *Urban Revitalization,* ed. D. B. Rosenthal (Beverly Hills, CA: Sage, 1980); Robert Friedland, *Power and Crisis in the City: Corporations, Unions, and Urban Politics* (New York: Macmillan, 1983), 78–124.

38. Martin D. Carnoy, Derek Shearer, and Russell Rumberger, *A New Social Contract: The Economy and Government after Reagan* (New York: Harper and Row, 1983), 122–49; M. Hout, "Occupational Mobility of Black Men: 1962 to 1973," *American Sociological Review* 49 (June 1984): 308–22.

39. Michael Lipsky, *Street Level Bureaucracy: Dilemmas of the Individual in Public Services* (New York: Russell Sage, 1980); Richard A. Cloward and Frances Fox Piven, *The Politics of Turmoil: Essays on Race, Poverty, and the Urban Crisis* (New York: Pantheon, 1974); Clarence N. Stone, "Whither the Welfare State: Professionalism, Bureaucracy, and the Market Alternative," *Ethics* 93 (April 1983): 588–95; Matthew A. Crenson, "Urban Bureaucracy in Urban Politics: Notes toward a Developmental Theory," in *Public Values and Private Power in American Politics,* ed. J. David Greenstone (Chicago: University of Chicago Press, 1982).

40. James Button, *Black Violence: Political Impact of the 1960s Riots* (Princeton: Princeton University Press, 1978); Shefter, *Political Crisis/Fiscal Crisis*; Piven and Cloward, *The Politics of Turmoil.*

41. Paul E. Peterson, *City Limits* (Chicago: University of Chicago Press, 1981), 178–81.

42. Shefter, *Political Crisis/Fiscal Crisis*; Michael K. Brown and Steven P. Erie, "Blacks and the Legacy of the Great Society: The Economic and Political Impact of Federal Social Policy," *Public Policy* 29 (Summer 1981): 299–330; Button, *Black Violence,* 169; also see chapter 2 in this volume.

43. Brown and Erie, "Blacks and the Legacy," 301; Carl Stokes, *Promises of Power* (New York: Simon and Schuster, 1973); Ira Katznelson, *City Trenches: Urban Policy and the Patterning of Class in the United States* (New York: Pantheon, 1981), 177–78.

44. Peter K. Eisinger, "The Community Action Program and the Development of Black Political Leadership," in *Urban Policy Making,* ed. Dale Rogers Marshall (Beverly Hills, CA: Sage, 1979), 133; also see Bette Woody, *Managing Crisis Cities: The New Black Leadership and the Politics of Resource Allocation* (Westport, CT: Greenwood, 1982), 81–83; Karnig and Welch, *Black Representation and Urban Policy,* 50–78.

45. J. Hadden, Louis Masotti, and V. Thiessen, "The Making of Negro Mayors, 1967," in *Big City Mayors: The Crisis in Urban Politics,* ed. L. Ruchelman (Bloomington: Indiana University Press, 1969).

46. Robert Smith, "Black Power and the Transformation from Protest to Politics," *Political Science Quarterly* 96 (Fall 1981): 431–43; Martin L. Kilson, "Political Change in the Negro Ghetto, 1900–1940s," in *Key Issues in the Afro-American Experience,* vol.

2, ed. Nathan Huggins, Martin Kilson, and Daniel Fox (New York: Harcourt, Brace, Jovanovich, 1971), and "The New Black Political Class," in *Dilemmas of the Black Middle Class,* ed. Joseph Washington Jr. (Philadelphia: J. Washington, 1980).

47. Clarence N. Stone, "Systemic Power in Community Decision-Making: A Restatement of Stratification Theory," *American Political Science Review* 74 (December 1980): 981. Stone defines systemic power as "that dimension of power in which durable features of the socioeconomic system (the situational element) confer advantages and disadvantages on groups (the intergroup element) in ways predisposing public officials to favor some interests at the expense of others (the indirect element)." The coalition of selected interest groups forming a durable hierarchy in support of pro-growth politics is an instance of systemic power.

48. George Sternlieb and J. W. Hughes, "Metropolitan Decline and Inter-Regional Job Shifts," in *The Fiscal Crisis of American Cities,* ed. Roger Alcaly and David Mermelstein (New York: Random House, 1977); Gregory D. Squires, "Capital Mobility versus Upward Mobility: The Racially Discriminatory Consequnces of Plant Closings and Corporate Relocations," in *Sunbelt/Snowbelt: Urban Development and Regional Restructuring,* ed. Larry Sawers and William Tabb (New York: Oxford University Press, 1984); Bradbury, Downs, and Small, *Urban Decline,* 182; Robert Goodman, *The Last Entrepreneurs: America's Regional Wars for Jobs and Dollars* (Boston: South End, 1979), 44–45.

49. Bradbury, Downs, and Small, *Urban Decline,* 6–7. Portsmouth and Oakland were not ranked, presumably because they are not clearly the dominant cities in their SMSAs. Of the 121 cities listed, 36 percent were growing and 35 percent were stagnant.

50. Ibid., 52–55. One-third of the total of 153 cities ranked scored in the three worst categories on the disparity index, compared to eleven out of thirteen black-led cities. Nearly one-third of the 153 scored in the three best categories. On the divergence index, five of thirteen black-led cities scored in the three worst categories, compared to eleven of the total sample.

51. Oakland, "Central Cities," 323–25.

52. Richard P. Nathan and Charles Adams, "Understanding Central City Hardship," *Political Science Quarterly* 91 (Spring 1976): 51–52; Bradbury, Downs, and Small, *Urban Decline,* 9.

53. Ibid., 51–55.

54. J. T. Black, "The Changing Economic Role of Central Cities and Suburbs," in Solomon, *The Prospective City,* esp. 104, 109.

55. R. B. Cohen, "The New International Division of Labor, Multinational Corporations, and Urban Hierarchy," in Dear and Scott, *Urbanization and Urban Planning*; Miller and Tomaskovic-Devey, *Recapitalizing America,* 30–31.

56. Black, "Changing Economic Role," 104, 106; Doug L. Birch, "Who Creates Jobs?" *The Public Interest,* Fall 1981: 3–14. Between 1970 and 1975, four of the cities currently governed by black regimes (Atlanta, New Orleans, Philadelphia, and Washington) lost 78,500 manufacturing jobs and gained 36,200 in the service sector.

57. Black, "Changing Economic Role"; Friedland, *Power and Crisis in the City,* 73–75.

58. Friedland, *Power and Crisis in the City,* 73; Kasarda, "Urban Change and Minority Opportunities," 55–57.

59. Lester Thurow, *Generating Inequality* (New York: Basic, 1975); Christopher Jencks, "Affirmative Action for Blacks: Past, Present, and Future," *American Behavioral Scientist* (July/August 1985): 731–60.

60. David M.Gordon, R. Edwards, and M. Reich, *Segmented Work, Divided Workers: The Historical Transformation of Labor in the U.S.* (London and New York: Cambridge University Press, 1982), 206–10. Although J. P. Smith and F. Welch ("Racial Differences in Earnings: A Survey of New Evidence," in *Current Issues in Urban Economics,* ed. P. Mieskowski and M. Straszheim [Baltimore: Johns Hopkins University Press, 1979], 54) suggest that blacks may be becoming less vulnerable to business cycles relative to whites, that effect reflects the progress of an intraracial labor segmentation; the marginalized inner-city population remains as vulnerable as ever, as was indicated in the tremendous increases in black unemployment during the early 1980s.

61. Black, "Changing Economic Role," 111. The four cities were Chicago, Detroit, Philadelphia, and Washington. The other six were Baltimore, Cleveland, Milwaukee, New York, and St. Louis. Of those, only St. Louis, which actually had the most disadvantageous divergence of any of the central cities, was comparable to the other four. In Dallas and Cleveland the gap between central city and suburban unemployment rates even narrowed.

62. Robert Rosenfeld, "Income Inequality and Crime," in *The Changing Structure of the City,* ed. G. A. Tobin (Beverly Hills, CA: Sage, 1979).

63. In fairness to Young, the desire to purify a sector of the central business district (CBD) has been a recurring theme in Atlanta politics. Earlier attempts (in the Maynard Jackson administration) included restrictions on consumption of alcohol near liquor stores (to remove winos from view) and two attempts to establish curfews on adolescents (to clear them from downtown). The second curfew attempt, which originated from the same council member who proposed the earlier one, succeeded because its proponents grafted it onto public concern over the then current missing and murdered children issue; see Adolph Reed Jr., "Narcissistic Politics in Atlanta," *Telos,* Summer 1981: 97–105.

64. Charles L. Schultze, E. R. Fried, Alice M. Rivlin, N. Teeters, and Robert Reischauer, "Fiscal Problems of Cities," in Alcaly and Mermelstein, *Fiscal Crisis of American Cities,* 192–93; Robert Lineberry and Ira Sharkansky, *Urban Politics and Public Policy,* 3rd ed. (New York: Harper and Row, 1978), 225; Friedland, *Power and Crisis in the City,* 194.

65. Stephen M. David and Paul Kantor, "Political Theory and Transformations in Urban Budgetary Arenas: The Case of New York City," in Marshall, *Urban Policy Making,* 191–92; Shefter, *Political Crisis/Fiscal Crisis.*

66. I. S. Lowry, "The Dismal Future of Central Cities," in Solomon, *The Prospective City,* 175; Bradbury, Downs, and Small, *Urban Decline,* 6–7.

67. H. A. Garn and L. C. Ledebur, "The Economic Performance and Prospects of Cities," in Solomon, *The Prospective City,* 216–18.

68. Ibid., 210–11. On their index of "Changes in Urban Conditions, 1960–1977," J. W. Fossett and Richard P. Nathan rank fifty-three of the largest fifty-seven U.S. cities on the basis of amount of older housing, population loss, and concentration of poverty; 88 percent of the black-led cities ranked fell in the worst-off 40 percent of the total; see their "The Prospects for Urban Revival," in *Urban Government Finance,* ed. Roy Bahl (Beverly Hills, CA: Sage, 1981), 66.

69. Schultze, et al., "Fiscal Problems of Cities," 192–93; Roy W. Bahl and A. Campbell, "City Budgets and the Black Constituency," in *Urban Governance and Minorities,* ed. Herrington Bryce (New York: Praeger, 1976). In every region except the Midwest, whose sample excluded Gary, the mean percentage increase for black-led cities was higher than that for the region as a whole; in all four regions black-led cities received more intergovernmental assistance.

70. Oakland, "Central Cities," 350; Thomas J. Anton, *Federal Aid to Detroit* (Washington, DC: Brookings Institution, 1983); C. J. Orlebeke, *Federal Aid to Chicago* (Washington, DC: Brookings Institution, 1983); J. W. Fossett, *Federal Aid to Big Cities* (Washington, DC: Brookings Institution, 1983).

71. Swanstrom, *The Crisis of Growth Politics*; Eric H. Monkkonen, "The Politics of Municipal Indebtedness and Default, 1850–1936," in *The Politics of Urban Fiscal Policy,* ed. S. K. Ward and T. J. McDonald (Beverly Hills, CA: Sage, 1984); William K. Tabb, *The Long Default* (New York: Monthly Review, 1982); Pierre Clavel, *The Progressive City: Planning and Participation, 1969–1984* (New Brunswick, NJ: Rutgers University Press, 1986); Peter Steinberger, *Ideology and the Urban Crisis* (Albany: SUNY Press, 1985); Shefter, *Political Crisis/Fiscal Crisis*; R. M. Stein, E. G. Sinclair, and M. Neiman, "Local Government and Fiscal Stress: An Exploration into Spending and Public Employment Decisions," in *Cities in Stress,* ed. M. Gottdiener (Beverly Hills, CA: Sage, 1986); Irene S. Rubin and R. Rubin, "Structural Theories and Urban Fiscal Stress," in Gottdiener, *Cities in Stress.*

72. Shefter, *Political Crisis/Fiscal Crisis,* 232.

73. Mack H. Jones, "Black Political Empowerment in Atlanta: Myth and Reality," *Annals of the American Academy of Political and Social Science* 439 (September 1978): 114–15.

74. William E. Nelson Jr. and Philip J. Meranto, *Electing Black Mayors: Political Action in the Black Community* (Columbus: Ohio State University Press, 1977), 339–40.

75. Ronald W. Walters, "The Black Politician: Fulfilling the Legacy of Black Power," *Current History* 67 (November 1974): 200–201.

76. Of course, the trenches themselves are products of political competition for uses of urban space and therefore reflect a hierarchy already influenced by direction of public policy and patterns of service delivery; see C. Kaufman, "Political Urbanism: Urban Spatial Organization, Policy, and Politics," *Urban Affairs Quarterly* 9 (June 1974): 421–36;

Richard C. Rich, "Distribution of Services: Studying the Products of Urban Policy Making," in Marshall, *Urban Policy Making*.

77. Peterson, *City Limits*, 159.

78. Woody, *Managing Urban Crises*, 190, 202.

79. Swanstrom, *The Crisis of Growth Politics*, 100–107.

80. Edward Greer, *Big Steel: Black Politics and Corporate Power in Gary, Indiana* (New York: Monthly Review, 1979), 129–32; Woody, *Managing Urban Crises*, 196; D. H. Guyot, "Newark: Crime and Politics in a Declining City," in *Crime in City Politics*, ed. A. Heinz, H. Jacob, and R. L. Lineberry (New York: Longman, 1983); Eisinger, *The Politics of Displacement*, 85–90; Rufus P. Browning, Dale Rogers Marshall, and David H. Tabb, *Protest Is Not Enough: The Struggle of Blacks and Hispanics for Equality in Urban Politics* (Berkeley: University of California Press, 1984), 154–56.

81. Woody, *Managing Urban Crises*, 39; Eisinger, "Black Mayors and the Politics of Racial Economic Advancement," 251. Eisinger's study of six cities with black mayors highlights a distinction between black regimes and individual black mayors in this respect. In each of the five cities with black regimes (Newark, Atlanta, Detroit, Washington, D.C., and Gary) black representation on police forces increased by at least 100 percent. By contrast, in Los Angeles the increase was negligible.

82. Eisinger, *The Politics of Displacement*, 159–61; Woody, *Managing Urban Crises*, 44–90.

83. Eisinger, *Black Employment in City Government*, 37–41; A. Ganz, "Where Has the Urban Crisis Gone? How Boston and Other Large Cities Have Stemmed Economic Decline," in Gottdiener, *Cities in Stress*, 47–50; Terry N. Clark and L. C. Ferguson, *City Money: Political Processes, Fiscal Strain and Retrenchment* (New York: Columbia University Press, 1983), 138–44.

84. Adolph Reed Jr., *The Jesse Jackson Phenomenon: The Crisis of Purpose in Afro-American Politics* (New Haven and London: Yale University Press, 1986), 31–40.

85. Jeffrey R. Henig, "Collective Responses to the Urban Crisis: Ideology and Mobilization," in Gottdiener, *Cities in Stress*.

86. Leonard Cole, *Blacks in Power: A Comparative Study of Black and White Elected Officials* (Princeton: Princeton University Press, 1976), 147; Clark and Ferguson, *City Money*, 133; Karnig and Welch, *Black Representation and Urban Policy*, 12–13.

87. Kilson, "Black Political Class," 86–89; Karnig and Welch, *Black Representation and Urban Policy*, 11–12.

88. John Conyers and W. L. Wallace, *Black Elected Officials: A Study of Black Americans Holding Governmental Office* (New York: Russell Sage, 1976), 28.

89. Dennis R. Judd and M. Collins, "The Case of Tourism: Political Coalitions and Redevelopment in the Central Cities," in Tobin, *Changing Structure of the City*, 182–83.

90. Harvey Molotch, "The City as a Growth Machine," *American Journal of Sociology* 82 (September 1976): 309–32; see also John Logan and Harvey Molotch, *Urban Fortunes: The Political Economy of Place* (Berkeley: University of California Press, 1987).

91. Swanstrom, *The Crisis of Growth Politics,* 152.

92. Clarence N. Stone, "Power and Social Complexity," in *Community Power: Directions for Future Research,* ed. Robert J. Waste (Beverly Hills, CA: Sage, 1986). Stone develops this point in relation to explaining a notion of "ecological power," i.e., "the capacity to reshape the context—that is, the social ecology—within which one operates," or, more specifically, the ability "to enlist government in restructuring the terms under which social interactions occur" (84).

93. Dennis R. Judd, "Electoral Coalitions, Minority Mayors, and the Contradictions in the Municipal Policy Agenda," in Gottdiener, *Cities in Stress,* 146; Eisinger, *The Politics of Displacement,* 91–92; Swanstrom, *The Crisis of Growth Politics,* 3; Bryan D. Jones and Lynn Bachelor (with C. Wilson), *The Sustaining Hand: Community Leadership and Corporate Power* (Lawrence: University of Kansas Press, 1986), 38–39; Richard Child Hill, "Crisis in the Motor City: The Politics of Economic Development in Detroit," in Fainstein et al., *Restructuring the City.*

94. A. Harris, "The Capitalistic Gospel according to Rev. Andrew Young," *The Atlanta Journal-Constitution,* September 22, 1985; Clarence N. Stone, "New Class or Convergence: Competing Interpretations of Social Complexity on the Structure of Urban Power," *Power and Elites* 1 (Fall 1984): 1–22, and *Regime Politics: Governing Atlanta, 1946–1988* (Lawrence: University of Kansas Press, 1989), 108–59.

95. Woody, *Managing Urban Crises*; Rod Bush, "Oakland: Grassroots Organizing against Reagan," in *The New Black Vote: Politics and Power in Four American Cities,* ed. Rod Bush (San Francisco: Synthesis, 1984); Clark and Ferguson, *City Money,* 140–42.

96. Hill, "Crisis in the Motor City," 94–98; Stone, *Economic Growth and Neighborhood Discontent*; E. C. Hayes, *Power Structure and Urban Policy: Who Rules in Oakland?* (New York: McGraw-Hill, 1972), 75–127; Clavel, *The Progressive City,* 21–22; Jones, "Black Political Empowerment in Atlanta"; Carl Abbott, *The New Urban America: Growth and Politics in Sunbelt Cities* (Chapel Hill: University of North Carolina Press, 1981), 102, 143–66; Karl E. Taeuber and A. F. Taeuber, *Negroes in Cities* (Chicago: Aldine, 1965).

97. Clarence N. Stone, "City Politics and Economic Development: Political Economy Perspectives," *Journal of Politics* 46 (February 1984): 286–99; Michael Peter Smith, "The Uses of Linked Development Policies in U.S. Cities," in *Regenerating the Cities: The U.K. Crisis and the American Experience,* ed. Michael Parkinson, Bernard Foley, and Dennis R. Judd (Manchester, Eng.: University of Manchester Press, 1987); Doug Muzzio and R. W. Bailey, "Economic Development, Housing, and Zoning: A Tale of Two Cities," *Journal of Urban Affairs* 8 (Winter 1986): 1–18.

98. Barry M. Moriarty, *Industrial Location and Community Development* (Chapel Hill: University of North Carolina Press, 1980), 246–57; Bluestone and Harrison, *The Deindustrialization of America,* 185–87; Michael Peter Smith, R. L. Ready, and Dennis R. Judd, "Capital Flight, Tax Incentives, and the Marginalization of American States and Localities," in Judd, *Public Policy across States and Communities*; M. Wasylenko, "The

Location of Firms: The Role of Taxes and Fiscal Incentives," in Bahl, *Urban Government Finance*; R. W. Schmenner, "Industrial Location and Urban Public Management," in Solomon, *The Prospective City*; Swanstrom, *The Crisis of Growth Politics,* 141–55, 232–39. In addition to other limitations on the growth/jobs/reduced inner-city unemployment formula, Harrison cites evidence indicating that even the low-wage, secondary labor market employment that the growth agenda generates in the central city goes disproportionately to white suburbanites; see Bennett Harrison, *Urban Economic Development* (Washington, DC: Urban Institute, 1974), 52–53.

   99. Peterson, *City Limits,* 129; Friedland, *Power and Crisis in the City,* 221. Recognition of this tension may be a main reason that local elites often suspect first-time black regimes of being vaguely and generically "antibusiness." See Judd, "Electoral Coalitions, Minority Mayors," 145–46; Charles H. Levine, *Racial Conflict and the American Mayor* (Lexington, MA: Lexington, 1974), 76–77, passim; Eisinger, *Politics of Displacement,* 81ff.; M. D. Henson and J. King, "The Atlanta Public-Private Romance: An Abrupt Transformation," in *Public-Private Partnership in American Cities: Seven Case Studies,* ed. R. S. Fosler and R. A. Berger (Lexington, MA: Lexington, 1982), 306–7.

   100. Swanstrom, *The Crisis of Growth Politics,* 3; Kenneth Gibson, "Managing a Metropolis," in Tobin, *Changing Structure of the City,* 110.

   101. Jackson eventually settled on insistence on a minority set-aside and joint-venture program for airport construction and operation as his administration's "black" position.

   102. Judd, "Electoral Coalitions, Minority Mayors," 164.

   103. Henig, "Collective Responses to the Urban Crisis," 236; see also Todd Swanstrom, "Urban Populism, Fiscal Crisis, and the New Political Economy," in Gottdiener, *Cities in Stress*; and Stone, "Power and Social Complexity."

   104. Alvin J. Schexnider, "Political Mobilization in the South: The Election of a Black Mayor in New Orleans," in *The New Black Politics,* 1st ed., ed. Michael Preston, Lenneal Henderson, and Paul Puryear (New York: Longman, 1982), 232–34. The sales tax in New Orleans, however, replaced two flat-rate service taxes that were even more regressive; also see Eisinger, *The Politics of Displacement,* 175–80.

   105. Clark and Ferguson, *City Money,* 138–39; Eisinger, *The Politics of Displacement,* 197–98. Many critics have contended that a white mayor who acted as Wilson Goode did in the infamous MOVE incident in Philadelphia would be met by tremendous outrage from blacks. Though the nature of the MOVE case is considerably more complex than most of Goode's critics have acknowledged, the suggestion that more voluble reaction would have greeted a white mayor is almost certainly sound; see, for example, C. Stone, "Goode: Bad and Indifferent," *Washington Monthly,* July/August 1986: 27–28, and Richard A. Keiser, *Subordination or Empowerment? African-American Leadership and the Struggle for Urban Political Power* (New York: Oxford University Press, 1997), 115–16.

   106. Judd, "Electoral Coalitions, Minority Mayors," 148.

   107. Stone, "Power and Social Complexity," 100; Peterson, *City Limits,* 121–22.

108. E. E. Schattschneider, *The Semi-Sovereign People* (New York: Holt, Rinehart, and Winston, 1960), 71.

109. Molotch, "The City as a Growth Machine," 328.

110. Rubin and Rubin, "Structural Theories and Urban Fiscal Stress," 190.

111. Swanstrom, "Urban Populism," 103.

112. Smith, "Uses of Linked Development"; Smith, Ready, and Judd, "Capital Flight, Tax Incentives, and Marginalization."

113. Swanstrom, "Urban Populism," 225–45; Ganz, "Where Has the Urban Crisis Gone?"

114. Harold Washington's ambitious-sounding development plan was one of the more recent and clearest cases in point. The centerpiece of this plan was public-private cooperation to generate some 8,000 jobs through the use of tax and rent giveaways. Despite formal stipulation of preferential hiring for city residents (which in most instances is unenforceable) and overtures toward neighborhoods, the general thrust of the plan was to provide public subsidies for private development and to concentrate municipal purchasing as much as possible with local and minority firms. For a sober assessment of what was and might have been with respect to the Washington administration's approach to development, see Larry Bennett, "Harold Washington and the Black Urban Regime," *Urban Affairs Quarterly* 28 (March 1993): 423–40; Bennett examines the tensions and contradictions that drove the Washington coalition. Also see Judd, "Electoral Coalitions, Minority Mayors," 157–60. Moreover, linkage policies, by settling for front-end side-payments, actually may not be very good alternatives to taxation after all. In addition to not adequately compensating for the costs of growth, they may have a demobilizing effect on those groups in local politics who would press for more equitable compensation; see Smith, "Uses of Linked Development."

115. Swanstrom, *The Crisis of Growth Politics,* 236.

116. Judd, "Electoral Coalitions, Minority Mayors," 165.

117. Bush, "Oakland," 4. The Bush volume (*The New Black Vote*) suffers from a general failure to examine carefully the policy contexts within which the regimes operate and a naiveté about local public policy that at times slides into complete avoidance. For example, Bush's forty-three-page essay on black politics in Oakland devotes less than four pages to discussion of the Wilson regime, and more than a page of that concerns how he came to be elected.

118. Bush, "Oakland," 4; Thomas R. Dye, "Community Power and Public Policy," in Waste, *Community Power,* 46–47.

119. "Black Mayors Back Minimum Wage for Youth," *New York Times,* May 6, 1984; Bluestone and Harris, *The Deindustrialization of America,* 228; W. W. Goldsmith, "Bringing the Third World Home: Enterprise Zones for America?," in Sawers and Tabb, *Sunbelt/Snowbelt*; J. Sloan, "Enterprise Zones May Not Be the Bargain That's Advertised," *Wall Street Journal,* March 26, 1985.

120. Clavel, *The Progressive City.*

121. Swanstrom, *The Crisis of Growth Politics.*

122. In this respect I recall arguing as a functionary in the Maynard Jackson administration that we should lobby for passage of a point-of-earnings income tax ordinance even though it was clearly in violation of the Georgia Constitution. By passing it and forcing the state to react, we could at least have precipitated public debate on the issue and on the problem of the strain placed on service delivery by freeloading commuters. The argument fell on deaf ears.

123. By "neopluralist" I refer to versions of pluralist theory that have been amended to provide a role for extrasystemic activity (usually construed as systemic activity by other means, when regular channels are blocked) and to acknowledge that different groups possess different degrees of concentrated power and access to systemic channels. For a debate over neopluralism's character and content, see John F. Manley, "Neo-Pluralism: A Class Analysis of Pluralism I and Pluralism II" (with comments by Charles E. Lindblom and Robert A. Dahl), *American Political Science Review* 77 (June 1983): 368–89.

124. Doug McAdam, *Political Process and Black Insurgency, 1930–1970* (Chicago: University of Chicago Press, 1982); also see Frances Fox Piven and Richard A. Cloward, *Poor People's Movements: Why They Succeed, How They Fail* (New York: Pantheon, 1977).

125. McAdam, *Political Process and Black Insurgency,* 97.

126. Ibid., 186–87.

127. Ibid., 231–34.

128. Eisinger, *The Politics of Displacement,* 194–96.

129. Ibid., 167.

130. Browning, Marshall, and Tabb, *Protest Is Not Enough,* 241.

131. Karnig and Welch, *Black Representation and Urban Policy,* 54–55; William R. Keech, *The Impact of Negro Voting* (Chicago: Rand McNally, 1968).

4. Sources of Demobilization in the New Black Political Regime

1. Illustrations of the first tendency include chapter 3 in this volume; Dennis R. Judd, "Electoral Coalitions, Minority Mayors, and the Contradictions in the Municipal Policy Agenda," in *Cities in Stress,* ed. M. Gottdiener (Beverly Hills, CA: Sage, 1986); William E. Nelson Jr., "Cleveland: The Evolution of Black Political Power," in *The New Black Politics: The Search for Political Power,* 2nd ed., ed. Michael B. Preston, Lenneal J. Henderson, and Paul Puryear (New York: Longman, 1987); Clarence N. Stone, *Regime Politics: Governing Atlanta, 1946–1988* (Lawrence: University of Kansas Press, 1989); and Larry Bennett, "Harold Washington and the Black Urban Regime," *Urban Affairs Quarterly* 28 (March 1993): 423–40. Exemplifying the second are Carol Swain, *Black Faces, Black Interests: The Representation of Blacks in Congress* (Cambridge, MA: Harvard University Press, 1993); Jim Sleeper, "The End of the Rainbow," *New Republic,* November 1, 1993; Shelby Steele, *The Content of Our Character* (New York: St. Martin's, 1990); Walter Williams, *The State against Blacks* (New York: New Press, 1982); David J. Blum, "Black Politicians Fear They Can't Do Much to Help Their People," *Wall Street*

Journal, October 29, 1980; and Abigail Thernstrom, *Whose Votes Count? Affirmative Action and Minority Voting Rights* (Cambridge, MA: Harvard University Press, 1987).

Liberal social scientists' conventional characterizations of this issue are perhaps best represented by Peter Eisinger, *The Politics of Displacement* (New York: Academic Press, 1980); Wilbur C. Rich, "Coleman Young and Detroit Politics, 1973–1986," and Huey L. Perry and Alfred Stokes, "Politics and Power in the Sunbelt: Mayor Morial of New Orleans," both in Preston, Henderson, and Puryear, *The New Black Politics*; Richard A. Keiser, *Subordination or Empowerment? African-American Leadership and the Struggle for Urban Political Power* (New York and Oxford: Oxford University Press, 1997), and "Explaining African-American Political Empowerment: Windy City Politics from 1900 to 1983," *Urban Affairs Quarterly* 29 (September 1993): 84–106; and several of the case studies in Rufus Browning, Dale R. Marshall, and David Tabb, eds., *Racial Politics in American Cities* (New York: Longman, 1990). See also Jason Deparle, "The Civil Rights Battle Was Easy next to the Problems of the Ghetto," *New York Times,* May 17, 1992; and Stuart Taylor Jr., "Electing by Race," *The American Lawyer* 13 (June 1991): 50–54. Left and right can become indistinguishable under the sign of an abstract interracialism that defines black political assertiveness as intrinsically ineffectual and parochial, as is demonstrated in Pat Watters, "Talking about Race in Lafayette," *The Nation,* November 22, 1993; Michael Tomasky's two essays, "Public Enemies: Let's Make It Racial," *Village Voice,* October 12, 1993, and "The Tawdry Mosaic: Identity Politics in New York City," *The Nation,* June 21, 1993; Alan Wolfe, "The New American Dilemma," *New Republic,* April 13, 1992; Michael Oreskes, "The Civil Rights Act, Twenty-five Years Later: A Law That Shaped a Realignment," *New York Times,* July 2, 1989; and Peter Applebome, "Deep South and Down Home, but It's a Ghetto All the Same," *New York Times,* August 21, 1993, and "Suits Challenging Redrawn Districts That Help Blacks," *New York Times,* February 14, 1994.

2. I have discussed this problem in slightly different contexts in chapter 7 in this volume and in "Mythologies of 'Cultural Politics' and the Discrete Charm of the Black Petite Bourgeoisie," in *African Americans and the New Policy Consensus: Retreat of the Liberal State?,* ed. Marilyn Lashley and M. Njeri Jackson (Westport, CT: Greenwood, 1994).

3. For important, contextualizing examination of these other factors, see Peter Marcuse, "The Targeted Crisis: On the Ideology of Fiscal Crisis and Its Uses," *International Journal of Urban and Regional Research* 5 (September 1981): 330–55; Saskia Sassen, *The Global City* (Princeton: Princeton University Press, 1991), esp. 193–338; Michael Peter Smith and Dennis R. Judd, "American Cities: The Production of Ideology," in *Cities in Transformation: Class, Capital, and the State,* ed. Michael Peter Smith (Beverly Hills, CA: Sage, 1984); and Michael Peter Smith and Joe R. Feagin, eds., *The Capitalist City* (Cambridge, MA: Basil Blackwell, 1987), esp. parts 3 and 4.

4. The trajectory and characteristics of black political incorporation have been considered most extensively in Rufus P. Browning, Dale Rogers Marshall, and David H.

Tabb, *Protest Is Not Enough: The Struggle of Blacks and Hispanics for Equality in Urban Politics* (Berkeley: University of California Press, 1984); Rufus P. Browning, Dale Rogers Marshall and David H. Tabb, eds., *Racial Politics in American Cities,* 2nd ed. (New York: Longman, 1997); Martin L. Kilson, "Political Change in the Negro Ghetto, 1900–1940s," in *Key Issues in the Afro-American Experience, vol. 2,* ed. Nathan Huggins, Martin Kilson, and Daniel Fox (New York: Harcourt, Brace, Jovanovich, 1971), "From Civil Rights to Party Politics: The Black Political Transition," *Current History* 67 (November 1974): 193–99, and "The New Black Political Class," in *Dilemmas of the Black Middle Class,* ed. Joseph Washington (Philadelphia: J. Washington, 1980); Ronald Walters, "The Black Politician," *Current History* 67 (November 1974): 200–201; and Robert Smith, "Black Power and the Transformation from Protest to Politics," *Political Science Quarterly* 96 (Fall 1981): 431–43.

5. See Frank Parker, *Black Votes Count* (Chapel Hill: University of North Carolina Press, 1990); James W. Button, *Blacks and Social Change* (Princeton: Princeton University Press, 1989); Linda Williams, "Black Political Progress in the 1980s: The Electoral Arena," in Preston, Henderson, and Puryear, *The New Black Politics*; Alex Willingham, "Voting Rights, Government Responsibility, and Conservative Ideology," *Urban League Review* 10 (Winter 1986/87): 12–23, and "The Voting Rights Movement in Perspective," in *Without Justice for All: The New Liberalism and Our Retreat from Racial Equality,* ed. Adolph Reed Jr. (Boulder, CO: Westview, 1999).

6. By 1991 there were 7,490 black elected officials serving at all levels of government, compared to 1,469 in 1970. Cited in Lucius J. Barker and Mack H. Jones, *African Americans and the American Political System* (Englewood Cliffs, NJ: Prentice Hall, 1994), 72.

7. See chapter 2 in this volume and Peter Eisinger, "Black Mayors and the Politics of Racial Economic Advancement," in *Readings in Urban Politics: Past, Present, and Future,* ed. Harlan Hahn and Charles Levine (New York: Longman, 1984), "Black Empowerment in Municipal Jobs: The Impact of Black Political Power," *American Political Science Review* 76 (June 1982): 380–92, and *Black Employment in City Government, 1973–1980* (Washington, DC: Joint Center for Political Studies, 1983); Michael K. Brown and Steven P. Erie, "Blacks and the Legacy of the Great Society: The Economic and Political Impact of Federal Social Policy," *Public Policy* 29 (Summer 1981): 299–330; Martin D. Carnoy, Derek Shearer, and Russell Rumberger, *A New Social Contract: The Economy and Government after Reagan* (New York: Harper and Row, 1983), 122–49; Albert Karnig and Susan Welch, *Black Representation and Urban Policy* (Chicago: University of Chicago Press, 1980), 108–20; Dorothy K. Newman, Nancy J. Amidei, Barbara L. Carter, Dawn Day, William J. Kruvant, and Jack S. Russell, *Protest, Politics, and Prosperity: Black Americans and White Institutions, 1940–1975* (New York: Pantheon, 1978), 99–134.

8. Earl Picard, "New Black Economic Development Strategy," *Telos,* Summer 1984: 53–64.

9. On the growth, location, and characteristics of the black public functionary stratum, see "Symposium: Minorities in Public Administration," *Public Administration Re-*

view 34 (November/December 1974): 519–63; and Lenneal J. Henderson, *Administrative Advocacy: Black Administrators in Urban Bureaucracy* (Palo Alto, CA: R and E Associates, 1979). Bart Landry, *The New Black Middle Class* (Berkeley: University of California Press, 1987), 133–233, discusses sociological characteristics of the class milieu and social networks within which this stratum is embedded.

10. Clarence N. Stone provides a fine-grained description of the ways that local stratification systems are reproduced through mundane, "commonsensical" practices and premises; see his "Social Stratification, Nondecision-Making, and the Study of Community Power," *American Politics Quarterly* 10 (July 1982): 275–302.

11. Also see Brett Williams, "Poverty among African Americans in the Urban United States," *Human Organization* 51 (Summer 1992): 164–74; Walter W. Stafford and Joyce Ladner, "Political Dimensions of the Underclass Concept," in *Sociology in America,* ed. Herbert Gans (Newbury Park, CA: Sage, 1990); Leslie Innis and Joe R. Feagin, "The Black 'Underclass' Ideology in Race Relations Analysis," *Social Justice* 16 (Winter 1989): 13–33; Carole Marks, "The Urban Underclass," *Annual Review of Sociology* 17 (1991): 445–66; Ruth Conniff, "The Culture of Cruelty," *The Progressive,* September 1992: 16–20; Herbert J. Gans, "Deconstructing the Underclass: The Term's Dangers as a Planning Concept," *Journal of the American Planning Association* 56 (Summer 1990): 271–77.

12. See, for example, Lawrence Mead, *Beyond Entitlement: The Social Obligations of Citizenship* (New York: Free Press, 1986), and *The New Politics of Poverty* (New York: Basic Books, 1992); Mickey Kaus, "The Work Ethic State," *The New Republic,* July 1986: 22–33, and *The End of Equality* (New York: Basic Books, 1992); Charles Murray, *Losing Ground* (New York: Basic Books, 1984).

13. William Julius Wilson, *The Truly Disadvantaged: The Inner City, the Underclass, and Public Policy* (Chicago and London: University of Chicago Press, 1987), and "Studying Inner-City Dislocations: The Challenge of Public Agenda Research" (1990 Presidential Address), *American Sociological Review* 56 (February 1991): 1–14; see also Gretchen Reynolds, "The Rising Significance of Race," *Chicago,* December 1992: 81–82.

14. Dennis R. Judd details in a clear, elegant way the role of federal urban policy in reproducing and extending racial inequality since the 1930s; see his "Symbolic Politics and Urban Policies: How African Americans Got So Little from the Democrats," in Reed, *Without Justice for All.*

15. Sara Rimer, "Raid on Wrong Boston Home Results in Death of a Minister," *New York Times,* March 28, 1994; Frank Bruni, "A Battleground without Winners in the War on Drug Abuse," *New York Times,* June 28, 1998; Dirk Johnson, "Two out of Three Young Black Men in Denver Are on Gang Suspect List," *New York Times,* December 11, 1993; James McKinley, "Police Shoot an Unarmed Robbery Suspect Dead as He Flees," *New York Times,* February 10, 1990; Fox Butterfield, "Massachusetts Says Police in Boston Illegally Stopped Black Youth," *New York Times,* December 20, 1990; Neil A. Lewis, "Police Brutality under Wide Review by Justice Department," *New York Times,* March

15, 1991; Don Terry, "Man Dies after Arrest in Assault," *New York Times,* May 23, 1989, and "Death after Police Beating Inspires Fear in Detroit," *New York Times,* November 8, 1992; Alison Mitchell, "Brooklyn Officer Indicted in Unarmed Man's Death," *New York Times,* May 27, 1992; Ronald Sullivan, "Judge Finds Bias in Bus Terminal Search," *New York Times,* April 25, 1990; Sharman Stein, "Elderly May Pay for Sins of Young," *Chicago Tribune,* September 3, 1992; Matt O'Connor, "ACLU Charges CHA Violates Tenants' Rights," *Chicago Tribune,* November 19, 1992; Sharman Stein and William Recktenwald, "Sixty-five Seized in Sweep at CHA Homes," *Chicago Tribune,* April 7, 1992; Michel Marriott, "Drug Program Angers Many Residents of Boerum Hill," *New York Times,* July 2, 1989; Diana Jean Schemo, "Anger over List of Names Divides Blacks from Their College Town," *New York Times,* September 27, 1992; Elaine S. Povich, "Moseley-Braun Bill Would Try Some Thirteen-Year-Olds as Adults," *Chicago Tribune,* October 27, 1993; Coramae Richey Mann, *Unequal Justice: A Question of Color* (Bloomington: University of Indiana Press, 1993), esp. 150–55; Elliott Currie, "Capital Gangbusters: What's Wrong with the Crime Bill," *The Nation,* January 31, 1994. Also see Norval Morris, "It's the Time, Not the Rate of Crime, That's Filling American Prisons," *Chicago Tribune,* March 29, 1993, and "Race, Drugs, and Imprisonment," *Chicago Tribune,* March 30, 1993; and Jeffrey Fagan, "Drug Selling and Licit Income in Distressed Neighborhoods: The Economic Lives of Street-Level Drug Users and Dealers," in *Drugs, Crime, and Social Isolation,* ed. G. Peterson and A. Harrell (Washington, DC: Urban Institute Press, 1993). Despite the popular imagery, moreover, blacks reported the *lowest* rates of adolescent drug use in the United States; see U.S. Government Accounting Office, *Teenage Drug Use: Uncertain Linkages with Either Pregnancy or School Dropout* (Washington, DC: GPO, 1991), 15–17.

16. See chapter 6 in this volume and Christopher Jencks, *Rethinking Social Policy: Race, Poverty, and the Underclass* (Cambridge, MA: Harvard University Press, 1992), 189–98. See also Virginia Morris, "Docs Let Pregnant Whites Off Drug Hook," *New Haven Register,* April 26, 1991; Tamar Lewin, "Appeals Court in Florida Backs Guilt for Drug Delivery by Umbilical Cord," *New York Times,* April 20, 1991; Adolph Reed Jr., "The Liberal Technocrat," *The Nation,* February 2, 1988; and Willie Legette, "The Crisis of the Black Male: A New Ideology in Black Politics," in Reed, *Without Justice for All.* It is worth noting in this regard that the effects of alcohol and other drug consumption on fetal health have been wildly exaggerated in the current public hysteria; see Katha Pollitt, *Reasonable Creatures* (New York: Knopf, 1994), 169–86; and Claire D. Coles, Kathleen A. Platzman, Iris Smith, Mark E. James, and Arthur Falek, "Effects of Cocaine and Alcohol Use in Pregnancy on Neonatal Growth and Neurobehavioral Status," *Neurotoxicology and Teratology* 14 (1992): 23–33. There is, for example, apparently no such thing as a permanently damaged "crack baby." Moreover, the general perception of crack cocaine's uniquely addictive power for adults is itself a myth; see Stanton Peele, *Diseasing of America: Addiction Treatment out of Control* (Boston: Houghton Mifflin, 1989), 160–63. On the persistence of the "crack baby" myth and the mass media's role in perpetuating it, see

Janine Jackson, "The Myth of the 'Crack Baby': Despite Research, Media Won't Give Up Idea of 'Bio-Underclass,'" *Extra,* September/October 1998: 9–11. By the late 1990s the antifeminist, antiabortionist agenda of the fetal protection movement became still clearer, as states began defining "unborn children" as full human beings from the "time of fertilization to the time of birth," ostensibly for the purpose of providing latitude for the state in interventions to protect the interests of the fetus. In some instances this intervention could extend to imposing criminal penalties — as in a South Carolina statute providing for prosecution for child abuse of pregnant women who engage in behavior held to endanger the fetus; in some instances, though technically not criminalizing, such intervention, as in a Wisconsin initiative, could permit courts to compel pregnant women held to engage in endangering behavior to undergo treatment, including inpatient treatment, and could permit courts to appoint legal guardians for the supposedly endangered fetus, embryo, or pre-embryo. For discussion of these legislative initiatives, see Bob Herbert, "Pregnancy and Addiction: South Carolina's Misguided Law," *New York Times,* June 11, 1998, and "Hidden Agendas: Fetal Protection Isn't the Real Issue," *New York Times,* June 14, 1998.

17. Preston H. Smith, "'Self-Help,' Black Conservatives, and the Reemergence of Black Privatism," in Reed, *Without Justice for All,* provides the most thorough examination and critique to date of contemporary self-help rhetoric and its ideological and institutional foundations.

18. See, e.g., Lee Daniels, "The New Black Conservatives," *New York Times Magazine,* October 4, 1981; Murray Friedman, "The New Black Intellectuals," *Commentary,* June 1980: 46–52; Gordon Crovitz, "A Challenge to Liberalism," *Wall Street Journal,* September 16, 1980; Juan Williams, "Black Conservatives, Center Stage," *Washington Post,* December 16, 1980; Walter Williams, "Black Leaders Tell Only Part of the Story," *Moral Majority Report,* November 17, 1980; Peter Applebome, "Black Conservatives: Minority within a Minority," *New York Times,* July 13, 1991; Thomas Sowell, "A Black 'Conservative' Dissents," *New York Times Magazine,* August 8, 1976, and "Blacker Than Thou," *Washington Post,* February 13, 1981; Dallas Lee, "Black Prophets Preach New Ideas," *Atlanta Journal and Constitution,* March 8, 1981; Joseph Perkins, ed., *Critical Issues: A Conservative Agenda for Black Americans* (Washington, DC: Heritage Foundation, 1989); "Black America under the Reagan Administration: A Symposium of Black Conservatives," *Policy Review,* Fall 1985; Juan Williams, Glenn C. Loury, Julian Bond, Frank Mingo, and Paula Giddings, "Moving Up at Last?" *Harper's,* February 1987; Joseph Perkins, "An Alternative at Hand to the Black Orthodoxy," *Wall Street Journal,* January 15, 1985; and the recently reborn crackhead, alleged practitioner of violence against women, child support scofflaw, and courageous foe of black male irresponsibility, Glenn Loury, "Who Speaks for Black Americans?" *Commentary* 83 (January 1987): 34–38, "Breaking the Code," *Newsweek,* October 21, 1985, "Drowning New Black Voices in Partisanship," *Wall Street Journal,* February 2, 1985, and "The Failure of Black Leaders," *Penthouse,* November 1986.

19. Ellis Cose, "Breaking the Code of Silence," *Newsweek,* January 10, 1994; Howard Fineman, "An Older, Grimmer Jesse," in *Newsweek,* January 10, 1994; Joint Center for Political Studies, *Black Initiative and Governmental Responsibility* (Washington, DC: JCPS, 1987); Eugene Rivers, "On the Responsibility of Intellectuals in the Age of Crack," *Boston Review,* September/October 1992; Anthony Appiah, Eugene Rivers, Cornel West, bell hooks, Henry Louis Gates Jr., Margaret Burnham, and special expert Glenn Loury, "On the Responsibility of Intellectuals (in the Age of Crack)," *Boston Review,* January/February 1993; Anthony Flint, "How to Establish Link with Poor Debated by Black Intellectuals," *Boston Globe,* December 1, 1992; Roger Wilkins, "The Black Poor Are Different," *New York Times,* August 22, 1989, and "Black Like Us," *Mother Jones,* May 1988; Eleanor Holmes Norton, "Restoring the Traditional Black Family," *New York Times Magazine,* June 2, 1985: section 6, p. 43; Cornel West, *Race Matters* (Boston: Beacon Press, 1993), esp. 9–20, 47–60; Salim Muwakkil, "Black Male Crisis Hits the Mainstream," *In These Times,* June 12–25, 1991, and "Marriage of Convenience No Longer Convenient," *In These Times,* April 24, 1991; Samuel D. Proctor, "To the Rescue: A National Youth Academy," *New York Times,* September 16, 1989; Donald Stone, "On Writing 'Fallen Prince' " *Catalyst,* Winter 1988: 57–61; Marian Wright Edelman, "An Agenda for Empowerment," *Essence,* May 1988, 65–66; Emmett D. Carson, "Helping Our Own," *Essence,* May 1988, 160; Wilmer C. Ames Jr., "Reclaiming Our Families from the Welfare System," *Emerge,* April 1992; Priscilla Painton, "NAACP Convention Told Road to Success Starts Close to Home," *Atlanta Constitution,* July 10, 1987; Courtland Milloy, "Black Men's Hope, Reality," *Washington Post,* May 23, 1991, and "Mentoring Isn't Always the Cure-All," *Washington Post,* January 10, 1993; Henry Louis Gates Jr., "Two Nations . . . Both Black," *Forbes,* September 14, 1992; Don Terry, "A Graver Jackson's Cry: Overcome the Violence," *New York Times,* November 13, 1993; Orlando Patterson, "Toward a Study of Black America," *Dissent,* Fall 1989: 476–86; Robert Kerr, "Trenton Legislator Proposes Overhaul of Welfare System," *New York Times,* April 9, 1991; Michel Marriott, "Harsh Rap Lyrics Provoke Black Backlash," *New York Times,* August 15, 1993; J. I. Adkins Jr., "Self-Help Should Be Focus into the Twenty-First Century," *Chicago Tribune,* February 9, 1994.

20. William Galston, "The Future of the Democratic Party," *The Brookings Review,* Winter 1985: 16–24; Senator Bill Bradley, "Race and the American City," 102nd Cong., 2nd sess., *Congressional Record* (March 26, 1992), vol. 138; Senator John Kerry, "Race, Politics, and the Urban Agenda," Yale University, March 30, 1992, published in *Zeta* (May/June 1992).

21. Bradley, in fact, wrote a jacket blurb for Cornel West's *Race Matters.*

22. Paul Starr, "Civil Reconstruction: What to Do without Affirmative Action," *The American Prospect,* Winter 1992; and "Passion, Memory, and Politics, 1992," *The American Prospect,* Fall 1992; Richard Epstein, *Forbidden Grounds: The Case against Employment Discrimination Laws* (Cambridge, MA: Harvard University Press, 1992); Eugene

Genovese, "Voices Must Unite for Victory in the Cultural War," *Chicago Tribune*, December 22, 1993.

23. Gordon Lafer, "Minority Unemployment, Labor Market Segmentation, and the Failure of Job Training Policy in New York City," *Urban Affairs Quarterly* 28 (December 1992): 206–35, and "The Politics of Job Training: Urban Poverty and the False Promise of JTPA," *Politics and Society* 22 (September 1994): 349–88.

24. See also Alex Willingham, "Ideology and Politics: Their Status in Afro-American Social Theory," in *Race, Politics, and Culture: Critical Essays on the Radicalism of the 1960s*, ed. Adolph Reed Jr. (Westport, CT: Greenwood, 1986).

25. Bayard Rustin's famous essay, "From Protest to Politics," *Commentary,* February 1965: 25–31, noted at the time the challenge that the civil rights movement's successes posed for progressive black interests. Rustin called for expanding the movement's focus beyond pursuit of an agenda of racial inclusion to attack structured inequality that was not always explicitly racial. In context, Rustin's specific critique and call—which preceded Stokely Carmichael's "black power" speech on the Meredith march by more than a year—could have implied a strategic response like the variants of black power consciousness inflected toward radical political economy as easily as they did his argument for fastening black aspirations to the Democratic liberal-labor coalition. In retrospect at least, the course of subsequent events underscores this strategic ambivalence. Rustin wrote at a crucial point—before the first major escalation of the Vietnam War and the Watts uprising—at a moment when it was not quite clear how far Lyndon Johnson's administration and its governing coalition could be pushed toward an agenda of racial equality and social democracy. As responsiveness to black interests stiffened, Rustin's persisting commitment to subordinating black strategy within the Democratic liberal-labor alliance embodied an increasingly conservative force in black politics. Ultimately, by the 1970s, he had become irrelevant, except as an almost self-parodic shill for Zionist interests, reduced to patrolling the boundaries of the black political mainstream with his annual Black Americans in Support of Israel Committee statement as a putative litmus test for legitimacy. It is his relative conservatism in the late 1960s that makes Rustin attractive to those Clintonist intellectuals, like E. J. Dionne, William Julius Wilson, and others, who now invoke the 1965 *Commentary* essay as pointing to a road sadly not taken. Ironically, however, the essay includes a ringing indictment of liberals who argued, mutatis mutandis, for precisely the sort of tepid withdrawal from directly confronting racial inequality advocated by those who now embrace him. Rustin scored the *"New York Times* moderate who says that the problems are so enormous and complicated that Negro militancy is a futile irritation, and that the need is for 'intelligent moderation' . . . that Negro demands, while abstractly just, would necessitate massive reforms, the funds for which could not realistically be anticipated; therefore the just demands were also foolish demands and would only antagonize white people" (29). (See, for instance, Wilson, *The Truly Disadvantaged,* 125–26, and E. J. Dionne, *Why Americans Hate Politics* [New York: Simon

and Schuster, 1991], 86.) In this respect, Rustin's essay and its appropriation illustrate another significant problem in black politics, the tendency to construe interracialism less as an instrument for the pursuit of substantive political goals than as a goal in itself. Thus in his epigones' perspective — and perhaps increasingly also his own — Rustin's support for the strategy of interracial coalition overwhelms the ends to which that strategy was harnessed. The need to overcome this problem, which at bottom reduces black politics to a secondary debate over how to think about relations with whites, is of course one of the frustrations that impelled the development of the black power sensibility that Wilson and others believe to have been so corrosive in the first place.

26. For a statement of this version of black power, see Nathan Wright, *Black Power and Urban Unrest* (New York: Hawthorn, 1967).

27. Robert L. Allen's *Black Awakening in Capitalist America: An Analytic History* (Garden City, NY: Doubleday, 1969) is an important, early critical examination of this tension in the context of the black power mood. He provides the first thoroughgoing critique of black power's openness to corporate liberalism and the programmatic equivalent of Bantustan administration.

28. Howard Brotz, *Negro Social and Political Thought, 1850–1920* (New York: Basic Books, 1966), 1–33; August Meier, Elliott Rudwick, and Francis L. Broderick, *Black Protest Thought in the Twentieth Century,* 2nd ed. (Indianapolis, IN: Bobbs-Merrill, 1971), xix–lvi; Harold Cruse, *The Crisis of the Negro Intellectual* (New York: Morrow, 1967), esp. 4–13.

29. For illustration of this earlier period of sharp black political debate, see, e.g., Broderick, *Black Protest Thought,* 110–219; Ralph J. Bunche, *A World View of Race* (Washington, DC: Associates in Negro Folk Education, 1936), "The Negro in the Political Life of the United States," *Journal of Negro Education* 10 (1941): 567–84, "A Critique of New Deal Social Planning as It Affects Negroes," *Journal of Negro Education* 5 (January 1936): 59–65, "A Critical Analysis of the Tactics and Programs of Minority Groups," *Journal of Negro Education* 4 (July 1935): 308–20, and *The Political Status of the Negro in the Age of FDR* (Chicago: University of Chicago Press, 1973); E. Franklin Frazier, "The Status of the Negro in the American Social Order," *Journal of Negro Education* 4 (July 1935): 293–307, and "La Bourgeoisie Noire," in *Anthology of American Negro Literature,* ed. V. F. Calverton (New York: Modern Library, 1929); Abram L. Harris Jr., "The Negro and Economic Radicalism," *Modern Quarterly* 2 (1925):198–208, and *The Negro as Capitalist* (New York: American Academy of Political and Social Science, 1936); Sterling Spero and Abram L. Harris, *The Black Worker* (New York: Columbia University Press, 1931); Rayford W. Logan, ed., *What the Negro Wants* (Chapel Hill: University of North Carolina Press, 1944); L. D. Reddick, "A New Interpretation for Negro History," *Journal of Negro History* 22 (January 1937): 17–28; W. T. Fontaine, "The Mind and Thought of the Negro in the United States as Revealed in Imaginative Literature, 1876–1940," *Southern University Bulletin* 28 (March 1942): 5–50, " 'Social Determination' in the Writings of Negro Scholars," *American Journal of Sociology* 49 (January 1944): 302–

15 (with responses by E. Franklin Frazier and E. B. Reuter), "An Interpretation of Contemporary Negro Thought from the Standpoint of the Sociology of Knowledge," *Journal of Negro History* 25 (January 1940): 6–13, and the special section of the *Journal of Negro Education* 5 (January 1936).

30. Robert J. Kerstein and Dennis R. Judd, "Achieving Less Influence with More Democracy: The Permanent Legacy of the War on Poverty," *Social Science Quarterly* 61 (September 1980): 208–20; Karnig and Welch, *Black Representation and Urban Policy,* 49–51, 77–79; Brown and Erie, "Blacks and the Legacy," Richard A. Cloward and Frances Fox Piven, *The Politics of Turmoil: Essays on Poverty, Race, and the Urban Crisis* (New York: Pantheon, 1974), esp. part 4; Peter Eisinger, "The Community Action Program and the Development of Black Political Leadership," in *Urban Policy Making,* ed. Dale R. Marshall (Beverly Hills, CA: Sage, 1979); Bette Woody, *Managing Crisis Cities: The New Black Leadership and the Politics of Resource Allocation* (Westport, CT: Greenwood, 1982), 44–90.

31. See chapter 5 of this volume.

32. See chapters 3 and 6 in this volume; Marcuse, "Targeted Crisis"; Smith and Judd, "American Cities"; David Rothman, "The Crime of Punishment," *New York Review of Books,* February 17, 1994; Douglas Jehl, "Clinton Delivers Emotional Appeal on Stopping Crime," *New York Times,* November 14, 1993; Jerry Gray, "Using His Right, Florio Goes from Dead into Dead Heat," *New York Times,* September 20, 1993; Currie, "Capital Gangbusters"; Steve Daley, "Crime Debate Sparks Jackson Renaissance," *Chicago Tribune,* January 6, 1994; Michael deCourcy Hinds, "Philadelphia Adopts Tough Truant Policy with Handcuffs, Too," *New York Times,* February 9, 1994. The Hinds article was featured in the *Times*'s Education section. The fetish of punishment spreads even in the face of evidence gainsaying its putative justification in hysteria over increases in crime; see Neil Lewis, "Crime: Falling Rates but Rising Fear," *New York Times,* December 8, 1993; Elliott Currie, *Crime and Punishment in America* (New York: Henry Holt/Metropolitan Books, 1998); Franklin E. Zimring and Gordon Hawkins, *Crime Is Not the Problem: Lethal Violence in America* (New York and Oxford: Oxford University Press, 1997). Diana R. Gordon examines the spreading crime hysteria as an element and engine of a generally rightward, punitive turn in social policy in her *The Return of the Dangerous Classes: Drug Prohibition and Policy Politics* (New York: Norton, 1994).

33. "Murder Capital: A Mayor's Call for Help," *Newsweek,* November 1, 1993; Terry, "A Graver Jackson's Cry"; William Raspberry, "Jesse Jackson Calls on Nation's Blacks to 'Tell It' Like It Is," *Chicago Tribune,* October 11, 1993; Elaine S. Povich, "Moseley-Braun Bill Would Try Some Thirteen-Year-Olds as Adults," *Chicago Tribune,* October 27, 1993; Ronald Smothers, "Atlanta Sets Curfew for Youths, Prompting Concern on Race Bias," *New York Times,* November 21, 1990; Felicia R. Lee, "Polishing Image, Principal Bans Gold Teeth," *New York Times,* February 8, 1990; Josh Kovner, "Daniels Urges Boot Camp for First Offenders," *New Haven Register,* June 6, 1989; Michel Marriott, "Great Expectations Hobble Black Superintendents," *New York Times,* March 21, 1990.

See also Jonathan Kozol, *Savage Inequalities: Children in America's Schools* (New York: Crown, 1991), 195–96.

34. Woody, *Managing Crisis Cities*, 76–81; *African Congress: A Documentary of the First Modern Pan-African Congress*, ed. Imamu Amiri Baraka (LeRoi Jones) (New York: Morrow, 1972); National Black Political Assembly, *National Black Political Convention: Speeches, 1974*; Ronald Walters, "The New Black Political Culture"; William Strickland, "The Gary Convention and the Crisis of American Politics"; William L. Clay, "Emerging New Black Politics"; Charles V. Hamilton, "New Perspective Needed: Urban Economics, Conduit-Colonialism, and Public Policy"; and Imamu Amiri Baraka (LeRoi Jones), "Toward the Creation of Political Institutions for All African Peoples"; all in the special section on "The National Black Political Agenda," *Black World* 21 (October 1972).

35. See also Allen, *Black Awakening*. Allen's critique, made in the ferment that produced the new regime, could have been the foundation for a historically and contextually grounded radical black political discourse, and others (e.g., Julius Lester) seemed to be moving in a similar critical direction. Unfortunately, the possibilities were short-circuited by radicals' turn to "ideology" in the 1970s, which I discuss later in the text.

36. The following discussion draws from personal experience buttressed by mainly ephemeral documents. Not much pertinent secondary literature exists; the most comprehensive and least narrowly partisan include Jennifer Jordan, "Cultural Nationalism in the 1960s: Politics and Poetry," in Reed, *Race, Politics, and Culture*, as well as the essay by Willingham, "Ideology and Politics," in the same volume and chapter 2 in this volume. Also see Alex Willingham, "California Dreaming: Eldridge Cleaver's Epithet to the Activism of the Sixties," *Endarch* 1 (Winter 1976): 1–23; and Harold Barnette, "Criteria for Cultural Criticism" *Endarch* 1 (Spring 1975): 37–43. Robert C. Smith discusses the problems of commitment to an abstract ideal of unity as a principle and a utopian politics that beset at least the nationalist strain of this radicalism; see his *We Have No Leaders: African Americans in the Post–Civil Rights Era* (Albany: SUNY Press, 1996), esp. 75–78. A flavor of the debates can be gleaned from Mwalimu Owusu Sadaukai (Howard Fuller), *The Condition of Black People in the 1970s* (Chicago: Institute for Positive Education Press, 1972); Tony Thomas and Robert Allen, *Two Views on Pan-Africanism* (New York: Pathfinder Press, 1972); Ideological Research Staff of Malcolm X Liberation University, *Understanding the African Struggle* (Greensboro, NC: The "X" Press, 1971); Norman Harris, "A Recurring Malady: Baraka's Move to the 'Left,'" *Endarch* 1 (Fall 1974): 5–20; Adolph Reed Jr., "Marxism and Nationalism in Afroamerica," *Social Theory and Practice* 1 (Fall 1971): 1–39, "Pan-Africanism: Ideology for Liberation?" *Black Scholar* 3 (September 1971): 2–13, and "Scientistic Socialism: Notes on the New Afro-American Magic Marxism," *Endarch* 1 (Fall 1974): 21–39; Tony Thomas, "Black Nationalism and Confused Black Marxists," *Black Scholar* 4 (September 1972): 47–52; Francis Ward, *"Superfly": A Political and Cultural Condemnation by the Kuumba Workshop* (Chicago: Institute for Positive Education Press, 1972); Imari Abubakari Obadele, *Revolution and Nation Building: Strat-*

egy for Building the Black Nation in America (Detroit: House of Songhay, 1970); Black Workers Congress, *The Black Liberation Struggle, the Black Workers Congress, and Proletarian Revolution* (Detroit: BWC, 1974), and *The Struggle against Revisionism and Opportunism: Against the Communist League and the Revolutionary Union* (Detroit: BWC, 1974); Abdul Alkalimat, *A Scientific Approach to Black Liberation* (Nashville, TN: People's College, 1974); Abdul Alkalimat and Nelson Johnson, "Toward the Ideological Unity of the African Liberation Support Committee: A Response to Criticisms of the A.L.S.C. Statement of Principles" (1974); "From the Quotable Karenga" in *The Black Power Revolt,* ed. Floyd Barbour (Boston: Little Brown, 1966); Stokely Carmichael, *Stokely Speaks: Black Power Back to Pan-Africanism* (New York: Random House, 1971), and "Marxism-Leninism and Nkrumahism," *Black Scholar* 4 (February 1973): 41–43; Carlos Moore, *Were Marx and Engels White Racists? The Prolet-Aryan Outlook of Marx and Engels* (Chicago: Institute for Positive Education Press, 1972); Ronald Walters, "Unifying Ideology: African-American Nationalism," *Black World,* October 1973: 9ff., and "Marxist-Leninism and the Black Revolution: A Critical Essay," *Afrocentric World Review* 1 (Fall 1975): 3–71; Imamu Amiri Baraka (LeRoi Jones), *Kawaida Studies: The New Nationalism* (Chicago: Institute for Positive Education Press, 1972), *Raise, Race, Rays, Raze* (New York: Random House, 1971), "Toward Ideological Clarity," *Black World,* November 1974: 24ff., "Why I Changed My Ideology," *Black World,* July 1975: 30–42, "Newark Seven Years Later—Unidad y Lucha!" *Monthly Review,* January 1975: 16–24, and "The Congress of African People: A Position Paper," *Black Scholar* 6 (January/February 1975): 2–15; Phil Hutchings, "Report on the ALSC National Conference," *Black Scholar* 5 (July/August 1974): 48–53; Maulana Ron Karenga, "Which Road: Nationalism, Pan-Africanism, Socialism?" *Black Scholar* 5 (October 1974): 21–30; Haki Madhubuti (Don L. Lee), *From Plan to Planet* (Detroit: Broadside, 1973), "Enemy: From the White Left, White Right, and In-Between," *Black World* (October 1974): 36–47, and "The Latest Purge: The Attack on Black Nationalism and Pan-Afrikanism by the New Left, the Sons and Daughters of the Old Left," *Black Scholar* 6 (September 1974): 43–56; and Mark Smith, "A Response to Haki Madhubuti," *Black Scholar* 6 (January/February 1975): 44–53.

37. For a critical discussion of this sort of notion of political representation and its problematic features, see Hanna Fenichel Pitkin, *The Concept of Representation* (Berkeley: University of California Press, 1967), 60–91.

38. The absence of the Black Panther party (BPP) from this account may seem curious. It is nonetheless justified. The BPP was in effect the creature of a transitional moment between simple black power rhetoric and the clearly articulated formation of incrementalist mainstream and radical wings. The BPP crested as an autonomous black political organization in the late 1960s, before the institutional entailments of systemic incorporation had begun to take their ultimate forms. By the time the practical outlines of the new regime were clearly discernible, the party was in disarray practically everywhere except Oakland, California. Moreover, a combination of forces—ranging from police repres-

sion and the consequent need for broad-based fund-raising for legal defense to the quirks of its own ideological development—had led the BPP into a pattern of early alliances with white left groups. The result was an orientation that, outside the party's Bay Area stronghold in any case, was only weakly linked to the main tensions and driving forces in black political life. Although individuals certainly would go on from the Black Panther experience to subsequent activism rooted in black politics, the BPP was not really a force in the crucial period defined by the consolidation of the forms of black incorporation.

39. See, e.g., Hugh Hamilton, "Ron Daniels, The 'Guts and Faith' Candidate," *Brooklyn City Sun,* July 29–August 4, 1992.

40. Here I should acknowledge my own partisanship in ALSC's Marxist camp.

41. Stone, *Regime Politics,* 93, 166; Mack H. Jones, "Black Political Empowerment in Atlanta: Myth and Reality," *Annals of the American Academy of Political and Social Science* 439 (September 1978): 90–117.

42. I have argued this point in *The Jesse Jackson Phenomenon: The Crisis of Purpose in Afro-American Politics* (New Haven and London: Yale University Press, 1986).

43. Utrice C. Leid, "Jackson's 'Unilateralist' Approach to Politics Comes under Fire," *City Sun,* August 14, 1987; Thomas B. Edsall, "Jackson's Rainbow Coalition Has Faded to Shades of Gray," *Washington Post National Weekly Edition,* August 19–25, 1991.

44. See, e.g., Leslie Cagan, "Rainbow Realignment," *Zeta,* May 1989; Thulani Davis and James Ridgeway, "Jesse Jackson's New Math: Does It Add Up to a Winner?" *Village Voice,* December 22, 1987; Jim Schoch, "The Rainbow Coalition: Complex Realities," Shakoor Aljuwani, "Golden Opportunity," and Jerry G. Watts, "Whither the Rainbow?" all in *Democratic Left* 7 (November/December 1986); Andrew Kopkind, "Strategy for Now—And Next Time," *Nation,* September 25, 1989; "Exchange: Whither the Rainbow?" *Nation,* December 18, 1989; Jesse Jackson, "What We Won," *Mother Jones,* July/August 1988. By "meaningful" I mean those primaries held before Dukakis had garnered enough delegate votes to secure the nomination.

45. Galston, "Future of the Democratic Party"; Steven A. Holmes, "Must Democrats Shift Signals on Blacks to Win the Presidency?" *New York Times,* November 10, 1991; Democratic Leadership Council, *The New Choice: Draft for a Democratic Platform* (1992); Ernest Dumas, "DLC Cozies Up to Big Business," *Arkansas Gazette,* May 17, 1991; Dan Balz, "Democrats Face Minority Skepticism," *Washington Post,* May 8, 1991; Thomas Byrne Edsall and Mary D. Edsall, *Chain Reaction: The Impact of Race, Rights, and Taxes on American Politics* (New York: Norton, 1991); Thomas Byrne Edsall, "Clinton, So Far," *New York Review of Books,* October 7, 1993. For a critique of the DLC's view, see William Crotty, "Who Needs Two Republican Parties?" in *The Democrats Must Lead: The Case for a Progressive Democratic Party,* ed. James MacGregor Burns, William Crotty, Lois Lovelace Duke, and Lawrence D. Lovejoy (Boulder, CO: Westview, 1992); Julian Bond and Adolph L. Reed Jr., "Equality: Why We Can't Wait," *The Nation,* December 9, 1991; and Reed, *Without Justice for All.*

46. A similar story was being enacted simultaneously among white radicals. See, e.g., Todd Gitlin, *The Whole World Is Watching! Mass Media in the Making and Unmaking of the New Left* (Berkeley: University of California Press, 1980); Nigel Young, *An Infantile Disorder? The Crisis and Decline of the New Left* (Boulder, CO: Westview, 1977); Sara Evans, *Personal Politics: The Roots of Women's Liberation in the Civil Rights Movement and the New Left* (New York: Random House, 1979); John Case and Rosemary C. R. Taylor, eds., *Co-ops, Communes, and Collectives: Experiments in Social Change in the 1960s and 1970s* (New York: Pantheon, 1979); Russell Jacoby, "The Politics of Objectivity: Notes on the U.S. Left," *Telos,* Winter, 1977/78: 74–88. David Gross, "Culture, Politics, and 'Lifestyle' in the 1960s," and Andrew Feenberg, "Paths to Failure: The Dialectics of Organization and Ideology in the New Left," both in Reed, *Race, Politics, and Culture*; Rhonda Kotelchuk and Howard Levy, "The Medical Committee for Human Rights: A Case Study in the Self-Liquidation of the New Left," in Reed, *Race, Politics, and Culture.* The tension between adherence to principle and concession to realpolitik is of course a constant problem for radical politics. I suspect strongly that any attempt to specify a general rule of thumb governing radical practice in this regard could only be uselessly abstract. The fluidity and complexity of the concrete dialectics constituting most political situations preclude direct and uncontroversial application of any such guide. We can, however, profit from attending to this problem's persistence and to the ways that movements have responded to it in different historical contexts. For example, see Frances Fox Piven and Richard A. Cloward, *Poor People's Movements: Why They Succeed, How They Fail* (New York: Pantheon, 1977); Aileen S. Kraditor, *The Radical Persuasion, 1890–1917* (Baton Rouge: Louisiana State University Press, 1981); James Weinstein, *The Decline of Socialism in America, 1912–1925* (New York: Random House, 1967); and Russell Jacoby, *Dialectic of Defeat: Contours of Western Marxism* (New York and London: Cambridge University Press, 1981).

47. See, e.g., George Lipsitz, "The Mardi Gras Indians: Carnival and Counter-Narrative in Black New Orleans," *Cultural Critique* (Fall 1988): 99–121; Elsa Barkley-Brown, "African-American Women's Quilting: A Framework for Conceptualizing and Teaching African-American Women's History," *Signs* 14 (Summer 1989): 921–29; Robin D. G. Kelley, " 'We Are Not What We Seem': Rethinking Black Working Class Opposition in the Jim Crow South," *Journal of American History* 80 (June 1993): 75–112, and "The Riddle of the Zoot: Malcolm Little and Black Cultural Politics," in *Malcolm X: In Our Own Image,* ed. Joe Wood (New York: St. Martin's); Michael Eric Dyson, *Reflecting Black: African-American Cultural Criticism* (Minneapolis: University of Minnesota Press, 1993); Michelle Wallace and Gina Dent, eds., *Black Popular Culture* (Seattle: Bay Press, 1992). Perhaps the most explicit statement of this depoliticized notion of politics is Paul Gilroy's enthusiastic embrace of a putative "movement," allegedly rooted in diasporic "black expressive cultures" (such as popular music), that is defined crucially by "its antipathy to the institutions of formal politics and the fact that it is not principally oriented

toward instrumental objectives. Rather than aim at the conquest of political power or apparatuses, its objective centers on the control of a field of autonomy or independence from the system" ("One Nation under a Groove: The Cultural Politics of 'Race' and Racism in Britain," in *The Anatomy of Racism*, ed. David Theo Goldberg [Minneapolis: University of Minnesota Press, 1990], 279).

48. Starr, "Civil Reconstruction"; Genovese, "Voices Must Unite"; Gary Peller, "Race against Integration," *Tikkun* 6 (January/February 1991): 54–70.

49. For example, see Houston A. Baker Jr., *Modernism and the Harlem Renaissance* (Chicago: University of Chicago Press, 1987); Roy L. Brooks, *Rethinking the American Race Problem* (Los Angeles: University of California Press, 1990); Errol Smith, "It's the Values, Stupid," *New Democrat* 5 (November 1993): 10–12.

50. These issues are discussed usefully in Willingham, "Voting Rights, Government Responsibility," and "Voting Rights Movement"; Lani Guinier, *The Tyranny of the Majority: Fundamental Fairness in Representative Democracy* (New York: Free Press, 1994), 41–70.

51. Frances Fox Piven and Richard A. Cloward have argued for a similar strategy for the left in general; see *The New Class War: Reagan's Attack on the Welfare State and Its Consequences* (New York: Pantheon, 1982), esp. 120–22, 143–45; also see Piven, "Women and the State: Ideology, Power, and Welfare," in *For Crying Out Loud: Women and Poverty in the United States,* ed. Rochelle Lefkowitz and Ann Withorn (New York: Pilgrim Press, 1986), 339–40; Michael Lipsky, *Street-Level Bureaucracy: Dilemmas of the Individual in Public Services* (New York: Russell Sage Foundation, 1980), 188–91; Ann Withorn, *Serving the People: Social Services and Social Change* (New York: Columbia University Press, 1984).

52. For a discussion of the workings of racial stratification in these contexts, see chapter 3 in this volume; Howard Botwinick, *Persistent Inequalities: Wage Disparity under Capitalism* (Princeton: Princeton University Press, 1993), esp. 96–101, 101–8; Patrick Mason, "Accumulation, Segmentation, and the Discriminatory Process in the Market for Labor Power," *Review of Radical Political Economics* 25 (June 1993): 1–25, and "Race, Competition, and Differential Wages," *Cambridge Journal of Economics* 19 (August 1995): 545–68; Lafer, "Minority Unemployment," and "The Politics of Job Training"; David Gordon, Richard Edwards, and Michael Reich, *Segmented Work, Divided Workers: The Historical Transformation of Labor in the U.S.* (London and New York: Cambridge University Press, 1982); Edna Bonacich, "Advanced Capitalism and Black/White Race Relations in the United States: A Split Labor Market Interpretation," *American Sociological Review* 41 (February 1976): 34–51; Donald Tomascovic-Devey, *Gender and Racial Inequality at Work: The Sources and Consequences of Job Segregation* (Ithaca, NY: ILR Press, 1993). Mason (in "Race, Competition, and Differential Wages") and Botwinick (in *Persistent Inequalities,* esp. 38–49, 260–65), while affirming the structural foundations of existing labor market stratification by race and gender, forcefully challenge dual economy theories such as those advanced by Gordon, Edwards, and Reich and Bonacich.

53. A particularly insidious element of this reactionary momentum is the projection of the "black church" or religiosity as the locus of black political authenticity and efficacy. This construction legitimizes privatism — as opposed to action directed toward public institutions — as a political strategy and to that extent urges quietism. It also reinforces both fundamentally rightist tendencies to construe manifest racial inequality in terms that stress a putative "moral breakdown" in inner cities and the repressive agendas that ensue from that focus. See, e.g., Jon Meacham, "The Gospel Truth," *Washington Monthly,* December 1993: 8–14; Rev. C. Jay Matthews, "The Black Church Position Statement on Homosexuality," *Cleveland Call and Post,* June 10, 1993; Russell Walker, "Area Clergy Unite against Civil Rights Bill," *Cleveland Call and Post,* June 17, 1993; Leslie Maria Huff, "Black Ministers Declare War against Lesbians and Gay Men," *Cleveland Call and Post,* June 24, 1993; Lena Williams, "Blacks Reject Gay Rights Fight as Equal to Theirs," *New York Times,* June 28, 1993; West, *Race Matters,* esp. 11–20; Dyson: *Reflecting Black,* 221–329, and "Tangled Roots of an Urban Epidemic," *Chicago Tribune,* July 8, 1993; Kelley, " 'We Are Not What We Seem,' " 88–89; Jehl, "Clinton Delivers Emotional Appeal"; Ari L. Goldman, "Black Women's Bumpy Road to Church Leadership," *New York Times,* July 29, 1990; Cathy Hayden, "Principal Banned from Campus for Prayer Episode," *Jackson Clarion-Ledger,* November 20, 1993; "Mississippi Fights Ban on Prayers in Schools," *New York Times,* December 7, 1993; Esther G. Walker, "100 Black Clergy Endorse Sharpton's U.S. Senate Bid," *New York Amsterdam News,* August 8, 1992; Evelyn Nieves, "Flake's Sermon of Defense Greeted with Ovations," *New York Times,* August 6, 1990; Joseph P. Fried, "Flake Pleads Not Guilty to All Charges," *New York Times,* August 21, 1990; E. R. Shipp, "Church Backing of Tyson Splits Baptists," *New York Times,* March 16, 1992; "Tyson Ally in Baptist Church Is Indicted on Charge of Lying," *New York Times,* July 25, 1992; Ronald Smothers, "Black Baptists Meet in Limelight of Politics and Shadow of Criminal Charges," *New York Times,* September 12, 1992; Kristen Johnson, "Vote for Me, Brother," *Atlanta Journal,* June 18, 1976; Cecil Williams, "Crack Is Genocide, 1990's Style," *New York Times,* February 15, 1990; Proctor, "To the Rescue." For critiques see Smith, " 'Self-Help' "; Legette, "Crisis of the Black Male"; Reed, *The Jesse Jackson Phenomenon,* 41–60; Joe Wood, "Bad Faith: Playing on the Moral High Ground," *Village Voice,* February 15, 1994. Wood situates Louis Farrakhan's dangerous, antidemocratic political style as typical of a species of the politicized black Christian minister, noting the features they share.

5. A Critique of Neoprogressivism in Theorizing about Local Development Policy

1. Paul E. Peterson, *City Limits* (Chicago: University of Chicago Press, 1981), 132.
2. Ibid., 129.
3. Ibid.
4. Ibid., 147.
5. Ibid., 121–28.

6. Ibid., 133.

7. Ibid., 129.

8. Todd Swanstrom, *The Crisis of Growth Politics: Cleveland, Kucinich, and the Challenge of Urban Populism* (Philadelphia: Temple University Press, 1985), 15–17.

9. See Clarence N. Stone and Heywood T. Sanders, "Reexamining a Classic Case of Development Politics: New Haven, Connecticut," in *The Politics of Urban Development*, ed. C. N. Stone and H. T. Sanders (Lawrence: University of Kansas Press, 1987), 159–81.

10. Peter K. Eisinger, *The Politics of Displacement: Racial and Ethnic Transition in Three American Cities* (New York: Academic Press, 1980), 5.

11. See, e.g., Richard P. Nathan and Charles Adams, "Understanding Central City Hardship," *Political Science Quarterly* 1 (Spring 1976): 47–62; and Katherine L. Bradbury, Anthony Downs, and Kenneth A. Small, *Urban Decline and the Future of American Cities* (Washington, DC: Brookings Institution, 1982), esp. 6–7.

12. See, e.g., Clarence N. Stone's study of urban renewal in Atlanta, *Economic Growth and Neighborhood Discontent: System-Bias in the Urban Renewal Program of Atlanta* (Chapel Hill: University of North Carolina Press, 1976); and John H. Mollenkopf, *The Contested City* (Princeton: Princeton University Press, 1983).

13. Albert K. Karnig and Susan Welch, *Black Representation and Urban Policy* (Chicago: University of Chicago Press, 1980), 12–13, 23.

14. See M. Dale Henson and James King, "The Atlanta Public-Private Romance," in *Public-Private Partnership in American Cities: Seven Case Studies,* ed. R. Scott Fosler and Renee A. Berger (Lexington, MA: Lexington, 1982), 293–337. Cf. Bradley R. Rice, "Atlanta: If Dixie Were Atlanta," in *Sunbelt Cities: Politics and Growth since World War II,* ed. Richard M. Bernard and Bradley R. Rice (Austin: University of Texas Press, 1983), 31–57; and Ivan Allen Jr. (with Paul Hemphill), *Mayor: Notes on the Sixties* (New York: Simon and Schuster, 1971).

15. Stone, *Economic Growth and Neighborhood Discontent*; also see Mack H. Jones, "Black Political Empowerment in Atlanta: Myth and Reality," *Annals of the American Academy of Political and Social Science* 439 (September 1978): 90–117.

16. A taste of Young's insistence on cultivating a rapport with the business community can be gleaned from Art Harris, "The Capitalist Gospel According to Rev. Young," *Atlanta Constitution,* September 22, 1985.

17. Allen, *Mayor,* remains the most illuminating source on this motif in Atlanta's political structure; see also Floyd Hunter, *Community Power Succession: Atlanta's Policy Makers Revisited* (Chapel Hill: University of North Carolina Press, 1980).

18. Allen's story of his own recruitment and grooming for political office is illustrative; see *Mayor,* 9–16.

19. Eisinger, *The Politics of Displacement,* 81.

20. Henson and King, "Atlanta Public-Private Romance," 306.

21. For an examination of one representative of the element that refused to accept the idea of black rule see Russ Rymes, "The Tide Turns Again for Dillard Munford," *Atlanta Journal/Constitution Magazine,* November 23, 1980, 14ff.

22. Jones, "Black Political Empowerment," 109.

23. Ibid.

24. Thus Birmingham, Alabama; New Orleans, Louisiana; and Charlotte, North Carolina; have also elected black mayors with considerable support from the business elite.

25. Rice, "Atlanta," 51–52; Eisinger, *The Politics of Displacement,* 81.

26. Henson and King, "Atlanta Public-Private Romance," 306–7; Eisinger, *The Politics of Displacement,* 83.

27. This programmatic orientation was articulated in Mayor Jackson's "State of the City, 1980" address (21 January 1980) and in the "Action Plan to Combat Poverty in Atlanta," prepared for the Mayor's Poverty Task Force by his Department of Budget and Planning, May 21, 1981.

28. Raleigh Bryans, "Airlines Hint OK of Move of Terminal," *Atlanta Constitution,* July 22, 1973.

29. Sam Hopkins, "FAA Gives Push to Second Airport Here," *Atlanta Constitution,* September 8, 1973; Gene Tharpe, "Possible Airport Site Acquired near Dallas," *Atlanta Constitution,* July 28, 1973; Jim Gray, "Airport Study Urged," *Atlanta Constitution,* October 10, 1973, and "Airport Welcome," *Atlanta Constitution,* January 20, 1974.

30. As the debate unfolded, the airlines—especially Delta—became increasingly candid and adamant in stating their preference, which was for the Paulding-Polk option (see Jim Merriner, "Mayor Raps Airport Site Option Cost," *Atlanta Constitution,* May 13, 1974; Tharpe, "Possible Airport Site Acquired").

31. Tharpe, "Possible Airport Site Acquired."

32. Ibid.

33. See Jones, "Black Political Empowerment," 107.

34. Ibid., 109–11.

35. Margaret Shannon examines the Portman-Cousins rivalry in "The Battle of Downtown Atlanta," *Atlanta Journal and Constitution Magazine,* July 22, 1979, 10ff.

36. Jones, "Black Political Empowerment," 10; also see Frederick Allen, "Airlines Fear Second Airport Never Will Be," *Atlanta Constitution,* January 26, 1975.

37. Raleigh Bryans, "Delta Chides ARC Report on Airport," *Atlanta Constitution,* March 2, 1975.

38. Jim Merriner, "City Still Seeks Southside Airfield Site," *Atlanta Constitution,* April 3, 1975.

39. Jim Merriner, "City Not Bound by ARC Vote," *Atlanta Constitution,* July 2, 1978.

40. See Jones, "Black Political Empowerment."

41. The following discussion draws freely from almost daily coverage of the joint venture controversy in the Atlanta press, as well as from Jones, "Black Political Empowerment."

42. Jim Gray, "Compromise Okayed on Joint Ventures," *Atlanta Constitution,* February 10, 1976.

43. Peterson, *City Limits,* 178–82.

6. The "Underclass" as Myth and Symbol

1. Doug Glasgow, *The Black Underclass* (San Francisco: Jossey Bass, 1980). Gans, e.g., attributes the coinage of the term to Myrdal; see Herbert J. Gans, "Deconstructing the Underclass: The Term's Dangers as a Planning Concept," *Journal of the American Planning Association* 56 (Summer 1990): 271–77. Gans's essay, which I did not read until I had completed this article, parallels several of my criticisms of the underclass construct and shares a general concern with the notion's ideological core and limitations as an analytic or planning device.

2. Ken Auletta, *The Underclass* (New York: Random House, 1982).

3. Oscar Lewis, *La Vida* (New York: Random House, 1966), li.

4. Auletta, *The Underclass,* 25.

5. Ibid., 27–28.

6. Ibid., 29.

7. Ibid., 33.

8. Lawrence M. Mead, *Beyond Entitlement: The Social Obligations of Citizenship* (New York: Free Press, 1986), 22.

9. Mickey Kaus, "The Work Ethic State," *The New Republic,* July 1986: 22.

10. Ibid., 24.

11. Ibid., 25.

12. Ibid., 28.

13. Ibid., 33.

14. Ibid.

15. Nicholas Lemann, "The Origins of the Underclass," part 1, *The Atlantic Monthly,* June 1986, 33.

16. Nicholas Lemann, "The Origins of the Underclass," part 2, *The Atlantic Monthly,* July 1986, 68. In his subsequent book, *The Promised Land: The Great Migration and How It Shaped America* (New York: Knopf, 1991), Lemann gives a much richer and more complex account in which his sharecrop culture formulation is less pivotal. Nevertheless, he repeatedly invokes that dubious notion, along with the imagery of social pathology, where one might expect to find analysis or explanation. Thus, he undermines an otherwise helpful and intelligent narrative that stresses the role of public policy in reducing black inner-city poverty — including local politicians' intransigent commitment to residential segregation and their concentration of the social costs of urban renewal on blacks, as well as an ambivalent federal antipoverty initiative.

17. Lemann, "Origins," part 1, 53.

18. Lemann, "Origins," part 2, 56.

19. Richard P. Nathan, "The Underclass: Will It Always Be with Us?" (unpublished paper given at the New School for Social Research, New York, November 14, 1986).

20. Richard P. Nathan, "Is the Underclass Beyond Help?" *New York Times,* January 6, 1989.

21. Isabel V. Sawhill, "The Underclass: An Overview," *Public Interest,* Summer 1989, 3.

22. Ibid., 5.

23. Ibid.

24. Erol R. Ricketts and Isabel V. Sawhill, "Defining and Measuring the Underclass," *Journal of Policy Analysis and Management* 7 (1988): 318.

25. Ronald B. Mincy, Isabel V. Sawhill, and Douglas A. Wolf, "The Underclass: Definition and Measurement," *Science* 248 (April 1990): 450–53.

26. Sawhill, "The Underclass," 5.

27. Ricketts and Sawhill, "Defining and Measuring the Underclass," 316.

28. Eleanor Holmes Norton, "Restoring the Traditional Black Family," *New York Times Magazine,* June 1985, 79.

29. Ibid., 96.

30. Ibid., 97.

31. William Julius Wilson, *The Truly Disadvantaged: The Inner City, the Underclass, and Public Policy* (Chicago and London: University of Chicago Press, 1987), 6–7.

32. Ibid., 20–21, 137, and passim.

33. David T. Ellwood, *Poor Support: Poverty in the American Family* (New York: Basic Books, 1988), 200.

34. Ibid.

35. Ronald B. Mincy, Isabel V. Sawhill, and Douglas A. Wolf, "Response," *Science* 249 (June 1990): 1472–73.

36. Sawhill, "The Underclass," 11. Although Sawhill in her text adduces specific authors to support other claims in this article, for this one she adopts the vagueness of an aspirin commercial. Her "common-sense intuition" is confirmed by unspecified "ethnographic studies in low-income communities . . . more quantitative research [on the behavioral effects of] neighborhood environment . . . and . . . studies that suggest that welfare dependency and a failure to form stable families may be passed from parent to child" (11). Interestingly, this commonsensical claim does not appear at all in either of her two more carefully documented articles on this topic.

37. Wilson, *The Truly Disadvantaged,* 3.

38. Ibid., 7.

39. Ibid., 46ff. For the record, even Charles Murray includes isolation effects among his sources of intractable poverty; see his *Losing Ground: American Social Policy, 1950–1980* (New York: Basic Books, 1984), 189.

40. Brett Williams discusses the strengths and limitations of ethnography in a very intelligent, careful, and useful way in her critical examination of anthropological and

other social scientific approaches to American poverty; see "Black Urban Poverty in the United States," *Human Organization* 51 (1992): 164–74. Williams, to very good effect, charts the partiality of tensions between and ideological underpinnings and entailments of anthropological and sociological approaches to the study of inner-city poverty.

41. Ellwood, *Poor Support,* 191–95; Mincy, Sawhill, and Wolf, "The Underclass," 451–52; Ricketts and Sawhill, "Defining and Measuring the Underclass," 318–19. Wilson provides a particularly explicit example of the logic of this reification and its centrality to underclass mythopoeia; see William Julius Wilson, "Studying Inner-City Social Dislocations: The Challenge of Public Agenda Research" (1990 Presidential Address) *American Sociological Review* 56 (February 1991): 1–14.

42. Pete Hamill, "Breaking the Silence," *Esquire,* March 1988, 98.

43. Auletta, *The Underclass,* 51.

44. Ellwood, *Poor Support,* 16–18.

45. Adolph Reed Jr., "The Liberal Technocrat," *Nation,* February 6, 1988.

46. Wilson, *The Truly Disadvantaged,* esp. chap. 3.

47. Reed, "The Liberal Technocrat," 169.

48. "Only One US Family in Four Is 'Traditional,' " *New York Times,* January 30, 1991.

49. Mary Jo Bane, "Household Composition and Poverty," in *Fighting Poverty: What Works and What Doesn't,* ed. Sheldon H. Danziger and Daniel H. Weinberg (Cambridge, MA: Harvard University Press, 1986), esp. 228.

50. See, e.g., Kristin Luker, "The Social Construction of Teenaged Pregnancy" (paper presented at the annual meeting of the American Sociological Association, Washington, D.C., August 1990), and "Dubious Conceptions: The Controversy over Teen Pregnancy," *The American Prospect,* Spring 1991: 73–83; Arline T. Geronimus, "The Effects of Race, Residence, and Prenatal Care on the Relationship of Maternal Age to Neonatal Mortality," *American Journal of Public Health* 75 (1986): 1416–21, "On Teenage Childbearing and Neonatal Mortality in the United States," *Population and Development Review* 13 (1987): 45–79, and "Black/White Differences in Women's Reproductive-Related Health Status: Evidence from Vital Statistics," *Demography* 27 (1990): 457–66.

51. Wilson, *The Truly Disadvantaged,* 73–74. Wilson also argues that teen childbearing is pathological principally because it is out-of-wedlock (28–29).

52. Lee Rainwater and William L. Yancey, eds. *The Moynihan Report and the Politics of Controversy* (Cambridge: MIT Press, 1967), 88–89 (pages 42–43 of Moynihan's *The Negro Family: The Case for National Action*).

53. "Furor on Child-Support Move," *New York Times,* February 2, 1991.

54. Tamar Levin, "A Plan to Pay Welfare Mothers for Birth Control," *New York Times,* February 9, 1991.

55. Isabel Wilkerson, "Wisconsin Welfare Plan: To Reward the Married," *New York Times,* February 12, 1991.

56. Katha Pollitt, *Reasonable Creatures: Essays on Women and Feminism* (New York: Knopf, 1994), 173–74.

57. Virginia Morris, "Docs Let Pregnant Whites off Drug Hook," *New Haven Register,* April 26, 1990.

58. Marian Wright Edelman, *Families at Peril* (Cambridge: Harvard University Press, 1987).

59. Staff of the Chicago Tribune, *The American Millstone: An Examination of the Nation's Permanent Underclass* (Chicago and New York: Contemporary Books, 1986).

60. Philip Kasinitz, "Facing Up to the Underclass," *Telos,* Summer 1998: 178.

61. Norton "Restoring the Traditional Black Family," 93.

Permissions

The University of Minnesota Press gratefully acknowledges permission to reprint the following essays.

A different version of chapter 1 was presented in a series of lectures delivered by Adolph Reed Jr. during his appointment as John J. McCloy '16 Professor at Amherst College during the 1998/1999 term.

Chapter 2 originally appeared as "The 'Black Revolution' and the Reconstitution of Domination," in *Race, Politics, and Culture,* ed. Adolph Reed Jr. Copyright 1986 by Greenwood Press. Reproduced with permission of Greenwood Publishing Group, Inc., Westport, Connecticut.

Chapter 3 originally appeared as "The Black Urban Regime: Structural Origins and Constraints," in the journal *Comparative Urban and Community Research* 1 (1988). Copyright 1988 by Transaction Publishers; all rights reserved. Reprinted by permission of Transaction Publishers.

An earlier, shorter version of chapter 4 originally appeared as "Demobilization in the New Black Political Regime: Ideological Capitulation, and Radical Failure in the Post-Segregation Era," in *The Bubbling Cauldron,* ed. Michael Peter Smith and Joe R. Feagin, University of Minnesota Press, 1995. Reprinted by permission of the publisher.

Chapter 5 originally appeared as "A Critique of Neo-Progressivism in Theorizing about Local Development," in *The Politics of Urban Development,* ed. Clarence N. Stone and Heywood T. Sanders, published by the University Press of Kansas. Copyright 1987. Reprinted by permission of the publisher.

Chapter 6 originally appeared as "The 'Underclass' as Myth and Symbol: The Poverty of Discourse about Poverty," in *Radical America* 24, no. 1 (winter 1992): 21–40. Copyright 1992. Reprinted by permission of *Radical America.*

Index

Adolph Reed Jr. is professor of political science at the New School for Social Research and a member of the editorial board of *Comparative Urban and Community Research.* He is the author of *W. E. B. Du Bois and American Political Thought: Fabianism and the Color Line* and *The Jesse Jackson Phenomenon: The Crisis of Purpose in Afro-American Politics,* and editor of *Race, Politics, and Culture: Critical Essays on the Radicalism of the 1960s* and *Without Justice for All: The New Liberalism and Our Retreat from Racial Equality.*

Julian Bond is chairman of the NAACP National Board of Directors, professor in the Department of History at the University of Virginia, and distinguished professor in residence at American University.